# FROM SONG TO BOOK

Folquet de Marseille as lyrical writer, troubadour chansonnier *N*, Pierpont Morgan Library M 819, fol. 63, detail. (Photograph courtesy of The Pierpont Morgan Library)

# FROM SONG TO BOOK

*The Poetics of Writing in Old French Lyric*

*and Lyrical Narrative Poetry*

## SYLVIA HUOT

CORNELL UNIVERSITY PRESS

ITHACA AND LONDON

Cornell University Press gratefully acknowledges grants from the College of
Liberal Arts and Sciences of Northern Illinois University and the Andrew W.
Mellon Foundation which aided in bringing this book to publication.

First published 1987 by Cornell University Press.

International Standard Book Number 0-8014-1922-0
Library of Congress Catalog Card Number 87-47547
Printed in the United States of America
Librarians: Library of Congress cataloging information
appears on the last page of the book.

The paper in this book is acid-free and meets the guidelines for permanence
and durability of the Committee on Production Guidelines for
Book Longevity of the Council on Library Resources.

# CONTENTS

v

# Contents

# Contents

Contents

# ACKNOWLEDGMENTS

One of the greatest pleasures of extended research is the opportunity that it affords for exchange with other scholars, and I feel particularly fortunate in the number of people who have offered advice and moral support along the way. My first thanks go to Karl D. Uitti and Michael J. Curschmann of Princeton University, who as directors of my dissertation presided over my initial investigations of medieval lyric and lyrical narrative poetry and its manuscript tradition. My debts to both of them are considerable. Among the many other people who have contributed to my thinking during the years I have spent with this work, I thank Emmanuèle Baumgartner, Kevin Brownlee, Peter Dembowski, Nancy Freeman Regalado, Lori Walters, and Winthrop Wetherbee; the book is significantly richer for the questions, comments, and corrections they have offered. Robert F. Cook made many very helpful suggestions as reader for Cornell University Press. And to Leo Krumpholz I owe a very special thanks for support and encouragement during all phases of this project.

Research for this book was conducted in many American and European libraries and could not have proceeded without the helpful cooperation of librarians and other staff members of the following institutions: the Biblioteca Apostolica Vaticana; the Biblioteca Laurenziana and the Biblioteca Riccardiana, Florence; the Bibliothèque de l'Arsenal and the Bibliothèque Nationale, Paris; the Bibliothèque Municipale, Arras; the Bibliothèque Municipale, Dijon; the Bodleian Library, Oxford; the British Library, London; Firestone Library, Princeton University; the Musée Condé, Chantilly; the Newberry Library, Chicago; the Pierpont Morgan Library, New York; Regenstein Library, the University of Chicago; and the Walters Art Gallery, Baltimore. I have also made use of the invaluable research facilities of the Institut de Recherche et d'Histoire des Textes, Paris, a branch of the Centre National de Recherche Scientifique. I am grateful to the Hill Monastic Manuscript Library, St. John's Abbey and

University, Collegeville, Minnesota, for providing a microfilm of MS 2609 of the Nationalbibliothek, Vienna.

This study was supported in part by a Fellowship for Independent Study and Research from the National Endowment for the Humanities, which enabled me to devote full-time efforts to the final preparation of the typescript. I am especially grateful for this generous support.

SYLVIA HUOT

*DeKalb, Illinois*

# FROM SONG TO BOOK

# Introduction

I began this book with a seeming paradox: medieval literature is at once more oral and more visual than a modern printed book. The medieval manuscript, with its colorful initials, miniatures, and decorative margins, appeals to the eye as an object of visual delight. Yet the texts that it contains are designed to appeal to the ear—lyric poems set to music, narratives that address a listening audience. In a literary tradition conceived for oral delivery, what is the role of the book?[1] And as the practice of silent reading grew during the later Middle Ages, what was its effect on poetic practices?[2]

These are large questions and have been treated from various perspectives by a number of scholars.[3] I have limited myself to French literature of the thirteenth and fourteenth centuries and have focused on courtly lyric and lyrical narrative poetry. I have chosen this material because the relation of lyricism and writing is a particularly interesting case in point, and an examination of the lyrico-narrative tradition reveals a well-defined movement from a more performative toward a more writerly poetics. My approach combines poetic, iconographic, and codicological analysis, aimed at describing the relationship between poetics and manuscript format. Poetic analysis will focus on the thematization of writing and performance, on the figure of the poet as singer or writer, and on the transformations and modifications of lyric poetics that each author in turn effects. My readings are based on a study of the texts in manuscript—in each case I have examined as many manuscripts of the text as were accessible to me—and aim to provide a reading not merely of the poem but of the poem as manifested in book form.

I employ the term "lyrico-narrative" not as a specific generic designa-

1. See Crosby; Zumthor, *Poésie et la voix.*
2. See the study by Saenger.
3. For some works that have provided broad historical and conceptual bases for the present study, see Chaytor, Clanchy, Ong, Stock, and Zumthor in the Bibliography.

1

tion but rather as a loosely defined but useful category, comprising texts on the topic of love, with first-person narrative discourse, lyric insertions, or both. For the purposes of this study, the term "lyric" refers to the courtly love lyric, or *chanson courtoise*. I freely acknowledge that this represents an arbitrary exclusion of such important lyric genres as the political *sirventes*, the Crusade song, religious lyric, or the frequently ironic *pastourelle*. I have limited myself in this way so that the remaining body of literature, which is still quite large, may be treated in some degree of depth. I have, moreover, adapted the term "lyrical" to refer not only to nonnarrative poetry in stanzaic form but also to narrative poetry in octosyllabic couplets (romance or *dit*) and even prose works that share certain thematic and grammatical features of the chanson courtoise. For example, the first-person identification of author and protagonist is common to lyric poetry and to such works as the narrative *Roman de la rose* and the prose *Bestiaire d'amours*. The dedication of a work to the narrator's lady, rather than to a patron, further contributes to the lyrical quality of many a romance and dit, as does a focus on the narrator's amorous adventures. And the lyrical narrative manifests the self-reflective quality of courtly lyric. For the *trouvère*, to sing and to love are complementary facets of a single activity, and the song records the event of its own making. Similarly, a lyrical romance or dit frequently records the event of its composition or transcription, and sometimes both, portraying poetic composition as a form of love service.

This transposition of lyric thematics and discourse into narrative format poses certain paradoxes. Most obvious is the conflict between narrative progression and resolution on the one hand, lyric stasis and open-endedness on the other. This issue has been explored in recent work on the *Roman de la rose*.[4] Equally important is the issue of medium. Whereas the twelfth-century romance narrator explicitly presented himself as heir to a long-established written tradition, the twelfth-century trouvère was explicitly a singer, whose songs derived from his own personal experience rather than from books. The evolution of the lyrical romance and dit entailed a progressive redefinition of lyric poetry as a written medium and of lyric discourse and thematics as appropriate to a writerly narrative format, as well as the identification of an explicitly written literary tradition conjoining lyric and narrative poetics.

To trace a movement from performative to writerly poetics requires not only close attention to poetic conventions but also an understanding of the status of vernacular writing in the later medieval period. It must be remembered that, throughout the medieval period, writing retained a certain dimension of orality, being understood as the representation of speech. Not only poets but even rubricators of manuscripts appropriated the language of oral declamation. Even in the late fourteenth cen-

---

4. See Hult, *Self-Fulfilling Prophecies;* Lejeune; Strohm; Verhuyck; Vitz.

tury, writing could still be described as the pale imitation of an oral original. For the translator Jean Daudin, for example, the movement from speech to script provided an analogy for linguistic translation. In the prologue to his translation of Petrarch's *De remediis unius utriusque fortunae*, dedicated to Charles V, Daudin regretfully comments that eloquence is lost in translation, just as in the case of the eloquent Cicero, Demosthenes, Homer, and Virgil, "quant on lit aucun d'eulx et on ne les ot parler, une grande partie d'eulx lui est defaillant" (when one reads any of them and does not hear them speak, he is missing a good deal).[5]

As the visual representation of an essentially oral text, the medieval illuminated manuscript has a certain theatrical—at the risk of anachronism, one might even say cinematic—quality; it does not merely describe events but, rather, stages them. The performative quality of the medieval book is of profound importance, and I will have occasion to refer many times to this idea in the course of the present work. Writing in the second quarter of the thirteenth century, Richard de Fournival testifies to the theatricality of the illustrated book in the prologue to his *Bestiaire d'amours*. Commenting on the fact that the *Bestiaire* is constructed of speech and illustrations—*parole* and *painture*—Richard explains that the combination of the two allows for a vivid auditory and visual experience of that which is depicted: "Car quant on voit painte une estoire, ou de Troie ou d'autre, on voit les fais des preudommes ke cha en ariere furent, ausi com s'il fussent present. Et tout ensi est il de parole. Car quant on ot .i. romans lire, on entent les aventures, ausi com on les veïst en present." (For when one sees a story illustrated, whether of Troy or of something else, he sees the actions of the worthy men that lived in those times, just as though they were present. And it is just the same with speech. For when one hears a romance read [aloud], he follows the adventures, just as though he saw them before him.)[6]

In *Claris et Laris*, which postdates the *Bestiaire d'amours* by about thirty years, Claris is described as witnessing the events that he reads of in a book of love stories: "En .I. petit livre veoit / La mort Tibé et Piramus" (In a little book he saw the death of Thisbe and Pyramus [Alton ed., vv. 162–63]). And the analogy between theater and the illuminated book is still apparent in fifteenth-century English defenses of the mystery plays, in which the dramatic performance is referred to as a "living book."[7]

The poets that we will examine exploited this performative quality of

5. This prologue is printed by Delisle in his "Anciennes traductions françaises"; I quote from p. 294. I am grateful to Peter Dembowski of the University of Chicago for drawing this passage to my attention.

6. Segre ed., p. 5. References to editions of works discussed are to those listed in the Editions section of the Bibliography. The first citation of a work gives the editor's last name, "ed." to indicate that the reference is to an edition, and the line or page numbers. Except where ambiguity would result, later references to the work give only line or page numbers. All translations are mine.

7. See Woolf, pp. 85–101.

literature in general and lyricism in particular in various ways: some explored the notion of writing as a visual projection of song or speech, whereas others stressed the inherent differences between performance and writing. Overall, it is possible to document a general shift of focus, in the later thirteenth and fourteenth centuries, from lyric performance to lyric composition, with the latter defined ever more insistently as an act of writing rather than one of song or declamation. Romances and dits with lyric insertions tend increasingly to recount the genesis of the lyrics in question, rather than to describe their performance. This concern with composition is associated with a more writerly concept of the song as specifically referential, documenting a particular experience; the fiction of many a fourteenth-century *dit amoureux* is that of the poet-lover who uses both lyric and narrative verse forms to record, in writing, the vicissitudes of his love. As the lyric voice is assimilated to that of the narrator or writer, a new poetics is defined.

In order to designate the act of poetic creation as it is represented in lyrico-narrative texts of the thirteenth and fourteenth centuries, I have introduced the term "lyrical writing." The concept of the "lyrical writer" is exemplified in the frontispiece illustration, a portrait of the troubadour Folquet de Marseille taken from a late thirteenth-century anthology of Provençal verse copied in Italy. The poet, seated at a writing desk, holds his pen aloft and gestures expansively as though on the verge of bursting into song: lyric composition is conceived at once as an act of writing and as an inspired performance.[8] The image reflects an understanding of writing as the visual representation of speech (or song); indeed, this vision of the lyric poet captures the metaphor expressed by the Psalmist, "My tongue is the pen of a ready writer" (Ps. 45:1). The thirteenth-century image, however, is the opposite number of the biblical text: whereas the psalmist is a singer whose song is a figurative script, the lyric poet is a writer whose script is a representation of song. The gradual establishment of the writer's primacy over the singer will be a central theme of this study.

The lyric and lyrico-narrative tradition plays a crucial role in the emergence of a "book" culture and the definition of the vernacular poet as a writer. Central to Old French lyrico-narrative poetry is the *Roman de la rose,* in which the process of writing is thematized and foregrounded as a creative, rather than merely duplicative, activity. At the same time, the act of writing the *Roman de la rose* is presented as inspired love service, ordinarily a lyric characteristic. Profusely illustrated, carefully rubricated, the *Rose* was received *as a book,* and an important aspect of its pervasive influence on subsequent French literature is its mapping out of a poetics at once lyrical and writerly. Contemporary with Jean de

8. On analogies between speaking and writing, see Camille, "Seeing and Reading."

Meun's continuation of the *Rose* are the earliest surviving single-author anthologies in the French secular literary tradition, and these are devoted to either songs or dits: first-person and frequently lyrical poetry. The growth of this lyrico-writerly poetics, centered on the lyric poet as writer and author of books, reaches new heights in the fourteenth century, in the carefully arranged anthologies of lyric and lyrico-narrative verse produced by Guillaume de Machaut and Jean Froissart.

In order to discuss the poem or poetic corpus as a book, and the poet's appropriation of bookmaking processes, it is necessary to establish an understanding of just what a vernacular literary book was in the thirteenth and fourteenth centuries. To this end, I begin with a detailed examination of selected codices, and a discussion of the relationship between poetics and manuscript format and between scribal and poetic processes.[9] I proceed from the assumption that although some codices are disorganized miscellanies, a great many—perhaps the majority—are carefully organized literary constructs. The scribe responsible for the production of the book played a role that combined aspects of editor and performer; in the words of James Farquhar, the scribe was the "organizer and *metteur-en-scène* of the book."[10] In examining the architectonics of the manuscript and the poetics of the visual text—comprising poem, rubrics, and miniatures and other decorative elements—I wish, first of all, to establish the paratextual and codicological features that would be manipulated by poet-compilers and poet-writers who conceived of their works as books. Additionally, I wish to address the presence of poet and scribe, respectively, and to distinguish the role associated with each.

In establishing the affinities between scribal and poetic practices, I have drawn on concepts that have already been identified and discussed by others. Daniel Poirion has stressed the importance of *auctoritas, translatio,* and *conjointure* as modes of cultural transmission in the Middle Ages.[11] These principles operate at the level of both poem and codex. The authority of a classical or vernacular poet can be evoked either through a grouping of his works within an anthology or by a citation within a single text. The poet's blending of material drawn from different texts or different literary traditions—what Chrétien de Troyes called a "molt bele conjointure" (very beautiful conjoining [*Erec et Enide,* Roques ed., v. 14])—is analogous to the scribe's artful *compilatio*.[12] The appropriation of classical learning and culture by the Christian Middle

---

9. For general background, see Kleinhenz; Hindman and Farquhar. For a discussion of the scribal role in an analogous process, the transformation of the previously oral *chanson de geste* into a written tradition, see Delbouille; Tyssens.

10. Hindman and Farquhar, p. 66.

11. Poirion, "Ecriture et ré-écriture," p. 118.

12. On *compilatio,* see Minnis; Parkes. On *conjointure,* see Freeman, *Poetics of "Translatio Studii" and "Conjointure"*; Kelly, "Sens" and "Conjointure."

Ages designated in the term *translatio studii et imperii* is practiced by poets, translators, and compilers alike.[13] As we will see, a scribe could effect a conjointure through a suggestive coupling of texts; he could exploit the blend of Christian and classical materials in courtly romance in order to build a bridge, within a diverse anthology, from romances of antiquity (*romans antiques*) to hagiography. These concepts, normally associated with a clerkly narrative tradition, undergo certain modifications as they are appropriated into a lyric tradition that is rapidly developing its own sense of learnedness. The compilation of anthologies devoted solely to the career of a single vernacular poet entails a new kind of poetic authority, new principles of textual conjoining. In a very real sense, such compilations are authorized by Jean de Meun's enunciation of a lyric translatio that places the medieval lyric or lyrico-narrative poet in a written lyric tradition extending back to Ovid and his predecessors, Tibullus, Catullus, and Gallus.

Following the first two chapters, devoted to narrative and lyric anthologies, respectively, I will turn to the examination of individual texts. After studying a series of thirteenth-century texts in Chapters 3–6, I will return to an examination of manuscript format in Chapter 7, a study of the emergence of the single-author anthology codex in the late thirteenth and fourteenth centuries. In the last three chapters I will examine the anthologies of Machaut and Froissart.

My analysis of both codices and texts focuses on scribes, compilers, illuminators, and poets as participants in and readers of the Old French literary tradition. Admittedly, the finer points of the compiler's craft were undoubtedly lost on a certain portion of the medieval audience, who would have experienced the texts only as they were read aloud, one at a time, and who would have had no recourse to the visual elements of the book. Even the person who commissioned the book did not necessarily concern himself or herself with the literary consciousness that informed the work of scribes and artists (or the workshop master who supervised them). Poets, who frequently state explicitly that they came to produce this or that romance after having read a particular Latin book or perused their patron's library, constitute a somewhat special case. The shared concerns of poets, scribes, and illuminators may well reflect a literate consciousness of the written medium and its creative potential that was appreciated, initially, by only a small percentage of the medieval audience.

On the other hand, the sharp increase in vernacular manuscript production in the thirteenth and especially the fourteenth centuries, and the careful arrangement and execution characteristic of so many, argue

---

13. On *translatio studii*, see Freeman, *Poetics of "Translatio Studii" and "Conjointure"*; Kelly, *"Translatio Studii"*; Uitti, *Story, Myth, and Celebration*, especially pp. 134, 146–51, 204–5.

for a growing literacy rate and an increasing demand for books that are more than mere repositories of texts to be read aloud. The popularity of acrostics and anagrams in late thirteenth- and fourteenth-century poetry further suggests an audience that delights in the manipulation of the written word. And it is impossible to imagine that the owners of illuminated manuscripts would never have looked at the pictures for which they had paid so much, even if they were unable to read a single word. Through a visual appreciation of author portraits, recurring iconographic motifs, and general page layout, even an illiterate "reader" could have been conditioned to certain concepts of authorship, codicological continuity, or literarity, which in turn might inform his or her appreciation of texts received aurally.

Although specific information about literacy rates in the thirteenth and fourteenth centuries is difficult to come by—let alone information about the owners of particular manuscripts, virtually none of whom can be identified at all—the texts themselves offer some evidence for lay literacy. Even in the twelfth century, certain romance couples—Lavinia and Eneas, or the lovers of Marie de France's *Milun*—correspond in writing, and the practice recurs in various texts of the thirteenth and fourteenth centuries: the *Roman du castelain de Couci*, the *Livre du voir dit*. In *Yvain*, a young girl reads a romance to her parents. Froissart, in *L'Espinette amoureuse*, claims that his lady first won his affections by reading to him from *Cléomadès*. The attribution of literacy may be meant to confer a special status on the character in question, but surely some lay men and women did know how to read and write, did read books to themselves and to one another, and therefore could have been sensitive to scribal or poetic manipulation of codicological elements.

We will probably never know the full story of the reception of medieval literature by its general audience, given the lack of detailed information about the production and consumption of oral and written works alike. In the end, we are left with the texts and the books themselves as our primary evidence, and if these do not render up the secrets of their medieval owners, readers, and listeners, at least they may have something to tell us about their authors, copyists, and illustrators. It is primarily with the latter group that this book is concerned.

# PART ONE

# ON THE NATURE OF THE BOOK
# IN THE THIRTEENTH AND
# FOURTEENTH CENTURIES

Et je vous monstrerai comment cis escris a painture et pa-
rolle. Car il est bien apert k'il a parole, par che ke toute
escripture si est faite pour parole monstrer et pour che ke on
le lise; et quant on le list, si revient elle a nature de parole. . . .
Et meesmement cis escris est de tel sentence k'il painture
desire.

[And I will show you how this writing has illustration and
speech. For it is quite clear that it has speech, since all writing
is made in order to show forth speech, and in order to be
read; and when it is read, it reverts to the nature of speech.
. . . And similarly this writing is of such a topic that it desires
illustration.]

Richard de Fournival, *Bestiaire d'amours*

Chapter 1

# Scribal Practice and Poetic Process
# in Didactic and Narrative Anthologies

The subject of vernacular codex organization and production in the thirteenth and fourteenth centuries is a vast and largely unexplored area; the following discussion makes no claims at being comprehensive. Its aim is to identify certain organizational principles typical of French literary codices of this period and certain aspects of manuscript format and text presentation. The implications of these codicological features for thirteenth- and fourteenth-century poets will be discussed in subsequent chapters; before a given poet's manipulation of his work as a written medium can be assessed, a certain understanding must be established of what a vernacular literary book was in the later Middle Ages and how it functioned as a poetic system in its own right. In this chapter, I set forth some basic avenues of inquiry into the architectonics of the codex and the poetics of the manuscript text.

Many medieval codices are miscellanies, containing a seemingly random mixture of didactic, courtly, and bawdy texts in prose and verse;[1] others, at the opposite end of the spectrum, contain but a single text. Even in those having more uniform contents, it is not always possible to discern any logic to the order of pieces. Many codices, however—many more, I suspect, than are currently recognized—are organized according to principles ranging from rudimentary groupings of thematically related texts to an elaborate overall design. Similarly, whereas some are decorated for purely ornamental and even ostentatious purposes and others lack any decoration at all, many are true "critical editions," with carefully designed programs of rubrication and illumination that clarify the structure of the book and provide textual commentary. No doubt the tastes, the degree of literary sophistication, and the financial capacities

---

1. For a detailed description of such a manuscript, see Lepage, "Recueil français." See also Faral's facsimile edition, *Manuscrit 19152 du Fonds français;* Faral's remarks, pp. 10–11, are relevant here.

of the manuscript owner influenced the selection of texts and the degree and type of ornamentation; and the degree of patron control over manuscript production was probably itself variable. Whether the scribe was executing a plan of his own creation or one dictated by his patron, though, is less important for the present context than an understanding of what this plan was and how it was put into effect: in either case we are witnessing the processes by which a scribe or team of scribes shaped a group of texts into a book. In the following examples, therefore, I have not attempted to distinguish patron-initiated from scribally initiated features. I analyze the evidence of the manuscripts as artifacts and the work of the scribe as it appears therein in order to arrive at a critical reading of the books themselves.

## Examples of Thematic Unity: MSS Bibl. Nat. fr. 24428 and 12786

In referring to this category of manuscript organization as "thematic," I purposely choose a term of general rather than precise meaning, for it is meant to cover a range of possibilities. The distinction of "thematic" and "narrative" organization is itself somewhat artificial, and it is used here purely as a device for imposing some kind of order on an extremely diverse field. The two examples I have chosen exhibit different kinds of organization. In both, certain themes and motifs governed the selection of texts. In MS 24428 the pieces have been arranged in a linear progression, emanating from the first text and building up to the last; in MS 12786 the pieces are grouped in loosely defined categories around a central text.

MS 24428, copied in the late thirteenth or early fourteenth century,[2] is an anthology of didactic texts translated or adapted from various Latin sources:

*L'Image du monde* (first verse redaction)
*Li Volucraires*, a poem attributed to Omond, treating the allegorical significance of birds and trees
*Li Bestiaire divin* of Guillaume le Clerc
An anonymous allegorical lapidary (Pannier ed., *Lapidaires français*, pp. 228–85)
Marie de France's *Fables d'Ysopet*

2. A colophon attached to the *Image* states that it was copied in 1265, but this must have been taken from the source from which MS 24428 was copied. For a discussion of the dating of MS 24428, and its attribution of both the *Image* and the *Volucraires* to "Omond," see Fant, pp. 45–51.

A treatise on sin and penance, beginning "Qui veut faire confession . . ."
(He who wishes to make confession . . .).

The uniform appearance of the manuscript suggests that it was written
and compiled at one time, so the existing arrangement can be assumed
to reflect an original plan.

The *Image du monde* is, as its name suggests, a description of the
natural world.[3] Its fifty-five chapters include an account of the creation
of the world; enumerations of the plants, birds, animals, and precious
stones to be found in various places; and discussions of geography and
astronomy. The texts that follow elaborate upon the discussions of the
natural world, providing more detailed information about individual
species and also revealing the allegorical significance of each. These
treatises thus constitute a continuation of the *Image du monde*, one
which, moreover, is invited by the text itself. At the end of the chapter
on the stones of India, for example, the reader who wishes further
information is instructed to "lire ou lapidaire, / Qui dist leur nons & leur
vertus" (read in the lapidary, which tells their names and their powers
([fol. 17]). And at the end of the entire discussion of beasts and birds,
plants and minerals, is the following comment:

> Maintes choses sont bien apertes
> Dont les raisons sont molt covertes.
>
> .  .  .  .  .
>
> Par clergie puet bien li hom
> D'aucune chose avoir raison.

[Many things are quite evident, for which the reasons are hidden. . . . By
means of learning, man can know the reason for something.] [Fol. 22v]

The *Image* itself is an open text, allowing plenty of possibility for amplification. In particular, it concentrates on that which is "evident," describing the habits and appearances of earthly things and the motions and
properties of heavenly bodies, without attempting to uncover the "hidden reasons." The latter approach is taken in the three allegorical treatises; they are not only the continuation but also the exegesis of the
opening piece.

The middle section of the codex actually offers two different kinds of
exegesis: the allegorical treatises are followed by a transposition of birds
and animals into the literary language of fable, itself interpreted moral-

3. On the *Image,* see Charles-Victor Langlois, *Vie en France au Moyen Age,* vol. 3, pp.
135–97. On rubrics and chapter headings in the *Image,* see Grand, pp. 10–12; for citations
of the prologue and certain other passages, see Grand, pp. 30–57. A diagram from the
*Image* is reproduced by Evans, p. 43, fig. 16.

istically. Allegory and morality provide the bridge from the *Image,* a straightforward account of the natural world placed in the context of God as creator and sustainer, to the penitential treatise, a straightforward account of spiritual salvation. The overall plan reflects the medieval system of fourfold exegesis: we begin with the literal reading of the world, progress to allegorical and tropological readings, and arrive finally at the anagogical reading, an unveiled explanation of the moral life of the human soul.

The *Image du monde,* then, provides the basis for the entire compilation, whereas the treatise on penance is, so to speak, its final cause. By referring back to the opening treatise, the reader can situate a given motif in the larger context of the world and its relationship to God. Additionally, the admonishments to the reader in the prologue to the *Image,* by focusing attention on the orderly arrangement and illustration of the text, are applicable to the codex as a whole. The introduction stresses the importance of the astronomical diagrams, stating that without these, "li livres ne porroit estre legierement [entendus]" (the book could not easily be understood [fol. 1]).[4] These figures are clearly necessary to the exposition of such phenomena as eclipses or planetary conjunctions and of the general structure of the cosmos. But miniatures also play an important role in the allegorical exposition of the two texts that follow, as well as in the *Fables;* the introduction to the *Image* is at the same time an introduction to the entire codex. In the *Bestiaire divin,* each bird or animal is identified in a rubric and in a miniature that illustrates both the particular trait ascribed to the animal in question and the allegorical interpretation. The image of the pelican (fol. 57), for example, shows her stabbing her breast to shed life-giving blood on her babies; beside her is the Crucifixion, where Christ is being stabbed by Saint Longinus (Reinsch ed., vv. 521–614). Similarly, the turtle dove (fol. 72v) is shown as a single bird in a tree, next to which Christ is shown bearing the Cross between two guards while a female figure looks on: the turtle dove mourns her lost mate as the Church mourns Christ (vv. 2649–2736). The miniatures are truly a rendition in visual terms of the text in its dual focus, both here and in the single miniature of the *Volucraires.* Each fable, in turn, is likewise illustrated; and although these miniatures do not portray the "allegorical leap," they do provide a vivid representation of the central action, thereby helping to fix the moral tale more firmly in the mind of the reader.

The prologue of the *Image* reminds the reader that the "livre de clergie" (book of learning) has been carefully ordered and that this order

4. The word "entendus" was omitted in MS 24428; I have taken it from MS Bibl. Nat. fr. 1553, fol. 163.

should be respected. The reader is instructed to read "ordeneement" (in order), "Si qu'il ne lise rien avant / S'il n'entent ce qui est devant" (Such that he read no further unless he understands what comes before [fol. 1v]). Like the statement that the illustrations are an integral part of the text, this admonition to attend to the order of the book, and not to proceed until each point has been fully grasped, applies very well to the codex as a whole: here, even more than within the *Image* itself, each text builds on the last, leading the reader through a series of steps to the final revelation.

Indeed, this very structure—the movement from Divine Creation to the natural world and back again to the spiritual—is itself signaled in the closing section of the *Image* in a statement equally relevant to the opening text and to the book as a whole. Returning at the end of his treatise to God, who is reached at the outermost limits of the cosmos, the narrator comments, "Ci fenist l'Image dou monde. / A dieu commence, a dieu prent fin" (Here ends the *Image of the World*. It begins with God, it ends with God [fol. 47v]). The *Image du monde,* then, provides not only the basic subject matter but also the structural model for the entire anthology. By following this plan, the compiler constructed a book that is itself a *livre de clergie,* a large-scale description and decoding of the world.

I have chosen a relatively straightforward example to begin with, because it will make it easier to see the editorial practices of the compiler. Clearly, the compiler of MS 24428 was a careful reader, and he chose each element of his compilation with an eye to its participation in an overall plan. Each text contributes to the structure of the whole, and each in turn is more fully understood when read in conjunction with the others. We can begin to see the intimate relationship between poetic and scribal practices, between the microstructure of the individual text and the macrostructure of the anthology codex. It is appropriate here to think of Marie de France's famous enunciation of literary tradition in the prologue to her *Lais:* when the ancients wrote books, they customarily left it up to future generations of readers to "gloser la lettre / E de lur sen le surplus mettre" (gloss the letter and discover further meaning [Rychner ed., vv. 15–16]).[5] As readers of Marie de France have already noted, there is more than one way to "gloss the letter"; not only actual glosses, but also creative translations, adaptations, and reworkings of earlier texts contribute to this process of clarification. As the above example has demonstrated, the scribal compiler as well participates in this ongoing cultural project: his suggestive arrangement of texts is another means by which a literary work can be seen, as Marie de France put it, to have "blossomed."

5. See Alfred Foulet and Uitti; Hult, *Self-Fulfilling Prophecies,* pp. 95–97.

I turn now to a second example of thematic organization, the codex Bibl. Nat. fr. 12786, which dates from the early fourteenth century. The collection comprises an assortment of lyrical, allegorical, and didactic texts.[6] Although they are not arranged as systematically as the contents of MS 24428, there are evident groupings of allegorical, lyric, didactic, and religious poems. The contents are

> *Le Roman de la poire*, by Tibaut, an imitation of the *Roman de la rose* that employs personification allegory, lyric insertions (copied with space for music, which was never filled in), and a series of allusions to exemplary lovers of vernacular and classical tradition (see below, Chapter 6)
>
> *Le Livre des pierres*, an anonymous prose treatise enumerating the properties and allegorical significance of precious stones (Pannier ed., *Lapidaires français*, pp. 291–97)
>
> *Li Bestiaire d'amours*, by Richard de Fournival, in which the traditional bestiary animals become allegories of love (see below, Chapter 5)
>
> "Son poitevin" (Poitevin song), the first stanza of a song attributed elsewhere to Gautier d'Espinal, copied without space for music
>
> *Le Roman de la rose* of Guillaume de Lorris, with only the short anonymous continuation
>
> A series of motets, copied with space for musical notation that was never provided
>
> "Les Prophecies que Ezechiel li prophetes fist," a series of predictions concerning weather patterns and the behavior that is thereby indicated, based on which day of the week Christmas falls
>
> *Explication des songes*, an anonymous prose treatise explaining the prophetic significance of a long series of dream images
>
> *L'Ordre de l'amors*, a dit describing a monastic order of faithful lovers, possibly by Nicole de Margival[7]
>
> *La Trinitez Nostre Dame*
>
> *Les .IX. Joies Nostre Dame*
>
> *Le Dit d'Aristote*, probably by Rutebeuf
>
> *Le Lunaire de Salomon*, a treatise predicting the traits to be expected in children born on each day of the lunar cycle.

It is interesting that the *Rose* appears here in short form, at the center of the manuscript. The lack of Jean de Meun's continuation, first of all, is surprising; MS 12786 is the only one of the nearly three hundred surviving *Rose* manuscripts known to date that does not contain his por-

---

6. My understanding of MS 12786 has been enriched through conversations with Lori Walters of Princeton University, who discusses this manuscript in her dissertation, "Chrétien de Troyes and the *Romance of the Rose*" (pp. 363–87). Walters has informed me that this dating of MS 12786 derives from a private consultation with François Avril of the Bibliothèque Nationale. The presentation of the *Roman de la poire* in MS 12786 will be discussed in Chapter 6. For information concerning editions of the works found in MS 12786, see Segre ed., *Bestiaire d'amours*, pp. xxxviii–xl.

7. See Iburg.

tion of the poem.[8] Even the six other manuscripts containing the anonymous continuation attach Jean's continuation to the end of the first one.
It is possible that the scribe meant to add Jean's portion, and that this
work—along with musical notation, illuminations (for which spaces were
reserved in the *Poire,* the *Bestiaire d'amours,* and the *Rose*)—and the rubrics
in the second half of the codex (for which space was also reserved)—was
simply never completed. This hypothesis is supported by the fact that
the scribe removed two folios from the final gathering of the *Rose* before
copying the text, thereby causing it to end on the last folio of a gathering. He left blank the remaining half of the recto side and all of the verso
side of the final folio. The scribe thereby made it possible to add Jean's
continuation without any erasures, recopying, or dismantling of gatherings. Also, the final couplet of the anonymous continuation is missing,
and there is no explicit, although the *Rose* is otherwise rubricated. These
signs do suggest that the scribe intended to continue the text of the *Rose,*
but unfortunately we cannot be sure of it.

As for the central location of the *Rose,* this too is open to question.
Since neither folios nor gatherings are numbered, and none of the
catchwords has survived, we cannot be certain that the present order of
texts is the original one.[9] We do know, however, that the contents are all
original to the collection, since the entire manuscript is written in a single
hand; and since most of the texts begin on the same page, or at least
within the same gathering, where the previous text ends, we can at least
be sure of the arrangement of individual sections within the codex. Thus
we know that the three sequences—*Poire,* lapidary; *Bestiaire d'amours,*
"son poitevin," *Rose;* and the entire remainder of the codex from the
motets on—represent the original order of texts, even if we cannot be
certain that these three sections originally followed one another in the
current order. Most of the thematic groupings noted above, then, are
original to the manuscript. And although the midpoint location of the
*Rose* must remain a hypothesis, evidence suggests that it was seen as the
nuclear text of the anthology; since it begins in the middle of a gathering, it cannot have occupied first place, and it was, in my opinion, most
likely used as the centerpiece of the collection.

Let us examine a little more closely the thematic relationship of the
*Rose* to the remainder of the book. The *Poire,* as I have said, is closely
modeled on the *Rose;* the *Bestiaire d'amours,* in turn, is likewise related to
the *Rose,* not only through its use of allegory, but also as a similar exam-

8. See Ernest Langlois.

9. Ernest Langlois (pp. 49–52) notes that the ink of the first page of the *Bestiaire
d'amours* is faded, and suggests that it may have occupied first place at a time when the
manuscript was without a cover. But this could have occurred at any time during the six
centuries since the manuscript was copied; it need not have occupied first place during the
fourteenth century.

ple of the conflation of lyricism with a literary form normally associated with a more learned tradition. We know from the rubrication that the *Bestiaire d'amours* would have ended with a miniature representing the God of Love; this image, not part of the normal iconography of the *Bestiaire d'amours*, provides a link between this treatise and the *Rose*, which begins on the facing page.[10] The "son poitevin," as well as the motets, expands on the lyrical quality of the *Rose*, the *Bestiaire d'amours*, and the *Poire* and echoes the lyric insertions in the *Poire*. The *Ordre de l'amors*, finally, corresponds to the "art d'amors" enclosed in the *Rose*.

The treatise on dreams is of obvious relevance to the *Rose* and may in fact have been edited to this end. No modern edition exists for this text, but I have seen two other versions of it in fourteenth-century manuscripts.[11] The version in MS 12786 is very much shorter than either of these other two and presents its images in a different order: it opens with the dream image of birds, and at its midpoint we find, among others, dreams of being in a *vergier* (garden); of fountains; of hearing music; of beholding one's own face; and of erotic encounters. This arrangement, which highlights those images found in Guillaume de Lorris's dream, may well be the work of a compiler building a lyrico-didactic anthology with the *Rose* at its core.

The other texts, finally, are of less immediate relevance to the *Rose* but do participate in its general field of associations. The lapidary is another allegorical text; the "Ezechiel," as well as the *Lunaire de Salomon*, continues the theme of prophecy; the religious poems offer spiritual love, in honor of the "Rose without thorns." Even the figures of Aristotle and Solomon are appropriate to the lyrico-didactic tenor of the collection. Aristotle, after all, is not only one of the most famous scholars of all time, but also, in a well-known medieval legend, the lover whose weakness for a singing maiden is celebrated in the *Lai d'Aristote*. And Solomon likewise is known both as philosopher—again, one of the most important known to the Middle Ages—and also as an aristocratic lover, author of an allegorical love poem whose pervasive influence is apparent not only in the *Roman de la rose* but throughout the medieval lyric tradition. Both of these figures, then, embody the conflation of lyricism and clerkliness exemplified by the *Rose*.

In spite of the diversity of the collection, then, every text within it does relate in one way or another to the *Rose*, which thus functions to hold the

10. The God of Love appears at the beginning of the *Bestiaire d'amours* in MS Bibl. Nat. fr. 25566; he is shown at the end in the two manuscripts which contain the narrative continuation of the *Bestiaire d'amours*. This continuation, including the introduction of the God of Love, is an imitation of the *Roman de la rose*. It is interesting that in MS 12786, we find an independent introduction of the God of Love into the *Bestiaire d'amours* as a means of associating it with the *Rose*.

11. The treatise on dreams also appears in MSS Bibl. Nat. fr. 24432 and 1317.

collection together by providing the "intertext" in which all elements are united. Interestingly, a further piece of evidence that this particular assortment of texts may represent a conscious response to the *Rose* is the presence of virtually the same poetic elements in Nicole de Margival's *Dit de la panthère d'amours*. The latter poem is approximately contemporary with MS 12786, having been composed sometime around 1300. I will discuss the poetic types brought together in the *Panthère* in Chapter 6; as we will see, the *Roman de la rose* is used here as a primary subtext that authorizes the incorporation of bestiary, lapidary, didactic, and lyric elements. Although it is impossible to establish a relationship of influence or imitation between MS 12786 and the *Panthère,* the similarities between poem and book do serve, again, as eloquent demonstration of the affinities between scribal and poetic process, between *compilatio* and *conjointure*.

## Examples of Narrative Organization: MSS Bibl. Nat. fr. 1447 and 375

I will begin, as before, with a relatively simple example of narrative organization. The MS Bibl. Nat. fr. 1447, copied in the first half of the fourteenth century, contains only three texts: the anonymous *Floire et Blanchefleur;* Adenet le Roi's *Berthe aus grans piés;* and the anonymous *Claris et Laris.* Although each poem is a separate fascicle unit, they are copied in the same hand and must surely have been intended to occupy the current order. On the surface it may seem that three very different sorts of texts have been combined here: the first and the last are both romances in octosyllabic couplets, but only the last contains Arthurian material, whereas the middle text is composed in the monorhymed *laisses* of the *chanson de geste*. Nonetheless, there is a logic behind this choice of texts.

The relationship between the first two poems is straightforward: as the prologue to *Floire et Blanchefleur* reminds us, these characters are the parents of Bertha, mother of Charlemagne. Thus the prologue to the first text actually serves to introduce the second as well, where Floire and especially Blanchefleur reappear. *Floire et Blanchefleur* also serves as an appropriate "first chapter" to the book in that it presents two major cultural infusions at the basis of European civilization: Christianity and the classical tradition. The first appears when, upon marrying Blanchefleur, Floire becomes a Christian to please his wife; it is as a Christian, the prologue reminds us, that he becomes king of Hungary and progenitor of Charlemagne. As the result of exemplary love Christianity is established in this Eastern European kingdom, and ultimately passes to one of the most important heroes of Western Europe.

The classical tradition is represented by the cup for which Blanche-fleur is traded (Pelan ed., vv. 434–97). The cup is decorated with the story of the Trojan War; it once belonged to Aeneas, who gave it to Lavinia. Following this, we are told, the cup remained for some generations in the treasury of the Caesars until it was stolen, passing into the hands of merchants and, ultimately, to Floire himself. Through his possession of this cup, Floire's quest for Blanchefleur parallels that of Aeneas for Lavinia; and just as Aeneas and Lavinia were the ancestors of Romulus, founder of Rome, so Floire and Blanchefleur are the ancestors of Charlemagne, medieval continuator of the Roman Empire. The material presence of this artifact stresses the sense of continuity leading from Troy through Rome and into medieval Europe; what we have come to recognize under the terms *translatio studii*, transmission of culture and learning, and *translatio imperii*, transmission of imperial authority.

*Claris et Laris*, which is unique to this manuscript, is an interesting choice to follow the *Floire-Berthe* progression. It is a massive compendium of Arthuriana, featuring numerous figures from romance tradition: Cligés, Yvain, Gauvain, Eliduc, Erec, Merlin, King Mark, and many others. The entire Arthurian world is brought into play and placed in a pan-European context: Claris and Laris are Gascons, and the battles fought by Arthur and his knights involve figures from Spain, France, Germany, and Hungary. The location of Arthur in this central European setting—victorious king among the French and Germans, fighting off threats from Spain and from the East—implicitly associates him in turn with the figure of Charlemagne.

The three texts were composed independently, over a period of approximately one hundred years. They are not associated in any other surviving manuscript. The compilation in MS 1447 is the work of an individual who saw in the personages, themes, and motifs shared among these works the possibility for a poetic conjointure that transcends the boundaries of individual texts. To the reception of Christianity and the classical tradition portrayed in the first text is added historical material proper to the epic tradition and a detailed picture of the Arthurian world. The book as a whole offers a synthesis of Old French literary possibilities. Central to this picture of historical and cultural progression, of translatio studii and imperii, is Charlemagne, the mythico-historical figure whose presence, both implicit and explicit, informs the entire book.

MS 1447 is typical of many narrative anthologies, which map out a progression from antiquity to the medieval world. The romans antiques are usually transmitted in chronologically ordered pairs or groups, very often followed by Arthurian material.[12] For example, the famous Guiot

12. For example, there are only two manuscripts of *Eneas*, out of a total of nine, where it

manuscript, Bibl. Nat. fr. 794, originally began with *Athis et Prophilias*, set in Athens; it moved on through the *Roman de Troie*, the *Roman de Brut*, and the *Empereurs de Rome* and ended with the five romances of Chrétien de Troyes.[13] A particularly intricate example of this sort of compilation, MS Bibl. Nat. fr. 1450, will be discussed in a later section of this chapter. One of the most exhaustive of these narrative compendia, in turn, is MS Bibl. Nat. fr. 375, an Artesian codex of the early fourteenth century that contains an encyclopedic array of texts.[14] The first thirty-three folios—an illuminated Apocalypse, a French commentary on the Apocalypse, the *Prophetie de la sibylle Tiburniea*, and the *Livre de Seneke*—are clearly from a different manuscript and will be excluded from discussion. What remains of the original compilation is as follows:

*Le Roman de Thebes*
*Le Roman de Troie*
*Athis et Prophilias*, here identified as *Li Sieges d'Ataines*
Jean Bodel's *Congé*
*Le Roman d'Alexandre*, to which has been added, with no break, the *Significa-tion de la mort Alexandre* and the *Vengeance Alexandre*
A prose genealogy of the counts of Boulogne, a later addition written on some folios that were left blank
The third part of the *Roman de Rou*, which recounts the history of the dukes of Normandy
*Guillaume d'Engleterre*
*Floire et Blanchefleur*
*Blancandin*
Chrétien's *Cligès*
Chrétien's *Erec et Enide*
*La Viellette*, a fabliau about a knight and an old woman
*Ille et Galeron*, by Gautier d'Arras
Gautier de Coinci's miracle of Theophilus
*Amadas et Ydoine*
*La Chastelaine de Vergi*
A musically notated *prosa* in honor of Saint Stephen
*Vers de la mort*
*La Loenge Nostre Dame*
A repetition of *La Viellette*
Nine miracles of Our Lady

The whole is preceded by a table of plot summaries, in rhymed couplets, for each text in the collection; these summaries range from about thirty to about a hundred lines in length.[15] From this, and from the number-

---

is not accompanied by at least one other text providing background or continuation; see Salverda de Grave ed., *Eneas*, vol. I, pp. iv–v.
13. See Roques, "Manuscrit fr. 794."
14. On MS 375, see Micha, pp. 29–32, 316–24; and François.
15. These summaries were published by Jordan.

ing of the pieces, we know that the compilation from *Thebes* on is complete. *Thebes* bears the number three, however, and, unfortunately, the pages bearing the first nine summaries are lost, so we do not know what the missing texts were.

Several different scribes worked on MS 375; that different texts were copied independently (probably simultaneously) is suggested by the fact that the numeration of gatherings starts over again with number one at the beginnings of *Thebes, Troie,* and *Alexandre.* Indeed, the copyists may not even have been aware of the position for which the texts they copied were destined. The rubrics between pieces provide a sense of continuity; in most cases, they give the name and number of the text that has just ended and the name of the one to follow. The number and the title of the text to follow, however, are often written in a hand different from (though contemporary with) that of the text. At the end of *Thebes,* for example, the copyist wrote, "Explicit li sieges de Tebes. & d'Ethioclet & de Pollinices" (Here ends the siege of Thebes and [the tale] of Eteocles and Pollinices [fol. 67v]). Following this, in a different ink, is added "li tierce brańke" (the third branch). Similarly, the copyist of *Theophile* completed his text, "Chi fine de Theophilus / benis soit qui l'escrist" (Here ends [the tale] of Theophilus. Blessed be he who wrote it [fol. 315]). To this was added, "Li sezeisime. Et ci aprés d'Amaldas & d'Idoine" (The sixteenth. And after this [the tale] of Amaldas and Idoine). Most likely, the final arrangement was done by a compiler who oversaw the work of the other scribes and who was responsible for assembling the completed texts, numbering them, and completing the rubrication.

The table of summaries, which functions as a prologue to the entire compilation, leaves no doubt that MS 375 was conceived as a unified whole. Here, as in the rubrics, the texts are numbered as the "branches" of the book:

> Li dousime branque del livre
> Parole & demoustre a delivre
> Et de Cligét et de Fenisse. . . .

> En la quatorsime branquete
> Orés d'une puant viellette.

[The twelfth branch of the book speaks and reveals about both Cligès and Fenice. . . . In the fourteenth branchlet, you will hear of a vile old woman.] [Fol. 34]

The word *branche* is normally applied to the segments of a large narrative cycle, such as the *Roman de Renart* or the Grail romances. Its use here indicates the extent to which independently composed texts could be subsumed by the overall plan of the book. On a smaller scale, the three Alexander narratives, recognized today as separate texts with different authors, have been conjoined to form a single entry.

The selection and disposition of texts is analogous to that found in MSS 1447 or the Guiot manuscript; again, there is a progression from ancient to contemporary times. The overall movement is from paganism to Christianity; within this, the story of love and chivalry as ongoing human activities creates a cultural continuity between the ancient and medieval worlds. The first four texts (that is, numbers three through six of the original compilation) take us through a progression of cities: Thebes, Troy, Athens, Arras. Following this first cycle, we return to the Greek world and move from the legend of Alexander to the history of the Anglo-Norman dynasty. A third cycle begins with *Floire et Blanchefleur*, where we return yet again to the pagan world; this time, the narrative recounts the contact between pagan and Christian cultures and the absorption, through conversion, of pagan into Christian. *Floire* is followed by a series of romances set in a semimythical but Christian and European world; this series culminates in the contemporary French setting of the *Chastelaine de Vergi*.

Within the series of romances, two texts offer alternative poetic responses to the theme of love and adventure. The fabliau of *La Viellette* gives a parodic version of the romance heroine; in *Theophile*, Theophilus and the Virgin are the clerical, spiritualized counterpart of the chivalric couples of the romance world. *Theophile* also, of course, anticipates the series of religious poems with which the collection ends, preparing for the contrast of these final miracle stories with the pagan tales at the beginning. The book is a global compendium of Old French narrative. Classical and Christian learning, human and divine love, chivalric and spiritual experience are the complementary poles of the cultural heritage here presented, and they find expression in epic, romance, fabliau, hagiographic and even liturgical format.

Numerous thematic and narrative parallels govern the series of romances, serving not only to unify them as a group but also to draw together the entire collection. The prologue to the *Roman de Rou*, for example, declares the importance of writing as a means of preserving history, by recording the great cities and the great men. Citing Thebes, Babylon, and Troy, the narrative comments:

Meinte cité ad ja esté
e meinte riche poësté,
dunt nus or(e) rien ne seüssum
si en escriz rien ne eüssum.

[There have been many cities and many rich imperial powers, of which we would know nothing now if we had nothing in writing.] [Vv. 85–92]

23

Because it comes after the initial cycle of great cities, this statement is of obvious relevance to the compilation as a whole. The historical discussion of this passage further helps to link the history of the Normans to the immediately preceding tale of Alexander, who is cited here as an important part of the heritage that writing has preserved for us.

If the *Roman de Rou* expresses the principle of translatio imperii—the historical succession of empires, the passage of power and authority from one locale to the next—the Christianization of imperial power is represented in *Floire et Blanchefleur* with the conversion of Floire, the Hungarian king, and is continued in *Blancandin* with the double conversion of the Greek prince Sadoine and his Saracen bride. In both cases, conversion is the result of human love and friendship; this association strengthens the link between the representations of non-Christian love and friendship in the romans antiques and the purely Christian love of the miracle stories. Since *Blancandin* recounts the story of an Athenian prince and his alliance with a French prince, it further continues the story of Greece, which has been presented from the siege of Thebes through the death of Alexander: Greece is Christianized, and brought into contact with France.

These themes are continued in Chrétien's two romances. *Cligès* contributes its famous prologue enunciation of cultural translatio, noting the passage of *chevalerie* and *clergie* from Greece to Rome and then to France. It is in *Cligès* that the Greek world is brought into contact with the Arthurian world, through the efforts of a new Alexander; and Constantinople is the next in the series of great cities. The implied cultural link between Greek and French (or Anglo-Norman) societies is further cemented.[16] *Erec et Enide,* in turn, contributes its statement of narrative conjointure, which similarly reflects on the masterful conjoining of texts within the collection.

*Erec* also works together with *Floire* to continue the story of Troy, recounted in the first half of the book. *Floire* portrays the fall of Troy on the cup traded for Blanchefleur; *Erec* portrays the story of Eneas on Enide's saddle. The relationship between these two artifacts creates a substantial link between the two texts, whereas their encapsulation of the themes of the first part of the book contributes to the unification of the collection. The presence of the artifacts in the texts creates an interpenetration of roman antique and courtly romance, which further expresses the interpenetration through visual and textual artifacts of ancient and medieval cultures.

In addition to the general themes of classical antiquity, Christian con-

---

16. That the portrayal of "Greek" society was a significant factor in the inclusion of *Cligès* is suggested by the fact that the summary focuses entirely on the portion of the story set in Constantinople.

version, love, and chivalry, specific narrative parallels link the various romances. In both *Floire* and *Cligès,* the imagined death of the lady nearly brings about the suicide of her lover. The same motif appears in *Amadas et Ydoine,* where Ydoine, who appears to be dying because of a magic ring secretly placed on her finger by an enemy knight, pleads on her "deathbed" for her lover to go on living. Ydoine, like Fenice, resorts to magic to escape the sexual advances of her husband, while Blanche-fleur manages to resist the caliph, her would-be husband. In most of these romances, lovers are separated and one must quest in search of the other; in many, the knight must perform a series of military exploits to win or to secure his lady. Again, these romance themes contribute to the overall unification of the codex. The experience of human love is shown to encompass not only eroticism but also feats of arms, the virtues of chastity and fidelity, and even the miracle of regeneration in the face of apparent death; the themes of the opening historical texts and the closing miracle stories are interwoven. The relationship between the romance heroine's escape from death and religious miracle is suggested by the juxtaposition of the châtelaine de Vergi and Saint Stephen: the one heroine who really does die is, as the others would have been, a martyr to love, and so parallels the Christian martyr.[17] The miracle of salvation is further expressed in the juxtaposed stories of Ydoine and Theophilus: a tale in which a man saves a lady from apparent death caused by the sinister magic of an enemy knight follows a story in which Our Lady saves a man from apparent spiritual death caused by the Archenemy himself.

Overall, this arrangement of texts results in a coherent book and also makes a statement about the medieval romance, in which seemingly disparate thematic and cultural currents are drawn together. Although thematic analysis can help to explain the particular choices made by the compiler, in the end we must recognize that MS 375 represents a response to a fundamental quality of romance poetics: its power to blend and to conjoin, to mediate between the cross-currents of medieval European culture, and to express that culture's fears, hopes, and ideals. Again, MS 375 demonstrates the extent to which poets, scribes, and compilers were collaborators in a common project of literary creation and transmission.

As we might expect, the figures of scribe and compiler play an interesting role in MS 375. The author of the table of summaries, Peros de Neele, names himself in an explicit. Whether or not Peros was the one

---

17. The *Chastelaine de Vergi* is also associated with saints' lives in the early fifteenth-century MS Bibl. Nat. fr. 1555. It appears in the context of religious and didactic poetry in another manuscript of the late fourteenth or early fifteenth century, announced and described by Lodge. At least some readers evidently regarded it as the story of an exemplary martyr of love.

who "masterminded" the compilation, it is at any rate he who presents it in its entirety; he is our guide, so to speak, in perusing the book. Interestingly, his manner of presentation imitates oral declamation. The summaries are replete with expressions such as "Listen . . ." and "You will hear . . ." They frequently end with short prayers and invocations, in which the use of the first-person plural suggests the bond established between performer and audience: "Or nus doinst Dius si bien rescore" (Now may God grant us such good deliverance [fol. 34]). Such language recalls the language of literary forms known to have been part of the oral repertory of the *jongleurs,* such as saints' lives and chanson de geste. The scribe assumes a role analogous to the performer: he is an intermediary between the audience and the story, and the book is the space in which his written "performance" takes place.

A second scribe names himself at the end of *Troie* in an oft-quoted colophon of thirty-eight verses.[18] He identifies himself as Jehan Mados, nephew of Adam de la Halle. The date given in this colophon, 1288, is too early to apply to this manuscript, which can be dated on paleographic grounds as early fourteenth century; it must, then, derive from the source of MS 375. Possibly, as suggested by Charles François, the date was copied accidentally by a scribe who thought it was part of the text.[19] On the other hand, perhaps he copied it by design: it is not, after all, inappropriate to the themes of the collection. The eulogy of Adam anticipates the *Congé* of Jehan Bodel, which follows after the next entry; the stories of Troy and Athens are interwoven with the story of Arras and its poets and clerks. Madot himself adopts a stance derived from the Goliardic tradition. In terms reminiscent of the Archpoet, or Rutebeuf, he complains of the cold that he suffered while performing his task, laments the loss of his coat in a dice game, and expresses the hope that he will be paid promptly for his work. The colorful portrait that is here drawn reminds us of the ongoing presence of the scribe throughout the book. Just as the narrator interventions within a romance render explicit the presence of a live performer, so the colophon brings us face to face with the persona responsible for the written production of the text.

The texts found in MS 375 were probably read aloud individually; as such they could have been tailored to the interests of the audience in question or otherwise adapted to the circumstances of performance. Because of its large size and weight, though, the book is not particularly easy to handle; if its owner had wanted copies of texts purely for oral reading, he might have done better to have bound them separately. The book has been carefully arranged, however, and its opening presenta-

18. The colophon appears in the Constans edition of the *Roman de Troie,* vol. 6, pp. 28–29.

19. See François, pp. 769–74.

tion is in summary form, which suggests to my mind that it was conceived as a literary compendium and commissioned by someone who appreciated its encyclopedic coverage of the Old French literary and cultural heritage. The book is an artifact in its own right and as such records the circumstances, or at least a fictional view thereof, under which this particular rendition was created. Through this manner of presentation, the codex takes its place, along with Floire's cup and Enide's saddle, as an artifact bearing *matière antique*, the cultural heritage of antiquity, into the medieval world.

## *Compilatio* and *Conjointure:* The Poet-Compilers of MSS Bibl. Nat. fr. 1450 and 1446

I turn now to two manuscripts in which the activities of poetic composition and scribal compilation are even more closely united than in the previous examples. In these, not only have individual poems been arranged to form a meaningful whole, but portions of text have been rewritten in order to effect a smoother transition.

MS 1450, which dates from the second quarter of the thirteenth century, presents a by now familiar progression of romans antiques and Arthurian romances:

*Le Roman de Troie*
*Le Roman d'Eneas*
*Le Roman de Brut*, into which have been inserted all five of Chrétien's romances, in the order *Erec*, *Perceval* (with the First Anonymous Continuation), *Cligès*, *Yvain*, and the *Charrete*
*Le Roman de Dolopathos*, a shortened version of the prose *Sept Sages de Rome*, of which the final pages are missing[20]

The collection thus stresses, again, the cultural continuity leading from Troy to Rome and Britain; the legends of Arthur, framed by the larger story of Britain, are juxtaposed with a second series of legends framed by a story of Imperial Rome.

Although this combination of texts is, as we have seen, a typical one, MS 1450 is somewhat unusual in its insertion of a group of romances into another romance. Similar examples of scribal editing can be found. In the early fourteenth-century MS Bibl. Nat. fr. 12603, for example, the ending of the *Eneas* is adapted so as to lead directly into line 67 of the

---

20. On MS 1450, see Micha, pp. 35–37 and 297–315. Cf. also Walters, "Rôle du scribe." Walters and I have arrived independently at some of the same conclusions regarding this manuscript.

*Brut,* a portion of which then follows.[21] By omitting the account of Eneas's many descendents (vv. 10132–56 have been removed) and the prologue of *Brut,* the scribe is able to move without a break from the tale of Eneas and Lavinia to that of their son. An even more elaborate editing appears in MS Bibl. Nat. fr. 903, a fourteenth-century copy of a mid-thirteenth-century compilation: the story of Pyramus and Thisbe, the genealogy of the Virgin, and an abridged version of the *Roman de Troie* have been inserted into a verse translation of the Old Testament, thereby contextualizing pagan and sacred history.[22] As these and other examples indicate, the liberties taken by the scribe of MS 1450 were an accepted part of medieval scribal practices; since this particular combination is unique, though, it affords us the opportunity to examine the editorial practices of a particular, if anonymous, compiler.

The compiler of MS 1450 has skillfully exploited the tension between the integrity of the individual text and the tendency of the collection as a whole to subsume its parts. *Eneas,* for example, follows *Troie* without so much as a single blank line in between; only the ornamental initial tells us that a new poem is beginning. Since *Eneas* lacks a prologue, the transition is very smooth. Similarly, the transition from *Brut* into *Erec* and on to *Perceval* is facilitated by the omission of Chrétien's prologues. Due to the loss of some pages, we do not know if the prologue to the *Charrete* was included; *Yvain,* of course, has no prologue proper. As the manuscript stands today, the only prologue among Chrétien's works is, appropriately enough, that of *Cligès,* with its description of the transmission of chevalerie and clergie from Greece to Rome to France. It is here, too, that Chrétien portrays himself both as the author of romances—the stories of Erec and Tristan—and also as the translator of Ovid; that is, as the one through whom Celtic legends and classical Latin poetry were brought together into the domain of romance (in the literary and the linguistic sense of the word). Enfolded into the heart of the book—it appears in the third of the five Chrétien romances, themselves enclosed within a poem that is in turn framed by other works—this classic statement of *translatio* extends its significance throughout the collection, providing an important key to the logic and the unity of compilation.

The articulation of the book into its poetic and narrative units is expressed through a system of ornamental initials. The start of a new text is marked by an extra large initial (eleven or twelve lines high) in blue, green, red, and brown, decorated with vine patterns and with human, animal, or hybrid figures. Major divisions within a text are marked by smaller initials, ranging in height from four to nine lines but usually four or five lines high, in red and blue, decorated with a pattern of scroll

---

21. See Salverda de Grave's edition of *Eneas,* vol. 1, pp. iv–v.
22. On MS 903, see Constans's edition of the *Roman de Troie,* vol. 6, pp. 34–40.

work. Minor divisions—what we might think of as paragraphs—are marked by even smaller, single-color (red or blue) initials. The use of this code enabled the scribe to mark the subordination of Chrétien's romances to their frame narrative, as well as the return to *Brut.* Although Chrétien's romances do open with multicolored initials, they are smaller than those of the other texts, ranging from five to nine lines in height. Only *Cligès,* which, as we have seen, is afforded special treatment, opens with an initial of ten lines. The return to *Brut* is marked by a large version (seven lines high, with a long ornamental tail) of the red and blue initials used to mark episodic divisions. Since we pass from one text to another, a large initial is needed; but the color and size of the initial indicate that we are returning to a text already begun.

The code of initials is also used to interesting effect in *Eneas.* Only one major episodic division is indicated, and this one is marked with an initial a full eight lines high. The section thus marked begins, "En sa chambre estoit la roine, / Premers araisona Lavine" (The queen was in her room; first she addressed Lavinia [fol. 106; corresponding to Salverda de Grave ed., vv. 7858–59]). It is surely no accident that this marker of narrative articulation appears at the major interpolation added onto Virgil's story by the *Eneas* poet; in leaving space for this initial, the scribe pays homage to an act of poetic continuation, the expansion of the story of Aeneas, that is very similar to his own continuation-expansion of Wace's story of Arthur.[23]

This system of initials heightens the tension between the two views of the codex: one as a single (though complex) narrative unit and the other as a collection of independent, though thematically related, narratives. The integrity of the individual text is preserved, its boundaries clearly marked. At the same time, the text is susceptible to divisions and subdivisions, and we are invited to read the individual works themselves as simply the largest-scale series of divisions within the book. By the creation of sequences of texts, the incorporation of one textual sequence

---

23. A series of rubrics in the upper margins of MS 1450 provides a more explicit mapping out of this process of narrative articulation. The rubrics are not in the same hand as the text, although they cannot be very much later. Nor do they appear to reflect the same dialect, reading, for example, "remans" where the text has "romans," and "coumenche" for "commance." They are probably the work of some later thirteenth-century reader. Although some of the rubrics have been trimmed away, it is evident that originally each new text was announced. Additionally, the oversized initial in *Eneas* is marked with the rubric, "Ci declaran l'an le signe d'amo[r] en la vie de Eneas et de Lavine & coment se combatist por [el]le" (Here is declared the sign of love in the life of Aeneas and Lavinia and how he fought for her [fol. 106]). No other rubrics survive from within the middle of a text (except, of course, to announce Chrétien's romances within *Brut*); although others may have been lost, it is noteworthy that the one passage we know was so marked is this major narrative interpolation into Virgil's story. The rubric implies that the rubricator, whoever he may have been, read the pattern of narrative continuations and interpolations in the way that I have suggested.

between two parts of another text, and the incorporation of one narrative episode into a larger narrative framework, both poet and scribe compile and conjoin narrative units. The book itself is a large-scale, composite romance, crafted and produced by the scribe just as the individual romance is produced by the poet.

An important detail supports this reading—the separation of the extended prologue of *Troie* from the narrative proper. The codex opens, not with a multicolored initial of the sort that normally begins a new text, but with an initial outlined in red and blue. Possibly its blank interior was originally intended for historiation; certainly it would not be surprising for the first page of a codex to begin with a historiated initial. In any case, the multicolored initial does not appear until the line "Peleus fu un riches reis" (Constans ed., v. 715). The discussion of clergie, the enumeration of the various authors—Homer, Dares, Benoît—who have treated the Trojan material, the account of the tale's textual history, and the summary of the war and its aftermath are all set apart as though a separate text. In effect, this discussion is used as a prologue to the entire collection, laying out the themes to be explored in the succession of texts that follows. The creation of a prologue that is detached from any specific text contributes greatly to the sense of the codex as a unified whole.

The sense of continuity across textual boundaries is heightened at what is potentially the point of greatest fragmentation, the insertion of Chrétien's romances into *Brut,* by a manipulation of narrative voice. During a discussion of the fantastic tales told by poets about Arthur's knights, Chrétien's works are announced by the statement, "Mais ce que Crestiens tesmogne / Porés ci oïr sans alogne" (But you can hear Chrétien's testimony here without delay [fol. 139v]). It thus appears that it is the narrator of *Brut* who recounts the romances of Chrétien as an amplification of his own material; since *Erec* begins at once, without an intervening prologue, we can easily imagine a continuity of voice from one text to the next. The transition back into *Brut* is similarly smoothed by the adaptation of the ending of the *Charrete.* In other manuscripts, the *Charrete* ends with Godefroiz de Leigni's epilogue, beginning:

> Seignor, se j'avant an disoie,
> ce seroit oltre la matire,
> por ce au definer m'atire.

[Lords, if I said any more about it, that would be outside the subject, and so I draw to a close.] [Roques ed., vv. 6098–100]

The scribe of MS 1450 has modified these lines in such a way as to lead directly back into *Brut:*

Segnor, se jo avant disoie,
Ce ne seroit pas bel a dire,
Por ce retor a ma matire.

[Lords, if I said any more, it wouldn't be worth saying, and so I'll return to my subject.] [Fol. 225]

Clearly, this voice can only be that of the scribe: it is he who creates the digression and he who determines what is to follow. By identifying himself with the romance narrators, he reminds us that he, in fact, is responsible for this rendition of the story—the larger story, of which each romance is but a part. We encounter a new persona: the scribal narrator, who, although he uses the language of oral recitation, effects his "performance" of romance through the medium of writing.[24] His implicit presence throughout the book transcends the boundaries of the individual text, contributing to the unification of the whole.

An understanding of the thematic unity of the book, finally, helps to explain some of the textual variants that it presents. An exhaustive analysis is beyond the scope of the present study, but a brief discussion can demonstrate certain points. Let us consider Chrétien's romances. Micha has suggested that for *Erec* and *Cligès* two different sources were used: one, less complete, for the opening half of *Erec* and the closing third of *Cligès* and one, more complete, for the end of *Erec* and the beginning of *Cligès*.[25] The use of two sources would explain the distribution of lacunae, but the question remains as to why the scribe would combine a shorter and a fuller version. Perhaps the text he copied from was already a composite. On the other hand, we know that the scribe of MS 1450 was concerned with compilation and text production; might not the characteristics of the texts be a reflection of his own biases?[26] The absence or presence of prologues, for one, is quite likely by design, as we have seen. Possibly the distribution of lacunae is an indication of the scribe's priorities. He clearly tells us why Chrétien's romances were included: as further stories relating to the deeds of English heroes. If a history of royal houses is at stake, then the end of *Erec,* a coronation and public celebration, is of great importance, whereas the details of the lovers' adventures and the ups and downs of their relationship are less so. Again, if the textual focus is on England, then the first part of *Cligès,* which takes place at the court of Arthur, is more relevant than the part that takes place in Constantinople.

24. The idea of scribes, editors, and poets as participating in a common project is stressed by Uitti, "Foi littéraire," and by Hult, "Gui de Mori."
25. Micha, pp. 297–308, 314.
26. For further discussions of scribal intervention in literary transmission, see Kennedy; Woledge.

The specific nature of the lacunae is telling. Micha has identified two general types: the suppression of descriptive details relating to festivals, clothing, utensils, and so on; and the omission or abridgment of passages relating to love psychology. In both cases it seems likely that the scribe wanted to remove extraneous material that, in his opinion, did not contribute to his historical narrative. It is interesting that two descriptive passages that survived intact are those referring to Enide's saddle, with its depiction of the story of Eneas, and Erec's coronation robe, with its depiction of the quadrivium and reference to Macrobius. These passages, which serve to associate *Erec* with the classical *auctores* and the learned tradition, would clearly appeal to the scribe; they are indeed appropriate to the project he has undertaken.

That the scribe felt love psychology to be secondary to his historical theme is supported by an examination of his rendition of *Eneas*. Aside from omissions of a single line—most likely due to carelessness, since they violate the rhyme scheme—his *Eneas* exhibits lacunae amounting to twenty-two lines that are shared by at least one other manuscript, and lacunae of eighty-four lines that are unique to MS 1450.[27] Of the shared lacunae, only six lines refer to love psychology; but of those unique to MS 1450, four lines relate to the love between Eneas and Dido, and seventy lines relate to the love of Eneas and Lavinia. Either MS 1450 is the sole surviving copy of an *Eneas* in which love monologues and debates had already been abridged, or these omissions are the editorial work of the scribe. Considering the similar treatment of love passages in other texts and the historical bias of the collection, the latter possibility seems more likely. All in all, MS 1450 is an excellent illustration of the extent to which a scribe could participate in literary production.

Our other example, the late thirteenth-century MS 1446, contains a much more varied assortment: the prose *Histoire de Kanor,* the *Couronnement de Renart,* the *Fables d'Ysopet* of Marie de France, and dits by Baudouin and Jean de Condé, as well as four versions of the first part of another prose romance, *Constant.* The current volume is actually made up of the remains of at least three manuscripts.[28] What interests me is a single pair of texts, the *Couronnement* and the *Fables,* which are here presented as a unit and which may have originally been a separate volume unto themselves. For reasons that will become apparent, I do not believe that the scribe of MS 1446 originated this conjointure but rather that he copied from a source in which these poems were already conjoined. We will examine these two texts in isolation from the rest of the

27. These figures are based on the list of variants given by Salverda de Grave in his edition of *Eneas.*

28. For a description of MS 1446, and a discussion of its formation and probable date, see Foulet's edition of *Le Couronnement de Renard,* pp. ix–xv.

codex as an example of textual conjoining performed by a compiler whose work is not otherwise accessible to us.

The *Couronnement* and Marie de France's *Fables* have been conjoined by means of the epilogue of the *Couronnement*, in which the narrator announces his intention to append the "Provierbes d'Izopet" to his poem, and an introductory passage that prefaces Marie's prologue, in which the narrator exhorts his audience to listen to Marie's rendition of the "proverbs." It would seem from this that the person responsible for the textual coupling is the author of the *Couronnement*, but we must exercise some caution here. If MS 1450 were our only copy of the *Roman de Brut*, we might assume that Wace had taken it upon himself to insert Chrétien's romances into his poem, a serious and anachronistic misreading. Unfortunately, there is no other manuscript of the *Couronnement* against which to check this interpretation. I will, therefore, leave open the question of just who was responsible for the composite text as it now stands. In referring to this person as a compiler, or a poet-compiler, we are in any case doing him no injustice, for whether he composed the entire *Couronnement* or only its epilogue, his creative act was one comprising both verse composition and textual compilation.

One could easily imagine a conjoining of the *Couronnement de Renart* and Marie's *Fables* on the basis of the shared literary language of beast allegory and shared message of morality and social criticism; and the compiler does not fail to note the latter point. Interestingly, however, he also offers another reason for this rapprochement. Marie, he claims, wrote the *Fables* for the same patron, a Count Guillaume, for whom he wrote the *Couronnement*. Marie does acknowledge a "cunte Willalme / le plus vaillant de cest reialme" (Count William, the most valiant of this realm) in her epilogue (Warnke ed, vv. 9–10). The *Couronnement*, however, was written at least half a century after Marie did her work, and there can hardly be any question that the two poets were not employed by the same patron.[29] The poet-compiler nonetheless invokes common patronage as the pretext for attaching the two poems. This attention to the circumstances of composition, albeit fictional, and the suggestion that texts can be associated on the basis of common patronage is fundamentally different from anything that we have seen in the other manuscripts examined here, where poems were associated purely on the basis of intertextual relationships. The only reference to authorship was in MS

29. From historical allusions it is possible to determine that the *Couronnement* was written after 1251, perhaps not until after 1263, and before 1280. See Foulet's edition of the *Couronnement*, pp. xxiii–xxvi. Foulet also points out that the *Couronnement* could not possibly have been written for the same Count William that Marie mentions and that the poet must have known this; his claim is a literary device used for the association of the two poems (pp. xxxii–xxxiii).

1450, with its presentation of Chrétien as an authority on Arthur's knights. If the person responsible for this instance of textual conjoining was in fact the author of the *Couronnement*, it may be that he was attempting to gain recognition for his work by attaching it to Marie de France's extremely popular fables.[30] If it was a later compiler, he may have noticed the dedication to a Count William in both texts and used it as a pretext to attach the lesser-known *Couronnement* to a thematically related work with which everyone was familiar.

In fact, it would not be inaccurate to say that the author of the *Couronnement* presents himself or is presented by a later compiler as the continuator of Marie de France, just as the scribe of MS 1450 has presented Chrétien as the continuator of Wace. This is not continuation as we ordinarily think of it, that is, a prolongation by adding onto the end. Nonetheless, the *Couronnement*, as presented here, is the continuation of Marie's project of didactic poetry addressed to the nobility. Her poem has been appropriated and incorporated into the later work, just as surely as Guillaume de Lorris's *Roman de la rose* was appropriated by Jean de Meun and incorporated into his long narrative. Indeed, the technique is somewhat similar in both cases: just as Jean de Meun made Guillaume's narrator-protagonist the protagonist of his own romance, so our compiler has in a sense made Marie de France, narrator of the *Fables*, into his protagonist. In the prologue that he placed at the head of her prologue, he speaks in the first person as the one who is going to tell (*raconter*) moral tales, whereas Marie is introduced in the third person: "Or entendés pour Diu, singneur, / Coment Marie nos traita / Des provierbes" (Now, by God, listen, Lords, how Marie presented the proverbs to us [fol. 88v; Foulet ed., vv. 3404–6]). Marie's voice is thus bracketed in implied quotation marks: her entire narrative, from prologue through epilogue, takes place within the context established by the *Couronnement* narrator.[31]

A further interpolation has been effected in the *Fables*, which, since it is also unique to MS 1446, is probably the work of the same poet-compiler. At the end of Marie's prologue is a passage that is surely an adaptation of the prologue of Richard de Fournival's *Bestiaire d'amours*.[32] In this prologue, Richard explains that his book appeals to both the ear, since one must listen to the words (*parole*); and the eye, since one must look at the illustrations (*painture*). He adds that the bestiary needs to be

30. If such was the poet-compiler's desire, it must be said that he failed, since Marie's *Fables* survives, in whole or in part, in twenty-three manuscripts, and the *Couronnement* survives in but one.

31. For a discussion of the way in which Jean de Meun appropriates Guillaume's narrator into his own romance, see Hult, "Closed Quotations."

32. The interpolated prologue passage about *painture* is printed by Warnke in the appendix to his edition of Marie's *Fables* (edited as *Die Fabeln*), p. 329. On Richard de Fournival, see Chapter 5.

illustrated, because the habits of birds and animals are more easily grasped through visual representation than through verbal description. The redactor of the *Fables* surely had this text in mind when he wrote:

> Pour çou qu'il dist que pointure est
> Une chose, qui a l'ueil plest,
> E parole si ert a oïe:
> Par coi ici nos senefie
> Que cis livres doit iestre poins.

[For this reason he says that illustration is a thing that pleases the eye, and speech is to be heard: by this he signifies to us here that this book should be illustrated.] [Fol. 89]

An association between the *Fables* and the *Bestiaire d'amours* is not surprising: both employ animal imagery for didactic purposes; they are sometimes found in the same manuscripts; the rubric in the thirteenth-century MS Bibl. Nat. fr. 2168 even identifies Marie's *Fables* as a bestiary. The various medieval collections of fables, including Marie's, are often illustrated. In fact, if this interpolation is the work of the same redactor who attached the *Fables* to the *Couronnement,* then the latter may even have felt that the presence of animal illustrations in both poems would contribute not only to his didactic purposes but also to the unity of the composite text. MS 1446, however, does not illustrate the *Fables;* the only miniatures for these poems are an image of the crowned Renart at the beginning of the *Couronnement* and a portrait of Marie de France writing her book at the beginning of the *Fables.* No other spaces for miniatures have been left. For this reason I do not believe that it was the scribe of MS 1446 who was responsible for this redaction of the text. It could be argued that it was he who adapted the *Fables* to the *Couronnement,* using a version of the *Fables* that already had the extra prologue calling for illustration, but even this seems unlikely: surely a scribe who took this much initiative in editing his texts would have thought either to reserve space for illuminations or else to omit the passage calling for them.

The scribal narrators that we have encountered in MSS 1446 and 1450, as well as in the table of summaries in MS 375, are active participants in literary production. The scribe, as much as the poet or the performer, helps to shape and to interpret the literary text and the tradition in which it is inscribed. In these interpolated passages, the scribal voice speaks to us from inside the text, and at times it is indistinguishable from the voice of narrator, editor, or poet. But the voice of the scribe also addresses us from outside the text, in the rubrics with which manuscript texts are embellished. Rubrication, in fact, is the primary means by which the scribe guides the reader through the book, identifying and commenting upon the texts that he offers to us.

## The Voice of the Scribe: Rubrication in MS Bibl. Nat. fr. 25545

There are many different types of rubrication in medieval manuscripts, ranging from a simple explicit at the end of an otherwise unmarked text, to lengthy commentaries interspersed at frequent intervals throughout the text.[33] Very generally speaking, rubrication is more thorough in the fourteenth century than in the thirteenth century, perhaps reflecting a growing literacy rate and an increased reliance on the book rather than the performance for literary consumption. The *Roman de la rose* was subject to particularly elaborate rubrication, some of which will be discussed in Chapter 3. Here, I will examine the rubrication of a fourteenth-century anthology, MS Bibl. Nat. fr. 25545, in which we can find examples of various types of rubrics.

MS 25545 is a composite manuscript, which appears to have been rearranged at some time in the past. Most of its contents, however, date from the early years of the fourteenth century.[34] Its contents are largely satirical, didactic, and religious texts, including a series of fabliaux, Rutebeuf's *Confession Renart*, Marie de France's *Fables d'Ysopet*, *La Chastelaine de Vergi*, a fragment of Richard de Fournival's rhymed version of the *Bestiaire d'amours*, *Les Sept Sages de Rome*, and several saints' lives. Since we are concerned here not with the architectonics of the manuscript or the personality of a particular compiler, I have not attempted to account for the codex as a whole but simply to identify examples of rubrication that are typical of medieval practices.

Some of the rubrics in MS 25545 are a relatively terse identification of the text: "Ci commence Ysopet en françois, qui contient .lxxxi. chapitres" (Here begins Aesop in French, which contains 81 chapters [fol. 28v]). This tells us not only the title and length of the text but also that it is a translation "en françois." Interestingly, the *Bestiaire d'amours* is similarly identified as "li Bestiaires d'amors en françois" (fol. 89v). The *Bestiaire d'amours* does not, in fact, present itself as a translation but rather as the writer-lover's personal message to his lady. It does, however, draw on a Latin allegorical tradition; and it was often associated with texts that are presented as translations, such as the *Bestiaire divin* or the *Image dou monde*. Its close relationship to this tradition of Latin and Latinate texts presumably led the scribe to regard the *Bestiaire d'amours* as a translation also, even if of a slightly different type. Here, then, the scribe aids the reader not only to distinguish one text from another but also to recognize the different kinds of texts found in the codex.

---

33. On rubrics, see Baumgartner, "Espace du texte"; Hult, "Closed Quotations"; Huot, "Scribe as Editor."

34. See Långfors, who cites a verse colophon written by the same copyist who composed the other verse rubrics, dating this scribe's work as 1317.

Most of the narratives are given descriptive rubrics, often framing the text. One fabliau, for example, is headed "Ci commence d'une dame de Flandres / C'uns chevaliers tolli a .i. autre par force" (Here begins about a lady of Flanders, whom one knight took from another by force) and concludes, "Explicit de la dame ax .ii. chevaliers tors. / Ci fenist li fabliax, dou droit contre le tort" (Here ends about the lady with the two wrong knights. Here ends the fabliau, of right versus wrong). Another is headed,

> Ci aprés commence d'une damoisele qui
> onques pour nelui ne se volt marier.
> Mais volt voler en l'air.

[After this begins about a girl who never wanted to get married. But she wanted to fly through the air.] [Fol. 4v]

It concludes, "Explicit de la damoisele qui / volt voler" (Here ends about the girl who wanted to fly [fol. 5v]). And the *Chastelaine de Vergi* is headed "Ci commence de la Chastelaine de Vergi / Qui mori pour loialment amer son ami" (Here begins about the châtelaine de Vergi, who died for loyally loving her lover [fol. 84]) and concludes, "Explicit de la Chatelaine de Vergy, / Qui mori par trop amer son ami" (Here ends about the châtelaine de Vergi, who died for greatly [or excessively] loving her lover [fol. 89v]).

The term *fabliax* in the second rubric above contributes, like the qualification *en françois,* to the rudimentary generic classification of texts; it contrasts, for example, with the designation *rommans* in the rubric announcing the *Rommans des sept sages.* Beyond that, these rubrics, like numerous others in this codex and elsewhere, offer an encapsulation of the central narrative action or the dilemma on which the action is founded. Though far simpler than Peros de Neele's summaries in MS 375, they do provide a similar service in guiding the reader through the book. Inasmuch as the scribe has chosen what he considers to be the most important moment or image of each text, they also offer a reading of the poems. For example, the fabliau of the girl who wanted to fly could just as well have been described as the story of an innocent young girl who is tricked into sleeping with a more worldly clerk and so becomes pregnant, thereby being forced to marry him. The outrageous nature of the girl's original desire, however, colors the entire course of the narrative, and it is for this that she is remembered. Moreover, the scribe has exploited the comic potential of the girl's desire through his phrasing of the rubric. As we read the first two lines, we do not know the girl's motivations: she may be a proud romance heroine or even a saint. As we read the "punch line," however, any such expectations are dashed: this girl's alternative to marriage is the unlikely choice of flying through the air. Although it could be argued that the story was too well known for anyone to be surprised by it, the story and the rubric still probably had comic value; like a favorite joke, the delayed "surprise" could be enjoyed even by one who knew it was coming.

The rubrication of the preceding fabliau reveals a similar use of humor. In the opening rubric, the lady appears to be the victim of an abduction; by the time of the explicit, she has become "the lady with two knights," suggesting that the story may be less about a villainous knight than about a woman with a large sexual appetite. We see here that the rubricator does much more than identify texts to facilitate reader access to the collection (though he does do that); he actively participates in the presentation of these texts to their audience. Again, the scribe's work is a written performance; and, like any performer, he makes little asides to his audience, cracking jokes at the expense of his characters or philosophizing about his material. His remarks force us to evaluate the text before us: Is the châtelaine de Vergi a tragically wronged heroine who exemplifies the virtues of loyal love? Or did she perhaps love *too much,* so that her story illustrates, instead, the dangers of love?

The scribe's participation in the poetic process is further expressed in his frequent adoption of the versification of the texts to which his rubrics refer. In the fabliau of "The lady with two knights," for example, every line ends with either *tors* or *tort;* the explicit attaches itself as the continuation of the poetic fabric. Or, to take a new example: Rutebeuf's *Vie du monde,* in monorhymed quatrains, is followed by Huon le Roi de Cambrai's *Descrissions des relegions,* in which the same rhyme is often repeated for several lines running. Both are identified by rubrics in monorhymed quatrains, in which the rubricator sententiously registers his agreement with the didactic content of the poems. Again, the scribe is an explicit presence in the book, announcing and commenting upon the material he brings us. Like the scribe of MS 1450, he attaches his discourse to that of the texts; through his act of writing, he appropriates the narrative or didactic voice and continues it into his own pronouncements. Unlike the scribe of MS 1450, though, the rubricator of MS 25545 "speaks" in red ink. In this way his own persona is distinguished from that of the various authors. The integrity of the individual text is preserved, while, at the same time, it becomes part of an ongoing scribal performance.

As in other anthology codices that we have seen in this chapter, the tension between fragmentation and wholeness remains unresolved in MS 25545. Through the accumulation of examples, we can begin to see more clearly some of the terms of this tension. Compilers could bind their anthologies together through narrative or thematic links among texts: manipulation of narrative voice could create a continuity across textual boundaries. On the other hand, the materiality of the book allows for visual signals, such as the red ink of rubrics and the design of ornamental initials, that clearly mark the boundaries and subdivisions of each text. These elements are handled variously by different scribes, but we may say that, in general, a continuity of content and voice is played off against a visual discontinuity. Or, even more generally, the basic textual fabric presented by the book would have one aspect if experienced aurally, another if experienced visually. Undoubtedly, a large number of medieval readers did experience the book exclusively through oral presentation, thereby missing out on the complex layers of authorial and scribal mediation; in the person of the performer, all voices are united. The existence of the manuscripts indicates, however, that the scribes themselves, at least, were conscious of their role in shaping literary tradition. And the number of manuscripts marked by this kind of literary sophistication, along with a similar literary consciousness expressed in poetic works of the period, does suggest that the poets and scribes who shared these concerns must have found an audience capable of reflection about the manipulation of voice and the creative tension between oral and written format.

## The Figure of the Author in a Thirteenth-Century Codex: MS Arsenal 3142

The preceding survey, though brief, has demonstrated the important role played by the scribe as editor, commentator, and narrator. We have seen, as well, several examples of the narrative and thematic schemas that govern anthologies. In all of these organizational programs, content appears to be the most important factor in determining the choice and arrangement of texts. What of authorship? For that matter, what of the author's role in the written transmission of his texts? The evidence of the manuscripts overwhelmingly suggests that, before the fourteenth century, authorship was not a particularly important factor in the compilation of vernacular narrative or didactic anthologies; that twelfth- and thirteenth-century poets did not normally oversee the production of manuscripts; and that scribes were not concerned with preserving the author's precise words. It has often been noted that twelfth- and even thirteenth-century texts are not normally preserved in manuscripts dating from within the author's lifetime. Furthermore, although an author may name himself in prologue or epilogue, his name is hardly ever given in rubrication, suggesting again that content—as expressed in the name of the protagonist, normally used to identify a romance—was more important than authorship for medieval readers and copyists.

Multiple works by the same author could certainly appear in a single codex, but this can hardly be said to have been the rule. Even the *Lais* of Marie de France, a collection of texts explicitly marked as such by the existence of a prologue that serves to introduce the whole, is transmitted as a complete group in only one manuscript.[35] The works of Chrétien de Troyes are often found in pairs or groups, a tribute to Chrétien's powerful reputation; but even they are not normally announced as "the works of Chrétien" and are never marked by an author portrait. Ironically, MS 1450—the one case in which Chrétien's complete narrative corpus is introduced, collectively, as such—is also one of the manuscripts in which the texts are subjected to the greatest degree of scribal editing. Clearly, respect for Chrétien's authority and poetic prowess did not necessarily imply a respect for the letter of the text.

One vernacular author who does appear to have overseen the written production of his works is Gautier de Coinci. His *Miracles Nostre Dame* are transmitted as a group, complete with prologues and epilogues for each of the two books, in several thirteenth-century manuscripts, and he explicitly refers to his work as a book that he plans to have copied, illuminated, and disseminated.[36] Gautier, however, was a monastic and not a court poet; he belongs to a different milieu and a different tradition, one in which an author was more likely to be involved in book production. An example more relevant to the present context is Adenet le Roi, whose work dates from the second half of the thirteenth century. Adenet's poems are often transmitted in pairs or groups also; the most complete compilation known today is in the MS Arsenal 3142, which probably dates from within Adenet's lifetime and could even have been made under his supervision.

MS 3142 is a collection of epic and didactic poetry, containing

Adenet's *Cléomadès, Enfances Ogier,* and *Berthe aus grans piés*
Alard de Cambrai's *Livre de philosophie et de moralité,* here titled *Dits des sages*
A treatise on Job, added in the fourteenth century
Adenet's *Beuves de Commarchis*
The *Miserere* and *Dit de la charité* of Le Reclus de Moliens
Jean Bodel's *Congé*
Bodel's *Chanson des Saisnes*
Marie de France's *Fables d'Ysopet*
*Les Proverbes au vilain*
A series of religious and moral dits, including a series of dits by Baudouin de Condé and the *Proverbes Seneke le philosophe*

35. See Hoepffner, "Tradition manuscrite des *Lais*"; Baum, pp. 42–58, 117–26.
36. On Gautier manuscripts, see Ducrot-Granderye. For the illuminations of the famous Soissons manuscript (including several author portraits) see Focillon. In addition to monastic authors, aristocratic authors, whose social standing enabled them to act simultaneously as patron, would also be in a position to oversee manuscript production of their works; for such an example, see Friedman's edition of Joinville's *Credo*.

As far as we know, this assemblage of works by Adenet represents his complete works. Since the addition of "Job" required the insertion of a new gathering, we know that the codex was rebound in the fourteenth century; possibly it was then that *Beuves,* which should logically be placed among Adenet's other works, was moved to its current location. In any case, several factors suggest that this grouping of texts was conceived as an author corpus.

The half-page miniature heading *Cléomadès* leaves no doubt that it was intended from the start as the opening piece in the codex, and appropriately so. The prologue of *Cléomadès* functions as an introduction to Adenet's entire corpus, listing his poetic compositions: "Je qui fis d'Ogier le Danois / et de Bertain qui fu ou bois" (I who made [stories] about Ogier the Dane and about Bertha who was in the forest [Henry ed., vv. 5–6]). *Cléomadès* further serves to introduce the persona of Adenet through its epilogue, a detailed account of Adenet's various patrons. Thus, although *Cléomadès* is actually Adenet's last poem, it can function as a prologue to his oeuvre by announcing the works to come and by creating the context of patronage within which these works were composed.

The opening and closing miniatures of *Cléomadès* contribute to the definition of Adenet's place as court poet. In the opening scene Adenet, identifiable by his crown and vielle, is shown in the presence of Marie de Brabant, queen of France; Princess Blanche, daughter of Saint Louis and widow of the infant of Castille; and Jean II de Brabant.[37] These latter are recognizable by the coats-of-arms represented on their clothing. The miniature presumably depicts the commissioning of the poem by Queen Marie and Princess Blanche, as described in Adenet's prologue and epilogue. Directly below this, in the opening initial of the text, is a representation of Adenet holding writing tablets. Following the epilogue, an envoi dedicates the "book" to the count of Artois; an accompanying miniature shows Adenet handing his book to a knight who bears the arms of Artois.

Eulogy of the patron is, of course, a common enough feature of medieval poetry; and the owners of books frequently had their coats-of-arms inscribed on the opening page. This situation, however, is a little different. Adenet does not merely sing the praises of the person for whom the poem was composed or for whom the copy was made but of *all* his patrons. The only thing that unites this group of aristocrats is their common patronage of Adenet; the poetic career of the author is evoked here and given a centrality that we have not seen in other works. It is as

---

37. This miniature is described by Henry in *Biographie d'Adenet,* p. 96. Henry also confirms that MS Arsenal 3142 is contemporary with Adenet (p. 96). Henry publishes the opening miniatures for Adenet's poems from the various manuscripts, including MS Arsenal 3142.

though Chrétien had inserted reminiscences about Marie de Champagne into the *Conte du Graal.*

The opening and closing miniatures, together with the opening historiated initial, refer to three distinct moments in the evolution of the poem: its original commission by Marie and Blanche; its composition by Adenet; and its presentation, as a finished volume, to the count. Central to the process of text production is Adenet himself; and his consistent use of the first-person voice creates an identity between narrator and author, one who is both a court figure and a producer of books. In this respect his work exemplifies certain innovations of the thirteenth century. We can appreciate what is new here by returning to the comparison with Chrétien. The prologue of *Cléomadès* echoes that of *Cligés* but with an important shift from third-person to first-person voice; Adenet's "I who made . . . / I have undertaken another book" contrasts with Chrétien's statement, "He who made the story of Erec and Enide . . . begins a new story."[38] Even in the *Charrete,* which opens with an extended first-person statement of poetic service somewhat reminiscent of trouvère lyric, the transition from prologue to narrative proper entails the transformation of this authorial persona into a third-person figure: "Del *Chevalier de la charrete* / comance Crestïens son livre" (Chrétien begins his book about the knight of the cart [vv. 24–25]). As a result, the narrative voice is available for appropriation by performers (or scribes) without any subsequent displacement of Chrétien as an authoritative presence in the text. The romance can be thought of as a script prepared by the poet for future presentation by others. Adenet, on the other hand, writes at a time when vernacular poetry already has a long-standing written tradition, and his narrative voice is influenced by the scribal persona that we have seen in the above examples. He does not write words to be spoken by someone else (though his poems undoubtedly were read aloud for some time to come) but rather projects his own voice into writing and thereby assumes responsibility, as author, not only for the story but also for the written rendition.

*Ogier,* the second work in MS 3142, is headed with a miniature illustrating the narrative content of the poem; but the text opens with a historiated initial depicting Adenet (recognizable, as usual, by his crown) with a book, and he appears in the margin with his vielle. These images provide a visual link with *Cléomadès;* the presence of the author, in his dual identity as writer and performer, is the basis of this association. In this way Adenet's poetic identity, established by *Cléomadès* and its illuminations, is extended to the next text in the series. *Berthe* and *Beuve* are illustrated only by representations of narrative content; but their

---

38. On the use of first-person and third-person discourse, see Badel, "Rhétorique et polémique"; Cerquiglini, "Clerc et l'écriture."

citation in the original prologue, and the initial insistence on Adenet's presence, ensures the perception of these texts as part of the Adenet corpus.

The opening and closing miniatures of *Cléomadès* and the envoi dedication could be used to support the claim, first raised by Paulin Paris, that the manuscript was prepared under Adenet's supervision.[39] These miniatures and the envoi are lacking from fourteenth-century manuscripts of *Cléomadès;* readers more removed from Adenet's immediate context were presumably more interested in the story of Cléomadès than in the textual history of *Cléomadès*.[40] Further evidence for the privileged status of MS 3142 is found in the format of the acrostics (vv. 18541–61 and 18563–75) that name Adenet's two female patrons, "La Roiine de France Marie" and "Madame Blanche." The passage containing these acrostics appears in later manuscripts as well, but in MS 3142 it has been specially marked: the first word in lines 18562 and 18576 has been omitted and a blank space left at the beginning of the lines. These omissions create breaks in the vertical progression of initial letters and set off the acrostics from the rest of the text.[41] The omission of the words does not in itself prove Adenet's intervention in the scribal process, but it does certainly indicate a scribe who understood the acrostics and considered them important. These features not found in later manuscripts all suggest the supervision of someone directly concerned with accurate representation of the poet-patron relationships that gov-

---

39. Paris, pp. 685, 710.

40. In the fourteenth-century MS Bibl. Nat. fr. 1456, *Cléomadès* opens with a double miniature. One half represents the marriage scene found after the prologue at the start of the narrative proper in thirteenth-century manuscripts; the other represents a figure lying in bed, surrounded by other figures (see Henry, *Biographie d'Adenet*, pl. viii). Possibly this is the work of an illuminator who no longer understood the miniature as it appears in MS 3142 (where Queen Marie reclines in bed, surrounded by Adenet, Jean de Brabant, and Princess Blanche). Other fourteenth-century manuscripts, if they are illuminated at all, depict only narrative scenes. On the other hand, in MS Bibl. Nat. fr. 24404, a late thirteenth-century manuscript executed in Paris and containing only *Cléomadès* and *Berthe*, the former ends with the same envoi and dedicatory miniature as MS 3142. The first leaf of *Cléomadès* is missing, but a line drawing in the lower margin of fol. 80 represents Cléomadès bearing the arms of Princess Blanche, and the princess in the wedding scene on what is now fol. 1 wears Blanche's arms. According to François Avril of the Bibliothèque Nationale, the drawing on fol. 80 was added in the first half of the fourteenth century. Possibly its artist copied Blanche's arms from a now lost frontispiece resembling the one in MS 3142. *Berthe* opens with a representation of Adenet reading a book held by a monk, in illustration of the prologue statement that he researched his poem at Saint Denis. In the manuscripts closer to Adenet's immediate circle, the context of patronage and the learning of the poet are stressed; in later manuscripts, these factors are less important. Again, this lends support to the hypothesis of Adenet's personal influence on the earlier manuscripts.

41. In the thirteenth-century MS 24404 (see note 40), the same words are omitted. The first ("Nommer" at the end of the first acrostic, on fol. 166v) was originally written but scratched out; at the end of the second acrostic, there is no sign that the opening word of the line was ever there. In the later manuscripts, however, there is no such highlighting of the acrostics.

erned the poem's composition; this person may well have been Adenet himself.

It is not necessary, in the present context, to decide whether MS 3142 is itself a manuscript directed by Adenet or merely the faithful copy of such a manuscript. What is most important for the present study is the evidence of author involvement in manuscript preparation, whether in this volume or its source, and the attention to author identity and poetic composition as a possible frame of reference for a collection of poems.

Indeed, author identity and shared authorship as a basis for the conjoining of texts is a pervasive feature of MS 3142. While the Adenet corpus is certainly the most impressive such example, the collection does also include two poems by Le Reclus de Moliens, identified as a unit through the closing rubric, "Explicit Miserere et Charité / Que li Reclus de Moliens rima" (Here ends the *Miserere* and the *Charity*, which the Reclus de Moliens rhymed [fol. 226v]), two poems of very different literary types by Jean Bodel; and a series of poems by Baudouin de Condé, identified as an author corpus through the opening rubric "Ci commencent li dis Baudouin de Condé" (Here begin the *dits* by Baudouin de Condé [fol. 300v]). Again, the arrangement and illumination establish a strong authorial presence in the first text attributed to each poet. The *Miserere* opens with a miniature depicting a monk transcribing a text and a prologue in which the narrator explains that he offers us here the fruits of his own readings; the subsequent *Dit de la charité* is headed by a representation of almsgiving. The first poem by Bodel is the *Congé*, with its lyric focus on the persona of Bodel and his place in the community of Arras; the miniature represents Bodel reading his statement to an assembled audience. The *Saisnes,* on the other hand, is headed by a miniature depicting the king of France. Finally, the first of Baudouin's dits is the *Salus Nostre Dame,* headed by a representation of the poet, scroll in hand, addressing a Madonna and Child; subsequent dits are illustrated with the central image from which each draws its title (pelican, rose, and so on). Thus the general illustrative pattern noted in the Adenet corpus is followed wherever there is more than one poem by the same author.

Even some of the other works in the codex have the format of a compilation and are unified through an author's prologue and an accompanying portrait. The *Dits des sages* is a compilation of wisdom drawn from the classical auctores and the Bible, summarized in octosyllabic couplets. Each section is headed by an image of a robed man holding a scroll and by a rubric identifying the sage in question and the general content of his teaching. The whole is headed by the prologue, in which Alard describes his work as reader, compiler, and summarizer; and a miniature that shows a monk transcribing a text. Similarly, the *Fables* are a collection of short narratives, each headed by its own miniature; the whole is framed by the author's prologue and epilogue, which describe the project of poetic translation. The author portraits accompanying prologue and epilogue represent Marie de France; at the beginning she is in the act of writing, whereas at the end she holds up her finished book. As was suggested by the frame miniatures of *Cléomadès,* the author's act of writing seems to have taken place during the passage from prologue to epilogue. The codex is the representation of various kinds of performances: oral performance, in the case of the *Congé* and the dits; written performance, in the case of *Cléomadès, Ogier,* the *Dits des sages,* the *Miserere,* and the *Fables.*

As stated above, the identification of monastic authors as scribes and the likelihood of a monastic author's supervising text production were established at an earlier date. Therefore, to see monastic poets portrayed as clerks and scribes is not surprising. It is interesting, though, to see the way that a codex can be built up out of vernacular author corpora; and especially interesting that nonmonastic poets like Adenet, Bodel, and Baudouin de Condé should be included in such a scheme. The implications are far-reaching. Collections of the type studied earlier in this chapter suggest a view of vernacular narrative texts as repositories of themes, images, and episodes: they are all in some sense fragments of a larger whole, which can be variously defined and to which they can be variously adapted. A collection like MS 3142 suggests a different view of vernacular texts as self-contained units, crafted in a certain way by a poet operating under certain circumstances; they bear a historicity as texts, referring not only to the fictional or moral world that they describe but also to an original and unique act of composition. They are thus much less readily adaptable to new contexts and tend rather to evoke their own context.

Concomitant with these developments is a shifting sense of the roles and relationships of poet, scribe, and performer. These changing ideas about poetry and its production and transmission will be explored in the works of individual poets. First, though, we must turn to the analysis of lyric codices, in order to see how lyric compilations fit into the picture that has begun to emerge.

Chapter 2

# Scribal Practice in Lyric Anthologies:
# Structure, Format, and Iconography
## of *Trouvère Chansonniers*

Old French chansonniers have been cataloged in bibliographies, as
have the songs they contain;[1] individual manuscripts have been described with varying degrees of detail by many editors. Several have
been published in facsimile editions.[2] But there exists no really comprehensive study of this body of manuscripts.[3] The present study likewise is
not a comprehensive review; I will focus only on selected manuscripts.
By examining manuscripts from numerous perspectives—organization,
rubrication, layout, iconography—I hope to identify typical features of
chansonnier format and to draw some conclusions about the nature of
lyric compilation in the thirteenth and early fourteenth centuries. Not
surprisingly, lyric and narrative anthologies have many elements in common. Certain characteristics that distinguish lyric poetry from other
verse forms, however, are reflected in features that are peculiar to lyric
manuscripts. The figure of the author, in particular, assumes an importance quite unlike that of the romance author. This examination of the
treatment of courtly lyric by the compilers of chansonniers, and of
changes that took place in the course of the thirteenth and early fourteenth centuries, complements the preceding discussion of narrative anthologies, provides a basis for the examination of the appropriation of

1. Jeanroy, *Bibliographie sommaire;* Spanke. I refer to chansonniers according to the
sigla adopted by Jeanroy: A = Arras, Bibl. Mun. 657; C = Bern, Bibl. Mun. 389; K = Paris,
Arsenal 5198; M = Paris, Bibl. Nat. fr. 844; N = B.N. fr. 845; O = B.N. fr. 846; P = B.N.
fr. 847; T = B.N. fr. 12615; U = B.N. fr. 20050; V = B.N. fr. 24406; W = B.N. fr. 25566;
X = B.N. n.a. fr. 1050; a = Rome, Vat. Reg. 1490.
2. For a bibliography of facsimile and diplomatic editions, see Lerond's edition of
Châtelain de Couci, *Chansons attribuées au Chastelain de Couci.*
3. There are, however, some important contributions to the study of trouvère chansonniers. See, in particular, Karp; Schwan; Van der Werf, *Chansons of the Troubadours and
the Trouvères.*

lyricism by narrative poets, and helps to clarify changing concepts of lyric poetry and the lyric poet.

## A Survey of Chansonnier Format

In most Old French chansonniers, songs are arranged by author; such anthologies always open with aristocratic trouvères, most frequently granting first place to Thibaut, king of Navarre. Anonymous songs, if there are any, form a separate group at the end of the collection. The attribution of a given song may vary from one codex to another, as is typical of a manuscript tradition. A few chansonniers contain no attributions at all. In the late thirteenth-century MSS *C* and *O*, for example, songs are arranged in alphabetical order (based only on the first letter of the song), with no indication of authorship.[4] Some chansonniers additionally have special sections for pastourelles, *jeux-partis* (debates about love casuistry), and other such generic categories.

The layout of lyric texts differs from that used for narrative texts. Musical notation is provided only for the first stanza, following which the remaining stanzas are transcribed in order. Stanzaic divisions are indicated by ornamental initials, like those used to mark narrative divisions. Each stanza, however, is written out like prose, with line divisions only sometimes indicated by punctuation marks. This layout contrasts with the careful lineation of narrative verse. Even in texts such as Jean Renart's *Roman de la rose*, where songs or lyric stanzas appear within a narrative, the scribe sometimes copied them as blocks of prose, reverting to a line-by-line layout with the return of the narrative. Evidently the line of narrative verse was considered a meaningful unit; but for songs, the meaningful unit was the stanza. This difference may reflect the musical quality of the song: the unit of performance is certainly the sung stanza, which revolves around a configuration of rhyming words but does not correspond to a visual shape.

The careful attention to authorship in most trouvère anthologies also contrasts with the format of most thirteenth-century narrative anthologies. Where narrative poems are normally identified by the protagonist or central image of the text—*Roman de Troie, Roman de la rose;* or, without the generic designation, *Ci commence d'Erec et Enide*—songs are normally identified by author, and there is a clear syntactic dif-

---

4. The songs in MS *O* are arranged within each alphabetical division in an order corresponding more or less to authorship: the first several songs are usually by Thibaut de Navarre, the next few by Gace Brulé; and every so often one finds groups of songs by one or another trouvère. These groupings are probably due to a process of compilation from manuscripts in which songs were arranged in author corpora. The scribe does not seem to have been particularly concerned with categorization of songs according to author.

ference between "li romans *de* Cligés" (the romance *about* Cligés) and "les chansons *au* Chastelain de Couci" (the songs *belonging to* [that is, attributed to, authored by] the châtelain de Couci) or "les chansons Gace Brulé" (Gace Brulé's songs). The importance of author identity for the courtly lyric is due in part to the aristocratic standing of so many trouvères; it is also indicative of the self-reflexive quality of the lyric.[5] Narrative and didactic texts are about historical events, moral or intellectual concepts, or the adventures of a fictional protagonist; courtly lyric, as is often pointed out, is about the event of its own making.[6] The experiences of loving, of making a song, and of singing it are indistinguishable, just as the figures of protagonist, author, and performer are united in the lyric "I." A further result of this phenomenon is that lyric discourse, unlike narrative or didactic discourse, is not easily accessible for scribal appropriation. A scribe may be a storyteller, but he is less readily a singer or lover. Producer and rubricator of lyric texts, he assumes the role of narrator with regard to the lyric personae. He participates not in the space of the individual song or song corpus but in the space of the codex as a whole, announcing and orchestrating the series of lyric performances that he brings us.

Let us examine a little more closely the treatment of the author corpus as a textual unit. The distinction of individual corpora is most pronounced in three manuscripts that originally marked nearly every corpus with an author portrait (of which many have been removed): the closely related MSS *a* and *A*—the latter dated 1278 in a colophon, the former dating probably from the early fourteenth century—and the late thirteenth-century *M*. In a second group of manuscripts dating from the end of the thirteenth century, only the opening page and, in two cases, a separate section of anonymous songs, is illuminated: the very closely related MSS *K, N, P,* and *X,* and the somewhat less closely related MS *V*. In these, author corpora are marked through the use of rubrics and ornamental initials, the use of which varies from one manuscript to another.

MS *X,* the most thoroughly rubricated of this group, uses large ornamental initials and rubrication for the beginning of almost every corpus; as in all chansonniers, individual songs are marked with smaller ornamental initials, whereas stanzas are marked with colored but still smaller initials. A series of anonymous *chansons Nostre Dame* at the end is likewise

---

5. Räkel (p. 259) suggests that the insistence on trouvère names represents an aristocratic "cult of the name" and its imitation by the bourgeois trouvères.

6. In this respect it is interesting to note that certain lyric forms were usually anonymous: the pastourelle, a narrative form using past tense discourse and reported dialogue; the *chanson Nostre Dame,* for which the Virgin provides a fixed point of reference quite unlike the unique and unnamed lady of love lyric; and the motet, which, as a result of its multiplication of voice, may have been understood more as a virtuoso performance piece than as the expression of a lyric self.

marked with a rubric and further identified as an entirely new section by a miniature portraying the Madonna and Child. MSS *K, N,* and *P,* on the other hand, single out only the more important trouvères. In MS *P,* for example, large ornamental initials mark the beginnings of the first four corpora: those of Gace Brulé, the châtelain de Couci, Blondel de Nesle, and Thibaut de Navarre. From there on, the only sign of a new corpus is in the author rubrics labeling each song. MS *N* uses a hierarchy of rubrics and initials of different kinds. Authorship is indicated throughout by means of a rubric located in the margin next to the beginning of each song; in addition, large ornamental initials mark the first three author corpora, which are further identified by the following rubrics:

Ce sont les chançons que li Rois Thiebaut de Navarre fist.

[These are the songs that King Thibaut of Navarre made.] [Fol. 1]

Ici faillent les chançons le Roi de Navarre. Et commencent les chançons mon seigneur Gace Brulé.

[Here end the king of Navarre's songs. And begin my lord Gace Brulé's songs.] [Fol. 15v]

Ci faillent les chançons mon seigneur Gace Brullé. Et commencent les chançons au Chastelain de Couci.

[Here end my lord Gace Brulé's songs. And begin the châtelain de Couci's songs.] [Fol. 39]

The corpus of Blondel de Nesle, which follows that of the châtelain, is marked by the same ornamental initial used for the first three corpora but has no introductory rubric. There follows then one song each by the count of Anjou and Hugue de Bresi; these are marked only by the regular oversized initials used for the beginning of any song. We then arrive at a new rubric, "Or viennent ici enprès les chançons Perrin d'Angecourt" (Now from this point begin Perrin d'Angecourt's songs [fol. 47v]). The song that follows is marked by an oversized initial. Following Perrin's songs is a series of corpora without introductory rubrics; large ornamental initials mark the corpora of Tierri de Soissons, Gillebert de Berneville, and Moniot d'Arras, as well as a series of anonymous songs. Finally, we arrive at a series of *motets entés* (motets containing popular refrains), also marked by a large ornamental initial and the rubric "Ci commencent li motet enté" (Here begin the motets entés [fol. 184]). The layout of MS *K* is very much the same as MS *N;* only the distribution of rubrics and ornamental initials varies slightly, due most likely to the relative popularity of these trouvères as perceived by the copyist or his patron.[7]

The individual trouvère corpus, then, had a certain integrity as a textual unit, comparable to a special generic division like the motets or to a narrative or dramatic text. Certain trouvères enjoyed an especially high measure of respect. And it is interesting that the anonymous songs are marked as a special group, as though the lack of an author persona, even if it be nothing more than a name, was itself a distinguishing feature.

How did the compilers of chansonniers go about gathering their materials? Although this question still has not been answered with certainty, I believe that the strongest evidence is for a combined oral and written tradition.[8] Undoubtedly, the lyric poetry of the twelfth and early thirteenth centuries was largely an oral tradition. Poets may have composed the texts in writing, and performers may sometimes have kept written copies of their repertory, but there is no evidence that systematic chansonnier compilation began before the mid-thirteenth century. By the time the first songbooks were compiled, then, the songs would already have existed in multiple versions developed through oral transmission, and a given scribe would have written down the version that he knew or liked the best. It is unlikely that the songs were immediately transformed into a written tradition with the appearance of the first manuscripts. The difficulties encountered by anyone who attempts to establish a chansonnier stemma suggest that it was not a simple matter of copying one manuscript directly from another. For example, even within a single author corpus, the analysis of different songs may reveal different stemmas; for that matter, even a single song may turn out to have one stemma for the words and another for the music.[9]

It is hard to imagine that all this confusion springs from scribal incom-

---

7. For the format of MS *K*, see the facsimile edited by Aubry and Jeanroy.

8. The question of the relative roles of oral and written transmission of trouvère lyric has been long debated. Karp argues for a purely written tradition in "The Trouvère Manuscript Tradition," asserting with regard to the group *K, L, N, P,* and *X* that "Oral tradition may have influenced the archetype itself, but there can be no question of its direct influence on any of the five surviving chansonniers" (p. 36); and that textual variants in the group *M, T, A,* and *a* point to a written rather than an oral tradition. Van der Werf, however, points out that trouvère songs were removed from "the world of *learned* musicians," and that they "originated and circulated in a *notationless* musical culture," in "Trouvère Chansons as Creations of a Notationless Musical Culture" (p. 67, emphasis his). Van der Werf offers convincing arguments for simultaneous oral and written transmission in *The Chansons of the Troubadours and Trouvères*, stating that "initially most or all chansons were transmitted in an exclusively oral tradition and . . . from about the middle of the thirteenth century on there was dissemination in writing parallel to the continuing oral tradition" (p. 28; see also pp. 30–32).

9. On the process of establishing a stemma for songs and chansonniers, see Schwan; Lerond's edition of Châtelain de Couci, *Chansons*, pp. 31–40. On musical transmission in the Middle Ages, see also Treitler.

petence or perversity. We have already seen considerable evidence in narrative and didactic anthologies that the medieval scribe was highly conscious of his responsibilities as participant in the process of literary transmission, and there is no reason to suppose that a scribe copying a lyric anthology would view his task any differently. Most chansonniers are beautifully written and obviously expensive books that would not likely be entrusted to a scribe who did not know his business. Moreover, the close relationship among the members of the group $K$, $N$, $P$, and $X$, which appear to derive from a common archetype, shows that scribes could copy music and poetry accurately if they wanted to. Most likely, the high number of variants within the lyric tradition is due to the continued modification of songs by performers and to the scribes who in turn edited their work in conformance with the performance practices with which they were familiar. They may at times also have had access to multiple written repertories, perhaps belonging to performers, and put together a collection of songs drawn variously from more than one source.

A brief examination of the group $K$, $N$, $P$, and $X$ and the related MS $V$ reveals evidence for the combining of different sources. Textually, MS $V$ is very close to MSS $K$, $N$, $P$, and $X$; but musically, it is not very closely related to any surviving manuscript, even though MSS $K$, $N$, $P$, and $X$ are closely related among themselves with regard to both words and music. In fact, aside from the songs of Thibaut de Navarre, which seem to have enjoyed a special position in the chansonnier tradition, 75–80 percent of the melodies in MS $V$ are largely or completely different from those preserved for the same songs in other manuscripts.[10] One can only assume that the scribe of MS $V$ (or its immediate source) copied the texts from a manuscript closely related to the $K$, $N$, $P$, and $X$ family but used a different source for the melodies. According to Theodore Karp, there is a certain stylistic uniformity to the melodies unique to MS $V$, which, in comparison with melodies in other manuscripts, are more syllabic and of a smaller range, with fewer skips, less clearly established tonal centers, and less literal repetition.[11] Perhaps these melodies derive from a particular performer or group of performers known to the scribe; they may also have been edited according to the tastes of the patron who commissioned the manuscript.

We can also find evidence for compilation from different repertories within the group $K$, $N$, $P$, and $X$. All four manuscripts begin with a series of author corpora followed by a series of anonymous songs; this is the "core" material that is nearly the same in each manuscript. After this common beginning, however, the collections diverge. MS $K$ ends with a

10. Karp.
11. Ibid., p. 28.

second series of anonymous songs arranged alphabetically; MS *N*, with motets and lais; and MS *X*, with a collection of chansons Nostre Dame.[12] Here, it is not a question of combining two different sources for the same material but rather of appending different bodies of material onto an already established collection. Although the scribes of MSS *K*, *N*, and *X* did not attempt to incorporate the new material into the original collection, other scribes in a similar position may well have acted differently, thereby contributing to the mingling of different manuscript families within a single codex.[13] Considering that different methods of compiling from multiple oral and written sources all operated simultaneously, it is small wonder that the textual history of a song or song corpus is so difficult to establish.

If songs continued to be transmitted orally throughout the thirteenth century, the compilation of chansonniers did, nonetheless, contribute in the long run to a stabilization of the lyric tradition, as the written tradition came to assume a greater importance. Hans-Herbert Räkel has shown in his study of thirteenth-century contrafacta that contrafacta of the first half of the thirteenth century differ markedly from those of the second half.[14] According to Räkel, the earlier contrafacta reflect the fluidity of the oral tradition, whereas the later ones follow the imitated melodies precisely and are almost certainly based on a study of the original song in written form. Chansonnier compilation, in other words, can be associated with a more writerly concept of vernacular lyric and of lyric composition.

The movement toward a more writerly concept of vernacular lyric can be illustrated through a comparison of the early fourteenth-century MS *a* and the middle to late thirteenth-century MS *U*. MS *a* offers a comprehensive range of lyric genres, divided into the following sections: songs, arranged by author; anonymous pastourelles; motets and rondeaux, mostly by Guillaume d'Amiens; anonymous chansons Nostre Dame; and jeux-partis. As far as I can tell, not only the author corpora but also the sections of pastourelles, jeux-partis, and chansons Nostre Dame were originally headed with opening miniatures, and all songs have musical notation.[15] The manuscript opens with a table of incipits: it is a deluxe manuscript, beautiful to behold and well designed for easy reference. MS *U* in turn is also somewhat varied, containing not only trouvère songs but also a number of troubadour songs; it is especially valuable for

---

12. MS *P* may originally have been limited to the corpus of attributed songs; the other texts now bound in this volume are evidently all from other manuscripts.

13. On compilation from multiple sources in the early fourteenth-century trouvère MS *R*, see Schubert.

14. Räkel.

15. Most of the pages on which a new corpus began have been removed; the few that remain all have miniatures and ornamental borders. One assumes that it was because of the miniatures that the others were cut out. In a few cases traces of the ornamental border are discernible on the remaining stubs.

its unique inclusion of several *chansons de toile*. There are no miniatures, nor do we find the gold leaf, decorative borders, or large ornamental initials that characterize other chansonniers.[16] All pieces are anonymous (including troubadour and trouvère songs whose authorship is well attested elsewhere), arranged in seemingly random order. Some musical notation has been filled in, but more often the staves are empty. Reader access to this collection is somewhat facilitated by a table of incipits, which, however, is not complete.

MS *a* is clearly a very different kind of manuscript from MS *U* and serves a different purpose. The former codifies the Old French lyric tradition according to subject and versification and identifies a series of noble and bourgeois poets: it is a first step toward the establishment of an Old French lyric canon, which can be studied as such. MS *U*, on the other hand, is more a repository of songs that are thus saved from oblivion; its smaller format and general low-budget aspect suggest that it could possibly have belonged to a minstrel, who was more interested in preserving a large performance repertory than in designing a system of generic classifications or a literary history. MS *U*, one of the oldest surviving collections of trouvère lyric, represents an earlier period of lyric compilation, when most people still encountered the songs as performance pieces and had not yet begun to look upon the trouvère tradition as an object of study and codification. The attitude toward lyric poetry reflected here is similar to that which characterizes the earlier romances with lyric insertions, such as Jean Renart's *Roman de la rose*, in which the emphasis is on the performance of songs. By 1300, however, trouvère songs were being supplanted by the newer *formes fixes*, themselves evidence of a more systematic approach to lyric versification and a desire to stabilize the text. The treatment of lyric insertions in late thirteenth- and early fourteenth-century narratives, such as the *Roman du castelain de Couci* or the *Dit de la panthère d'amours*, further reflects this consciousness of vernacular lyric as a written literary tradition. As we saw in the preceding chapter, scribal practices and poetic process are intimately related and mutually influential phenomena; a study of chansonnier structure and illumination is of profound importance for the investigation of lyric and lyrico-narrative poetics in the thirteenth and fourteenth centuries.

## Knights, Poets, and Performers: The Iconography of the Trouvères

Illuminated trouvère chansonniers can be divided into three general categories, as noted above. The group *K, N, P, V,* and *X,* as well as the

---

16. See the facsimile of MS *U*, edited by Meyer and Raynaud, and the description by Parker.

compilation of Adam de la Halle's works in MS Bibl. Nat. fr. 25566 (chansonnier *W*), feature a single miniature on the first page, which can be taken as a portrait of the trouvère with whose songs the collection opens; in MSS *P*, *W*, and *X* additional miniatures introduce special sections, such as the chansons Nostre Dame of MS *X*. In MSS *A*, *a*, and *M*, on the other hand, nearly every trouvère is (or was originally) introduced by an author portrait. In the alphabetical chansonnier *O*, finally, each new letter of the alphabet is marked with a historiated initial illustrating the opening stanza of the song. MSS *W* and *O* will be discussed individually, since both of them are special cases. Here, I will examine the author portraits of MSS *K*, *N*, *P*, *V*, and *X* and MSS *A*, *a*, and *M*. These images highlight the central themes of courtly lyric—nobility, love, poetic composition, and musical performance—and contribute significantly to the definition of the lyric persona as author, lover, or performer.

Although the opening miniatures in the group *K*, *N*, *P*, *V*, and *X* are very similar, there are certain differences among them. MSS *K*, *N*, *V*, and *X* all open with the songs of Thibaut de Navarre; in the first three, Thibaut's songs are illustrated with the image of a vielle player before a royal couple. MS *X* in turn opens with an image of a crowned man gesturing toward a lady, who places her hand on her heart. We are reminded here that aristocratic followers of love are both the subject and the intended audience for the series of performance pieces to follow; in three cases, Thibaut appears in both capacities at once, as he and his lady listen to the songs that he has composed about their love. The miniature in MS *X*, in which the relationship of lover and beloved is conflated with that of singer and audience, resembles that of MS *P*, where the opening miniature represents a man holding a scroll and gesturing toward a lady, who again places her hand on her heart. Since this collection opens with the songs of Gace Brulé, the man is uncrowned and carries the attribute of a trouvère. Finally, a series of anonymous songs in MS *P*, which may not derive from the original manuscript, opens with the image of a man and a lady in a verdant landscape: a generalized reference to the lyric equation of love, song, and springtime.

At one level, these opening-page miniatures can be understood as author portraits. At another level, they illustrate the entire collection, designating the type of song it contains. In MS *X*, the opening image of *fin'amors* contrasts with the later image of Madonna and Child. Whether they are understood as specific author portraits or generalized generic indications, though, these representations of performance are a way of creating the visual presence of the minstrel from whom the medieval audience would normally have received these songs. The song is first of all an oral, musical medium; a book in which it is written down is still conceived as the visual record of oral performance.

The themes of love, chivalry, poetry, and music are developed more elaborately in the more profusely illustrated MSS *A, M,* and *a,* and these manuscripts are the ones that offer the most interesting perspective on the figure of the author and the delineation of the lyric tradition.[17] Unfortunately, all three manuscripts have been severely mutilated; but five miniatures survive in MS *A,* fifteen in MS *M,* and seven in MS *a,* allowing some tentative conclusions. The programs of illumination, as they survive, are as follows:[18]

### MS *A*

| | |
|---|---|
| 130 | Chastelain de Couci: knight in armor |
| 133 | Gautier de Dargies: knight in armor |
| 135 | Ugon de Bregi: knight in armor |
| 140 | Richard de Fournival: man seated at desk before open book |
| 142v | Adam de la Halle: man writing in book (fig. 3) |

### MS *M*

| | |
|---|---|
| 4 | Comte d'Anjou: knight in armor |
| 5 | Comte de Bar: knight in armor |
| 6 | Duc de Brabant: knight in armor (fig. 1) |
| 7 | Vidame de Chartres: knight in armor |
| 49 | Morisses de Creon: knight in armor |
| 49v | Gilles de Beaumont: knight in armor |
| 51v | Jehan de Louvois: knight in armor |
| 57 | Bouchart de Malh: knight in armor |
| 80 | Gilles de Vieilles Maisons: knight in armor |
| 86 | Pierre de Creon: knight in armor |
| 87 | Gautier de Dargies: knight in armor |
| 105 | Willaumes li Vinier: man stands holding a small rolled-up scroll, gesturing; next to him, man sits on an ornamental stool, holding a baton (fig. 4) |
| 126v | Colart le Bouteiller: man kneels and prays to standing lady |
| 160 | Robert de la Pierre: man stands holding an unfurled scroll |
| 163 | Pierrekin de la Coupele: crowned man sits and plays the vielle |

### MS *a*

| | |
|---|---|
| 18 | Gace Brulé: knight in armor |
| 21 | Vidame de Chartres: knight in armor |
| 69 | Colart le Bouteiller: man with a hunting bird on his wrist |
| 82 | Jehan de Griemler: man standing out of doors (singer?) |

17. For a facsimile edition of MS *A* and a discussion of its original state, see Jeanroy, *Le Chansonnier d'Arras.* Jeanroy's statement that the chansonnier was not originally part of the large anthology with which it is now bound is refuted by Segre's edition of the *Bestiaire d'amours,* pp. xlvii–li.

18. Folio numbers in MS *A* differ from those of Jeanroy's facsimile edition, as the manuscript has been rebound and restored to its original state.

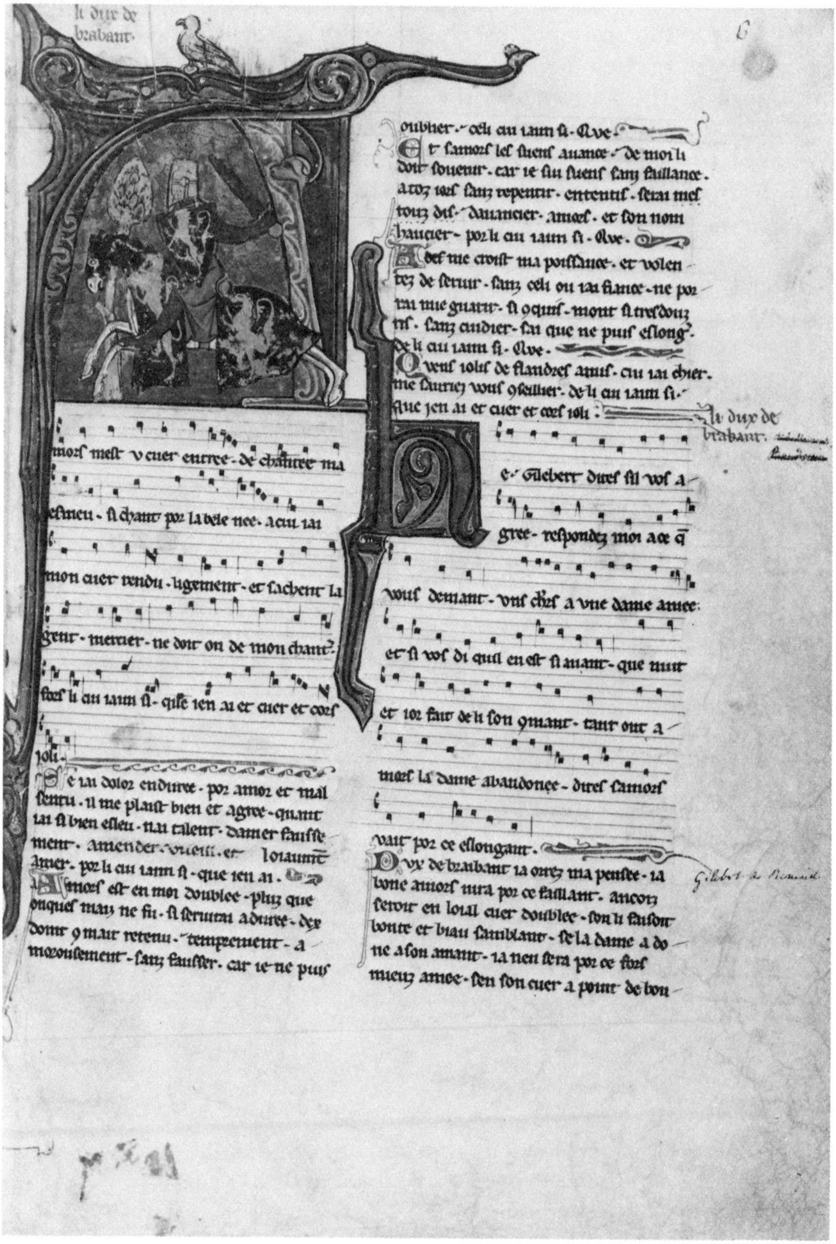

*Figure 1*. Duc de Brabant, trouvère chansonnier *M*, B.N. fr. 844, fol. 6. (Photograph: Bibliothèque Nationale, Paris)

86  Willammes d'Amiens li Paignieres: man painting a coat-of-arms (fig. 2)
94  Perrin d'Angecourt: man holding a portative organ (fig. 5)
100  Martin le Begin de Cambrai: man holding a bagpipe

In all three manuscripts the illuminations serve to distinguish aristocratic trouvères, who are depicted as knights in armor on horseback, from nonnobles, who are depicted variously as writers, singers, musicians, and courtly figures. This pattern is followed in all surviving miniatures of these three manuscripts; a similar image heads the collection of songs by Thibaut de Navarre bound into the beginning of MS *T*. The representation of aristocratic trouvères as knights was evidently an iconographic convention shared by this group of manuscripts, just as the group *K, N, P, V,* and *X* shares the convention of the opening-page miniature representing performance and the couple; no doubt the missing miniatures would have adhered to this scheme.[19] This would have meant a lengthy series, in MSS *A, M,* and *a,* of very similar images illustrating the aristocratic trouvères, creating an insistence upon the noble, courtly presence embodied in the songs. We are reminded again that courtly lyric expresses the ideals of a particular social class.

The individual representation of each trouvère strengthens considerably the sense of distinct poetic identity, and the integrity of the author corpus as a textual entity. Though far less specific or detailed than the *vidas* (biographies) that appear in many Provençal chansonniers, these miniatures do, nonetheless, serve a similar function in providing an image for each new lyric persona. The particularizing quality of the miniatures is especially marked in the knightly images, in spite of their formal similarity, because of the representation of each knight's coat-of-arms (fig. 1). In most cases it can be determined that the coat-of-arms is accurately portrayed.[20] For figures that have not been historically verified, such as Gace Brulé, it is of course impossible to determine whether the coat-of-arms is accurately represented or not. Even if fictional, however, it still serves to endow the trouvère with a specific identity. The combination of the heraldic image and the aristocratic title of the rubric points to an actual historic existence for these figures, grounding the lyric "*I*" in an extratextual reality. The same thing is suggested, if less specifically established, by the place names or occupational epithets attached to the names of many of the nonnobles: Colart le Bouteiller

19. Manuscript format and manner of illumination are evidently features held in common by members of a given manuscript family: MSS *K, N, P, V,* and *X* form one closely related group, and MSS *A* and *a* and MSS *M* and *T,* respectively, are related to each other more closely than to the *K, N, P, V,* and *X* group.

20. Occasional small errors can be detected, most likely due to carelessness; the intention was clearly to reproduce accurate coats-of-arms for each noble trouvère. See Pinet.

*Figure 2.* Willammes d'Amiens li paignieres, trouvère chansonnier *a*, Bibl. Vat., Reg. Lat. 1490, fol. 86. (Photograph: Biblioteca Apostolica Vaticana)

(Colart the wine steward); Willaumes li Vinier (William the vintner); Willammes d'Amiens li Paignieres (William of Amiens the painter), who is in fact represented as a painter (fig. 2). The life of the song in the world at large is further indicated by the designation of *chansons couronnées,* songs awarded a special prize. The inclusion of these details establishes the geographical and social framework within which Old French lyric developed.

In the preceding chapter, we saw that numerous romance anthologies present a series of exemplary knights and ladies who participate in an ongoing story of love, chivalry, and adventure; this shared system of values and behavior suggests a cultural fabric uniting Troy, Greece, Rome, and medieval Europe. It parallels the corresponding poetic project of writing about these experiences, which also defines a cultural continuum, uniting ancient and medieval authors. As Chrétien tells us, *clergie* and *chevalerie* are the two sides of the medieval cultural heritage, conjoined through the process of the *clerc* recording the deeds of the *chevalier.*

In the chansonniers, the cultural milieu is more narrowly defined, including only medieval France; the exemplary heroes participate simultaneously in the poetic and experiential aspects of the cultural project, being at once authors and protagonists. The cultural blending is not diachronic but synchronic: nobles and nonnobles, chevaliers and clercs, as well as musicians and bourgeois, can participate in this society of courtly lovers-singers-poets. The roles are differently defined: instead of clerks, scribes, and performers collaborating to record the deeds of knights and kings, we find that the former are elevated to the status of protagonists, celebrating their own dreams and desires, whereas the latter in turn acquire a voice to relate their experience without the mediating presence of a narrator. Thus the terms of the codicological construct are somewhat differently drawn in narrative and in lyric anthologies; but in both cases, the book defines a collective cultural enterprise and situates the individual experience—poetic, musical, amorous, chivalric—within this context.

The distinction between noble and nonnoble trouvères is important and deserves closer attention. MS *A* sets up a contrast between knights and clercs, recalling the conventional opposition of chevalerie and clergie. This distinction is expressed in both miniatures and rubrics. Noble trouvères are uniformly portrayed as knights; the rubric states, "Ce sont les kançons mon seigneur *X*" (These are the songs [of/by] my lord *X*). Thus the miniature announces nobility, chevalerie; the rubric announces the songs and their link with an aristocratic title and name. For the two nonnobles whose miniatures survive, Adam de la Halle (also known as Adam le Bossu) and Richard de Fournival, the miniature portrays a scribe (fig. 3); the rubrics state, respectively, "Adans li boçus

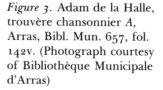

*Figure 3.* Adam de la Halle, trouvère chansonnier *A*, Arras, Bibl. Mun. 657, fol. 142v. (Photograph courtesy of Bibliothèque Municipale d'Arras)

fist ces kançons" (Adam le Bossu made these songs) and "Richars de Fournival fist ces kançons a sa vie" (Richard de Fournival made these songs during his life). Thus the miniature announces poetic composition, *clergie*; the rubric announces the making of the songs by a particular personage. What is stressed is the poetic craft that produced the songs. The two sets of miniatures provide two complementary views of song, contrasting the aristocratic articulation of sentiment with its appropriation by a class of educated poets.

In MSS *M* and *a*, the second set of images evokes performance, whether declamatory or musical, and the courtly life (figs. 4, 5).[21] This distinction between noble and nonnoble trouvères suggests that the latter, in some cases at least, belonged to a class of professional performers. One is reminded of the opening miniatures in MSS *K*, *N*, and *V*, where the viellist is distinguished from the aristocratic author-protagonist of the song. The crown worn by the viellist Pierrekin de la Coupelle in MS *M* identifies him as "King of Minstrels," the title also claimed by Adenet le Roi. The iconography of the minstrel—scroll, musical instrument, honorific crown—contributes, like the iconography of *clergie* in MS *A*,

21. Other manuscripts do not distinguish between the rubric identification of noble and nonnoble trouvères as MS *A* did.

to the definition of a class whose primary association is with the transmission, both oral and written, of lyric poetry.[22] Even Willammes d'Amiens li Paignieres may be included, as book illuminator, among those responsible for the written literary tradition. His is the only surviving portrait in which a bourgeois trouvère is shown plying his trade; although this may be coincidence, it could mean that his trade was considered more relevant to the poetic tradition. Interestingly, his page is also more profusely decorated with marginal figures than any of the other surviving miniature pages of MS *a,* as if the illuminator took advantage of this opportunity to celebrate a fellow guildsman.

The one nonnoble trouvère not represented as scribe, illuminator, singer, or musician is Colart le Bouteiller, depicted in both MS *M* and MS *a* as an aspirant to courtliness: in the former, he prays before his lady, whereas in the latter he holds a hunting bird. This last image in particular may be a humorous comment on the bourgeois imitation of the aristocracy.[23] Is it a coincidence that Colart is so represented in both manuscripts? Again, this question cannot really be answered, since our knowledge of the iconographic tradition is too fragmentary. Perhaps Colart's position as wine steward was important enough to afford him a certain air of courtliness. Perhaps some oral tradition identified Colart, and possibly others whose portraits have not survived, as having particularly high-flown courtly pretensions. It may also be that this iconography was used for any nonnoble trouvère who did not have a strong reputation for either learning or musical talent.

Unfortunately, the depleted condition of all three manuscripts prevents us from knowing whether the iconography of clergie is actually unique to MS *A.* It is possible that all three manuscripts originally contained images of both writing and singing, along with images of knighthood and those of love and courtly activity. It is not surprising to find the iconography of clerkliness used for poets like Adam and Richard, both of whom had a reputation for learning and produced a variety of works in addition to chansons courtoises; we cannot assume from these two somewhat unusual poets that all nonnoble trouvères in the codex would have been so illustrated. What we can say is that about 1300 the lyric persona could be conceived primarily as noble protagonist or primarily as a maker of songs; and that lyric composition in turn could be linked with either book production or musical performance. These

---

22. There is some evidence that one trouvère, at least, may have also been employed as a scribe. The colophon at the end of the codex containing chansonnier *A* identifies the scribe of that portion as "Jehans d'Amiens li petis"; and a "crowned" song in the slightly later MS *a* is attributed to "Jehans li petis" (fol. 62v), identified in the table as "Jehan li petit clerc." For discussion of other possible poet-scribes, see Walters, "Rôle du scribe."

23. On the movement of courtly lyric from noble to bourgeois circles, see Räkel, pp. 135–37, 259.

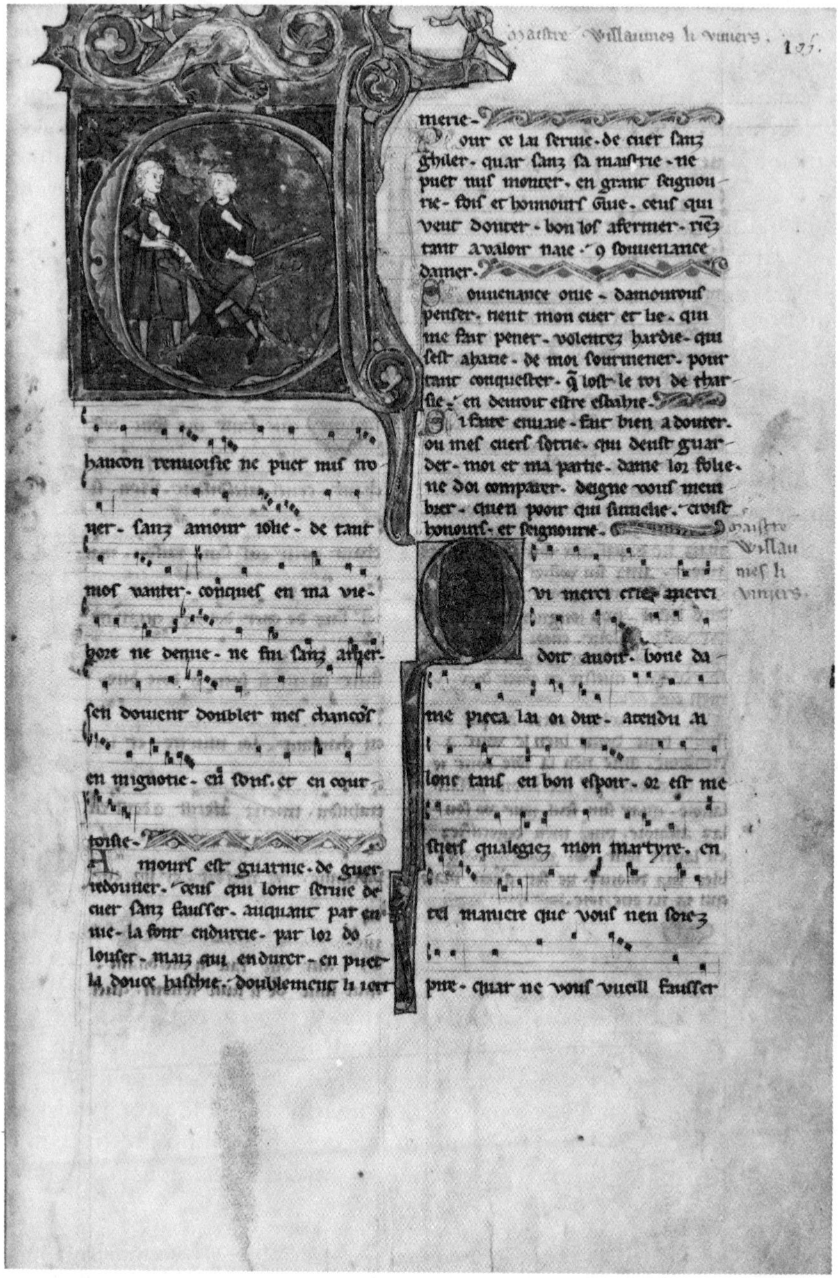

*Figure 4.* Willaumes li Vinier, trouvère chansonnier *M,* B.N. fr. 844, fol. 105. (Photograph: Bibliothèque Nationale, Paris)

distinctions, expressed by the compilers and illuminators of chansonniers, were also exploited by contemporary poets, as will be seen in later
chapters.

The figure of the author that emerges from the chansonniers is of
profound importance for the eventual emergence of the fourteenth-
century author-compilers like Guillaume de Machaut and Jean Froissart.
The chansonniers graphically express a valorization of the roles of clerk
and minstrel. These figures assume a more central position than in
narrative anthologies, where, though certainly important, they were rel-
egated to the marginal space of prologues, epilogues, narrator interventions, rubrics, and colophons. Although the distinction between nobility
and the professional classes still obtains, the inclusion of the latter nonetheless suggests an extension of courtly ideals to those outside the aristocracy. Such a concept is not entirely new; the poetic debates about the
clerc and the chevalier go back at least as far as the twelfth century.[24]
These poems, which already provided a forum whereby clerks could
declare themselves "courtly" figures, are an important background for
the appearance of the nonnoble trouvère. In the *Jugement d'amour*,[25] for
example, the judgment is passed that clerks are "vaillant et cortois"
(valiant and courteous [v. 414]), gifted with more fine qualities than any
other people in the world. An epilogue appended to the *Jugement
d'amour* in one manuscript even adds that just as the rose surpasses all
other flowers, so the clerk surpasses knights, kings, and counts.[26]

On what grounds are clerks superior to knights? One of the most
important arguments offered in the *Jugement d'amour* is that clerks have
transmitted the cultural values of courtliness, presumably through their
role in literary tradition. During the central debate (in which the participants are all birds), the goldfinch argues that knights would know nothing of delight or liberality if they had not learned it from clerks. And the
nightingale reiterates that "amors fust grant pieça perdue / Se clers ne
l'euist maintenue" (love would be long since lost if clerks had not maintained it [vv. 355–56]). This argument suggests a valorization of the
figures responsible for the transmission of literary texts over and above
those whose deeds are celebrated in these texts. Furthermore, although
the question is settled by means of combat, the battle is decidedly lyricized: the nightingale fights for the clerks, and the popinjay champions
the knights. Whereas the popinjay carried aristocratic and lyric connotations in medieval poetry, the nightingale was the lyric bird par excellence, the bird of love and of song. That the nightingale is the bird of the

24. See Faral, pp. 191–303.
25. Faral includes a critical edition of the *Jugement d'amour,* using the five known manuscripts, in *Recherches*, pp. 251–69.
26. This passage is printed by Faral in his notes to the *Jugement*, p. 269.

clerks suggests again that clerks are superior for their ability to articulate love sentiment poetically and musically.

What emerges from the survey of both manuscripts and the *Jugement d'amour* is that it was within the realm of lyricism that the clerk could challenge the knight and that the valorization of the clerk hinged on his participation, through poetry, in the codification of love experience. The chansonniers further suggest that this principle could be extended to professional performers. The clerkly trouvère is a new kind of author figure, combining aspects of the clerkly romance narrator, the scribal editor and compiler, and the amorous protagonist. As this figure moves into the poetic spotlight, a variety of new literary possibilities are generated: there is a new focus not only on love and song as such but also on the circumstances of performance, the circumstances of poetic composition, and even on the activities of writing and bookmaking. This combination of lyric inspiration and affective experience on the one hand, and a self-conscious preoccupation with literary production and transmission on the other, will form the basis for our examination, in subsequent chapters, of the history of lyrico-narrative and lyrico-didactic literature.

## The Arrangement of an Author Corpus: Adam de la Halle and MS Bibl. Nat. fr. 25566

The emphasis on author identity and the author corpus raises two related questions: Did trouvère corpora circulate independently of the chansonniers? And did trouvères ever supervise the compilation of their own songs? Neither question can be adequately answered in light of the available evidence. The earliest surviving single-author collection, packaged and presented as such outside a chansonnier, is the compilation of the complete works of Adam de la Halle in the late thirteenth-century Artesian MS Bibl. Nat. fr. 25566. Whether this actually was the first time that such a collection was made, however, cannot be determined with certainty. Other trouvères, or performers of trouvère verse, may have kept their own written records that do not survive today; and there is some evidence for a precedent in the songs of Thibaut de Navarre.

Thibaut's initiative in compiling his own songs is attested in the *Grandes Chroniques*. Here it is stated that Thibaut made some of the loveliest songs ever heard, "Et les fist escripre en sa sale à Provins et en celle de Troyes, et sont appellées *Les Chançons au Roy de Navarre*" (And he had them written down in his hall in Provins and in the one in Troyes, and they are called *The Songs by the king of Navarre*).[27] It is, of course, impossi-

27. This passage is quoted by Wallensköld in his edition of Thibaut de Champagne, p. xvii.

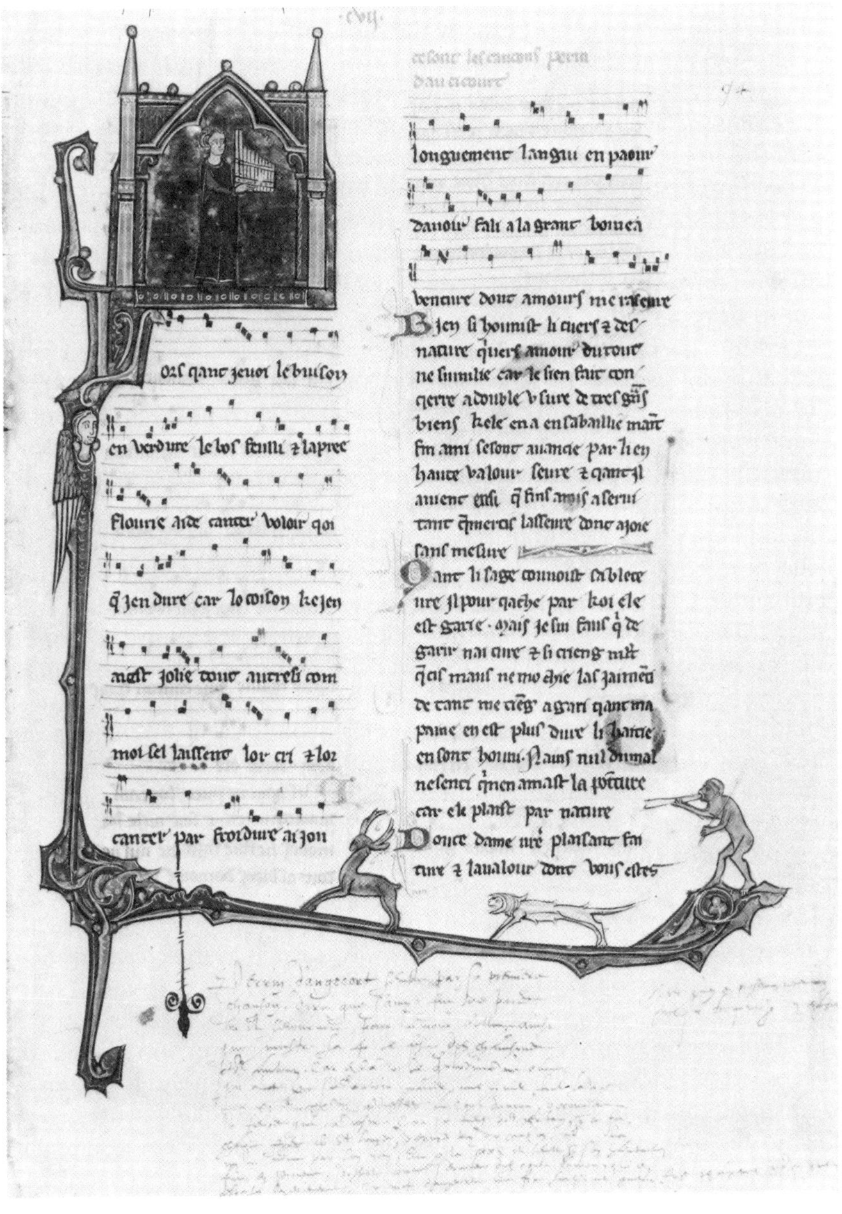

*Figure 5*. Perrin d'Angecourt, trouvère chansonnier *a*, Bibl. Vat., Reg. Lat. 1490, fol. 94. (Photograph: Biblioteca Apostolica Vaticana)

ble now to be sure of the truth of this statement. Thibaut's songs do, however, appear in almost exactly the same order in nearly every manuscript, suggesting common derivation from an early, authoritative compilation.[28] We may recall in this context that Thibaut was the descendent of Guillaume IX, the first known troubadour. That Guillaume's songs were the first to have been written down and associated with the name of a specific person is most likely due to his high social standing, which enabled him to provide for the written preservation of his songs. Thibaut can hardly have been unaware of the poetic fame of his illustrious ancestor; a similar pride in his own achievements may have led him to have a compilation made.

Certain particularities of the manuscript tradition suggest that Thibaut's songs enjoyed a special status as a song collection. In MS *M,* the original selection indicated by the table of incipits included only a small number of Thibaut's songs. The remainder of his songs were transcribed by a different, though contemporary, hand; they begin on a page originally left blank at the end of his songs, perhaps for precisely this purpose, and continue through two extra gatherings (this is the collection known as chansonnier $M^T$). Evidently, someone perceived Thibaut's corpus as incomplete and managed to remedy the situation. In MS *T,* three gatherings containing Thibaut's songs are bound in front of the original compilation. The first page is decorated by the usual image of the knight and the rubric "The king of Navarre made these songs." That this represents an interpolation is clear not only from the fact that these songs are transcribed in a different (though contemporary) hand but also because the gatherings of MS *T* bear their original numeration, beginning after Thibaut's songs with number one. Again, MS *T* in its original form contained only very few of Thibaut's songs; apparently someone felt that the rest needed to be there, occupying their usual place of honor. Finally, Thibaut's songs appear in MS Bibl. Nat. fr. 12581, a compendium of mostly prose works, such as the *Queste del Saint Graal* and Brunetto Latini's *Tresor;* it is dated 1288 in a colophon. Thirty-nine of Thibaut's songs and a few other lyric pieces were transcribed in the fourteenth century, without music or attribution, on the empty leaves left whenever a text was completed before the end of a gathering. The appearance of Thibaut's songs in this rather unlikely context testifies to his ongoing popularity; it shows that the songs could circulate independently of the chansonniers.

The case of Adam de la Halle is somewhat similar: there exist several isolated collections of his songs. The most impressive is that in MS Bibl. Nat. fr. 25566, which I will discuss shortly. In addition to the collection of Adam's complete works, there are nine folios of Adam's songs bound

---

28. See the table at the end of Wallensköld's edition of Thibaut's songs.

into the beginning of MS 25566; their different size and format clearly show that they did not originate with this codex. The thirteenth-century MSS *P* and *T* contain gatherings of Adam's songs and jeux-partis, transcribed in a fourteenth-century hand; the early fourteenth-century MS Bibl. Nat. fr. 1109, an anthology of diverse pieces, contains a compilation of Adam's songs and jeux-partis, copied later in the fourteenth century. This plethora of compilations suggests that Adam's songs may have circulated as a collection independently of the chansonniers. The order in which the songs appear is quite similar in all five of these collections, as in MS *A*. Generally, Adam's songs exhibit fewer manuscript variants than is typical of trouvère verse. These factors all point to the early existence of an authoritative compilation of Adam's songs; Adam's personal responsibility for this compilation, however, must remain a hypothesis.[29]

The compilation in MS 25566 is of particular interest because of its completeness and its proximity to Adam's immediate circle (late thirteenth-century Arras). It is articulated by a series of rubrics and miniatures, outlined below:

On the verso of the leaf containing the table: "Chi conmencent les chanchons maistre Adan de la Hale" (Here begin Master Adam de la Halle's songs).

| | |
|---|---|
| Fol. 10 | (Beginning of the songs; this was originally the first page following the table.) |
| | Miniature: singer before audience. |
| Fol. 23v | "Les partures Adan" (Adam's jeux-partis). |
| | Miniature: two men debating. |
| Fol. 32v | "Li rondel Adan" (Adam's rondeaux). |
| Fol. 34v | "Li motet Adan" (Adam's motets). |
| Fol. 37 | (Bottom of page) "Li jus du pelerin" (The play of the pilgrim). |
| Fol. 37v | (Beginning of *Pelerin*) |
| | Miniature: pilgrim addressing an audience. |
| Fol. 39 | "Chi commenche li gieus de Robin et de Marion c'Adans fist" (Here begins the play of Robin and Marion, which Adam made). |
| | Miniature: knight on horseback with falcon, shepherdess, sheep. |
| Fol. 48v | (Bottom of page) "Li jus Adan" (Adam's play). |
| Fol. 49 | (Beginning of *Jeu de la feuillée*) |
| | Miniature: man addressing an audience. |
| Fol. 59v | "Explicit li jeus de le fueillie" (Here ends the play of the bower). |
| | "C'est du roi de Sezile" (This is about the king of Sicily). |
| | Miniature: knight in armor on horseback. |
| Fol. 65 | "Explicit du roy de Sezile" (Here ends about the king of Sicily). |
| | "Ce sont vers d'amour" (These are verses about love). |

29. Schwan suggested that Adam's works might have been compiled originally by his nephew Jehan Madot, known as a scribe and an admirer of his uncle's poetic works from his colophon in MS 375 (see Schwan, p. 272).

Miniature: demon shooting arrows into the heart of a man and a lady.

Fol. 66v   "Chi definent li ver d'amour" (Here end the verses about love). "C'est li congiés Adan" (This is Adam's farewell). Miniature: man riding away on a horse, looking back to address an assembly.

Fol. 67v   "Chi fine li congiés Adan" (Here ends Adam's farewell). "C'est li vers de le mort" (This is the poem about death).

Fol. 68   "Explicit d'Adan" (Here ends about Adam).

The corpus is carefully arranged. First come the lyric works, divided according to type and arranged in ascending order of difficulty: traditional songs and jeux-partis are followed by the polyphonic compositions, culminating in the motets. These are followed by the dramatic works. The *Pelerin*, to be discussed later, features a eulogy of Adam and is generally believed to have been written after his death. The *Robin et Marion* is a dramatization of the lyric pastourelle, featuring the love of the shepherd couple Robin and Marion, the unsuccessful attempts of a knight to win Marion's affections, and the general antics, songs, and games of the shepherds and shepherdesses. The *Jeu de la feuillée* in turn represents the community of Arras itself and dramatizes Adam's role within this community. The plays are followed by the stanzaic compositions: the narrative *Roi de Sezile*, recounting the life of Charles d'Anjou, king of Sicily; the *Vers d'amour*, a lengthy meditation on the power of love; the *Congé*, in which Adam announces his intention to leave Arras and bids farewell to its citizens. The series ends, finally, with the three-stanza meditation on death, which is not attributed to Adam and, like the *Pelerin*, may have been added not as one of his works but as a means of rounding out the collection. This "special edition" of the works of a much-admired Artesian poet ends with his departure from Arras and subsequent death. I will return to this point later.

The divisions within the lyric corpus are the same as those used in chansonniers; we have seen these categories, for example, in MS *a*, also copied in Arras. Adam is thus presented as the author of a miniature but complete compilation. In the second part of Adam's collection, lyric themes reappear in dramatic or narrative form. Again, we move through a hierarchy of literary types, from the pastourelle through the bourgeois world of Arras to the courtly world of the *Roi de Sezile*.[30] In the last pieces, poetry appears in a nonmusical form: we have moved

30. These three levels of society—shepherds, townspeople, and nobility—are analogous to the generic distinction, deriving from the works of Virgil and known to the Middle Ages through the works of Donatus, Servius, and John of Garland, of literary works treating pastoral, peasant, and warrior classes, respectively. See Jauss. It may be that Adam, or his compiler, had in mind some such threefold system of genres: in this respect, too, Adam is shown to have produced a complete compendium of literary types.

from song to dit.[31] The combination of a lyric corpus with dramatic and narrative poetry by the same author is highly unusual. Chrétien de Troyes's songs, for example, do not appear in any of the manuscripts containing his romances, in spite of his considerable poetic reputation; nor are Richard de Fournival's songs transmitted in conjunction with the *Bestiaire d'amours*. Even within MS 25566, Richard's *Bestiaire d'amours*, *Consaus d'amours*, and *Poissance d'amours* are widely separated; Jean Bodel's *Jeu de St. Nicholas* and his *Congé* are two hundred folios apart. Indeed, to my knowledge no comparable formation of a generically diverse, vernacular single-author collection survives from before those of Machaut, dating from the middle and late fourteenth century. I will return to this point at greater length in Chapter 7.

As it happens, the musical and nonmusical portions of the collection are nearly identical in length: the lyric texts cover twenty-eight folios, and the texts following the *Pelerin* cover twenty-nine folios. It is at the precise midpoint, then, that we find this curious piece, which is not attributed to Adam but is instead about him: a pilgrim, recently arrived in Artois from Sicily, praises Adam's poetic accomplishments and describes his tomb to a group of Artesian peasants, who in turn offer their own memories of Adam as poet and singer. Here, at the heart of the collection, the persona "Adans li Bochus" is identified as a clerk and court singer for the count of Artois. Through the pilgrim's story, we learn that Adam was born in Arras; that he was "un clerc net et soustieu, grascieus et noble," who "savoit dis et chans controuver" (a pure and subtle, gracious and noble clerk, [who] knew how to make poems and songs [Langlois ed., vv. 23, 37]); and that he accompanied the count to Sicily, where his tomb can now be visited. Through the further eulogy spoken by the peasant Rogaus, we learn, more specifically, that Adam was gifted in both *diter* and *chanter* (vv. 86–87)—presumably, poetic and musical composition—and that he made many *canchons, partures, motès*, and *balades* (vv. 90–93).

This identification of Adam includes essentially the same information as that of Adenet in his prologue to *Cléomadès* (see Chapter 1): the poet's name, that of his patron, and an account of his poetic activity and its reception. The dual identification of Adam as clerk and singer also parallels the dual representation of Adenet in the miniatures at the beginning and end of *Cléomadès* in MS Arsenal 3142 (also an Artesian manuscript); first he appears with his musical instrument, then with his book. Though different sorts of poets—Adenet is primarily associated with chanson de geste, Adam with chanson courtoise—each creates a

---

31. With regard to the distinction between song and dit, and the presence of both in Adam's corpus, Zumthor has noted, "En dissociant la poésie 'personnelle' en poésie musicale et non-musicale, le XIIIe siècle préparera la grande transformation qui, au XIVe, affectera la première," in "Entre deux esthétiques," p. 1157.

poetic identity that draws on both the clerk and the minstrel. Adenet describes the research at Saint Denis that enabled him to compose a new, (supposedly) historically accurate chanson de geste; Adam refers in the *Jeu de la feuillée* to his Parisian education, the fruits of which can be seen in his application of polyphony to vernacular lyric. And just as Adenet's self-presentation in *Cléomadès* functions in MS 3142 as an introduction to his collected works, so this characterization of Adam is used in MS 25566 to unify his poetic oeuvre.

The *Jeu du Pelerin* does more than simply provide further information about the personage "Adan" named in the rubrics by explaining such things as the circumstances of patronage that led the author of songs and motets to write the *Roi de Sezile*. It occupies a crucial position between the lyric works and the other texts and as such has an important transitional function. It is closely linked to the *Jeu de Robin et de Marion*: not only does its closing line, the first half of a couplet, find its rhyme in the opening line of Marion's song; but also the Artesian characters of the *Pelerin*—that is, everyone except the pilgrim—reappear in *Robin et Marion*. Interestingly, the passages in which these characters appear are found only in MS 25566. Perhaps, as Langlois suggests, these interpolated lines were added by the author of the *Pelerin* in an attempt to strengthen the continuity between the two texts; or perhaps they were added by the scribe, as the result of his decision to insert the *Pelerin* into Adam's corpus.[32] For that matter, it is entirely possible that the author of the *Pelerin* is none other than the scribe to whom this arrangement of Adam's oeuvre is due.

The effect of grafting the *Pelerin* onto *Robin et Marion* is to locate the author of the preceding lyric corpus within the Artesian community; this short conversation about Adam within the context of *Robin et Marion* is the prelude to the extended picture of Adam among the citizens of Arras in the *Jeu de la feuillée*. The movement of the collection as a whole is from the lyric, with its focus on self, to drama and narrative, with a focus on the social context within which that lyric self operated as poet, lover, singer, and fellow citizen. Such a progression is already suggested within the lyric corpus itself in the movement from monologue to dialogue and from monody to polyphony. Indeed, even within individual songs Adam frequently juxtaposes a first-person statement of personal love experience with a third-person description of love experience in general, both ideal and villainous, so as to situate himself in a larger context. Adam's relationship to his social context is also, of course, the explicit theme of the *Congé;* and the *Roi de Sezile* opens with a prologue in which he names himself and states his poetic mission. The *Pelerin* inserts Adam as a character into the one text he was absent from, establishing

---

32. Langlois's edition of *Robin et Marion,* pp. 76–82.

his relationship to the pastoral world; the shepherds are aware of his reputation as poet, something they admire but also fail to comprehend. In this way a series of poetic experiments revolving around the relationship of self and society, poet and social context, becomes a complete program.

This reading is consistent with the framing of the collection as a whole. It opens with the self-presentation of the lyric persona as lover and singer in the first song, "D'amoreus cuer voel canter / Por avoir aïe" (With amorous heart I wish to sing, in order to have relief [Wilkins ed., vv. 1–2]). This persona speaks to us for the last time in the final stanza of the *Congé:* "A tous ceux d'Arras en le fin / Pren congié" (In closing I bid farewell to all the people of Arras [Coussemaker ed., stanza 13, vv. 1–2]). This in turn is followed by verses on death, not attributed to Adam. The final rubric, *Explicit d'Adan,* identifies the "Adan," hitherto known as author of the series of texts, as the protagonist as well; for, as I stated earlier, the preposition *de* is used to announce the protagonist or theme of a work and not its author.[33] The collection, in other words, begins with the arrival "on stage" of the trouvère and closes with his departure from Arras and his death, as is stressed by the miniatures; the series of lyric and lyric-based texts is not only the literary output of Adam de la Halle, but also the record of his life. The last words uttered by the poetic presence that has been sustained throughout this varied assortment of texts are a leave-taking, addressed to the community within which the poet lived and within which the manuscript was made; the protagonist's farewell to his circle of friends conflates with the author's farewell to his readers. The relocation of the narrative account of Adam's death from the end—where the general verses on death celebrate his passing—to the center serves to reinscribe his death and his ongoing reputation in the Artesian context. Indeed, this textual monument to Adam may be seen as the Artesian counterpart to the Sicilian tomb described by the pilgrim.

The *Jeu du pelerin* may be compared to the Provençal vidas. Normally written in red ink, the vida is an extended rubric; according to Schutz, the vidas were probably composed by scribes for use in chansonniers.[34] Like the *Pelerin,* the vida imposes unity on the song corpus to which it is attached by providing a specific third-person referent for the lyric "I" and situating this persona in a social and geographical context. Again, the scribe does not appropriate the lyric "I"; he assumes the role of narrator with regard to the lyric protagonist, and his use of the first person is clearly distinct from that of the troubadour. Similarly, the

33. The traditional pattern of rubrication is followed in MS 25566, as is indicated in such rubrics as "li rondel Adan," "Li motet Adan," "C'est du Roi de Sezile," "Explicit du Roy de Sezile."
34. Schutz, "Were the Vidas and Razos Recited?"

author of the *Pelerin* sets up a voice clearly distinct from the lyric voice; he makes the pilgrim and Rogaus narrators of the life, works, and death of the trouvère Adans.

The central location of the *Pelerin* bespeaks a compilational technique seen also in narrative anthologies. In MS 375, for example, a series of romances serves to mediate between antique pagan and medieval Christian legends; in MS 24428, allegory and fable mediate between the natural and spiritual worlds. The central location of *Cligès* in MS 1450 provides a thematic nucleus for the collection. In these cases, of course, the compiler exploited characteristics already inherent in the texts at his disposal; Adam's compiler may have composed the missing link himself.

Another very interesting analogy for this ordered compilation can be found in Jean de Meun's continuation of the *Rose*, which may predate MS 25566 by as much as twenty or thirty years. In a justly famous passage at the midpoint of the conjoined texts, the God of Love identifies Guillaume de Lorris by name, foretells Guillaume's poetic activity and death, and describes his tomb; and then he prophesizes the birth and poetic contribution of Jean Clopinel.[35] This passage also includes an encapsulation of Guillaume's text; many of its characters are reassembled, and the lover briefly reviews the God of Love's teachings and summarizes the events of the narrative up to that point. The ending of Jean's poem is anticipated in the God of Love's statement that the romance will not end until the lover attains the rose and wakes up. Thus this passage, like the *Jeu du pelerin*, effects a conjoining of texts around a central nucleus that establishes authorial identity and enunciates an overall narrative framework. And, as in the *Pelerin*, it is by characters within the fictional world that this material is formulated.

Jean was drawing on the structural importance of the midpoint in romance tradition. Indeed, in some notable cases, such as Chrétien's *Charrete* and Renaut de Beaujeu's *Le Bel Inconnu*, it is precisely the name and social identity of the protagonist that is revealed at the midpoint. Jean further accomplished a mirroring of the scribal voice within the fabric of his text: discourse about the subject matter, authorship, or genesis of texts is appropriate to the extratextual commentary of rubrication, and indeed Guillaume's "inability" to complete his poem, and Jean's decision to continue it, are frequently the subject of an extended rubric between the two parts of the *Rose*. In Jean's *Rose*, as in MS 25566, a compilation of texts accounts internally for its own coherence. Perhaps Adam's compiler was inspired by the *Rose;* or perhaps he was responding to the same poetic and codicological phenomena as Jean himself. In either case, the comparison serves, once again, to illustrate the closeness of scribal and poetic techniques.

35. On the midpoint of the *Roman de la rose*, see Uitti, "From *Clerc* to *Poète*."

A few words must be said about the relation of the Adam compilation to MS 25566 as a whole. Adam's oeuvre functions as a kind of prologue for the codex. It presents the Artesian setting, and the themes of love and social satire, that will remain important throughout the series of works that follows. The movement from lyric through drama to dit is also reflected in the overall structure of the codex.[36] The first half of the collection contains, in addition to Adam's works, the *Jeu de St. Nicholas*, with its satirical Artesian tavern scenes; the lyrical *Bestiaire d'amour* and its *Response*, in which the animal imagery of the bestiary tradition becomes the vehicle for a debate about love; and two folios of short pieces, the prose *Coument diex fourma Adan* and two dits. The midpoint of the codex is occupied by *Renart le Nouvel;* the second half consists of didactic works, including a large number of dits and a few longer works, such as *Li Tornoiement Antecrist*. Like Adam's oeuvre, the codex ends with a *Congé*, this time that of Jean Bodel. Again, Adam is held up as an exemplary Artesian poet. His works are a compendium of poetic types; they cover the field, so to speak, of Artesian poetry.

*Renart le Nouvel* is an interesting choice for the midpoint. With its prose love letters, lyric insertions, animal allegory, and social satire, it too wraps up the principal themes and literary forms of the codex. Moreover, the passage that falls on the central pages of the codex is the scene in which Renart's three ladyfriends get together, take turns reading aloud the prose and verse love letters each has received from him, sing a series of refrains, and draw lots to see which will retain him as lover. Several different kinds of love discourse are thus interwoven: song, verse declamation, prose, and debate.[37] This little compilation at the center of the codex echoes the compilation with which it began, exemplifying a similar variety of poetic voice and discourse and reiterating principles of textual conjoining.

The difference between the opening and the midpoint compilations is instructive, and it reflects a general development that can be seen over the course of the thirteenth century. In *Renart* the songs and letters are presented as integral parts of a narrative framework; they are important largely because they reflect upon or advance the narrative action. The refrains in particular are not composed by the characters themselves, nor do they refer specifically to the situation in which they are sung; they are appropriated from a large body of such refrains and used as a means of focusing a given character's experience into a conventional formula-

---

36. For a description of MS 25566, see Segre ed., *Bestiaire d'amours*, pp. xxxiii–xxxvii.

37. The precise midpoint of *Renart le nouvel*, based on a folio count, would be fol. 143, or vv. 4188–4256 in Roussel's edition. The midpoint of the codex, before the extra pages of Adam's songs were inserted at the beginning, was fol. 146, or vv. 4441–65 of *Renart*. The sequence with the letters is fols. 144–48, or vv. 4313–4602; this sequence is truly the midpoint of the codex, and virtually that of the poem.

tion. Adam's works, on the other hand, are conjoined on the basis of shared authorship. The transformation of Adam into the protagonist of the compilation suggests that the narrative framework that unites these pieces is the circumstances and act of composition itself: the poetic career of an individual. Although authorship was usually a factor in the compilation of chansonniers, the use of author identity as the basis for a generically diverse compilation was new, as I have said; and not until the late thirteenth century also, in the *Roman du castelain de Couci*, did the use of lyric insertions in a narrative text operate on the basis of authorship.

## The Iconography of Lyricism in the Alphabetical Chansonnier *O*

In the foregoing discussion, we have noted repeatedly that lyric and lyrico-narrative texts are most frequently identified by their association with a particular author: at the very least a name, perhaps also a geographical setting or social occupation, and sometimes also a visual image. But organization on the basis of authorship was not the only possible method of chansonnier compilation; and we turn now to an example of a very different sort of arrangement, the Burgundian MS *O*, dating from the closing years of the thirteenth century. As stated above, the songs in MS *O* are grouped according to the first letter of their opening line, without author attributions; a historiated initial marks the beginning of each new letter of the alphabet.[38] The program of illumination is as follows.

Fol. 1   "Ausi cum l'unicorne sui" (I am like the unicorn [R 2075]).
        Miniature: man stabbing a unicorn that is kneeling with its head in the lap of a lady, who holds a mirror. (This initial illustrates the opening stanza, in which the lover compares himself to the unicorn entrapped by a beautiful maiden and killed by a hunter.)

Fol. 14  "Bien me cuidoie partir" (I really thought to leave [R 1440]).
        Miniature: A seated man wearing a crown, gesturing in surprise or fear. (The song describes the emotions of fear and despair typical of lovesickness. Perhaps the crown indicates an awareness that the song is by Thibaut de Navarre, who names himself in the last line of the second stanza.)[39]

38. See Beck, *Reproduction phototypique du manuscrit Cangé*. There is no illustration for the letter "R," presumably due to oversight. The song accompanying each illustration is by Thibaut de Navarre, except in the following cases: "Grant pieça que ne chantai" (anonymous); "Haute chose a en amor" (Gillebert de Berneville); "Oëz por quoi plaing et sopir" (Gace Brulé). I have followed the orthography of MS *O*. Songs are identified by their number in Raynaud's catalog as revised by Spanke.
39. The line in MS *O* reads, "Nuns n'iert joianz que Thiebauz" (fol. 14).

Fol. 21v   "Contre le tans qui devise" (Against the season that divides [R 1620]).

Miniature: seated man with an arrow protruding from his heart. (This illustrates the closing lines of the first stanza, where the singer states that he has been struck by love's arrow.)

Fol. 32v   "Dame, cis vostre fins amis" (Lady, this your true lover [R 1516]).

Miniature: man kneeling and praying to a lady.

Fol. 46v   "En chantant vuil ma dolour descovrir" (By singing I want to reveal my sorrow [R 1397]).

Miniature: seated man reading from a long scroll.

Fol. 53v   "Fuille ne flors ne vaut riens en chantant" (Neither leaf nor flower has any worth in singing [R 324]).

Miniature: seated man gesturing in declamation next to a tree. (The tree may refer either to the singer's statement in the first stanza that only a mediocre singer needs to use trees and flowers for song material; or to his statement at the end of stanza 2 that, even when surrounded by people, he is as defenseless against love's arrows as if he were alone in an orchard.)

Fol. 56   "Grant pieça que ne chantai/Or chanterai" (For a long time I have not sung; now I will sing [R 65]).

Miniature: man standing and reading from a long scroll.

Fol. 56v   "Haute chose a en amor" (There is a noble thing in love [R 1954]).

Miniature: seated man holding out an open scroll but not looking at it. (The first stanza of the song is a general statement about the value of love.)

Fol. 57v   "J'aloie l'autrier errant" (The other day I was out riding [R 342]).

Miniature: knight on horseback approaching a seated shepherdess. (The miniature illustrates the narrative recounted in the song.)

Fol. 69v   "L'autre nuit en mon dormant" (The other night in my sleep [R 339]).

Miniature: man asleep in bed. (The song describes the lover's dream of a debate with the God of Love.)

Fol. 80v   "Mi grant desir et tuit mi grief torment / Vienent de la ou sont tuit mi penser" (My great desire and all my grievous torments come from there where all my thoughts are [R 741]).

Miniature: On the left, man sitting with chin in hand, looking downcast, gazing at lady sitting on the right, who gestures as if in warning or refusal. (The two people are separated by the central vertical bar of the "M," stressing the inaccessibility of the lady.)

Fol. 85v   "Nuls hons ne puet ami reconforter" (No man can comfort a friend [R 884]).

Miniature: man sitting, downcast, with head in hand.

Fol. 89v   "Oëz por quoi plaing et sopir" (Listen to why I lament and sigh [R 1465]).

Miniature: seated man addressing three other people.

Fol. 94   "Pour froidure ne pour yver felon" (Not for cold nor for cruel winter [R 1865]).

Miniature: seated man writing on a scroll. (In the first stanza the singer declares his intention to make a song in spite of the winter weather.)

Fol. 106v   "Qui plus aimme plus endure" (He who loves most endures most [R 2095]).

Miniature: seated man with head in hand.

Fol. 127   "Seignor, sachiez qui or ne s'en ira" (Lords, know that whoever will not go forth now [R 6]).

Miniature: standing man addressing two seated men.

Fol. 132v   "Tout autresi con fraint noif et yvers" (Just as snow and winter are crushed [R 906]).

Miniature: seated man reading from a long scroll.

Fol. 140   "Une chançon encor vuil / Faire . . ." (I wish to make another song [R 1002]).

Miniature: seated man reading from a scroll.

While the miniatures and the songs as well are all somewhat formulaic, there is nonetheless a method to the illumination. The scenes of declamation before an audience accompany songs that begin with an address to an audience: "Listen . . ." and "Lords, know . . ." The image of the scroll accompanies references to the making of a song or, in some cases, didactic stanzas with little or no reference to personal love experience. A man alone in a sorrowful pose illustrates the declarations of love and grief. Where the opening lines refer to the lady, she appears also. And in certain cases, there is a visual representation of a motif taken from the song: the unicorn, the arrow of love, the nature imagery, the shepherdess, the man in bed. These are not, therefore, random images; the whole is a carefully planned ensemble.

The illustration of the narrative content of the songs, rather than of the persona associated with a group of songs or of the performative aspect of the collection as a whole, distinguishes MS *O* from all other surviving illuminated chansonniers. Just as the collection is a series of individual songs rather than a series of author corpora, so the illuminations highlight a series of moments and motifs rather than a series of personae. On the other hand, since the content of the songs is, after all, the same in MS *O* as in the other manuscripts, the iconography presents, for the most part, a similar set of images: love, contemplation, song making, performance. The two major departures from standard chansonnier iconography as we know it today are the illustrations for "A" and "L." Let us examine these more closely.

The evidence suggests that "Ausi cum l'unicorne sui" was deliberately chosen by the compiler to occupy first place. Just as chansonniers generally opened with the songs of Thibaut de Navarre, so here nearly every alphabetical division opens with Thibaut's songs. Each group of Thibaut's songs preserves the relative order among themselves that they have in MSS *K, M*$^T$*, N, T, V,* and *X* (where these disagree, the ordering of MS *O* corresponds to that of at least one other manuscript, usually MS *M*$^T$). It seems safe to assume, then, that the copyist was working from a manuscript where Thibaut's songs appeared in a standard order and that with each new section he simply went through the collection, extracting songs of the appropriate initial letter. "Ausi cum l'unicorne sui," however, is the fourth (and final) song beginning with "A" in all the major thirteenth-century collections of Thibaut's songs. It was evidently by design that the image of the unicorn was placed at the beginning of MS *O.* The striking allegorical image is an impressive way to initiate the collection. Its motifs reappear in subsequent miniatures: the arrow in the heart of the man pictured in "C" echoes the spear of "A"; the man on his knees before the lady of "D" echoes the supplicating pose of the unicorn. The lady's mirror, and the motif of entrapment by sight, express central preoccupations of courtly lyric.[40]

The bestiary image also recalls an important thirteenth-century text: Richard de Fournival's *Bestiaire d'amours.* The popularity of this text may be gauged from its survival in numerous manuscripts of the thirteenth and fourteenth centuries, profusely illustrated; from Richard's decision to set it in verse; from an independent thirteenth-century verse redaction that survives in a manuscript and an incunabulum; and from allusions to the *Bestiaire d'amours* in such texts as the *Dit de la panthère d'amours,* which is contemporary with MS *O.* The reputation enjoyed by Richard de Fournival about 1300 is also documented by his clerkly portrait in MS *A.* An image of the unicorn, being stabbed as it lays its head in the lap of a maiden, appears at the approximate midpoint of *Bestiaire d'amours* manuscripts, illustrating Richard's discussion of the role of sight in love. The unicorn poem may have been chosen for first place not only because the image emblematically expresses major lyric themes but also because it provides a reference to this important text. In the *Bestiaire d'amours* Richard announces his intention to create a form of lyric discourse that operates through images and written words rather than through song. The project of MS *O* is complementary: the lyric discourse of song is presented through writing and visual imagery. By opening his collection with the bestiary image, the compiler of MS *O* may be suggesting a relationship between Richard's textual innovations and his own work.

The motifs of mirror and vision, and the inherent ambiguity as to

---

40. For a discussion of this poem and the importance of the unicorn in the imagery of the trouvères, see Faure.

whether the lover is attracted by his own image or that of the lady, are of course central to the courtly lyric tradition; but they do also recall, in particular, the celebrated handling of these themes in another important text, the *Roman de la rose*. The placement of a lady holding a mirror at the entrance to the collection, and the image of a man shot by Love's arrow shortly thereafter, may be a submerged reference to the *Rose*.[41] In this respect, the image for "L," which happens to occupy the approximate midpoint of the collection, is all the more striking. The dreamer in bed is the opening image in nearly every extant *Rose* manuscript; it was an established iconographic convention by 1300.

It required no special manipulation by the compiler to locate this dream-vision poem in illustrative position, for "L'autre nuit en mon dormant" is already the first poem beginning with "L" in all the principal thirteenth-century Thibaut collections. But it is unlikely that he failed to notice its relevance to his collection: the *Rose*, like the *Bestiaire*, explores the relationship between lyric discourse and writing and between aural and visual aspects of both song and book. Guillaume's development of a first-person narrative account of lyric experience is equally relevant to the narrative reading of songs implied by the miniatures of MS *O*. The placement of these two key initials is all the more pleasing in that, as luck would have it, they follow a symmetrical disposition: the collection opens with the midpoint image of the *Bestiaire* and has at its own midpoint the opening image of the *Rose*.

Although MS *O* contains iconographic links with two texts in which writing is thematized and presents itself as a cohesive book, it, like the other anthologies we have examined, can properly be conceived as the written embodiment of oral performance. The presence of musical notation, of course, marks the pieces as destined for performance, as in other chansonniers. The motif of performance is also stressed in the miniatures. Not only do two miniatures represent performance before an audience, but in every image of "song making," the song is represented by a scroll. This iconographic motif also appears in MSS *M*, *P*, and *W* (and elsewhere in representations of lyric poets or performers; see the frontispiece), and it contrasts with the books pictured in MS *A*. In MS *W*, at least, the object in question may be a rotulus, such as would be used by a singer; it is inscribed with the opening line. But the figures in MSS *M* and *P* are not looking at their scrolls, which in two cases are rolled up. The figures in MS *O* who bear scrolls are not before an audience, and those who do address an audience do not have scrolls. It would seem that the scroll is an iconographic motif suggesting song as such—the lyric

---

41. "Ausi cum l'unicorne sui" also recalls the *Rose* through its use of personification allegory: the lover describes the prison of love, guarded by Fair Semblance, Beauty, and Dangier. See Hult, *Self-Fulfilling Prophecies*, pp. 213–20.

text, destined ultimately for oral performance. The use of rotuli is probably a factor here. In addition, though, the scroll as a visual image carried connotations of orality from its use as the medieval equivalent of the "voice balloon": a figure held an unfurled scroll bearing the words that he or she was meant to be saying.

The scroll also indicated orality in the representation of sacred authors; it was used for prophets, whose medium was the spoken word. Evangelists, on the other hand, were shown either writing or holding books.[42] The representation of vernacular authors has not yet received systematic study. In the manuscripts that I have looked at, though, the book is the sign of a clerkly, learned poet whose work is explicitly presented as a written text; familiar examples are Jean de Meun and Adenet le Roi. In MS 3142, discussed in the preceding chapter, the book appears in portraits of authors identified as clerks, readers, and/or translators: Adenet, Alard de Cambrai, Le Reclus de Moliens, and Marie de France. The scroll, on the other hand, is used to illustrate works that suggest oral declamation: the *Congé*, the *Proverbes au vilain*, and various dits, *salus*, and prayers. In MS *O*, then, the image of the man with his scroll is the perfect way of expressing the concept of "making" a song; although composition is distinguished from performance, the trouvère is nonetheless shown making an oral text.[43]

MS *O* is a remarkably cohesive anthology. The lack of author attributions or portraits suggests a continuity of voice throughout the collection. No scribal voice appears in rubrics to mediate between the reader and the lyric persona; the voice of the book is the extended "I" of the song collection. There is no sense of narrative progression. The illumination suggests a constellation of significant moments—dream, discourse with the lady—placed in a larger context of meditation and song making. If a codex like MS 1450 is to be described as a composite romance, then MS *O* must be described as a composite lyric structure. In a fascinating manner, scribe and lyric persona become one.

This blending of scribal and lyric voice is analogous to the scribal appropriation of narrative voice found in numerous narrative manuscripts. To find this blending in a lyric anthology, however, is, as has been seen, highly unusual. Such an experiment could take place only in a larger context of literary innovation. The compilation and embellishment of lyric, narrative, and didactic compendia are but one aspect of

---

42. Schapiro.

43. We need not assume that the average trouvère really did compose his songs by writing them on a scroll, any more than we can assume from portraits of learned authors that the latter composed their works by writing in bound volumes of blank parchment. These author portraits express rather the *idea* of textual composition, associated in the first instance with orally performed texts and in the second with books. But songs no doubt did circulate on scrolls at least to some extent; see Byrne.

this larger context; equally important is the poetic activity of thirteenth-century authors. I have suggested certain relationships between compilational and poetic practices. It is time now to turn to the study of individual texts in order to assess the nature of these poetic experiments and their reception by scribes, illuminators, and a later generation of poets.

# PART TWO

## LYRICISM AND THE BOOK
## IN THE THIRTEENTH CENTURY

Loué soit cellui qui trouva
Premier la maniere d'escrire;
En ce, grant confort ordonna
Pour amans qui sont en martire.

[Praised be he who first invented the writing system; he gave
great comfort thereby to lovers who are in torment.]

Charles d'Orléans, *Poésies*

## Chapter 3

# Singing, Reading, Writing: Guillaume de Lorris, Jean de Meun, and the Manuscript Tradition of *Le Roman de la rose*

The discussion of anthology manuscripts in the preceding two chapters has served to establish a context within which we may now examine individual texts. In general, lyric and narrative texts were transmitted in separate codices, and we have seen that differences of format in lyric and narrative anthologies reflect essential differences between lyric and narrative poetry. Throughout the thirteenth century, however, a series of poetic experiments aimed at exploring the interaction and conflation of lyric and narrative poetics, resulting in a form of poetic discourse that can be termed "lyrico-narrative." Any discussion of lyrico-narrative poetry must begin with the *Roman de la rose*, certainly one of the most influential literary texts of the French Middle Ages. The original *Rose*, by Guillaume de Lorris, is the first known example of extended first-person narrative in the French language; as such, its importance has long been recognized.[1] The exact nature and dynamics of this lyrico-narrative blend, however, has been extremely difficult to pin down. The lyrico-narrative text is a hybrid entity, a conflation of narrative discourse, normally written and read aloud, and lyric discourse, normally sung. In short, lyricism, the direct oral expression of sentiment, is redefined so as to allow for a written lyric discourse. Romance, in turn, is also modified. Rather than the military and social exploits of an exemplary figure, the *Rose* offers a private, imaginative, affective experience—a youthful dream of love. The terms established in the two previous chapters prove extremely useful in analyzing the dynamics of lyrico-narrative discourse. Before

---

1. The *Rose* is not entirely without precedent, of course; it can be linked to the narrator interventions in *Le Bel Inconnu* and *Partenopeu de Blois*, for example, or Calogrenant's story in *Yvain*. The *Rose* is, however, the first known instance in French literature in which first-person narrative is the substance of an entire romance.

proceeding with a discussion of the *Rose,* let us reconsider for a moment the evidence of texts and manuscripts.

## "Lyric" and "Narrative": An Overview

The conventional romance narrator of the twelfth and thirteenth centuries mediates between his audience and a real or posited preexistent text or texts, usually identified as books and often in Latin. This stance commonly finds explicit formulation in romance prologues and epilogues, and is reiterated throughout the text by the recurrence of such phrases as "Ce dit la lettre"; "Si comme la lettre nous devise" (So says the letter; Just as the letter tells us). The narrator does not claim to have witnessed the events he recounts, which are usually located in a distant past. The authenticity of the story derives from the authority of the source books and from the narrator's own authority as reader and interpreter of books. The persona of romance narrator is that of someone reading aloud to his audience, explaining, updating, and otherwise editing the material as he goes along. This model coincides with the likely means by which the romance reached its audience: through oral reading.[2] The performer, reading to us out of the book held in his hands, is the extratextual manifestation of the narrator, reading to us out of his ancient books.

As we saw in Chapter 1, the scribe's activity is governed by a similar model. He, too, mediates between a written text and its audience; and he too is a reader and editor and a counterpart to both narrator and performer. Like the romance narrator, the scribe's act of reading manifests itself through writing. But like the performer, whose oral discourse is imitated by both narrator and scribe, the scribe is required to respect the integrity of the text before him. If his revisions are too extensive, he will be not a scribe but a new narrator, an author in his own right. We see how closely related are the roles of narrator, scribe, and narrative performer. Romance is governed by a series of interactions with books. Between us and the romance hero there unfolds a succession of texts, readers, and writers, culminating finally in our own reading—either a private encounter with the scribal rendition or a public encounter with the performer's rendition but in any case firmly rooted in a written tradition.

Narrative also, of course, implies action, history. Love, the classic lyric theme, is certainly central to romance as well. But in the romance world, though love may generate private meditation and monologue and is not

2. It is assumed that, since literacy was far from universal even among the aristocracy, the consumption of literary texts would often have been through the medium of performance. See the Introduction.

invariably requited or fruitful, it normally generates action, very often leading to marriage and procreation. To the succession of writers such as that leading from Homer, Dictys, and Daries through Benoît de Sainte-Maure to the scribe Jehan Madot, there corresponds a succession of heroes such as that leading from Priam, Hector, and Aeneas through Brutus and the Roman Caesars to the houses of medieval Europe. Textual and historical continuity—the history of civilization itself—are striking themes of many romance anthologies.

The chanson courtoise contrasts notably with narrative poetry as it has been outlined above. The singer claims, at least, not to mediate between a past event or text and his audience. Rather, he directly manifests a love experience to his audience, since, according to the poetic fiction, he is the lover of whom he sings. Lyric performance has a dramatic quality: the experience of love takes shape before our eyes. The individual song participates in a general paradigm of love experience: the lover remains loyal while suffering certain pains and sorrows, his love pangs are intensified by the arrival of spring, he fears gossip and guards his lady's anonymity, and so on.[3] The authenticity of a given song derives from the singer's ability to embody these attributes, the hallmark of true love, in verse. Thus each song is a unique crystalization of this fundamental lyric paradigm. It does not have textual ancestors and, indeed, does not even have a fixed text or melody; phoenixlike, it is re-created anew with each performance.[4]

Lyricism also implies a narrative stasis or discontinuity. Love as expressed through song does not generate any action other than thinking, weeping, and singing. Within the confines of the song, love does not lead to adventure, marriage, or procreation. It produces only desire, which continually renews and prolongs itself through verbal and musical expression. These lyric qualities are reflected in the format of chansonniers. The series of trouvères are arranged not chronologically, but hierarchically. They are not presented as successive heirs to a literary tradition nor as contributors to or participants in an ongoing story. Rather, they are an aggregate, co-equal embodiments of a common ideal.[5]

With this brief overview of lyric and romance poetics in mind, we can return to the *Rose*. I will begin with Guillaume de Lorris's poem, which

3. The best comprehensive study of lyric motifs remains Dragonetti's *Technique poétique des trouvères*.

4. With the increased production of chansonniers during the thirteenth century, the original fluidity of the song was largely stabilized, as I noted in the preceding chapter. Guillaume de Lorris's poem, however, predates any surviving chansonnier. For the purposes of reading Guillaume's *Rose*, we must think of lyric poetry as an oral, musical medium.

5. On the distinction between lyric and narrative, as well as the middle ground between them, see Zumthor, *Essai de poétique médiévale*, pp. 286–338.

must be considered on its own terms before we can assess the continuation by Jean de Meun and the composite text. How is the original *Rose* constructed? How does Guillaume handle the tension between a discourse of writing and lineage and one of song and desire, between narrative representation and lyric presentation?

## Lyrical Writing in Guillaume de Lorris: The Poetics of Narcissus

A fruitful starting point is with the motif of dream, chosen by Guillaume as the format for his romance.[6] The dream, in fact, is a lyrico-narrative construct. Guillaume's narrator does mediate between his audience and a text, but that text is not found in a book; it is experienced in a vision. Thus, he does also reveal to us his personal experience, but that experience is located in the past. The dream embodies imagination itself, source of both lyric and narrative poetry.[7] Insofar as it is a text read by the dreamer and later recast as a romance, it generates narrative discourse and makes of the "I" a dual entity: romance narrator and romance protagonist. Insofar as it is an experience of erotic desire, realized as love for the lady symbolized by the rose and source of inspiration for love poetry dedicated to this lady, it generates lyric discourse and gives the "I" the identity of lyric persona: lover and, if not exactly singer, poet.[8]

Thus the format of the dream miraculously serves to create a new kind of literary discourse, one both lyric and narrative. The "I" is at once romance narrator and protagonist (normally distinct personages) and lyric poet and protagonist (normally the same personage). Lyricism allows the identification of narrator and protagonist, thereby granting the authenticity and immediacy of performance to this romance. Narrative in turn allows the separation of singer and lover, placing the narrator at a critical distance that enables him to locate his own affective experience in a larger context of conflict and resolution: that is, in a context allowing for narrative action.[9]

But even a cursory look at Guillaume's *Rose* shows that the balance of lyric and narrative is not uniform throughout the poem. This is clear

6. On the dream motif, see Pickens.

7. Cf. Kelly, "Guillaume de Lorris' romance is a product of imagination," in *Medieval Imagination*, p. 57.

8. Guillaume never presents himself as a singer; his references to the process of poetic production make it clear that he is writing. See, for example, "Ja ne m'est parece d'escrivre" (I am never weary of writing [Lecoy ed., V. 3488]).

9. See Uitti, "From *Clerc* to *Poète*," p. 212, for a discussion of Guillaume's poetic "I" as a conflation of "clerkly romance narrator and lyric *trouvère*."

from the marked contrast between the opening lines, a typical romance prologue featuring a brief discussion of Macrobius and dream theory, and the closing lines, essentially a lyric *complainte*. Moreover, the poem's ending, though true to the underlying lyric model, does not offer the sort of resolution we might expect from a romance. In fact, I would suggest that Guillaume's lyrico-narrative romance can best be understood as a transformation between the poles of narrative and lyric; and the unifying model underlying this transformation is provided by Narcissus, a figure important in both lyric and narrative traditions.[10] Let us begin at the beginning.

"Songes est senefiance" (Dream is meaning), states Guillame in his prologue. A dream is a signifying code, a sign system; as I stated above, a dream is a text. And in the first half of the poem, largely descriptive with very little dialogue or narrative action, the narrator is essentially a reader of the dream text that unfolds before him. It must be remembered that in the thirteenth century a vernacular poetic text, even the clerkly romance, was understood also as performance, whether that performance was effected orally or in writing. To describe the dream as text, then, in no way contradicts its quality as a lived experience and a visual and aural spectacle. Indeed, the two sets of allegorical personages presented in the first half of the poem serve jointly to express the theatrical quality of the illuminated text, and the narrator's interaction with the images dramatizes the act of reading.

The narrator's first act of reading is focused on the wall surrounding the garden, quite literally a text of words and images, since the allegorical representations are equipped with labels.[11] This visual text is reproduced in nearly all manuscripts of the *Rose* by a series of miniatures representing each personified vice in turn and often accompanied by explanatory rubrics.[12] Reading this text of labeled images enables the reader to share in—indeed, to reenact—the narrator's original experience. The poem, spaced between and alongside these rubricated miniatures, is the narrator's commentary on the images; it is as though he is speaking to us from inside the book about the pictures that we, like him, see on its pages. Because the narrator is identified with the protagonist, and the miniatures at this point represent not what the protagonist does but what he sees, the dream experience acquires an immediacy close to that of lyric performance. On the one hand, we see the images through

10. The story of Narcissus in the *Rose* has attracted enormous scholarly attention. For a summary of the critical debate, see Hillman.

11. See, for example, "Son nom desus sa teste lui, / apelee estoit Felonie" (I read her name above her head, she was called Felony [vv. 153–54]). Guillaume also describes the wall as "portret dehors et entaillé / a maintes riches escritures" (embellished without and engraved with many rich writings [vv. 132–33]).

12. On the illustrations to the *Rose*, see Kuhn.

the eyes of a reader and narrator; on the other hand, we see them with our own eyes. As Richard de Fournival stated in the *Bestiaire d'amours*, textual illustrations cause distant or fictional events to materialize before the reader. The narrative world coincides with our world through the medium of the book.

What we find in the narrative world, then, is a text. Our experience as readers parallels that of the dreamer. As we confront the text, either as readers of the book or as audience at an oral reading where pictures could be shown, the images emerge as a visual presence, establishing a bond between us and the dream world. Similarly, as the narrator confronts the images, they seem on the point of coming to life, establishing a bond between him and the allegorical world of the garden. Old Age is described as having lost her beauty and her wisdom, implying that she is a character with a past and not a static image. Sorrow tears her hair; Hypocrisy prays; Avarice inspects her wealth. Each appears to have an ongoing existence. The tendency of these allegorical images to emerge as living characters culminates in the appearance of Oiseuse (Idleness or, more accurately, Idle Woman), an allegorical personification who is able to speak, move, and interact with the observer. As the dreamer penetrates the wall—a textual surface—he enters the world of allegorical representation: the garden is a living text, where everything is a sign.

The narrator's encounter inside the garden with the second series of images is an encounter with pure lyricism; the dream text has become a performance. And yet, whereas his reading of the wall images seemed to bring them to life as dramatizations of anticourtly vices, here his reading of the carol figures serves to transform this scene of music and dance into a series of virtually silent, static images. We are not given the words of their song or its musical accompaniment. Interestingly, although many *Rose* manuscripts feature a general illustration of the carol, the individual carol figures are not often represented in miniatures; as a result, they are less vivid presences for the reader. The dreamer has receded into the textual world, and we have not been able to follow him. The narrator plays a correspondingly more important role, even as the text asserts its lyric thematics; and we begin to sense a growing distinction between the narrator, whose voice remains accessible to us, and the protagonist, whose experience is becoming less immediately accessible. The metamorphosis of the central "I" has begun.

The protagonist next enters the scene of an important narrative event, the death of Narcissus. As he looks into the fountain and so falls in love, he reenacts the behavior of Narcissus and becomes even more clearly defined as a narrative protagonist, heir to previous narrative events. He is now fully a member of the world within the garden, protagonist and not merely reader of the dream. His exchange with the God of Love is the first extended dialogue in the poem: he is now located firmly within the narrative and no longer at its margins. He has become l'Amant (the Lover), a personification of the courtly lover.

During the second half of the poem, the number of characters with whom l'Amant interacts multiplies; he is now but one voice, one perspective, among many. No longer does he exhibit the globality of perspective enjoyed by the narrator of the first half, who explored every inch of the garden and saw its every detail revealed in the crystals. L'Amant becomes increasingly self-absorbed, obsessed with his desire for the elusive rose. No longer are we treated to the sumptuous descriptions of the first half; the new characters are described briefly or not at all, as though l'Amant is scarcely aware of anything peripheral to his immediate desire. As the limited perspective and voice of the protagonist grows in importance, the presence of the omniscient narrator-reader diminishes. By the end, the narrator has disappeared entirely, and the poem ends with l'Amant's extended complainte. Narrative discourse has given way to lyric discourse.

It is interesting to compare the final complainte with the description of the wall images, the first extended descriptive passage. In both cases the reader has the impression of confronting the dream text directly, without the mediation of a narrator. In the first case, though, it is because we can identify with the poetic "I" as readers of a common text. In the second, the poetic "I" *is* the dream text, as the singer is inseparable from his song. Very few manuscripts illustrate l'Amant's final complainte. It is as though he has become a disembodied voice or, perhaps, a voice whose only body is its own written text. From reader-narrator, the poetic persona has shifted to lyric performer. In between, narrative action and dialogue are generated by his interaction with the text that he reads, enters, and finally usurps.

What has this to do with the story of Narcissus? After his experience at the pool as reader and interlocutor of his own image, Ovid's Narcissus becomes a flower. This flower does not merely represent Narcissus but rather is Narcissus and shares his name. The story of Narcissus is also the story of the passage from representation—visual representation in the pool, aural representation in the words of Echo—to emblematic presentation, as Narcissus literally becomes an image of himself. As I have argued elsewhere, Guillaume de Lorris replaces the flower with the marble engraving; in his version, Narcissus has evidently become a written record of himself.[13] Likewise, Guillaume's persona passes from reader and interlocutor of the dream text to subject of that text; he too disappears, leaving only a written record of his desire.

Narcissus is also a lyric motif and in this sense represents a desire that

13. Huot, "From *Roman de la Rose* to *Roman de la Poire.*" See also Hult, "Allegorical Fountain," p. 144, n. 33.

is unfulfillable because it can never reach beyond itself, just as the lyric voice can never reach beyond itself to make contact with the object of its desire. Within the strict confines of the lyric monologue, dialogue is by definition impossible. Response and resolution are possible only if the lyric persona is located in a larger narrative or dramatic context. The establishment of this context, and the orchestration of its members, depends on an outside narrator who is not identified (at least not exclusively so) with any one of the narrative actors. This kind of critical distance between narrator and narrative subject is lacking in the chanson courtoise, as in Narcissus's exclamations and in the closing section of Guillaume's *Rose*. Narrative resolution of l'Amant's plight will be possible only if there is once again a narrator.

Guillaume de Lorris could, of course, have resurrected his narrator and brought the poem to a narrative conclusion had he wished to do so.[14] But as far as we can tell, he chose not to, remaining true to the dictates of lyric discourse and to the underlying construct of Narcissus. Guillaume's *Rose* poses lyrico-narrative discourse as a question, indeed a challenge, to subsequent poets. In later chapters, I will examine a number of middle and late thirteenth-century responses to his work. Here, I wish to consider what is certainly the most famous such response, that of Jean de Meun. Though sensitive to the lyric and dramatic qualities of Guillaume's poem, Jean chose to continue it primarily as a narrative. In examining his continuation of the *Rose*, we will focus on the narrative thematics identified above—the association of narrative activity, reading and writing, and procreation—and on his reconstitution of a textual narrator distinct from the protagonist.

## L'Aucteur and l'Amant: Lyrico-narrative Discourse in *Le Roman de la Rose*

The importance of the midpoint of the conjoined *Rose* has often been noted.[15] In Chapter 2, I discussed this passage as a poetic appropriation of scribal compilational technique; it establishes a continuity between two poems. The passage is also of great importance in its constitution of Jean de Meun as narrator; to adapt our previous term, I would say that Jean here establishes himself as lyrico-narrator. In accordance with the narrative model described above, Jean presents himself as reader-writer

14. On the incompleteness of Guillaume's *Rose*, see Kelly, "'Li chastiaus . . . Qu'Amors prist puis par ses esforz.'" In my opinion, the poem can be read as complete with a built-in fiction of incompleteness, and it is not necessary to assume that Guillaume found himself forced to abandon his conclusion. The latter view is supported by Hult, *Self-Fulfilling Prophecies*.

15. See Uitti, "From *Clerc* to *Poète*."

vis-à-vis Guillaume's text; and he locates himself, along with Guillaume, as heir to a succession of poets. The poets are not narrative or historical authors; Gallus, Catullus, and Ovid are lyric poets.[16] Moreover, Jean's own poetic venture is described as an act of love: "Cist avra le romanz si chier" (He will hold the romance so dear [Lecoy ed., v. 10554]). Inspired by Love, he is to sing of love—"fleütera noz paroles" (he will pipe our words [v. 10611])—to all who will listen. Thus Jean identifies his poetry as partaking of both lyric and narrative modes: he is part of a written tradition of lyric poets; his act of reading is an act of love; his act of writing is a song.

If Guillaume and Jean are both lyrico-narrative poets, Jean's role as narrator is nonetheless quite different from that of Guillaume. Guillaume loves the rose; Jean loves the *Romance of the Rose*. Guillaume is a participant in the dream world; Jean is an outside observer, who was not even born yet when the dream took place. Jean's eroticized activity as reader-writer of the *Rose* parallels Guillaume's erotic quest as lover of the rose, but the two remain distinct. Because of this, it is possible for Jean to assume the role of omniscient narrator, which is needed to effect a reconciliation of opposing viewpoints and a narrative resolution.[17]

This reading of the *Rose* is supported by a program of rubrication that appears, with minor variations, in a large number of manuscripts.[18] In these manuscripts the rubrication not only marks narrative divisions but also identifies the speaker of each dialogue or monologue passage. What is most interesting is that the first-person voice is also identified and is designated as either *l'aucteur* (the author) or *l'amant* (the lover), according to the role he is playing. This is illustrated here with the rubrics from the thirteenth-century MS Bibl. Nat. fr. 378, beginning with the rubrication for the text of Guillaume de Lorris. The complete text of these rubrics is given in Appendix A.

Throughout the first half of the poem, Guillaume's persona is identified as l'aucteur; as we have seen, his role at this point is primarily that of

---

16. Ovid is also, of course, the author of an epic-length narrative, the *Metamorphoses*, and in this capacity was an important model for Jean de Meun. In this particular passage, however, Ovid's lyric poetry is more at issue. The catalog of poets is an allusion to two passages, one in the *Tristia* (4.10, vv. 51–55) and one in the *Amores* (3.ix), both lyric texts.
17. On Jean de Meun as omniscient narrator, see Nichols.
18. My study of *Rose* manuscripts is limited to those copied before 1400 (of which approximately 150 are known today). I have found "Aucteur-Amant" rubrication in 53 of the 72 manuscripts that I have examined to date. For descriptions of the manuscripts discussed here, see Ernest Langlois. A question naturally arises as to the origin of the rubrics. It is conceivable that they originate with Guillaume de Lorris or, more likely, Jean de Meun. It seems most likely, however, that they were designed by scribes who assumed the responsibility for "packaging" the poem. They must stem from a very early period of *Rose* reception, for they exist in manuscripts of different families and appear as early as the thirteenth century. Whether or not they reflect the intentions of either of the poets, these rubrics exercised an influence on subsequent poets who read the *Rose* in rubricated form and as such deserve our attention.

reader and narrator. The first appearance of l'amant is with the God of Love's attack, directly following the fountain of Narcissus. During the interchange between Love and the protagonist, which, I repeat, is the first extended dialogue of the poem, l'amant gradually assumes the status of a character—l'Amant—and is distinguished from l'Aucteur. In the course of the conversation after his heart has been locked up by love, l'Amant acquires a voice of his own and, after some vacillation, comes to overshadow l'Aucteur.

The role of l'Aucteur in the second half of the poem is interesting. With one exception (v. 2891), his role is to narrate events that happen outside the view of l'Amant. L'Amant himself is able to narrate such events as the kiss or the appearance of Reason or Dangier (a term combining domination, power, and resistance). But he is presumably not a witness to the conversations of Jealousy, Fear, and Shame, for example, or the intercession of Franchise (a term implying nobility of character, generosity, and frankness) and Pity with Dangier. Unlike the first half of the poem, the second half does include narrative action that lies outside the immediate experience of the central protagonist. The split of the first-person voice into l'Amant and l'Aucteur represents a polarization: from the single observer-narrator, reader of the dream text as it passes before his eyes, are born the engaged participant and the detached omniscient narrator.

The role of this narrator, however, is strictly limited to very short passages; following the commandments of Love, only twenty-three and a half lines are attributed to l'Aucteur. His role approaches that of the rubricator: he identifies characters and explains who is speaking and to whom their words are addressed. In some cases his lines are virtually duplicated by the rubric that follows them. For example, this passage is attributed to l'Aucteur: "Lors ne puet plus Dangier durer, / il le covient amesurer" (Then Dangier could bear it no longer, he had to bring him back into line [vv. 3301–2]). There follows directly Dangier's speech, introduced by the rubric *Dangiers*. An eleven-line passage attributed to l'Aucteur, describing the arrival of Fear and the departure of Jealousy, ends: "Peor, qui tint la teste encline, / parole a Honte sa cosine" (Fear, who held her head down, speaks to her cousin Shame [vv. 3629–30]). The discourse of Fear that follows is introduced by the rubric *Ci parle Paours a Honte* (Here Fear speaks to Shame). Slightly later, in the exchange between Shame, Fear, and Dangier, l'Aucteur intervenes with a single line, "Lors aprés a parlé Poors" (After that, Fear spoke [v. 3694]). This line is followed by the rubric *Ci parle Paours a Dangier* (Here Fear speaks to Dangier). In other words, the information supplied by l'Aucteur in the second half of the poem does not go very far beyond that which could be, and often is, supplied by rubrication. Spoken discourse, not descriptive narrative, dominates the second half of the poem. From reader and commentator on a visual text, l'Aucteur has passed to the role of scribe and rubricator of a spoken text.

The role of l'Amant is also different from that of the protagonist of the first half. He does continue to be visually absorbed with the rose, and he interacts with various characters. As I have stated, however, he no longer roams the garden; he is now focused single-mindedly on the object of his desire. Again, the qualities of the persona of the first half—participation in the world of the garden and globality of perspective—have split and polarized. L'Aucteur now records events independent of the protagonist's experience but does not himself act within the drama; l'Amant is central to the ongoing drama but seems increasingly unaware of anything outside his immediate desire. By the end of the poem, as we have seen, l'Amant has come to dominate the scene entirely; his final monologue receives no reply, and there is no indication that he is even heard by any member of the garden.

The distinction between l'Aucteur and l'Amant, then, can be thus described: l'Aucteur is the omniscient narrator; l'Amant, the lyric persona. L'Aucteur describes the actions and words of others; l'Amant speaks for himself. L'Aucteur has no identity within the dream, no role within the garden, other than that of narrator; l'Amant is the main protagonist of the drama. The role of l'Amant becomes increasingly central; that of l'Aucteur increasingly marginal. Both l'Aucteur and l'Amant, however, are increasingly isolated voices.

The explicit distinction of l'Aucteur and l'Amant serves an important function in unifying the composite text. If narrator and protagonist are identified as two separate figures, the story of the protagonist can continue unbroken through a change of narrator; the reading imposed by the rubricator on Guillaume's poem sets it up for Jean's continuation. Moreover, the program of rubrication stresses a symmetry built into the lyrico-narrative dynamics of the conjoined *Rose*. It is at the midpoint of Guillaume's text that the God of Love intervenes and definitively transforms the protagonist into a lyric persona. Love assumes the role of narrator, recounting l'Amant's story in the future tense and even providing him with a monologue of love complaint whose repetitious rhymes—eight lines in *-vois, -voi, -voier,* and so on—allude to the intricate rhyme-play of courtly lyric (vv. 2289–96). As we have seen, the rubrics of MS 378 stress the transformation of l'Aucteur into l'Amant as the result of Love's words and actions. It is therefore all the more appropriate that the new narrator is established with Love's second intervention, at the midpoint of the conjoined *Rose*. Jean makes explicit what was already implicit in Guillaume: the God of Love is most efficacious, not as a patron of lovers but as a patron of love poets. His inspirational force sustains and brings to fruition the poetic quest, itself erotic; but he is remarkably helpless when it comes to furthering the amorous quest.

Indeed, Love himself even suggests that the former is the more compelling aspect of the overall enterprise. After exhorting his forces to aid the poor lover in his quest, he comments that if he was not pleading on behalf of the lover, he would do so "au mains por Jehan alegier, / qu'il escrive plus de legier" (at least to help Jean, in order that he write more easily [vv. 10633–34]). Once again, Love briefly assumes the role of prophetic narrator; what he recounts is the birth and career of a love poet. The symmetry of these two midpoint passages is stressed by the rubrication: just as it was during Love's first intervention that the designation *l'Amant* first appeared, so it is just after his second intervention that the designation *l'Aucteur* appears for the first time since Guillaume's text. L'Aucteur, the detached narrator, reenters the text during the exchange between Love and False Semblance. In MS 378, his first lines are the following:

> Faus Samblant, qui plus ni atant,
> Commence son sermon atant
> et dist a touz en audience . . .

[False Semblance, who waits no further, begins his sermon at once, and says to everyone in the audience . . .] [Fol. 44v; orth. of MS 378; Lecoy ed., vv. 10973–75]

In many manuscripts, l'Aucteur first appears slightly earlier, in what would seem a gratuitous specification: he is given the sentence "Et cil acort" (And he approaches [v. 10900]), appearing in the middle of a speech by the God of Love.[19] That the rubric *l'Aucteur* would be used for a "speech" of a mere half line suggests that it was placed there as an explicit marker of narrator presence following Love's discourse. There is once more an omniscient narrator, and this time he is not a disembodied voice or a reflection of the protagonist; he has a name and is firmly rooted outside the text. It is possible now to manipulate the narrative so as to effect a resolution of multiple perspectives. In demonstration of this, Jean provides the first instance, since the disappearance of Guillaume's Aucteur, of an extended dialogue in which l'Amant is not one of the interlocutors; he later includes episodes, such as the voyage to Cytherea, at which l'Amant is not even present. The distinction between l'Amant and l'Aucteur is carefully preserved in rubrics throughout the rest of the poem.

As I have stated, the distinction between l'Aucteur and l'Amant is not identical in all manuscripts that employ such rubrication. For example,

---

19. This particular rubrication appears as early as the thirteenth century; for example, it is found in MS Bibl. Nat. fr. 1559 (fol. 89v).

about half of the manuscripts that I have studied simply use *l'Amant* thoughout Guillaume's text, so that *l'Aucteur* does not appear until after Love's identification of Jean de Meun as continuator. This no doubt reflects the different roles played in the poem by Guillaume the lover the Jean the poet. Of the manuscripts that do use both designations within Guillaume's poem, only a few make the sustained distinction found in MS 378; others use *l'Amant* throughout except for one or two instances of *l'Aucteur*, which may occur either before or after Love's intervention.[20] These manuscripts may reflect a corruption of an original full program that was not understood by copyists. In any case, Jean's identity as l'Aucteur seems to have been more readily accepted. Rubrication of his poem varies in intensity, with some manuscripts exhibiting heavy rubrication and others little or none. But with very few exceptions, one of which will be discussed below, manuscripts agree, insofar as they are rubricated, on which passages are attributed to l'Amant and which to l'Aucteur. This consistency shows that the distinction was clearly perceived by medieval readers of the *Rose* and was felt to be a crucial aspect of the poem.

The vast majority of manuscripts exhibiting these rubrics also signal the break between the two poems, announcing Jean as author of the continuation (see the explanatory rubric of MS 378, fol. 25, cited below). These manuscripts often feature a miniature between the two poems, representing Jean as writer. Many also have rubrication, and sometimes a miniature as well, to mark the reference to Jean de Meun at the conjoined midpoint; the most common such rubric identifies *La priere au dieu d'Amors pour Maistre Jehan de Meun* (The God of Love's prayer for Master Jean de Meun [v. 10587]). On the other hand, of those manuscripts that fail to signal Jean at either the break or the midpoint, very few have "Aucteur-Amant" rubrication.[21] The mapping of the dynamics of lyrico-narrative discourse, then, is associated with an interest in the identity of the authors and in the relationship between the two. As represented by miniatures, this relationship is a function of writing.

20. There really is no set pattern to the rubrication of Guillaume's *Rose;* although some manuscripts follow the system found in MS 378, many do not. Given the number of variants, I do not feel that it will be possible to generalize until I have been able to examine a larger number of manuscripts. This ambivalence, so unlike the consistent rubrication of Jean's *Rose,* reflects the ambiguous nature of Guillaume's narrator, who somehow resists classification as either Amant or Aucteur.

21. Of the seventy-two manuscripts that I have studied, forty-two rubricate the reference to Jean at the midpoint; thirty-five of these also name him at the beginning of his poem, and thirty-eight have "Aucteur-Amant" rubrics. An additional fourteen fail to mark Jean at the midpoint but still rubricate his entrance after Guillaume's poem; twelve of these have "Aucteur-Amant" rubrics. I have found sixteen manuscripts that fail to name Jean de Meun in rubrics at any point, only three of which have "Aucteur-Amant" rubrics.

## Lyrical Writing in Jean de Meun: The Poetics of Pygmalion

Let us return to Jean's text and to his exploitation of the analogy linking sexual procreation, writing, and narrative activity. The metaphor of sexual coupling as writing, familiar from the Neoplatonic tradition, is explicitly developed during the Nature-Genius sequence. Genius as writer and, specifically, rewriter of Guillaume de Lorris provides a figure for Jean de Meun as writer.[22] Through writing, Genius effects a transposition of Guillaume's poetic construct into a new poetic register. This is a point to which I will return shortly. First, though, I wish to examine more closely his metaphoric designation of sexual intercourse as writing.

During his discussion of sexual procreation, Genius turns to the topic of homosexuality.

> Mes cil qui des greffes n'escrivent,
> par cui li mortel tourjorz vivent,
>
> . . . . .
>
> quant Orpheüs veulent ansivre,
> qui ne sot arer ne escrivre.

[But those who don't write with the styluses by which mortals always live . . . when they wish to follow Orpheus, who did not know how to plow or write.]
[Vv. 19599–600, 19621–22]

Orpheus is traditionally considered to be the initiator of homosexuality. But I would suggest that these lines may be taken another way as well. Orpheus indeed was not a writer but a singer, and his career typifies the prolongation and frustration of desire typical of courtly lyric. He did achieve marriage with Eurydice, but she died on their wedding day. He sought her in Hell and won her back with song, only to see her evaporate before his eyes. Like song itself, Eurydice was for Orpheus fleeting and ephemeral. Orpheus's identity as homosexual is a metaphor for the sterility of his love for Eurydice, the sterility of a love that finds expression only in song. It has been suggested that, by his retelling of Orpheus's tales of Pygmalion and Adonis, and by his identity as an inspired love poet, Jean offers himself as a new, redeemed, vernacular Orpheus.[23] I would take this formulation one step further: Jean is indeed a new Orpheus, and one of the things that is new about him is that his song is a written text.

Genius's condemnation of Orpheus parallels his condemnation of

22. See Brownlee, "Jean de Meun and the Limits of Romance"; and Smith.
23. See Brownlee, "Orpheus's Song Re-sung."

Guillaume's garden. Orphic sexuality and Orphic song, courtly love and courtly lyricism—on all sides we find the frustration of desire, sterility, and a privileging of ephemeral performance over concrete written text. The association of Orphic homosexuals with the inhabitants of the garden is heightened by Genius's statement that Nature did not supply people with "stylus" and "tablets" so that they could be "oiseuses" (idle [v. 19602]). Genius reads a new meaning into Oiseuse's role as gate-keeper of the garden: like homosexuality, courtly love is a form of idle-ness because it fails to accomplish procreation, just as song fails to produce an artifact. Writing with phallus or pen leads to the consummation of desire, to procreation and production, to signification.

Genius's recasting of the garden complements the poem's erotic finale; we might say that these passages are two sides of the same poetic coin. L'Amant impregnates the rose; Genius, wielder of the pen, transposes the garden into compelling imagery that is, so to speak, pregnant with meaning. And Jean de Meun, lover-writer of the *Rose*, might well say, to adapt only slightly his description of the rose's pregnancy, that as the result of his intervention, "tout le *roman* tandre / an fis ellargir et estandre" (I made the whole tender *romance* enlarge and swell [vv. 21699–700; I have substituted *roman* for *boutonet* (bud)]. Narrative, allegorical, and sexual consummation alike are effected by means of writing, either literal or figurative.[24]

Framed by Genius and the final acquisition of the rose is the story of Pygmalion. This interlude is nearly always announced by a rubric and is often articulated by means of several rubrics.[25] It is fairly often accompanied by a miniature that shows Pygmalion carving his statue and sometimes by additional miniatures; this even in manuscripts in which Jean's portion of the poem is but sparsely illustrated. It is thus marked out in most manuscripts as a significant episode, indeed an entire narrative in its own right; it is rubricated and illuminated more frequently, and more fully, than most other exempla cited in the course of the poem. It is no accident that the story of Pygmalion should be highlighted in this manner; as has been noted by others, Pygmalion plays a crucial role in Jean's revision of Guillaume's poetics and in his establishment of

24. Cf. Brownlee, ". . . we seem to have a fusion of the two je's: lover-protagonist and poet-narrator win, make love to, and pluck the rose together, *by means of poetry*," in *Poetic Identity*, p. 13 (emphasis his). The image of the enlarged rose also calls to mind Marie de France's statement in the prologue of the *Lais*, during the discussion of literary tradition and the interpretation of great literary works by succeeding generations, that a "great good" (including a literary work) flowers when it is heard and that "quant loëz est de plusurs, / Dunc ad espandues ses flurs" (when it is praised by many, then it has spread its blossoms [Rychner ed., vv. 7–8]).

25. Many manuscripts, for example, signal *La priere Pygmalion* and *Comment l'ymage reçut vie* (Pygmalion's prayer; How the image received life). Quite a few have rubrics to indicate the dialogue between Pygmalion and his statue.

his own lyrico-narrative poetics of writing. Pygmalion is Jean's answer to Narcissus.[26]

In Guillaume's poem, as we have seen, it is suggested that Narcissus metamorphoses into a written text. The production of this text means that Narcissus's love was not totally fruitless; he left at least this trace of himself. Similarly, Guillaume's protagonist has at least produced a poem. Because the distance between narrator and text collapses, though, narrative progression becomes impossible; his text, like that of Narcissus, is ultimately one of despair. Pygmalion, on the other hand, succeeds in producing an artifact, an external embodiment of his desire. Pygmalion, wielder of hammer and chisel, participates in the iconographic register of Genius, Nature, and Jean de Meun: he "writes" Galatea. But as a text, Galatea cannot be considered as narrative: she represents nothing in the empirical world and is not part of any historical or genealogical progression. It is Pygmalion's own desire that is recorded in the ivory, and in this sense his artistic act has more in common with lyric performance. Pygmalion is Jean's corrected image of the lyric poet as writer. The sexual implications of Pygmalion's creative act are graphically expressed in miniatures in many manuscripts that show Pygmalion aiming his chisel at a spot a little below Galatea's waist. The chisel is both pen and phallus: Pygmalion at once records his desire and fulfills it.

As artist-poet figure, Pygmalion provides an image for the conjoined poet-narrator of the composite *Rose:* he partakes of both Guillaume and Jean. Like Guillaume, he is both artistic creator and lover; he falls in love with his own conceptualization of feminine beauty, just as l'Amant falls in love with a reified *senhal.* Like Jean, he is external to the text of his desire; with the aid of Venus he is able to commune with and impregnate Galatea, just as Jean, inspired by Love, communes with his poem and brings it to fruition. The tale of Pygmalion thus provides a mythic underpinning for the poem as a whole, just as that of Narcissus did for Guillaume's poem.

Pygmalion's role as counterpart to the protagonist of the *Rose* is stressed by the extended musical performances he puts on during his initial wooing of his statue, which recall Guillaume's carol scene and the lyric monologue with which his poem closes. Like the trouvère, and like Orpheus, Pygmalion finds that musical performance produces no lasting effects. His relationship to l'Amant is further clarified through his comparison of himself to Narcissus and his prolonged anxiety that the

26. On Narcissus and Pygmalion, see the excellent discussion by Poirion, "Narcisse et Pygmalion." Not all critics, however, see Pygmalion as a positive example. Robertson reads Pygmalion as a figure of idolatry, whose delusion is analogous to the self-deceptions perpetrated by the Lover of the *Rose;* see his *Preface to Chaucer,* pp. 99–103. His reading is supported by Tuve, pp. 262–63; and by Fleming, pp. 228–37.

living Galatea may be but a dream.[27] Pygmalion's miracle is a coming together of dream and reality, art and life. This association of Pygmalion with the dream motif is most clearly expressed in MS Bibl. Nat. fr. 1565 (copied in 1352), where the story of Pygmalion is announced by the rubric, *Ci commence l'ystoire de Pygmalion et de son songe* (Here begins the story of Pygmalion and of his dream [fol. 136]). The accompanying miniature represents Pygmalion asleep in bed and is very much the same as the opening miniature of the poem, which, as in the vast majority of *Rose* manuscripts, represents Guillaume's dreamer asleep in bed. Pygmalion here is the explicit reworking, and *dépassement*, of the poet-dreamer of the *Rose*.

## The *Rose* as Book and the Question of Vernacular Poetic Authority

The *Rose* presents itself, and was received, not only as a romance but— specifically, emphatically—as a book. At the hands of Jean de Meun it becomes not only lyrico-narrative but lyrico-encyclopedic. In the *Miroër aus amoureus*, as he retitles it, the lyric theme of erotic desire is the vehicle for a vast array of material.[28] The programs of rubrication discussed above link the *Rose* to a Latin tradition of learned texts. For one thing, the rubrication stresses the dialogue format of the poem, thereby placing it in a rich tradition represented by such figures as Boethius, Augustine, and Plato. Beyond that, the explicit designation of authority, be it that of Reason, of Love, of Nature, or of the amorous protagonist, and the careful distinction between the narrator and his many protagonists call to mind a technique employed by medieval encyclopedists. Vincent of Beauvais, perhaps the most famous compiler of the thirteenth century, distinguished between the *auctores* that he cited, and himself as *actor*, or reciter of their words. By his own statement in the prologue to the *Speculum Maius*, he also took pride in his orderly arrangement of material and wanted to make the book visually accessible. Accordingly, manuscripts of the *Speculum Maius* bear rubrics identifying divisions of the text and also naming the *auctor* to whom each section is due. Whenever Vincent speaks for himself, the rubric *actor* appears.[29]

---

27. On the relationship between Pygmalion and the poet-dreamer of the *Rose,* and the importance of the word *songe* in the Pygmalion passage, see Brownlee, "Orpheus's Song," p. 206.

28. On the *Rose* as a poetic *summa*, see Uitti, "From *Clerc* to *Poète*," especially pp. 210 and 213–14.

29. See the extremely useful study by Minnis. On the various Latin terms used to designate authorship, see Chenu.

Similar procedures were often adopted by other compilers.[30] For a vernacular example we can examine briefly Alard de Cambrai's compilation known as the *Dits des sages* or the *Livre de philosophie et de moralité*.[31] This text is a thirteenth-century compilation of material on various topics drawn from the writings of the *auctores* and is arranged in some manuscripts according to author and in others according to theme. Each discussion is headed by a rubric that identifies both the author in question and the topic on which he is being cited; in some cases, the wording of these rubrics gives the book the format of a series of speeches. In MS Arras, Bibl. Mun. 657 (copied in 1278), a typical rendition of Alard's compilation, the series of authors begins with the rubric, "De ches .xx. maistres parole Tulles tout avant" (Of these twenty masters, Tully speaks before all others [fol. 2v]). The topics for which Cicero is cited are carefully rubricated, using such formulas as "Ichi nous devise Tulles . . ." (Here Tully explains to us . . .) or "Tulles dist . . ." (Tully says . . .). The transition from Cicero to the next author is treated as a transition from one speaker to the next:

> Ichi endroit se taist maistres Tulles qui a conté premiers. Si parole aprés Salemo[n]s. Salemons nous aprent que li consaus conduist l'oume.

> [Right here Master Tully, who spoke in first place, falls silent. And Solomon speaks next. Solomon teaches us that the counsel guides the man.] [Fol. 6v]

Similar rubrics articulate the "speeches" of the other authors, marking the transition from one to the next with the formula of silence and speech in turn. The passage from one author to the next is also marked by a historiated initial, which represents the author reading from an unfurled scroll to an audience of two or three people. As we have seen in previous discussions of author portraits, the scroll is frequently associated with oral discourse and works together with the rubric here to strengthen the impression that the text is a series of oral declamations by assorted authorities. Alard himself, the narrator-compiler of the treatise, is often represented at the beginning as a writer: it is he who has orchestrated this series of "speeches" into a book. The rubrication and iconography of this didactic compendium strongly resembles that found in many manuscripts of the *Rose*, in particular Jean's continuation, typically illustrated with recurring images of oral discourse, headed with the representation of Jean as writer and articulated by descriptive rubrics that

---

30. Minnis gives several other examples from the thirteenth century.

31. For a discussion of rubrication as a guide to the arrangement of material, and the organizational programs employed in different manuscripts, see Payen, "*Livre de philosophie et de moralité* d'Alard de Cambrai."

map out the thematic and rhetorical structure of the various long discourses.

The codicological format of the *Rose,* then, stresses its nature as an ordered compilation of material, an encyclopedia of sorts, representing a variety of perspectives that must be distinguished not only from each other, but also from that of the author-compiler. I have even found two manuscripts with tables of rubrics: here, the *Rose* is treated as an anthology.[32] Such rubrication is not typical of the romance tradition; among vernacular literary texts, I have found it nowhere except in the *Rose* and in certain fourteenth-century texts conceived as close imitations or reworkings of the *Rose.*[33] The *Rose* rubrics reflect a medieval perception, at least on the part of book designers, of the *Rose* as a new kind of vernacular literary text: an innovative poetics requires an equally innovative format.

The association of the *Rose* rubrication with that of encyclopedias raises an interesting question with regard to the word *aucteur.* Old French orthography was, of course, highly variable; in many manuscripts, the rubric is not *aucteur* but *acteur.* The distinction between narrator and protagonist is clear enough; what is not entirely clear is whether the narrator is meant to be understood as an *aucteur*—vernacular equivalent of the Latin poets, philosophers, and theologians—or as an *acteur,* vernacular equivalent of the Latin compilers. The latter interpretation is more consistent with the view of the *Rose* as a compendium; and in this case, Jean de Meun's address to the reader toward the end, normally introduced with a rubric stating "Ci s'excuse Maistre Jehan de Meun" or "Comment l'aucteur / l'acteur s'excuse" (Here Master Jean de Meun excuses himself; How the author excuses himself), would correspond to Vincent of Beauvais's *Apologia actoris.* Like Vincent, Jean assures the reader that he is merely the faithful transmitter of the words of others: a compiler. It is probable, however, that the ambiguous *aucteur-acteur* was at least sometimes understood in the former sense as well, especially since Jean de Meun was also known as the author of learned translations; participants in the literary debate, or *querelle,* of 1401–2 refer to him by such terms as *poëte, docteur, philosophe.*[34] Perhaps the very instability of the term *a(u)cteur* is itself indicative of a certain

32. I have seen tables in the fourteenth-century MSS Biblioteca Riccardiana 2755 and Bibl. Nat. fr. 1560.

33. For example, a very similar pattern of rubrication is used in manuscripts of Guillaume de Deguilleville's *Pelerinage de la vie humaine,* which is presented as an explicit reworking of the *Rose.* Similar rubrication also appears in Guillaume de Machaut's *Remede de Fortune* and in the *Voir Dit,* both of which stand in very close relationship to the *Rose.*

34. For the texts produced during the *querelle,* see Hicks's edition of *Débat sur le Roman de la Rose.* In *"Roman de la rose" au XIVe siècle,* Badel says of Jean de Meun's reputation in the fourteenth century that "on en use avec le texte de son *Roman* comme on en usait avec les textes des *auctores* latins" (p. 165).

ambiguity in the changing status of the vernacular poet during the later Middle Ages.[35]

Whatever may have been the precise identity of the narrator figure, it is nonetheless clear that the *Rose* was granted the status of a book and that it was seen as embodying a new kind of poetic authority, grounded at once in courtly lyricism and in Latin and vernacular written traditions, which provided a major source of unity for the composite text. The interplay of l'Aucteur and l'Amant creates an important continuity of voice throughout both parts of the poem. While some portion of the medieval audience would have received the poem purely through oral delivery, the proliferation of *Rose* manuscripts does indicate that this poem was experienced as a book by a relatively large number of people. One assumes that the format would not be so consistent if it did not have some appeal to a fairly broad audience. In any case, even if the insights of the average lay reader are inaccessible to us, the texts discussed in the following chapters show clearly that thirteenth- and fourteenth-century poets, at least, were sensitive to the lyrico-writerly dynamics of the *Rose*. And the careful use of illustration and page layout in so many *Rose* manuscripts cannot have gone wholly unappreciated by manuscript owners.

To take but a single example of the latter, let us briefly examine MS Bibl. Nat. fr. 1569, of the late thirteenth or early fourteenth century. The layout of the first page establishes the authorial and lyrical components of Guillaume's poetic persona (fig. 6). The text is disposed in two columns; on the left is the clerkly prologue about dream theory (vv. 1–20), and on the right is the lyrical prologue announcing the story of a particular dream (vv. 21–48). Across the top of the page is a two-part miniature. Over the left column, a man reads from a book to an audience; inscribed in the book are the opening words of the poem, "Maintes gens dient." Over the right column, a man is asleep in bed; Dangier stands at the foot of the bed. L'Aucteur and l'Amant are here laid out as complementary personae and as complementary textual voices.

At the break between the texts is a representation of Jean de Meun writing in an open book (fol. 28): the new authorial voice comes in. Finally, at the textual midpoint—at the line "Puis vendra Johans Chopinel" (v. 10535)—is a representation of one man handing a book to another (fol. 68v): the collaboration of the two authors. This sense of collaboration is stressed in the rubric between the two poems:

Ci dit l'aucteur comment Mestre Jehan de Meun parfist cest romans a la

35. For a related discussion of the application of the term *poète* to Guillaume de Machaut, see Brownlee, "Poetic Oeuvre of Guillaume de Machaut."

requeste Mestre Guillaume de Saint Amor, qui le commencement en fist; si
ne le pot parfaire.[36]

[Here the author tells how Master Jean de Meun completed this romance at
the request of Master Guillaume de Saint Amour, who made the beginning;
for he was not able to complete it.] [Fol. 28]

Jean's continuation of Guillaume's poem, then, is a collaboration by
means of the written word. Though Guillaume is portrayed in a performative mode and Jean is purely a writer, both are associated with the
book. Indeed, they represent different kinds of authorial presence:
Guillaume is understood as addressing his lady through the words of his
poem, whereas Jean is not. What Jean continues, according to the framework suggested here, is the unfolding of vernacular poetic authority.

The figure of l'Aucteur is expanded here beyond identification with
either Guillaume or Jean. It is his ongoing voice that accounts for the
conjoining of the two texts: for it is in the context of poetic authority that
the collaborative project of the *Rose* is inscribed. L'Aucteur speaks
through his narrators and his various characters, not being identified
with any one of them in particular but rather containing all of them. Not
only is l'Aucteur credited with the usual narrator interventions; he in-
trudes into the speeches of other characters as well. For example, the
passage on the Golden Age in the discourse of Friend is rubricated *Ci
conte l'aucteur du monde* (Here the author tells about the world [fol. 54v, at
Lecoy's line 8325]); in the discourse of False Semblance, a diatribe
against clerical hypocrisy is rubricated *L'aucteur contre Faus Semblant* (The
author against False Semblance [fol. 76, at Lecoy's line 11575]). Even the
final assault on the rose—a passage that for obvious reasons is normally
attributed to l'Amant—is attributed here to l'Aucteur, whose name is
inscribed at verses 21415 and 21553. Thus the final sexual consummation of l'Amant's desire is clearly more than a strictly erotic, fabliaulike
scenario: it is the final, climactic *poetic* consummation of the entire collaborative project.[37]

36. MS 1569 is not the only manuscript in which the first part of the *Rose* is attributed to
Guillaume de St. Amour, a confusion heightened not only by the common first name but
also by the reference to Guillaume de St. Amour in Jean's poem, not far from the discussion of authorship. This phenomenon certainly warrants a closer examination but lies
outside the scope of the present study.

37. The final passage is attributed to l'Aucteur in just a few other manuscripts. For
example, MS Bibl. Nat. fr. 1574, which stresses the nature of the *Rose* as a didactic compendium—by means, for example, of moralizing rubrics attached to such passages as the carol
scene, the discourse of False Semblance, and the discourse of the Old Woman—attributes
this final passage to l'Aucteur, thereby stressing its poetic rather than its erotic
implications.

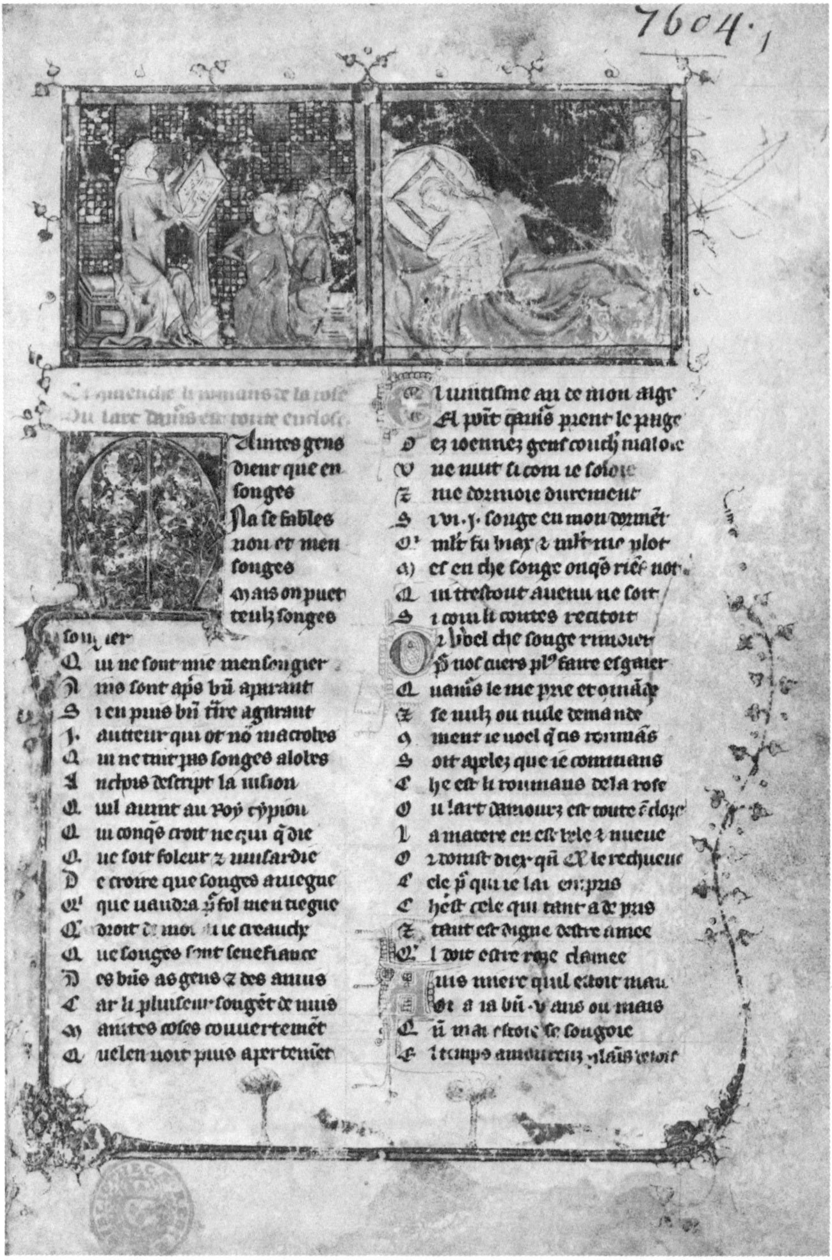

*Figure 6.* Opening page, *Roman de la rose*, B.N. fr. 1569, fol. 1. (Photograph: Bibliothèque Nationale, Paris)

There remains a great deal left to be said about the *Rose* and its reception; a large-scale study of *Rose* manuscripts is much needed.[38] I hope, however, to have identified here certain factors that will prove crucial to an understanding of thirteenth- and fourteenth-century lyric and lyrico-narrative poetry as a written medium. The *Rose* offers the model of a vernacular compendium, at once universal in scope and yet lyric in theme; an encyclopedic array of material, located within the context of dream and desire. The performative quality of courtly lyric and the dialogue format of much philosophical writing combine to produce a lyric *disputatio,* a learned debate about love and desire. A conflation of the conventional lyric equation of loving and singing with the Neoplatonic metaphor of procreation as writing provides a further model for an erotic discourse of lyrical writing, the ramifications of which were explored and reinterpreted by subsequent generations of poets.

Guillaume de Lorris, lyrical narrator; Jean de Meun, singer and lover of the written word: the combined work of these two poets brings into focus, with exceptional clarity, an entire complex of poetic issues. Jean's more writerly approach to lyrico-narrative discourse and his use of Pygmalion to establish the primacy of writing as a creative and not merely an imitative act reflect the general movement that we have seen, in the course of the thirteenth century, toward a more writerly, more systematic treatment of vernacular poetic composition and compilation. We will return to the *Rose* many times in the course of this study. Now, though, it is time to examine the work of other thirteenth-century poets in light of what we have learned from the *Rose.*

38. Ernest Langlois's catalog is, of course, an indispensable tool for any student of *Rose* manuscripts, and Kuhn's survey of *Rose* illumination provides a starting point for further iconographic studies. Badel also discusses manuscripts in his study of *Rose* reception. Tuve and, especially, Fleming comment on *Rose* illumination as a gloss on the text, raising many extremely important points. None of these authors, however, provides detailed analyses of individual manuscripts, taking into account textual variants, rubrics, glosses, illustrations, and so on, nor do any of them trace the evolution of the *Rose* manuscript tradition during the two and a half centuries of its existence as a record of changing patterns of *Rose* reception. It is my intention to address such issues in future studies.

## Chapter 4

# Text as Performance, Text as Artifact: Contrasting Models for the Romance with Lyric Insertions

In the foregoing chapters we have examined the relation between the persona of the romance narrator and that of the scribe, identified as compiler, editor, and/or rubricator of a text or series of texts. We have seen that the scribe is more readily assimilable to the persona of narrator than to that of lyric persona. Guillaume de Lorris, raising the question of written lyric discourse through the assimilation of narrator and lyric persona, left the resulting paradoxes unresolved. Jean de Meun's continuation established an extratextual narrator, combining aspects of scribal compiler and romance narrator with the lyrical equation of love and textual production in order to control the assortment of perspectives within the narrative and bring the whole to a conclusion. Scribal editors in turn devised a system of rubrication that imposed on the *Rose* a careful distinction between narrator and lyric persona; they then presented the whole as a system of oral declamation by assorted personages, ordered and arranged by the narrator-writer.

Although the conjoined *Rose* of Guillaume and Jean is certainly one of the most important (and surely the single most influential) of the texts raising the question of lyrical writing, it must be understood as part of a general thirteenth-century phenomenon. This period of intense scribal and poetic activity saw an enormously varied approach to written vernacular literature in general; most relevant to this study, the development of written lyric was explored through the compilation of chansonniers and through the poetic experiments of numerous poets. The use of first-person narrative was one important aspect of these experiments; another equally important development was the composition of romances with lyric insertions. This technique, apparently initiated during the first third of the thirteenth century by Jean Renart in his *Roman de la rose*, achieved an immediate and widespread popularity that lasted into the fifteenth century.[1] A third technique, finally, was the development of lyrical prose, of which the best-known example is Richard de Fournival's *Bestiaire d'amours*. The *Bestiaire d'amours* and its reception will be discussed in the following chapter; here, I wish to examine two important examples of the use of lyric insertions, Jean Renart's *Rose* and Jakemes's late thirteenth-century *Roman du castelain de Couci*.

Both Renart and Jakemes produced innovations that were to prove extremely important for subsequent poetic activity: Renart in the technique itself of using lyric insertions, and Jakemes in choosing a lyric poet as his protagonist so that his romance explains the genesis of an author corpus. The two romances are additionally interesting to compare because they express somewhat different attitudes toward the status of the lyric text. In Renart's *Rose*, songs maintain a decidedly oral character; he in turn takes on the persona of narrator-compiler, arranging and committing to writing a series of lyric performances. Jakemes, on the other hand, treats the châtelain's songs more as documents; that is, as texts originating at a fixed narrative moment for which some sort of history can be constructed. Interestingly, this view of the song as expressive of a specific narrative event is coupled with a lyricization of the narrative voice. It is as though some middle ground is being established where lyric and narrative can meet and interpenetrate.

In both cases the anthology format is an important dimension of the poetics of the whole, though again in somewhat different ways. Renart exploits the simultaneity of texts in a compilation, whereby different elements of the anthology can interact and gloss one another; Jakemes, on the other hand, in his assimilation of lyricism and writing, explores the nature of the book as a love token, an amorous space in which lover and lady can interact.

The contrast between Renart's *Roman de la rose* and Jakemes's *Roman du castelain de Couci* reflects the general contrast between the treatment of both lyricism and writing that we have already seen both in the history of the chansonnier and in the reinterpretation of Guillaume de Lorris's *Roman de la rose* at the hands of Jean de Meun. Following an examination of each poem individually, I will return to a consideration of how the poems fit into this larger context. With these points of comparison in mind, then, let us turn to the poems themselves.

1. Since the title *Roman de Guillaume de Dole* is a modern invention—the title *Roman de la rose* is given both in Renart's prologue and in the explicit of the single surviving manuscript—I prefer to use *Roman de la rose*.

## An Anthology of Performance: Jean Renart's *Roman de la rose*

Jean Renart's *Roman de la rose* tells the story of a German emperor, Conrad, who hears reports of the beauty of Lïenor, sister of Guillaume de Dole, and falls in love with her. A marriage is arranged. Envious of the imperial favor being bestowed on Guillaume through his sister's betrothal, the seneschal contrives to learn about a rose-shaped birthmark on Lïenor's thigh and uses this knowledge to back up his false claims of having had sexual relations with the girl. Great consternation results, but Lïenor eventually manages to prove her innocence, and the marriage is celebrated.

Renart's romance contains a large number and variety of songs: chansons courtoises, chansons de toile, dance songs, popular refrains, and even an excerpt of chanson de geste. In addition, the court minstrel Jouglet recites part of a tale identified by some with Renart's own *Lai de l'ombre*.[2] All are purely oral texts, recited or sung by a character in accordance with his or her personal circumstances. The chansons courtoises, for example, are most frequently sung in a private setting, usually by Conrad, or by Jouglet at Conrad's request. The courtly love lyric provides a dramatization of Conrad's sentiments, expressing first his love for Lïenor and then his grief over her imagined transgression. Within the tradition of the chanson courtoise, to sing is to become a lover. Conrad takes on the lyric "I" and so assumes the role of lyric persona. Similarly, the chansons de toile, though sung on one occasion by a knight, are otherwise sung, appropriately enough, by Lïenor and her mother in their sittingroom. As befits the modesty of an unmarried girl, Lïenor does not appropriate the first-person discourse of love lyric. The narrative format of her songs allows Lïenor to dramatize maidenly love while still attributing the sentiments to "Belle Aye" or "Belle Doe." She thus establishes her association with the amorous heroine of the chanson de toile without compromising her own chastity.

Although all songs are presented as oral performance, the quality of oral spontaneity is especially marked in the many carols and dance refrains of the romance. Through the succession of singers at a courtly gathering, recurring phrases and motifs are recombined in a virtual model of *mouvance*.[3] On one of these occasions, for example, the sister of the duke of Maience sings:

---

2. See Lecoy's introduction to his edition of Renart's *Rose,* p. viii.

3. The concept of *mouvance,* or the fluidity of the text before the age of printing, is developed by Zumthor in *Essai de poétique médiévale;* see pp. 65–72, 507.

Main se leva bele Aeliz,
dormez, jalous, ge vos en prie,
biau se para, miex se vesti
desoz le raim.
Mignotement la voi venir,
cele que j'aim!

[In the morning beautiful Aeliz rose—sleep, jealous one, I beg you! She
ornamented herself beautifully, dressed herself even better, beneath the
bough. Sweetly I see her come, whom I love.] [Lecoy ed., vv. 310–15]

This is answered by the count of Savoie, who sings virtually the same
lines in a rearrangement:

Main se leva bele Aeliz,
mignotement la voi venir,
bien se para, miex se vesti,
en mai.
Dormez, jalous, et ge m'envoiserai.

[In the morning beautiful Aeliz rose, sweetly I see her come, she ornamented herself well, dressed herself better, in May. Sleep, jealous one, and I
will enjoy myself.] [Vv. 318–22]

In other cases songs are linked by a few verbal parallels and a common
structure. The two songs above, for example, are framed by a second
pair, sung by an unnamed man and the count of Luxembourg (vv. 295–
99, 329–33). These two have a common rondel structure. Each elaborates, in the first and third lines, the image of a fountain surrounded by
flowers or branches; this is linked in the second line with a statement of
love, which is expanded in the final line. This succession of songs shows
very clearly the fluidity of the oral medium, in which singers draw on a
repertoire of lyric motifs and refrains that can be pieced together according to conventions of form and decorum.

The dance refrains are sung at public gatherings, by members of the
aristocracy. Here the song functions as an expression of the courtliness
of the group. The gathering becomes a theatrical event in which there is
no distinction between performers and audience. Rather, the society
collectively acts out the code of values and manners on which it is based,
through a code of diction and performance. The dance refrains have no
other frame of reference than that in which they are sung; the above
songs of flowering fountains, for example, are sung by people who have
gathered in the woods and are seated near fountains, surrounded by
multicolored flowers. The lengthy description that precedes the songs
makes it clear that everyone there is indeed "beautifully ornamented

and clothed"; and the count of Luxembourg sings "Tenez moi, dame" for the love of his lady. On the other hand, lest it be thought that the songs really are specific to a given moment or personage, it must be noted that one of the songs sung here, "Einsi doit aler qui bele amie a," is sung later on, during the tournament festivities, by Jouglet and Aigret de Grame. The songs are a general expression of, and commentary upon, courtliness as such and can be used by anyone in the appropriate circumstances.

Corresponding to the oral performative function of poetry and the theatrical quality of life at Conrad's court, is a more general social orientation around the spoken word. When Conrad wishes to summon Guillaume to court, he prepares a written letter. This document, however, is delivered by a messenger who announces the content of the letter as he hands it to Guillaume, and the letter itself must be read aloud for Guillaume by one of his knights. Indeed, the emperor fully expects that Guillaume's reception of the letter will be aural: he explains to his messenger that he wishes Guillaume to come to court "lués qu'il aura cest brief oï" (as soon as he has heard this letter [v. 8868]). The letter is less important textually than symbolically: like the gold seal attached to it, it is the embodiment and sign of imperial authority. Orally delivered messages and hearsay are the means by which information travels and important transactions take place. The phrase "par oïr dire" (by hearsay) applies to the seneschal's sexual knowledge of Lïenor (vv. 3373–74), to Conrad's love of Lïenor (vv. 3746–47), and to the general knowledge of the emperor's impending marriage (v. 4254).[4] The story of Lïenor—her beauty, her singing, and her real or imagined amorous alliances—circulates entirely by word of mouth, as an oral tradition. And like any other oral tradition, the story of Lïenor is subject to doubt and confusion, as conflicting versions vie for authority.

Jean Renart's prologue and epilogue suggest that his romance is conceived in a manner analogous to that of the songs and tales it contains. It is a decorative performance piece, intended for the listening pleasure of an aristocratic audience. And, just as the characters of the romance model themselves on poetry, so this poem may in turn serve as model to others:

> Bien le devroient en memoire
> avoir et li roi et li conte,
> cel prodome dont on lor conte,
> por avoir de bien faire envie
> ausi com cil fist en sa vie
> por cui l'en chante et chantera.

4. See Lacy.

[Well should kings and counts remember this noble man of whom they are told, that they might wish to do good, just as he did in his life, he for whom one sings and will sing.] [Vv. 5645–50]

The play on the word *conte* (count, tell), a favorite romance *jeu de mots*, stresses the relationship between the aristocracy and the body of poetry in which aristocratic values are celebrated. The phrase "sings and will sing" just three lines later reminds us that this tradition is one experienced largely through oral declamation and contains both lyric and narrative poetry.

Renart does more than merely preserve the songs, however; by setting songs in a narrative context, he offers a critique of courtly lyric and its various manifestations. There is a certain irony in the adoption of a trouvère voice by Conrad, a man who hopes for a speedy wedding: the trouvère persona does not normally see such hopes realized. In this respect the songs contribute a foreboding undercurrent to the romance. Let us examine the first song that Conrad sings explicitly in honor of Lïenor, the châtelain de Couci's Crusade song, "Li nouviaus tens et mais et violete" (The new season and May and violets) (vv. 923–30).[5] The stanza quoted in the text, in which the singer expresses his hopes of embracing his naked lady before departing overseas, is not entirely appropriate to Conrad, who has no apparent intention of departing anywhere; but it does express his optimistic expectations of success in love. If the remaining stanzas were sung, however, they would introduce a disturbing note into the as yet untroubled romance. The second stanza suggests that the lady may not have lived up to her lover's expectations: "Au conmencai la trouvai si doucete, / Ja ne quidai pour li mal endurer" (In the beginning I found her so sweet, I never expected to suffer because of her [Lerond ed., vv. 9–10]).[6] By the third stanza, the lady is designated "la douce rienz qui fausse amie a non" (the sweet thing named false friend [v. 18]). In the fifth stanza, the lover blames his tragic destiny of unrequited love on "li felon" (the evil ones [v. 36]); the sixth stanza, finally, explains that the lover would have succeeded with the lady if only his love had not been discovered by hostile parties just before he could consummate his desires:

> Amours m'eüst doné son guerredon.
> Maiz en cel point que dui avoir mon don,
> Lor fu l'amour descouverte et moustrée;
> Ja n'aient il pardon!

5. For the complete text of the song, see Lerond's edition of *Chansons attribuées au châtelain de Couci*, pp. 76–78.

6. I follow the order of stanzas found in MSS *M, O, R, T,* and *a*. For a discussion of the manuscript tradition, see the Lerond edition of *Chansons attribuées*.

[Love would have given me its reward. But at the point where I should have had my gift, the love was discovered and revealed: may they (that is, the afore-mentioned evil ones) never be pardoned!] [Vv. 45–48]

The sequence of events hinted at here certainly resembles that which in fact befalls Conrad: just as he is about to conclude the marriage agreement, his love is discovered by the hostile seneschal, who (albeit temporarily) prevents the hoped-for union by convincing Conrad that Lïenor has betrayed him.

Would all stanzas have been sung in an oral presentation of the romance? Here we can only speculate. Some songs are written out at full (or at least greater) length.[7] Perhaps, then, the stanza transcribed was the only one considered appropriate for the story at this point. If so, the audience would probably still have been familiar with the remaining stanzas, given the evident popularity of the song, and could be expected to think of the material left unstated: Conrad may be getting involved in a more complicated set of experiences than he realizes. If the entire song was sung, the audience might note the seeming inappropriateness of this material to Conrad's situation and wonder whether he was destined to live out the entire role there prescribed.

In this respect, the song that does reveal the emperor's love to the seneschal is most interesting. Conrad here sings a full two stanzas, as is stressed by the narrator's reference to "cez .II. vers" (these two stanzas [v. 3196]). This song that unleashes the seneschal's lying slander contains the fullest account of the lyric topos of *mesdire* (slander) found in any of the lyric material quoted in the text as it survives today:

> Ja fine amors ne sera sanz torment,
> que losengier et ont corrouz et ire.
> .  .  .  .  .
> Je soufferai les fauz diz de la gent
> qui n'ont pooir, sanz plus, fors de mesdire
> de bone amor.

[True love will never be without torment, for flatterers are annoyed and angered by it. . . . I will suffer the false words of the people who have power for nothing other than speaking ill of good love.] [Vv. 3188–89, 3193–95]

This song, moreover, appears to be Conrad's own exercise of the lyric instrument. Many of the other songs that he sings are the work of well-known trouvères; even though authorship is not always stated, nowhere else is there a suggestion that Conrad is inventing the songs he sings.

---

7. For example, two stanzas of the song attributed to Renaut de Beaujeu are given (vv. 1456–69); ten stanzas of the chanson de toile of Bele Aiglentine are given (vv. 2235–94).

Here, however, we are told that the emperor "made" the verses. The ironic potential of Conrad's appropriation of lyric discourse is fully exploited: he acquires a lyric voice of his own, enunciates a detailed statement of lyric inspiration (stanza 1) and torment (stanza 2), and thereby brings precisely these torments upon himself. As a result, he discovers the other side of lyric discourse, moving from songs of joy to songs of grief. And he is helpless in his predicament, like the persona of "Li nouviaus tanz et mai et violete," who states mournfully, "Je ne m'en sai vengier fors au plourer" (I know no vengeance but weeping [v. 30]). Trouvère lyric offers its hapless protagonist no model for the resolution of his plight.[8]

The stasis of courtly lyricism is also figured in the character of Guillaume. His role in the story is that of the consummate knight, personification of the courtly ideal. He first enters the narrative as the counterpart of the protagonist of the *Lai de l'ombre,* and it is as such that Conrad first desires to bring him to court. On the other hand, as Conrad becomes the lover of Lïenor, herself the counterpart of the lady of the *Lai de l'ombre,* he in turn becomes a second counterpart to the *Lai's* protagonist. Guillaume and Conrad are thus linked through their common association with the literary model, and Guillaume is used to dramatize aspects of the central experience.[9] It is he, for example, who sings "Lors que li jor sont lonc en mai" (When the days are long in May) (vv. 1301–7), the classic enunciation of the abstracted "love by hearsay" exemplified in Conrad's love for Lïenor. He shares fully in the emperor's grief over Lïenor's imagined transgression; it is he who echoes the sentiment of "Li nouviaus tanz," lamenting that he can avenge himself only by weeping (vv. 3830–31).

In an extremely suggestive article, Emmanuèle Baumgartner has described Renart's romance as the story of two poles of lyricism: the *grand chant courtois* is associated with Conrad and Guillaume, whereas the dance refrains and songs of May are associated with Lïenor.[10] The marriage of Conrad and Lïenor thus represents the dialectic of these two lyric types: the artificiality and sterility of the chanson courtoise is tempered by the natural fecundity of the dance songs. Mediating between these two pure lyric types are the narrative songs included in the romance: chanson de toile and chanson de geste.

Chanson de toile offers a possible model for resolution of the narrative dilemma: whereas the male lover of trouvère lyric plays a passive role, the female protagonist of chanson de toile is allowed a more active

---

8. In this regard, see Jung, "L'Empereur Conrad chanteur."

9. On the relationship between Conrad and Guillaume, see Zink, *Roman rose et rose rouge.* Diller also discusses traits in the character of Guillaume that would seem more appropriate to Lïenor's lover than to her brother.

10. Baumgartner, "Citations lyriques."

role. Within the romance our best example of these roles is the story of Bele Aiglentine, sung by a Norman knight during general court festivities. Distracted over her sewing, Bele Aiglentine confesses to her mother that she has been made pregnant by Count Henri; at her mother's instigation, she seeks out the count, asks to marry him, and so becomes a countess. Although this story does not precisely parallel that of Lïenor, each woman does take the initiative to salvage her reputation by journeying to her future husband and placing her case before him. Lïenor's association with chanson de toile strengthens this textual parallel. That the story of Bele Aiglentine plays an important role in foreshadowing the resolution of the romance is further suggested by the transcription of all ten stanzas within the text, a degree of thoroughness found nowhere else in the romance as it survives today.

The role played by chanson de geste is subtler but nonetheless important. The excerpt from *Gerbert de Metz* is sung just prior to Guillaume's arrival at court and is associated with a brother-sister jongleur couple. Chanson de geste would most likely be sung by a professional performer and not by a member of the aristocracy; here, it emanates from the nonnoble counterpart of Guillaume-Lïenor. A further association of chanson de geste is suggested by the sudden appearance of Guillaume's nephew following the seneschal's disclosures. Here, the focus suddenly shifts from the courtly lover tormented by a *fausse amie* (false beloved) and an evil *mesdisant* (slanderer), to the epic uncle-nephew team, prepared for swift action and vengeance. Where Guillaume knows no recourse other than courtly languour, the nephew immediately takes steps to clear the family honor; and his action in relaying the news to Lïenor and her mother makes the final resolution possible.

The epic associations become explicit, finally, with the comparison of Lïenor to Bertha, mother of Charlemagne, and Aude, sister of Oliver (vv. 4509–12). Guillaume-Lïenor, seeking marital affiliation with the imperial house, become the image for Oliver-Aude, similarly affiliated with the Carolingian dynasty through Aude's betrothal to Roland. Even more relevant to the character of Lïenor is the model of Bertha, who also triumphed over the perpetrators of deceit to clear her name, establish her identity, and regain her position as wife of the king who had fallen in love with her "per oïr dire."[11] Thus chanson de geste tempers lyric passivity with epic action and genealogical continuity and provides an appropriate model of feminine action.

Renart has exploited both narrative and compilational techniques in his *Roman de la rose*. The anthology format, embedded in a narrative

---

11. On the story of Bertha as it would have been known in the early thirteenth century, see Holmes's edition of *Berte aus grans piés*, by Adenet le Roi, pp. 9–10.

structure, allows for a network of intertextual relationships. On the one hand, a given song participates in a particular lyric paradigm—chanson courtoise, chanson de toile, and so on—within which repetition and reformulation, but not progression to a new register, are possible. On the other hand, a song is intimately tied to a narrative context, within which lyric motifs undergo transformation and development and are conflated or contrasted with motifs of different lyric types. Thus it is that, through the contrasting lyric discourse of Conrad and Lïenor, two different models of love converge on a single couple. At the moment of reconciliation, Conrad is moved to sing a joyful refrain:

> Que demandez vos
>   quant vos m'avez?
> que demandez vos?
>   —Ge ne dement rien
> se vos m'amez bien.

[What do you ask for, when you have me? What do you ask?—I ask for nothing, if you love me well.] [Vv. 5106–10]

Until this point, Conrad has sung exclusively chansons courtoises. His shift to a new form of lyric discourse marks the resolution of the problematic love of the chanson courtoise into the joyful, reciprocal love of the dance carol.

As a result of this narrative resolution of lyric motifs, the potential threat of chanson courtoise is neutralized. We have seen that the first song explicitly dedicated to Lïenor, "Li nouviaus tanz et mai et violete," provided a model for subsequent narrative developments; the helplessness of the lyric persona is reflected in Guillaume and Conrad, whereas the seneschal appears in the role of *mesdisant*. Now, however, Conrad and Guillaume are released from the constraints of such behavior, and the negative aspects of the song are turned back against the seneschal himself—it is his own behavior that is "discovered and shown" and he who must depart overseas, emphatically without having received the favors of the lady in question. Truly, as predicted by the narrator at the moment where the seneschal made his fateful discovery, evil reverts to the evil-doer (vv. 3198–99).

An interesting comment on the narrative is expressed in the closing image of Lïenor's wedding dress, with its representations of the life of Helen and of the Trojan War. The story of Helen figures a dual threat: the disruption of lineage caused by adultery and the disruption of culture caused by war. These problems were ultimately resolved: Helen was restored to her husband, and Aeneas escaped the ruins of Troy to transmit his cultural heritage to the line of Imperial Rome. Still, the story of Helen might seem an unlikely and inauspicious theme for a wedding dress; all the more so since the description of the dress focuses on Helen's elopement and the tragic destruction of Troy, without mentioning the subsequent restoration of either marriage or culture.

This dress must be understood in relation to Renart's text, itself compared to a dyed and embellished fabric in the prologue. The romance, too, is the story of potential disruption: the disruption of Conrad's lineage threatened by the apparent infidelity of his chosen bride and, more generally, the disruption of narrative and genealogical continuity threatened by the stasis of lyricism. It is the wedding that definitively overcomes these potential threats. Lyric love is subsumed by the social institution of marriage, instrument of generational and cultural continuation. Similarly, the story of Helen is neutralized by its incorporation into the wedding gown, which emblemizes the renewal, through marriage, of the imperial cultural heritage: by the end of the story, Lïenor's marriage to Conrad corresponds to Helen's return to Menelaus.[12] Lïenor's dress is analogous to such previous romance artifacts as Enide's saddle, which, with its images from the *Aeneid,* portrays the dangers that Erec and his wife have overcome; Floire and Blanchefleur's cup serves a similar function. Cultural history is presented as a process of *translatio,* an ongoing reenactment and reinterpretation of paradigmatic events.

As a purely visual narrative text, the fabric of Lïenor's wedding gown corresponds to the written transcription of the story ordered by the archbishop at the end of the romance. The story of Helen is not associated with an oral lyric tradition but rather with the written tradition of classical history and literature and, of course, with the vernacularization of this written tradition. Through the archbishop's intervention, Conrad and Lïenor also acquire a written history and so become a part of this literary tradition. Writing creates the final sense of resolution and closure; it also preserves the story for transmission to future generations and allows for narrative continuation through the addition or interpolation of new material. The importance of writing in Renart's romance must be stressed. Although he presents his tale in the prologue as a performance piece, it is in fact its anthology format, its imitation of a literary compilation, that allows lyric constraints to be overcome. Writing, both lyric and narrative, allows for revision, renewal, the infusion of new meaning, the fruition of newly conjoined literary materials.

---

12. Diller states that the poem's drama begins "lorsque Conrad prend au sérieux un instant un conte de fées; le drame s'achève au moment où Conrad réussit à subjuguer le merveilleux aux besoins de sa société" (p. 389). Jung, "L'Empereur Conrad," also offers some interesting observations on the role of Lïenor's dress.

# Biography of a Lyric Persona: *Le Roman du castelain de Couci*

The late-thirteenth-century *Roman du castelain de Couci*, attributed on the strength of the closing acrostic to Jakemes, focuses more explicitly on the genesis and transmission of lyric texts.[13] It tells the story of one of the most popular trouvères, the châtelain de Couci, who had lived nearly a century earlier. According to the romance, the châtelain falls in love with the lady of Faiel and woos her with his songs. Although initially resistant, she grows interested in the châtelain because of the fame that he acquires through his tournament exploits. Eventually she agrees to grant him an audience; but then, deciding to test his love, she keeps him waiting out in the rain all night long. Humiliated and sorrowful, the châtelain falls seriously ill from the combined effects of exposure and disappointment. Hearing this, the lady repents and renews her offer of a meeting. Recovering, the châtelain visits her, and soon an intimate relationship develops, providing the châtelain with ample occasion for song. The two meet frequently, arranging their meetings through the exchange of letters. All is well until another lady falls in love with the châtelain and, angered by his rejection of her advances, sends a servant to spy on him and discover whether he has a lover. Upon learning the truth, she reveals the situation to his lady's husband, who in turn surprises the lovers by returning home unexpectedly. The two manage to invent a lie to save themselves, but the husband remains suspicious and eventually determines to rid himself of the châtelain forever. He accordingly announces his intention to join the Crusade and take his wife along with him; at once the châtelain also takes the Cross, in order to accompany his lover. Only later does he realize that the husband has no intention of departing on Crusade and that he must leave his lady. This episode provides the appropriate context for the châtelain's two Crusade songs. Eventually, the châtelain dies while away on Crusade. He composes a final song and letter for his lady and has his heart and some locks of hair sent to her. But the husband intercepts this gift and, delighted at the death of his rival, cooks the heart and feeds it to his wife, telling her only after she has eaten it what it was. Upon hearing the news, the lady dies of grief.

The romance is certainly not based on factual information about the real châtelain de Couci. It combines elements derived from the songs, conventional romance material, and the popular legend of the *coeur mangé*. But this use of traditional subject matter must not blind us to Jakemes's extremely innovative treatment of songs in a narrative context

---

13. On the authorship of the poem and the various attempts to decipher the acrostic giving his name, see Matzke and Delbouille's Introduction, pp. lxvii–lxxvi.

and of lyricism and lyric and narrative voice, in general. Among thirteenth-century works, the *Roman du castelain de Couci* is unique in its presentation of a specific trouvère, whose corpus of songs is explained by the narrative. The format of the text resembles a sequence of songs interspersed with *razos,* or explanatory narratives, such as those existing in several Provençal chansonniers for Bertran de Born.[14] It is not certain that the collections of razos, which were diffused primarily in Italy and southern France, could have influenced Jakemes; but in any case his romance reflects a similar interest in conjoining lyric texts to a larger narrative framework that explains their genesis.

Insofar as his romance includes the arrangement of a lyric corpus, Jakemes, like Jean Renart, does the work of a compiler. His narrator is analogous to the rubricator of chansonniers (and in Provençal chansonniers, vidas and razos are normally written as rubrics) in that he orders and presents a series of lyric pieces and explains who made them and why. His relationship to the châtelain de Couci resembles that of Jean de Meun to Guillaume de Lorris: he continues the lyrical production of an earlier poet, developing its narrative potential and bringing it to a conclusion.

Jakemes differs from a chansonnier compiler, and from Jean de Meun and Jean Renart, in that he has a greater vested interest in the lyricism of his work; he identifies closely with his trouvère protagonist. Yet he is not writing about his own love, even though he states that he writes as love service. In a lyrical interpretation of the relationship between poet and audience, he replaces the poet-patron relationship with that of lover-lady, a move already hinted at in Chrétien's *Charrete* and developed more fully in such texts as *Le Bel Inconnu.* Thus he avoids the solipsism of Guillaume de Lorris, maintaining a distance between narrator and protagonist while at the same time effecting a fusion of lyrical, narrative, and scribal identities.

The prologue establishes the context for the figure of the trouvère, the aristocratic lover-singer. Jakemes begins, appropriately, with the word *amours;* and he explains that love is the criterion by which we can distinguish good people from bad. The criterion, however, is based not only on how they love but also on their attitude towards love poetry. Announcing that his poem is addressed to the "amorous," the narrator comments:

14. The vidas and razos were edited by Boutière and Schutz, *Biographies des troubadours.* Of particular relevance is the vida of Guilhem de Cabestaing, which states that the troubadour Guilhem was killed by his lady's husband and his heart fed to her; after the lady's death, people buried the lovers in a common tomb decorated with images recounting their story. On the relationship between lyric and narrative, see Poe.

Mauvais ne se poet acorder
A oïr bien dire ou compter;
Et puis k'oÿrs si li desplest,
Li faires bien pas ne li plest.

[A bad person cannot accept hearing anything good mentioned or recounted; and since hearing so displeases him, doing good does not please
him either.] [Matzke and Delbouille ed., vv. 7–10]

In these opening lines, Jakemes sets up a social standard that functions
for poet, performer, and audience alike. "Bad" is opposed to "amorous": faulty lovers are also bad listeners and bad poets, whereas the
amorous, seemingly by definition, excel at the creation or consumption
(or both) of good verse. Poet, performer, and audience participate in a
common enterprise that consists, ultimately, in the confirmation of a
courtly ideal that is at once social and aesthetic. The relations between
these dimensions of courtly society are expressed in a series of reformulations. Jakemes explains that in the past, princés and counts honored love by making *cans, dis, partures,* and *rimes* (songs, poems, jeux-partis,
and rhymes). The repetition of conte in rhyme position—"Count" (v.
11); "troops [of love]" (v. 12)—echoes its earlier use to refer to the
romance itself (v. 4), creating a verbal association of poetry (and, in
particular, this poem), aristocracy, and love. A true aristocrat is one who
loves *and* makes poetry; indeed, the importance of these criteria enables
the nonnoble poet or performer to identify himself as a member of
courtly society. Jakemes even extends the lyric concept of mesdire, a
central theme of the romance and the songs it contains, to refer to those
who speak ill of singers. There are, he says, just as many loyal lovers and
just as many skilled makers of romances and dits now as ever; but those
who can neither make nor understand such poetry have only unkind
words for the minstrels and jongleurs who keep it alive. Such people, he
concludes, are "rude et paÿsant" (rude and rustic [v. 33]), for a "courteous" person would never make such a statement. Clearly, the nonnoble
poet or performer is placed among the courteous, whereas his detrac-
tors, even if members of the nobility, are no better than rude peasants.
After this careful construction of the standards of courtliness, finally,
Jakemes reconfirms his own dual participation in this world, adopting a
stance of both romance narrator and lyric lover:

Or doinst Amours par sa bonté
Que celle le recoive en gré
Que mes coers aimme tant et prise
Que pour li ai ceste oevre emprise!

[Now may Love grant in his bounty that she whom my heart loves and praises receive it with goodwill, for I have undertaken this work for her!] [Vv. 51–54]

Just as the audience is defined in terms of its ability to appreciate both love and love poetry, so the poet in turn is defined in terms of his ability to please both his courtly audience and his lady.

Jakemes now introduces his hero, who is the perfect embodiment of these virtues. He is noble; his chivalrous nature and success in feats of arms make him the equal of Lancelot and Gauvain. He is a skilled maker of chansons and partures. And, of course, he is amorous. At several points, indeed, these qualities are simultaneously expressed in the image of the châtelain singing a love song while riding his horse on the way to or from a tournament, where his feats of prowess are always admired. Interestingly, this image is very much like the chansonnier illumination of the aristocratic trouvère galloping on a horse, in full armor, alongside the text of his songs. The romance is an elaborate narrative evocation of that trouvère ideal in which courtliness, chivalry, love, and song are all one. This nostalgia for the trouvère world entails a vision of courtly lyric as spontaneous oral declamation; although he is able to read letters, the châtelain never writes his songs down. They are pure lyricism, the live expression of sentiment.

Jakemes as narrator is identified with his protagonist through their common participation in this ideal. The first song composed by the châtelain is a lyric formulation of the central idea of the prologue, the identification of bad lovers as bad or improper singers. Asserting in the opening stanza that "Nulle cancons ne m'agree, / Se ne muet de boinne amour" (No song pleases me unless it is motivated by true love [vv. 364–65]), the châtelain contrasts such songs with the insincere songs sung by "li faignant prieour / Dont ja dame n'iert amee" (the fraudulent pleaders, by whom no lady will ever be loved [vv. 366–67]). In addition, Jakemes inscribes his own social role into the narrative itself; it was through the performances of the local minstrel, he tells us, that the lady of Faiel came to hear the châtelain's first song dedicated to her. She was impressed by his poetic abilities, which she knew had been placed at her service, and her interest in him grew. Similarly, the châtelain needs the services of a scribe to transcribe his final letter to the lady. Transmission of texts, both oral and written, is a central theme of the romance, as is audience reception. Let us examine more closely the construction of the narrative.

The narrative revolves around the opposition and juxtaposition of male-female couples. At the center are the châtelain and the lady of Faiel: they are the source of the narrative material and also of the "primary texts" recording their love, the songs and letters. Through their exchange of letters the lady and the châtelain engage in the process of writing their own story and advancing it from one episode to the next, and the songs reflect on the situation at hand. The central couple is doubled in the figure of Gobert and Isabelle, who aid in the transmission of texts, transcribing and delivering written letters and bearing oral accounts of the activity of one lover to the other. This construct is inverted in the figures of the lord of Faiel and the unidentified female admirer of the châtelain, each of whom relates to the corresponding member of the central couple as enemy and rival.

True to the construct established in the prologue, the husband and the rival lady manifest their villainy, within the closed system of the romance, by being both enemies of the central love relationship and a bad audience for the central love story. When the lady hears the account of the châtelain's visit to the lady of Faiel, she vows to destroy the couple. She, too, participates in the transmission of this story. But, as opposed to the courtly Isabel, who brings messages to the châtelain, the lady's narration is that of the mesdisant: she bears messages to the husband. He too (perhaps understandably) is a most unsympathetic audience. And he too abuses the power of language to gain his own ends: his insincere pledge to join the Crusade leads to the lovers' separation and ultimate death. If the lady is mesdisant, the husband is *faignant* (fraudulent). And the husband further shows his villainy, at the end, by his pleased reaction to the tragic tale of the châtelain's death.

There is an interesting contrast between the oral songs and the written letters produced by the central couple. The châtelain's song does communicate a private message to the lady, but only because he has already declared his love in private conversation. The songs lack specific references that could enable them to function as messages without some supporting text. They express general emotions of love, joy, sorrow, or the pain of separation in the face of the Crusade. As we saw in Renart's *Rose,* the song is intended for repeated performance and as such must be adaptable to any particular performance situation. Specifically, it is appropriate for any gathering of the courtly society defined in Jakemes's prologue. The bond between audience and performer is precisely that system of ideals expressed by the song. The lack of specific indicators in a song is part of the anonymity required if propriety is to be maintained in a public text; indeed, this anonymity is central to the courtly "code" violated by the rival lady of the romance. This anonymity in turn allows the song to inscribe itself in the general context of courtly society rather than in any specific set of relationships.

The letters, on the other hand, are private documents; and they are specifically linked to a sequence of events. They are replete with precise indications of place, time, and person: "your maid," "the bearer of this letter," "two weeks from now on Tuesday," Paris as the destination of the absent husband, and so on. In these letters the lovers refer back to past events or to their common story, as well as to projected future events. Where the song has only the eternal present of its repeated performances, the letter is attached to a fixed moment, the time of writing. Moreover, its existence as a unique artifact endows the first-, second-, and third-person characters of its text with specific identities— it is transcribed and delivered by and to specific individuals. Thus the quality of the letters as written documents is associated with their inscription in a very specific system of chronology, geography, and personal history. This narrative system is exemplary of the general system of courtliness expressed in the songs.

Jakemes's use of love letters is instructive, for it points toward the more writerly concept of lyric poetry implied by his innovative treatment of lyric insertions. Unlike Jean Renart and other thirteenth-century authors of narratives with lyric insertions, Jakemes has set up a context not for the performance of the châtelain's songs but rather for their composition. The narrative thus claims to provide not merely *an* interpretive context but rather *the* context in which the elusive chanson courtoise is revealed to contain a specific system of references. Jakemes has taken care to invent episodes that exploit any narrative potential that the songs might have.[15] The châtelain's second song, for example, is composed after he has spent a night huddled outside his lady's door in the rain, waiting in vain for her to fulfill her promise of a rendezvous. In this context, there is good reason for the lover to exclaim, "Las! cescuns cante, et je pleure et souspir" (Alas! Everyone sings, and I weep and sigh [v. 2595]), and to feel foolish and ashamed of his gullibility. The behavior of the lady, in turn, was indeed rather capricious, and the châtelain understandably wonders about it:

> Mierveilles ai dont vient ceste ocoisonz
> Qu'elle me fait a teil doulour languir:
> Chou est pour cou qu'elle croit les felons.

[I wonder what brought it about that she makes me languish in such sorrow: it is because she believes the evil ones.] [Vv. 2607–9]

Here, the classic lyric construct of the sorrowful, lovelorn trouvère lamenting the cruelty of his lady under the baleful influence of the mesdisants has been given a specific narrative illustration. Similarly, Jakemes invented an explanation for the two Crusade songs, distinguishing the

---

15. See Calin, "Poetry and Eros." For Calin, the songs are *"mises en abyme* that reflect, anticipate, prefigure even the lovers' destiny" (p. 200).

more purely amorous, even optimistic, tone of the single stanza quoted from "Au nouviel tans que mai et violette" from the mournful tone of "A vous, Amant" (To you, beloved). The first, we learn, was composed at a time when the châtelain believed that his lady would be accompanying him overseas; suspecting nothing, he innocently imagines his voyage in the context of a successful love affair. The second Crusade song, however, is composed after the châtelain realizes that he has been betrayed and that he is in fact forced to abandon his lady; his sorrowful farewell is entirely appropriate to his new situation.

Interestingly, as in Renart's romance, only the first stanza of "Au nouviel tans que mais et violette" appears in either manuscript of the *Roman du castelain de Couci*. Again, the intrigue hinted at in the unstated succeeding stanzas is appropriate to the turn that the narrative is about to take. Perhaps here, as in the preceding romance, the omitted stanzas are meant to occur to the audience as an implicit foreshadowing of trouble yet to come.

What Jakemes has done for the songs is to turn them into a series of written documents and provide them with a referential system. The chansonniers already gave the songs a written format as a corpus associated with the name "châtelain de Couci" and sometimes accompanied by the image of a knight. As such they were already accessible to be enjoyed by the amorous or derided by the ill-willed. Jakemes has in turn appropriated this corpus and generated from it a narrative system of love experience and textual transmission.

The romance indeed is designed as a showcase for the songs. They are literally grafted onto the narrative. The first line of a song always forms the second half of a couplet so that the song appears to have been fit into a space opened up between couplets. Thus the line immediately preceding the song not only serves to introduce it but also creates an opening in the textual fabric. To exclude the song from a recitation of the text one would need only to omit the line preceding it, or to complete the couplet with a closing formula. Indeed, there are places where a song is missing in both of the two manuscripts, and it is clear that the space originally created for it has been closed up in just this way. In MS Bibl. Nat. n.a. fr. 7514, the text still suggests at one point that the song is expected, even leaving a blank line where the song would have gone, as if to signal a pause where a performer could insert a song:

> Pour ytant fist il et trouva
> Ceste cancon a ciere lie
> En l'onnours d'amours et d'amie.
>         [blank line]
> Toute ot finee la canchon
> Ains qu'il venist a sa maison.

[Because of that, in a happy mood he made and found this song, in honor of love and girl friend. (blank line) He had completely finished the song by the time he got home.] [Fol. 59v; corresp. to Matzke and Delbouille's ed., vv. 3704–8]

In MS Bibl. Nat. fr. 15098, though, the space has been closed up:

> Pour ytant fist il et trouva
> Une chancon gaie et iolie.
> S'en va chantant a chiere lie.
> Tout ot finee sa ch[anc]on
> Ains qu'il venist a sa maison.

[Because of that he made and found a gay and pretty song. He went along singing happily. He had completely finished his song by the time he got home.] [Fol. 72v]

For the châtelain's final song, on the other hand, MS 15098 simply presents a gap in the continuity of the text (without, however, a space left). No song is given, and the line that seems to announce the song (v. 7563) is without rhyme. In the other manuscript, this gap has been filled by the song, "Sans faindre voel obeïr" (Without falsity I wish to obey [vv. 7564–7608]). Interesting questions are raised by this song, which could not possibly be by the real châtelain—it is not a form used by trouvères of his time—and which, moreover, is nowhere else attested. It has been suggested that Jakemes himself wrote this song.[16] If so, one cannot help wondering whether he consciously excluded songs commonly attributed to the châtelain in the chansonnier tradition that would have been appropriate here. One song that would have fit into the story at this point, and would even have "rhymed in" with the preceding half-couplet, is "Je chantaisse volentiers liement" (I would willingly sing gaily), attributed to the châtelain de Couci in five chansonniers.[17] Here the singer states that he would like to sing a happy song, but he cannot because love causes him nothing but grief, an appropriate sentiment for the song composed on the châtelain's deathbed, where "mout li ert joie lontainne" (joy was very far from him [v. 7610]). This song develops the standard trouvère theme of impending death and of bequeathing the heart to the lady. While this is a conventional image, it nonetheless does reverberate with the story Jakemes has constructed: the dying châtelain sends his heart to his lady, but her husband intercepts it and causes her to eat it, where-

---

16. Matzke and Delbouille suggest that the final virelay, as well as two rondeaux sung at a banquet that are also *unica*, may be due to Jakemes; see their introduction, p. lxvi.

17. The song is attributed to the châtelain in MSS *K, M, T, X*, and *a*. See Lerond ed., p. 66.

upon she dies of grief. In stanza 4, for example, the singer states that love "a mon cuer en li pour morir mis" (has placed my heart in her to die [Lerond ed., v. 32]). Certainly, by the end of the romance, the châtelain's heart has found its way into the lady, and both have died. It is as though this unstated song has been absorbed by Jakemes's narrative, the lyric themes and images fully appropriated and processed.

Even more appropriate—and, interestingly, also beginning with the proper rhyme—is the song "Merci clamans de mon fol errement," attributed to the châtelain de Couci in eight chansonniers.[18] This song too hints at a narrative intrigue similar to that developed in Jakemes's romance. It begins, "Merci clamans de mon fol errement, / Ferai la fin de mes chançons oïr" (Crying mercy for my foolish erring, I will put an end to my songs [Lerond ed., vv. 1–2]). The lyric persona indicates that he has put himself into a situation from which death is the only escape and, acknowledging that he is losing the pleasures of love through his own fault, laments that his downfall may cause pleasure to his enemies. The third stanza indicates that the lover's problems were brought on by indiscretion—he has not known how to hide his love—and contrasts this failure with the behavior of lovers who are discreet but false-hearted. The stanza suggests, of course, the châtelain's inability to hide his love from his lady admirer and hence from the lord of Faiel, as well as the contrast between the châtelain as a loyal if overly enthusiastic lover and the rival lady and husband as clever but treacherous lovers who bring about the deaths of their respective objects of desire. The closing lines of the song, finally, are very close to the narrative moment surrounding the composition of the last song in the romance: commending himself to his lady, the singer states, "Tout li perdoing en mon definement, / Et quant mon cors li toil, mon cuer li rant" (I pardon her for everything in my death, and as I withdraw my body from her, I give her my heart [Lerond ed., vv. 47–48]). An audience familiar with the songs of the châtelain de Couci (and the manuscript tradition suggests that his songs were extremely popular) would surely note that these unstated songs were being played out in the narrative. Jakemes has effected a fine interpenetration of lyric and romance, picking up the elusive narrative threads of the songs and continuing them in romance fashion. This transformation of song into narrative complements his lyricization of narrative voice in prologue and epilogue.

## The Material Text and the Reliquary of the Heart

Within the narrative, we are given an image for Jakemes's poetic system in the motif of the heart. The heart, physically removed from the

18. The song is attributed to the châtelain in MSS *A, C, K, M, P, T, X,* and *a.* See Lerond ed., pp. 85–86.

châtelain's body and sent in a locked coffer to his lady, is a reified lyric image. It is accompanied by the sealed letter, in which the châtelain's sentiment is textually enclosed and which provides a specific explanation of the heart and its function in the ongoing love story. This letter, it will be recalled, was transcribed by a clerc according to the verbal instructions of the châtelain; and the whole was delivered to its audience (unfortunately, the wrong audience) by Gobert, who additionally provided an oral narrative explaining the artifact. The entire construct provides an extended analogy for Jakemes's own enterprise. His text does contain the actual songs of the châtelain, made "according to his heart." It also contains letters, Jakemes's imaginative reworkings of the châtelain's presumed sentiment; and songs and letters alike are glossed by the narrative. Thus the various elements of the "heart" episode are integrated in Jakemes's composite text.

The importance of the heart as a generator of narrative is shown in the ways that it is used by the various personages in the romance. For the châtelain, the gesture of bequeathing his heart to the lady represents his attempt to dictate the final episode of his story. Just as his previous letters functioned to set up new amorous encounters, so now he intends a final "encounter" whereby the lovers can be symbolically united. Gobert, confronted by the wrathful husband, produces the heart and its story as a means of saving his own life. The husband in turn appropriates the precious artifact and uses it to create a different final episode, attempting to bring the story of the châtelain and the lady to quite another sort of conclusion. The lady, finally, through her reaction to the now rather complicated history of the heart, undoes the husband's attempts to control the narrative outcome. Much to his surprise and consternation, she dies of grief, providing the romance with an exemplary ending reminiscent of the ultimate fate of Tristan and Iseut.

This series of events is, again, analogous to the way in which Jakemes himself has appropriated the songs of the châtelain and arranged them in such a way as to create a particular narrative construct. Each of the romance characters acted within the constraints of his or her particular situation, attempting to manipulate the material at hand to the greatest advantage. Jakemes likewise performed his poetic task within the constraints imposed by the song corpus—it was necessary, for example, that the châtelain be amorous, that he find cause for both joy and sorrow, that he suffer at the hands of the mesdisants, and that he depart on Crusade—while at the same time manipulating his material to create a narrative of his own design.

Jakemes, indeed, has appropriated the "heart" and songs of the châtelain not only for purely poetic purposes but also, according to his prologue and epilogue, for use within the context of his own love relationship. The personages of the narrator and his lady provide a fourth

male-female couple, the extratextual counterpart of the protagonist couples. Like the châtelain, the narrator sings in honor of his lady. As he
states in the epilogue, "S'en canc souvent et haut et bas" (I often sing
both loudly and softly of her [v. 8264]). Moreover, he imitates the final
action of the châtelain, sending his lady an artifact that "contains" his
heart. Inspired by his love for her, he says, "Ai je mis mon coer et
m'entente / En rimer ceste histoire chi" (I have put my heart and my
attention into rhyming this story here [vv. 8248–49]).

The artifactlike quality of the text is stressed by the acrostic built into
it. This romance that contains the sung chansons and written letters of
the châtelain, like the box containing his heart and explanatory document, also embodies the "heart" of the poet and is inscribed with his
name. The narrator's references to the device of his signature express
his hopes that this textual artifact will not be abused by villainous characters—that he will be allowed a better fate than that of his protagonist.
Just as the narrative frames the songs of the châtelain, so it in turn is
framed by the lyric stance of the narrator. The romance as a whole is the
embodiment in lyric and narrative format of the trouvère identification
of love experience and poetic expression, and of poet and protagonist.
If, indeed, Jakemes did compose the châtelain's final song, then its lyric
"I" represents an even more complete fusion of protagonist and poet, as
Jakemes, like Jean de Meun, appropriates the lyric voice of his protagonist in order to continue not only the narrative development but also
the lyric discourse itself.

The motif of enclosure and containment operates at multiple levels of
the text, contributing to the unity of the poetological construct. Love
sentiment is enclosed in songs; the songs in the romance; the heart in its
box; Jakemes's love, as well as his name, in his poem. The motif of
containment is used to mediate between the thematics of love and that of
poetry—specifically, written poetry—through the association of the
book or other written text as container and the sexual connotations of
penetration and enclosure. We saw in Chapter 3 that, in Jean de Meun's
*Rose*, written lyric discourse is produced and defined through an assimilation of the lyric performance situation with the learned *enseignement*
(teaching), resulting in a written *disputatio* on the subject of love, and
also through the identification of the amorous quality of lyricism with
the sexual connotations of writing. Jakemes in turn, though operating in
a somewhat different manner, explores the poetic implications of the
latter analogy.

The quality of the letters as "containers" for private sentiment is
stressed by the repeated references to seals and to the process of folding
and unfolding the parchment as the letter is read. Similarly, the book
functions as a container for the text. In MS 15098, which contains only
the *Roman*, this effect is heightened by the placement of miniatures on

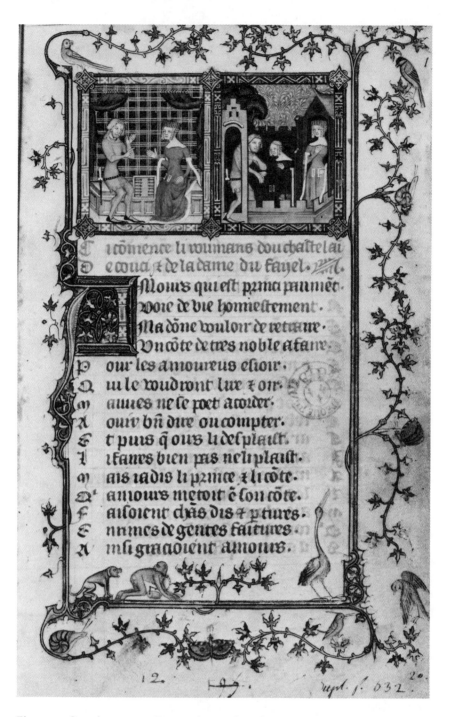

*Figure* 7. Opening page, *Roman du castelain de Couci*, B.N. fr. 15098, fol. 1. (Photograph: Bibliothèque Nationale, Paris)

the first page and near the end of the story (figs. 7, 8). These miniatures and the ornamental borders embellishing the pages that bear them provide a framework containing the entire story of the châtelain and his lady. This encapsulation of the story, moreover, itself stresses the thematics of enclosure and penetration.

On folio 1, a two-part miniature represents, on the left, the châtelain and the lady seated in a room, in conversation, with a closed box between them. The private union of the two lovers is represented; they are alone together, within the room. The closed box between them underscores the notion of privacy and containment that informs their relationship and its various forms of expression: the messages hidden in folded and sealed letters; the sentiments contained in songs; the love locked away in the heart of each. On the right, we see Isabelle welcoming the châtelain as he enters the gate of their house; beyond the gate, the lady stands in the open door. The lady is associated with the enclosed space of her room, itself encircled by the wall. The châtelain's entrance into this space signifies narrative progression—it is here that we enter the space of the romance, and it is through his visits to the lady that the romance is advanced—and, at the same time, his sexual presence in the private space of the Faiel household.

In the final miniature (fol. 157v; at v. 8163), also two-part, the scene on the left represents the lady, her husband, and their servant at the moment when he reveals to her that she has eaten the heart of her lover. He shows her the coffer, with the châtelain's hair hanging out of it, and the opened letter. The scene answers the second scene on the first folio: the châtelain's intrusion into the lord of Faiel's conjugal space is answered by the latter's intrusion into the private space of the lovers, represented by the coffer and letter. In the first image, the lady was metonymically doubled in the architectural space of the walled castle; here, the châtelain is metonymically replaced by his traces: coffer, hair, letter, and heart.

On the right, finally, we see the lady's death. She lies on her bed, her eyes shut and her hands over her heart while her husband and Isabelle stand grieving beside her. On the floor next to the bed is a locked chest. This final image answers the first image of folio 1. There, the two lovers were present as a couple; here, they have been fused into the single figure of the lady, who now literally contains her lover (or what is left of him), having just eaten his heart. As she lies dead or dying, she presents an impenetrable surface to her husband. Just as the love story remained for a long time hidden from his eyes, so now in this final moment his wife, having assimilated her lover, disappears with him into death. Like a bad reader of the poem—one, perhaps, who will be unable to decipher Jakemes's acrostic—the husband "reads" his wife's story and yet is at the same time excluded from it, unable to participate in its mystery or to

*Figure 8.* Closing miniature, *Roman du castelain de Couci,* B.N. fr. 15098, fol. 157v. (Photograph: Bibliothèque Nationale, Paris)

130

fathom its depths. This sense of impenetrability is echoed in the locked chest, which recalls the box of folio 1. The good reader, on the other hand, has been allowed to enter the story along with the châtelain at the beginning. Sympathetic readers, having been granted access all along to the inner worlds of the lovers, can draw from the final image of the lady an exemplary image of love that reflects their own experiences and values.

The written text has a bodily presence and allows for interaction between writer-narrator and reader-addressee; the sealed letters create the presence of one lover to another during times of absence. Jakemes himself uses the written text as a displacement of the desire he feels toward his lady: he puts his heart and his identity into it. He hopes that from there it may pass to her. An interesting analogy thus develops between the written text and the person of the lady. Just as Jean de Meun loved and wrote the *Rose*, and Pygmalion at once "begat" and copulated with Galatea—an action doubled, a few generations later, in the incestuous coupling of Cinyras and Myrrha—there is here a progressive identification of the text of love with the lady's space and ultimately her body. Our entrance into the book parallels the châtelain's entrance into her bedroom; as the book comes to an end she assimilates what is left of him into her body and, sealed in death, becomes the final image of closure.

As poet, Jakemes appropriates trouvère material and, operating in a mode that draws on both lyric and romance conventions, produces not an oral formulation but rather an artifact of love. Ultimately, the book where the songs are contained is figured in the coffer containing the heart and at the same time is itself a figure for the sexual interpenetration of lover and lady. Reminiscent of the nightingale reliquary that stands as memento to the violated love affair of Marie de France's *Lai du Laüstic*, the heart "reliquary" and its fate figure both the values and limitations of written lyric discourse. Because writing creates a tangible presence, it allows for communication that is more private and more direct than that of a publicly performed song; at the same time, because it leaves a visible record, it is more susceptible to outside interference and manipulation. Jakemes's response to this danger with regard to his own writing is the acrostic device: his identity is accessible only to those worthy characters capable of deciphering his coded message.[19]

19. It is interesting that this emphasis on the creation of a monument-reliquary for the lovers appears both here and also in the vida of Guilhem de Cabestaing, a possible source for Jakemes's knowledge of the coeur-mangé motif. This further connection between the two texts strengthens the possibility that Jakemes did have some knowledge of the vidas. Given the writerly approach to lyric texts that we have found in Jakemes's work, it is certainly not unlikely that he had studied vernacular lyric in book form.

## Lyrical Narrative and Lyric Compilation: From Performance to Book

The movement from Renart's *Roman de la rose* to Jakemes's *Roman du castelain de Couci* is analogous in certain respects to the movement from Guillaume de Lorris to Jean de Meun and to the development of the chansonnier as traced in Chapter 2. Although each text has its own configuration of elements, and it would be dangerous to impose a monolithic history on the extremely varied literary production of the thirteenth century, the general movement toward a more writerly concept of vernacular lyric identified in Chapter 2 is manifest in the history of lyrico-narrative poetry.

In Jean Renart's romance, even more than in that of Guillaume de Lorris, lyric discourse retains its oral character: it is not appropriated by the narrator but assigned rather to members of the fictional world. In this way, lyric discourse—sung, personalized, expressing a limited and individualized perspective on the central narrative theme—is clearly distinguished from the discourse of the narrator, which is global in perspective and which acknowledges its participation in a written tradition. The presence of the narrator, orchestrator of lyric and narrative motifs, allows for a plurality of voices and effects the reconciliation of the conflicting perceptions and desires of the various characters. Renart's narrator is analogous not only to the clerkly narrator of romance tradition but also the scribal compiler of chansonniers, who similarly announces and organizes a series of lyric performances without adopting a lyric voice himself. The narrator of Renart's *Rose* is fundamentally different from that of Guillaume de Lorris's *Rose*, where, as we have seen, the narrator is identified with, and increasingly eclipsed by, his lyric protagonist.

Renart's romance assumes a listening audience rather than silent readers. The narrator promises that "tuit cil s'en esjoïrent / qui chanter et lire l'orront" (all those who hear it sung and read will enjoy it [vv. 21–22]), and it would certainly be in performance that one could fully appreciate it. The lyric pieces indeed contribute significantly to blurring the distinction between the poetic world and that of the audience. In a recitation of the romance, the performance of songs serves to bring the characters to life: their discourse is clearly distinguished from that of the narrator. Moreover, the songs create an aural link between the audience and the romance characters, who are joined as common spectators of the lyric performance and as common adherents to the values enunciated in the songs. In this respect Renart's *Rose* differs from that of Guillaume de Lorris, where our initial identification with the dreamer was as common readers of a visual text.

While Jean Renart's romance is a narrative exploitation of lyric compilation, it cannot really be described as lyrical writing: song and written word, lyric and narrative discourse, remain distinct. It was Guillaume de Lorris who first effected a real interpenetration of lyric and narrative, song and written romance; his *Roman de la rose* is, most likely, a response to that of Jean Renart.[20] Jean de Meun's response to Guillaume in turn reinscribes this lyrical narrative in the larger framework of Jean's re-defined lyrico-narrative discourse. As we have seen, Jean effects a new blend of lyrical and writerly elements, some of which are familiar from Jean Renart: once again lyric discourse is subordinated to the voice of the central narrator-compiler, and diverse voices and viewpoints are coordinated by means of a compendium format. But Jean de Meun also preserves and exploits Guillaume's original conflation of lyric and narrative, in his exploration of writing rather than oral vocalization, as an eroticized creative act. Jean's contemporary, Jakemes, likewise allows for the interpenetration of lyric and narrative discourse; he focuses on poet rather than performer and on the lyrical text as a record of experience and an artifact of love.

Renart and Jakemes, as lyric compilers, participate not only in the history of poetics but also in the history of the chansonnier. Renart's prologue clearly indicates that he felt the inclusion of songs to be an essential feature of his text. He states, in fact, that they have been insert-ed "por ramenbrance des chançons" (in remembrance of the songs [v. 3]). The romance commemorates not the feats of the heroes so much as the songs themselves, which are gathered together and preserved through their incorporation into the romance structure. Renart's *Roman de la rose* offers one of the most diverse anthologies of Old French song known today; it bears witness to an early phase of lyric compilation and indeed predates any surviving chansonnier. Its stated theme, "armes et amors" (arms and love [v. 24]), recalls the iconographic programs of chansonniers *a* and *M*, which also present song both as musical enter-tainment and as the vehicle for knightly values. But in its relative lack of concern for lyric authorship, Renart's compilation is in fact closer in spirit to chansonnier *U*, which seems also to have been compiled pri-marily for the purpose of preserving songs and not for the purpose of setting up a canon of lyric poets. Renart's compilation is also closest to MS *U* in its contents: both collections combine trouvère and troubadour lyric as well as chansons de toile.

Jakemes's compilation, on the other hand, reflects the influence of the slightly later chansonnier tradition in which songs had come to be associ-

---

20. Zink argues in *Roman rose et rose rouge* that it is rather Jean Renart who is responding to Guillaume de Lorris. Although my own feeling is that Renart's text is the older, such matters are extremely difficult to prove. In the present context it is not really necessary to determine which text came first, since my primary interest is simply to demonstrate that these two poems reflect somewhat different approaches to lyricism and lyrical narrative.

ated with particular authors, of whom the châtelain de Couci was, to judge from the ornamental initials and special rubrics that announce his corpus in MSS *K, N, P,* and *X,* one of the most important. By the late thirteenth century a given song was nearly always transmitted in conjunction with the other songs by its author. Renart's compilation reflects a knowledge of the lyric tradition as a diverse body of songs, sometimes associated with an author's name but more fundamentally identified in terms of the performance situation to which each is appropriate. Jakemes's compilation, on the other hand, suggests a knowledge of the lyric tradition derived, at least in part, from a reading of chansonniers.

The *Roman du castelain de Couci* also resembles the later chansonniers *A, a,* and *M* in its treatment of the figure of the poet. As we have seen, Jakemes establishes criteria for courtliness that exclude some aristocrats and include nonnoble love poets and singers. Although his hero is of the upper class, Jakemes's focus on his own love affair and the analogy between himself and the châtelain as love poets demonstrate that these courtly values are accessible to a "professional" poet like himself and that, furthermore, his experience of love is worthy of poetic celebration. This state of affairs, clearly related to the valorization of the nonnoble trouvères in these illuminated chansonniers, is an essential part of the literary climate that allows a poet-compiler like Machaut or Froissart to produce books devoted to the amorous and poetic exploits of the author. In this respect, too, Jakemes differs from Jean Renart: in Renart's romance, minstrels either perform material from outside the courtly lyric, such as chanson de geste; or, if they do sing chansons courtoises, as Jouglet sometimes does, they do so at the request of a noble patron and in expression of the patron's, not the minstrel's, love experiences. Although the minstrel plays a crucial role as entertainer, adviser, and go-between in Renart's *Rose,* not until later in the thirteenth century does he acquire the status of lyric protagonist in his own right.[21]

21. See Dufournet.

Chapter 5

# The Audiovisual Poetics of
# Lyrical Prose: *Li Bestiaire d'amours*
# and Its Reception

Richard de Fournival's *Bestiaire d'amours* was composed during the second quarter of the thirteenth century. In several manuscripts it is identified by its alternate title, *Arriere ban* (Military reserves), in accordance with Richard's use of an extended military metaphor: just as a king attempting to take a city will, as a last resort, call upon his reserves, so the narrator-protagonist of the *Bestiaire d'amours,* having failed to conquer his lady through singing, makes his last stand by sending her his bestiary. The *Bestiaire d'amours* enjoyed an immediate and widespread popularity. It survives today in seventeen manuscripts of the thirteenth, fourteenth, and fifteenth centuries, including three of Italian origin; it inspired a variety of continuations and reworkings, as well as extensive programs of illumination. In Chapter 2 we saw that Richard de Fournival is one of two trouvères represented as a writer in chansonnier *A,* a tribute to his scholarly reputation. As both clerc and trouvère, author of chansons courtoises and of learned Latin treatises, Richard is an important figure in the history of lyrical writing.[1] His *Bestiaire d'amours,* a declaration of love and plea for "mercy" in which the first-person narrator uses traditional bestiary lore as a repository of metaphors for the experience of love, partakes of both the courtly lyric and the didactic bestiary tradition and presents a fascinating blend of clerkly and lyric elements. The manuscript tradition of the *Bestiaire d'amours* reflects its dual aspect of learned didactic form, a prose bestiary, and lyrical content, an expression of love. It is often transmitted in conjunction with the *Image du monde,* the *Bestiaire divin,* lapidaries, or a translation of the *Fables d'Ysopet.* Sometimes it is linked to other lyrical texts: the *Rose,* lyric poet-

---

1. In his edition of Richard de Fournival's *Oeuvre lyrique,* Lepage discusses Richard's identity and his various literary and scientific accomplishments. See also Richard de Fournival, "La Biblionomie."

ry, dits d'amours. In some codices, indeed, the *Bestiaire d'amours* serves to mediate between didactic and lyrical texts, as will be seen below. The blend of clerkliness and lyricism is further reflected in the varied iconography of the prologue miniatures, some manuscripts stressing the lyrical aspects of the text—oral declamation, music, love—and some the clerkly activities of teaching and writing.

The *Bestiaire d'amours* prologue is an important statement about the poetics of lyrical writing in the mid-thirteenth century. Richard states that his text is an illustrated written document, to be experienced visually, but that writing itself is the embodiment of speech. The components of his text, he states, are speech (*parole*) and painting (*painture*): it appeals to both ear and eye. As we saw in Chapter 3, the interplay of visuality and aurality, lyric performance and illustrated text, underlies the lyrico-narrative structure of the *Rose* as well. Richard, however, makes the audiovisual nature of the text his explicit point of departure. Although with texts so closely contemporary it is difficult to be certain of direct relationships, the *Bestiaire d'amours* was probably influenced by Guillaume's *Rose*. Guillaume de Lorris posed the question of written lyric discourse; the unfinished quality of the poem suggests the dangerous influence of lyric stasis and Narcissistic self-involvement on the narrative structure. Richard, in the opening pages of the *Bestiaire d'amours,* offers a different perspective, somewhat similar to that of Jean de Meun and other respondents to Guillaume de Lorris: the creation of the written text enables the lover to record his voice and send it to his lady, thereby averting the dangers of lyric ephemerality, sterility, isolation. In the *Bestiaire d'amours,* the movement from song to writing is presented as an essential step toward resolution of the lover's plight; through his arriere ban he hopes at last to reach his lady's heart.

In order to appreciate the innovative nature of the *Bestiaire d'amours,* we must first examine briefly the bestiary tradition from which it derives. The discussion in Chapter 1 of the *Bestiaire divin* and MS Bibl. Nat. fr. 24428 provides some background for the thirteenth-century reception of the bestiary. A further look at the *Bestiaire divin* will help to establish the clerkly context in which the *Bestiaire d'amours* operates and to identify the ways in which Richard has modified and lyricized the bestiary format.

## Lyricization of the Bestiary: Guillaume le Clerc and Richard de Fournival

Guillaume le Clerc, author of the *Bestiaire divin,* identifies his poem as a translation "en romanz" (into the Romance vernacular) from the "bon latin" (good Latin) of the original (Reinsch ed., vv. 8–9). The Latin text that stands behind Guillaume's romance version is itself grounded in anterior texts, for it mediates between two signifying systems, that of the natural world and that of sacred history. Guillaume moves through a series of birds and beasts, treating each in turn as an allegory of the drama of Fall and Redemption. The bestiary is presented as a collection of *essamples* (exemplary images) that, though arranged as a nonnarrative catalog, combine to form a picture of sacred history and in particular of the life of Christ. The poet evokes the grandeur and scope of this history, explaining that he cannot recount it in its entirety but that the bestiary format will allow for a series of partial formulations. Although the bestiary is built up out of isolated textual units, he explains, all participate in the larger story of Salvation, which provides an underlying continuity to the seemingly discontinuous series of essamples: although his material is diverse and varied, "neporquant si est tot une" (nonetheless it is all one [v. 347]). Toward the end of the poem, finally, Guillaume evokes once more the inexhaustibility of Christ's life as a source of literary material, of which "Boche d'ome ne porreit dire / La some" (Human lips cannot speak the sum total [vv. 3428–29]). But through "Les essamples del bestiaire" (The examples of the bestiary [v. 3442]) he has illuminated numerous aspects of this vast field.

Thus the *Bestiaire divin* participates in a complex system of textual filiation based on equivalences between sign systems of different sorts, linked through a process of translation. The beasts of the world are a living visual text that can be decoded to reveal its conformity to the text of God's Word; the Latin bestiary that was Guillaume's source articulates this system of correspondences. Guillaume in turn decodes this Latin text by translating it into the vernacular. In so doing, he also appropriates the diction of oral address, exhorting his audience to "listen"—for example, "Or oëz que dit li Normanz" (Now hear what the Norman says [v. 36])—and frequently using the first-person plural, which binds performer and audience as adherents to a common system of belief—for example, "Or priom Deu, qui nos crea" (Now let us pray to God, who created us [v. 4121]). As narrator-translator, Guillaume mediates between his French-speaking public and a written Latin authority: the allegorical system of the text in turn serves not only to mediate between the realms of natural and divine but also to delineate the shared experiences of temptation and salvation that unify the members of the Christian community.

Richard de Fournival's *Bestiaire d'amours* participates in the bestiary tradition but effects some interesting transformations of the basic model. For one thing, it posits not a learned, Latin authority but a lyrical, personal one: the author proposes that the beasts of the world are a text that records his own experience. Not divine but human love is the key to decoding this text, and he has recourse to this format not because it enables him to offer highlights of an infinitely expanding cosmic history but because it enables him to express his own inner feelings, otherwise inexpressible. After explaining in the prologue that he has decided to stop singing, which he now sees as a futile and even dangerous occupation, the narrator compares himself and his lady to various animals. He does not move systematically through a series of beasts, as Guillaume le Clerc did. The *Bestiaire d'amours* is first and foremost a declaration of love and a plea for the lady's "mercy"; animals are introduced, sometimes at length, sometimes only in passing, and in some cases repeatedly, to illustrate the lover's predicament.

The *Bestiaire d'amours*, then, is a lyricization and secularization of the *Bestiaire divin*. It addresses erotic rather than divine love, and its focus is on the first-person lyric persona at its core; the shared experience expressed in the allegorical system is aimed not at a large-scale community unification but at the private unification of lover and beloved. At the same time, Richard adopts a more writerly stance than his clerkly predecessor, for instead of moving from the language of writing (Latin) to that of speech (French), Richard moves from song to writing. In its intricate interpenetration of lyrical and writerly modes, Richard's work parallels that of Guillaume de Lorris, who constructed a romance ostensibly based not on a written source but on a dream. That lyricism can provide an authoritative basis for a written text is, again, a fundamental principle of French verse composition in the later Middle Ages.

## *Parole* and *Painture:* Richard's Audiovisual Poetics

The passage from song to book and the nature of lyrical writing are precisely what Richard addresses in his prologue. Here he identifies sight and hearing—*veïr* and *oïr*—as the doors to memory, and he states that he is using these two means of approach in an attempt to establish himself in his lady's memory. He explains that his text consists of both parole, which is heard; and painture, which is seen. He stresses the importance of the pictures, stating that "cis escris est de tel sentence k'il painture desire" (this writing is on a topic that calls for illustration [Segre ed., p. 7]). The instructional value of pictures, which work together with the words of the text to communicate a particular set of teachings, is a topos of the learned tradition. One is reminded, for example, of the prologue to the *Image du monde,* in which we are told that without its figures the book could not easily be understood. Although the *Image* has no theoretical formulation comparable to Richard's, its diagrams are clearly an integral part of the text, announced by such formulas as "Et regarder poëz par cest / Figure escripte, qui ci est" (And you can see [it] by this written figure, which is here). There follows at this point a map of the cosmos, after which the text continues: "Ces set estoiles que je di /

Que vous oëz deviser ci . . ." (These seven stars that I speak of, which you hear explained here . . . [MS Bibl. Nat. fr. 24428, fol. 29v]).[2] In many manuscripts (including MS 24428) these illustrations are not framed miniatures against an ornamental background but rather are figures drawn on the blank parchment like the words themselves; they too are "written" and are closely integrated into the text. Words and diagrams together form a visual text; in the act of reading, words become oral ("Which you hear explained here") while the diagrams remain visual ("You can see"). Although never raised to a theoretical principle, the distinction between the oral writing and the visual diagrams and the particular contribution made by each are ubiquitous features of the discourse of the *Image*. In the epilogue found in some manuscripts, the audience is addressed as "Vous qui avés oï l'escrit" (You who have heard the writing [MS Bibl. Nat. fr. 12469, fol. 71v]) and presented with a final map in which they can see (*veïr*) the shape of the cosmos.

The importance of diagrams for a scientific treatise may seem a special case, but miniatures were an important part of any text that revolved around descriptions of places, objects, or people.[3] In a thirteenth-century treatise on the mythical races of the Orient, for example, the miniatures that represent the creatures in question are sometimes announced by a line such as, "Ves les ci ensinc / Pains con li livres le tesmogne" (See them here, depicted just as the book tells of it [MS Bibl. Nat. fr. 1506, fol. 9]). Similarly, the miniatures of the *Bestiaire divin*, though never explicitly evoked within the text, play an important role. This is especially true when, in codices such as MS 24428, the miniatures represent both the animal and the sacred event to which it refers; the entire allegorical system is visually as well as verbally depicted. The life of Christ and the events of sacred history unfold before our eyes and ears as we move through the progression of birds and beasts, seeing the pictures and hearing the words.

Richard's prologue thus links the *Bestiaire d'amours* to a learned tradi-

---

2. On the use of diagrams in medieval books and the visuality of the page, see Evans. He discusses astronomical diagrams (pp. 43–44) and reproduces an example from the *Image* (fig. 16).

3. The didactic function of visual images was recognized from the early Middle Ages. A well-known testimony to this consciousness is Gregory the Great's characterization of church sculpture as a "Bible for the illiterate" in two epistles to the Bishop Serenus of Marseilles (*Patrolog. Lat.*, 77, cols. 1027–28 and 1128–30). An interesting example contemporary with the composition of the *Bestiaire d'amours* is Joinville's illustrated *Credo*, explicitly designed as a text of words and images that can serve to bring the Word of God to the sick or dying by means of the senses of sight and hearing; see Friedman's commentary in his edition of Joinville's work. For general discussion of the importance of illustration in medieval texts and examples of texts that explicitly call attention to their visual presentation, see Curschmann. Although Curschmann's primary focus is German literature, he discusses a number of French examples as well, including the *Bestiaire d'amours*. See also Camille, "Book of Signs."

tion of illustrated treatises, as is appropriate for a bestiary. But at the same time Richard also evokes a slightly different function of images. In discussing the importance of visual signs, he cites not scientific or philosophical treatises but, rather, the story of Troy. The importance of the illustrations as described here is not to provide diagrams of military maneuvers but, rather, to create the presence of historical figures: "on fait present de chu ki est trespassé par ces .ij. coses, c'est par painture et par parole" (one makes present that which is past by means of these two things, that is, image and speech [p. 5]). That is, the function of the miniatures in this context is not, or not only, didactic but also performative; we have, in effect, a script and a cast of characters who enact the story. Richard thus associates his text with the tradition of didactic or scientific treatises and also with a vernacular tradition of illustrated poetry. The dual appeal of *veïr* and *oïr*, indeed, can be a function of the illuminated manuscript as an audiovisual construct or of performance, in which an audible voice combines with visual gestures. The *Bestiaire d'amours* is at once a scientific treatise that instructs through language and visual images, and a re-creation of lyric performance that enables the lover to address his lady by proxy.

As the *Bestiaire d'amours* proper begins, the narrator continues to elaborate the themes of sight and hearing. Almost the entire first half of the *Bestiaire d'amours* concerns the initiation, continuation, or expression of love by means of visual signals, speech, or music. The sight and sound of the lady bewitch the lover, who in turn communicates his feelings to her by means of song, words, or gestures. At the midpoint (pp. 33–43), a discourse on the five senses leads into an account of the stages of love: it begins with sight, increases as the senses of hearing and smell are engaged, moves on to taste with the first kiss, and is fully consummated through touch. The narrator states that love so far has taken over his sense of sight, hearing, and smell; he has therefore lost his memory, since, as stated in the prologue, sight and hearing are the doors to memory.

This return to the prologue has the important effect of linking the discussion of memory as an epistemological faculty to the discussion of love. Sight and hearing, image and text, were originally presented as vehicles for the transmission of knowledge. Now they have become vehicles for the transmission of love. Memory is not only an intellectual but also an affective faculty, and the illustrated book is an instrument of seduction as well as instruction. The seductive quality of language is a theme well attested in the Latin tradition; Richard here exploits it to support his fusion of lyricism and bookishness.[4] Music and writing; song and book; *dous regart* (sweet look), *dous parler* (sweet speech), and a scientific treatise with instructional figures: between these seemingly

---

4. See, for example, book 1 of Augustine's *De doctrina christiana*.

disparate poles there emerges a common ground of audiovisual communication.

The distinction between singing and writing is formulated explicitly through the first five bestiary examples. The lover explains that, like the cock crowing at midnight and the ass braying in hunger, he has a desperate need to express himself. But, like the wolf that is struck dumb when caught off guard by a man, he has lost his voice, so that "cis escris n'est mie fais en cantant, mais en contant" (this writing is not done as singing, but as narration [p. 12]). Writing is already the solution to one classic lyric dilemma. The lover who is too shy to address his lady need not wait for her to hear one of his songs: he can write to her. Moreover, the lover continues, singing is dangerous business. Playing with the lyric topos of immanent death, he cites the cricket, so distracted by the pleasures of singing that it allows itself to be killed, and the swan, which sings beautifully and then dies.[5] He comments:

> Et pour che vous di jou ke por le paour ke j'oi de la mort au chine, quant jou cantai miex, et de la mort au crisnon, quant jou le fis plus volentiers, por chu lassai le canter a cest arriereban faire, et le vous envoiai en maniere de contreescrit.

> [And so I tell you that because of the fear I had for the swan's death, when I sang better, and for the cricket's death, when I did it more willingly, for that reason I left off singing in order to make this arriere ban, and I sent it to you in the form of a transcription.] [P. 14]

We saw earlier that Jean de Meun's use of Pygmalion as the answer to Narcissus suggests that writing has the advantage of allowing the lover to record his desire in a text or image external to himself. Richard, too, turns to writing as the escape from the lyrical death of nightingale and swan, a death of self-absorption that is ultimately equivalent to the death of Narcissus: the lover as writer can fix his sentiments permanently in a concrete form that will serve to ensure his lasting presence while at the same time remaining himself distinct from the text that he has written. Unlike a mirror image, a performed song, or the Narcissus flower, the book is separable from its author. It can exist without him, and he need not die in order for it to come into being.

## Song, the Written Word, and the Word Made Flesh: Procreation and Incarnation in *Li Bestiaire d'amours* and *Le Roman de la rose*

If certain lyric dangers have been circumvented by means of the movement from song to writing, Richard's poetics nonetheless retains

5. Some manuscripts, as well as the *Bestiaire rimé*, read *rossignol* (nightingale) for *crisnon* (cricket), intensifying the lyric connotations.

essential lyric features. This becomes clear when we examine his use of the motif of birth. In several places, he interprets birth as the image for the lady's acceptance of her lover. In recounting the reproductive habits of certain animals, he explains that "li enfanters senefie le retenirs d'amours . . . adont fait une feme d'un homme son faon, quant elle le retient com ami" (giving birth signifies acceptance in love. . . . thus a woman makes a man her baby, when she retains him as her lover [p. 95]). This distortion of the normal pattern of procreation and descent is fundamentally circular: the would-be lover woos his lady, wins her, and so begets himself in a new identity as lover. The lady is an external vantage point by means of which the author can create himself. The written text, as instrument of seduction, is a crucial part of this process. The author sends out the text in which he places himself as authority and suppliant; the lady, through a sympathetic reading, in turn re-creates him as lover. The written text functions as a locus for displaced sexual interaction, as the relationship of lover-performer and lady-audience is transformed into that of the mutually defining writer and reader.

Richard makes a further use of the birth motif in the example of the weasel, where women's unfavorable responses to their lovers' words are likened to the weasel's manner of conception through the ear and birth through the mouth: "quant elles ont oï tant de biax mos, k'il leur sanle k'eles doivent amer et k'eles ont ausi com conceü par l'orelle, si s'en delivrent par le bouce a .i. escondit" (When they have heard so many beautiful words that it seems to them that they should love and that they have as it were conceived through the ear, then they give birth through the mouth to a refusal [pp. 26–27]). Richard here intensifies the sexual implications of the reading-writing relationship: he has already stated in the prologue that his treatise is an appeal to his lady by means of eye and ear, and now he likens the lady's reception of his words to an act of sexual coupling. In this model, however, she is to give birth not to him but to further words, the text of her refusal. Thus the act of text production on the part of the male lover-writer engenders either himself as lover or more text; in either case, it engenders a response from the lady as reader-audience. In this way the strict lyric identity of narrator and protagonist is modified. The "I" passes from generating text from and about himself to being an element in a text generated reciprocally by himself and the lady; into the tight configuration of the lyric "I" Richard introduces a second "I" and makes the role of reader an integral part of the construct.

Richard's treatment of the thematic nexus of lyricism, writing, and procreation provides an interesting background for Jean de Meun's use of these elements thirty or forty years later. I have already suggested a relationship between Jean's use of Pygmalion and Richard's insistence on the medium of writing: a brief digression into the *Rose* will serve to identify further points of contact between Jean's *Rose* and Richard's *Bestiaire d'amours* and to elucidate the poetic statement that each author is making. As we saw in Chapter 3, the motif of procreation was associated in the *Rose* with that of writing and reflected Jean de Meun's relationship with the text of desire, which was external to him in a way that Guillaume's text of his own desire was not. A note of ambivalence is introduced, however, through the incestuous nature of the line that Pygmalion and Galatea produce; it turns in on itself with the love of Myrrha for her father Cinyras and, with the love of Adonis and Venus, finally returns full circle to the deity under whose auspices the line began. This circularity, reminiscent of "the circularity of song,"[6] is incorporated into the narrative structure of Jean's poem through his relocation of the Adonis story to an earlier narrative moment: by the time we get to the account of his birth as descendent of Pygmalion, we have already heard about his death, so the story, too, feeds back into itself.[7]

The story of Adonis has a particular relevance to the *Rose* in that Adonis's transformation into a flower, through disobedience to love and failure to heed the pleas of the lady that loves him, repeats the fate of Narcissus. Although Jean de Meun suppresses thé metamorphosis of Adonis in his retelling of the story, the full Ovidian account would have been well known to educated thirteenth-century readers; the motif of flower lies just beneath the textual surface, linking the figures of Narcissus, Adonis, and l'Amant himself, in love with a rose. As a result of the inverted narrative structure, the figure of Adonis mediates between the figures of Narcissus and Pygmalion, providing a link between the two myths that inform the poem. The story of Narcissus and Echo, in two parts, presents first the story of Narcissus pursued by the image of his own words; then that of Narcissus pursuing his own visual image. Pygmalion in turn desires his creation, the image of his desire; the coupling of Pygmalion and his "ymage" in turn engenders the situation of Cinyras, desired by his own (biological) creation. The story of Narcissus and Echo is mirrored in the linked stories of Pygmalion-Galatea and Cinyras-Myrrha, whereas the story of Adonis has elements in common with both.

The moral drawn by the narrator from the story of Adonis offers one clue to the function of this narrative configuration. Adonis, we are told, died because he failed to believe his lady. The need to believe absolutely the words of a "chose amée" (beloved thing) are reiterated at the end of the poem (vv. 21630–37), as if this is an essential element in l'Amant's

---

6. I refer, of course, to Zumthor's "De la circularité du chant," also elaborated in his *Essai de poétique médiévale*, pp. 211–12.

7. Brownlee discusses the figure of Adonis in the *Rose* in "Orpheus's Song."

successful conquest of the rose (and Jean's conquest of the *Rose* as well). Of the many couplings represented among the mythical characters, only one, that of Pygmalion and Galatea, is entirely successful. It would seem that what is required for generation to take place is for the progenitor, be he writer, artist, or begetter, to believe in the independent reality of his image or creation, to take it at face value and engage with its surface, and not to seek to understand its relationship to him or its underlying identity. Cinyras discovers that Myrrha is his own offspring and reacts with murderous rage, attempting to undo the fruits of his own begetting. Narcissus realizes that the image he desires has no reality to it; he fails to accept Echo's desire as real. Pygmalion, however, does believe in the reality of his image, even while knowing at the same time that it is his own creation.

A similar fiction is required of the writer: he must believe in the reality of the text, asserting that it embodies its own truth, that it constitutes an Other. Jean acknowledges that this is a fiction and that the lyrical writer in particular is really only engaging with himself; he has neither the live audience of the singer nor the external referent of the chronicler, hagiographer, or romancier. Nonetheless, the figurative language of poetic allegory and the materiality of the written text constitute a reality unto themselves that can carry the project to fruition.

The movement from the myth of Narcissus to that of Pygmalion is telling in this regard. The two sides of the Narcissus story contrast oral and visual imaging of the self; this mythical construct is appropriate to the poetics of a fundamentally lyrical narrative, in which song is transposed into writing. The stories of Pygmalion and Cinyras, on the other hand, contrast artistic and biological filiation; this construct is appropriate to a poetics of textual reification. Jean further demonstrates the concretization of figurative language through his preservation of the courtly allegory through to the end of the poem: l'Amant makes love to the rose as a rose, and we are left with the image of a pregnant rosebud.

While Richard and Jean handle the image of birth and procreation differently, both in effect create a "genealogy" of textual and biological filiation that is self-duplicating and circular—what we might term a lyrical genealogy. In Richard's model the successful lover engenders himself by means of the seductive language he addresses to his lady; in his new identity as "offspring" (*faon*) he presumably addresses to her still more words that engender further response. The text is both the locus of interaction between lovers and the product of that interaction; Richard's construct thus resembles that portrayed by Jakemes in the *Roman du castelain de Couci*. Jakemes differs from Richard, though, in his more strongly suggestive development of the analogy between the text as artifact of desire and the lady as object of desire. This latter step is central for Jean de Meun; in his model the primary relationship is now between writer and text. The reader in turn is generalized: Jean de Meun no longer addresses the lady "worthy of being called rose" but, rather, an indefinite audience of "amorous lords" and "valiant ladies" (vv. 15129, 15165) who observe him as he interacts with his text.

The *Bestiaire d'amours* has another point in common with the *Rose:* both pit the model of lyrical writing and human desire against that of sacred writing and divine love. Richard leaves the opposition implicit, but his choice of the bestiary format inevitably raises the association of his text with the *Bestiaire divin.* Jean in turn makes the association explicit, with the discussions of divine providence and the Incarnation during the discourse of Nature, and Genius's comparison of the garden to the *biaus parc* of Heaven. Again, the two authors handle the motif differently, but a comparison of their respective methods helps to reveal some of the common ground occupied by these two important instances of lyrical writing.

We can begin this investigation with what may seem, initially, an unlikely question: what does Christ have in common with the lyric persona and, in particular, with the persona of the *Bestiaire d'amours?* Interestingly, one can form a striking analogy between the Trinity and the lyric construct. God the Father, His Word, and the love that binds them are conjoined as one; similarly, the lyric persona, his song, and the love that he feels are interdependent and inseparable.[8] The creative process by which song becomes writing imitates the divine creative process of the Incarnation of the Word; the lyric writer creates a visible icon of himself. In the *Bestiaire d'amours,* as we have seen, there is in fact a suggestion that this initial production of text is but a prelude to the successful conquest of the lady, whereby the lover-writer "begets" himself. Indeed, Richard's image of aural begetting recalls that of the Virgin Mary, who conceived the Word of God through the ear.

The *Bestiaire divin* is constructed around the medieval fourfold allegory, built on a movement from a diversity of signs to a unity of meaning. As cited above, Guillaume le Clerc comments that his seemingly diverse subject matter of birds and beasts resolves itself into the uniform matter of moral teachings; this is the tropological reading of the natural world. In the allegorical reading, the diverse moral teachings themselves further resolve into the single model of the marriage of Christ and the Church; and the Church is the body of Christ as well as his bride so that all signs ultimately lead to Christ, the Word that contains the meanings of all other words. Finally, the anagogical reading, which concerns "last things," emerges with the discussion of the Last Judgment at the end of

---

8. The notion of the "lyric triangle," uniting self, love, and song, was developed by Professor Karl D. Uitti of Princeton University in his graduate seminars on Old French literature, which I attended from 1976 to 1979.

the poem. A similar movement from one level of meaning to another informs the *Bestiaire d'amours:* the diversity of animals is resolved first into the body of love teachings, then into the specific model of the protagonist and his lady. While the final consummation of this relationship is only hinted at within Richard's text, this aspect is fully developed in an anonymous continuation appearing in two fourteenth-century manuscripts of the *Bestiaire d'amours,* as will be discussed later. Whether the continuator was imitating the format of the *Bestiaire divin* is, of course, highly debatable, but it is interesting that the structure of the *Bestiaire d'amours* was such as to elicit the corresponding final passage.

Richard's use of allegory is consistent with his view of the text as a means of intercourse between writer and reader, lover and lady. Writing gives a body to his speech; it also creates a meeting place between the two experiential realms, the two codes, of natural world and human love. Writing has the fundamental quality of mediating and conjoining; it creates a nexus, a space for interaction and translation. The *Bestiaire d'amours,* as a system of signs, presents an allegory of the relationship between reader and writer, who are thus located simultaneously within and outside the textual construct; it provides an artificial space where they can meet and interact.

If the relationship between reader and writer is crucial for Richard, that of writer and text, along with the dynamics of signification, is central to Jean de Meun's *Rose,* as I have said. The lyric motif of the self as referent for an entire environment of signs lies at the basis of Jean's use of divinity as a counterpoint to Narcissus. As stated in Chapter 3, Narcissus represents a dual crisis of love and signification: his inability to realize his desire is a function of his inability to resolve the relationship between self and image of self, sign and referent. Caught in this dilemma, Narcissus wastes away and is ultimately replaced, in Ovid, by the flower that bears his name, or, in Guillaume de Lorris, by the written image of his name. Narcissus becomes an image of himself. And Narcissus is later contrasted with Pygmalion, whose miracle is that of image made flesh. Playing off both of these mythical figures is the Christian Trinity. Nature tells us that God (like Narcissus!) gazes into a "mirouer pardurable" (eternal mirror [v. 17438]); in fact, "Cil mirouers c'est li meïsmes" (He himself is this mirror [v. 17441]). In the Trinity, sign, referent, and that which mediates between the two are separate yet one, as are Father, Son, and the love that binds them. The three-point opposition of Narcissus, Pygmalion, and trinitarian God implicitly states the thematic nexus, fundamental to the poetics of the *Rose,* that I have described: in the figure of Christ, Son of God and Incarnation of the Word, the mysteries of love, of lineage, and of signification are perfectly fused.

A second aspect of Jean's use of sacred allegory is the debate, running

throughout the poem, about figurative discourse, poetic truth, and linguistic propriety. This debate is sparked, appropriately enough, by Reason's naming of the organs of sexual generation. The testicles of Saturn,
she states, gave birth to Venus: castration, the displacement or suppression of the sexual organs, entails the birth of erotic desire and at the
same time renders the consummation of such desire impossible. Analo-
gously, the suppression of the words *coilles* (balls) and *viz* (prick) in
courtly diction, and the displacement of eroticism through poetic artifice, prolongs desire and obstructs its fulfillment. Such linguistic "castration" results in the generation of endless words that at once signify
and obscure sexual functions; the courtly lover-poet accordingly finds
himself in the dilemma dramatized by Guillaume de Lorris's "incomplete" poem.

In this context, Christ represents linguistic propriety in its purest
form: a unique instance in which sign and referent are not separated at
all. His opposite pole, from this perspective, is False Semblance, who
represents the complete dissociation of sign and referent, the ultimate
linguistic "castration" leading to the ultimate promiscuity of signification. As shape-shifter and seducer, False Semblance is an endless generator of signs with no referent at all, the complete inversion of Christ as
absolute referent in whom all signs come to rest. The God of Love,
patron of courtly diction, plays off these two extremes as generator of
poetic truth, a tricky and changeable business that mediates between the
poles of absolute truth and absolute falsehood and may at times partake
of both.

With such figures as Narcissus, Pygmalion, False Semblance, and
Christ, Jean establishes multiple models of writing and its potential dangers and powers. As I implied in Chapter 3, the discourse of Genius and
the final passage of the poem suggest that some resolution has been
reached. Genius moves effortlessly between the iconography of lyric
Narcissism and that of Christian allegory, demonstrating the power of
the written word to mediate between different poetic registers, to express more than it says. The ending, finally, accomplishes what had
theretofore seemed impossible: the consummation of desire within the
bounds of courtly diction. That the rose becomes pregnant is consistent
with Jean's overriding interest in the production of signification; what is
important for him is less the relationship between the lover and the lady
who "reads" him than the generation of meaning through the writer's
interaction with his text.

The comparison of Richard de Fournival and Jean de Meun serves to
highlight the contrasting modes of lyrical writing developed during the
thirteenth century. Richard focuses on the theatrical nature of song,
transposing the performative aspects of lyricism into a text that offers a
forum for communication between writer and reader. Jean focuses on

the close identification of lyric persona and text and on the dynamics by which song is generated from the state of desire; he establishes a similarly self-generating and self-reflexive poetics of writing. These modes of lyrical writing were important elements of the literary experiments of this period; we have seen a somewhat similar contrast in Jean Renart's *Rose* and Jakemes's *Roman du castelain de Couci*. The *Rose* of Guillaume de Lorris, that of Jean de Meun, and the *Bestiaire d'amours* all exerted a strong influence on subsequent poets. As a first step toward assessing the influence of the *Bestiaire d'amours*, we can begin with the most immediate responses it elicited—the continuations and redactions to which it was subject and the programs of illumination with which it was embellished.

## Amplification of *Li Bestiaire d'amours:* Responses and Continuations

To judge from the surviving manuscripts, the most widely disseminated continuation of the *Bestiaire d'amours* was the anonymous *Response du Bestiaire,* which follows the *Bestiaire d'amours* in the thirteenth-century MSS Paris, Bibl. Nat. fr. 412 and 25566 and Dijon, Bibl. Mun. 526, and the fourteenth-century MS Vienna, Nationalbibl. 2609.[9] Here the lady writes back, stating that she has read the arriere ban and reworking the system of metaphors in such a way that the animals now become a series of lessons about love from her perspective. The lover called her a siren? No, she says, he is the siren, attempting to enchant her with his honeyed words (*beau parler*). Again, he has called himself a unicorn, bewitched by a virgin. Indeed, she says, just as the unicorn bears a lethal weapon in its sharp horn, so he bears the lethal and cutting implement of speech. As the lady works through the series of animals, replying to his arguments, we realize that the entire allegorical construct has become bivalent. It is here, in the textual system, that lover and lady are conjoined as writers and readers of one another.

In this sense the format of the *Bestiaire d'amours,* and especially its material existence as a book, has allowed the lyric circle of isolation to be broken. The *Bestiaire d'amours* and its *Response* are the germ of an epistolary novel; through writing, lover and lady can communicate. Again, we are reminded of the *Roman du castelain de Couci,* where the lovers collaborate in writing their own story through the exchange of letters, and, although less directly, of Renart's *Rose,* where the format of the written compilation allows the lyric register of Conrad's *grand chant courtois* to

---

9. For descriptions of the manuscripts of the *Bestiaire d'amours,* see Segre's edition, pp. xxxiii–lxv. I thank the Hill Monastic Manuscript Library, St. John's Abbey and University, Collegeville, Minn., for providing me with a microfilm of Vienna MS 2609.

interact with Lïenor's register of chanson de toile and with the general background of dance refrains. Within the space of the book, at once performative and literary, lover and lady can be conjoined through the juxtaposition of texts and ultimately by their common participation in a shared poetic system.

The open-ended potential for this sort of continuation is reflected in Vienna MS 2609, an Artesian manuscript dating from the second quarter of the fourteenth century. Here the *Bestiaire d'amours* and *Response* are embedded in a series of prose texts that form an ongoing dialogue between a man and a woman. The *Bestiaire d'amours* is preceded by *La Vraie Medecine d'amours,* a declaration of love that focuses on love-sickness and the lover's need to be cured by the lady, attributed to Bierniers de Chartres, and by *La Response del onguement de la vraie medechine d'amours,* a dialogue between the lover and his lady in which different types of lovers are enumerated and love psychology further elaborated. The *Response du Bestiaire* is followed by the lover's rejoinder (without title), itself followed in turn by a further response from the lady. A rubric on the last page indicates that at one time this text was followed by "li livres de Ovide de art en roumans" (Ovid's book of art in Romance vernacular [fol. 52v]), presumably a translation of the *Ars Amatoria.*

There can be little doubt that the remaining two final pieces were written for the purpose of following the *Bestiaire d'amours;* they are the work of another author-compiler. It is less clear for what purpose the two opening pieces were written, but they too are certainly the work of someone familiar with Richard's work, for the prologue of the *Medecine* invokes "li boins clers Maistre Richars de Furnival" (the good clerk Master Richard de Fournival [fol. 1]) and cites the prologue of the *Bestiaire d'amours.* Bierniers, the author of the *Medecine,* makes the leap suggested by Richard's implicit analogy between memory and love. After recapitulating the inability of any one person to know everything and the strength of Divine Love, which sought to remedy this situation—the discussion that in the *Bestiaire d'amours* led into the discussion of memory—the *Medecine* narrator announces that God's gift to the human race was love, "aloiance d'amor et de recreation par la vertu et la fragilité de la char, entre home et feme" (the linking of love with procreation by the virtue and the fragility of the flesh, between man and woman [fol. 1]). Further allusion to the *Bestiaire d'amours* prologue and to the analogy between memory and love appears in the *Response del onguement,* which includes a discussion of *veoir* and *oïr* as the two gates to memory and love. Both texts additionally employ bestiary imagery, though less systematically than Richard de Fournival.

In a most interesting and somewhat peculiar extension of the love-sickness topos, the *Medecine* also picks up the importance of writing and the status of the written text as a material representative of the lover-writer. After stating that his sickness can be cured only by a special ointment of love, the narrator reveals that, in fact, the ointment that currently relieves his distress is the ink with which his love plaints are written:

> Si me douteroie jou qu'il ne moustrast mie si soingneusement ma besoingne comme cis escris, qui est fais et escris dou plus cier ongement que nus mires poroit faire . . . que li communs de la gent doit apieler "enke." Mais en cestui escrit le voel jou apieler "ongement."

> [Thus I would doubt that anything would show my need as fully as this writing, which is made and written in the most precious ointment that any doctor could make . . . which the common people have to call "ink." But in this writing I want to call it "ointment."] [Fol. 2v]

The act of writing in itself soothes the distraught lover; in spreading ink on the page he is figuratively anointing himself. As the discussion continues, he refers to the ink as "the ink of my heart" (fol. 4) and stresses that it is a refined and subtle substance, for it is made not of harsh chemicals, but rather of thought (*pensee*), the "most subtle and invisible" substance known (ibid.). The ink, in other words, is the visible manifestation of the lover's thoughts; the voice of the *Medecine* is purely a written voice. Although the *Medecine* does not refer to Richard's discussion of writing as a substitution for song, Bierniers has clearly made the same association: for him, the written word is the visible emanation of his love, just as the song is the aural emanation of the trouvère's love. We could hardly ask for a more explicit account of what I have termed "lyrical writing."

That the written text functions as the representative of the writer, finally, is expressed in the narrator's final address to the lady. He states, first of all, that he will tell her how to heal him, just as the physician learns how to heal his patient by studying a urine sample. This reference to the urine sample recalls a miniature, placed alongside the first discussion of the ink as an ointment, which shows a bed-ridden patient and a doctor with a flask, captioned, "Li phisisyens qui regarde l'eurine au malade" (The physician who looks at the sick man's urine [fol. 2v]). This miniature follows a series of miniatures representing the lovesick narrator languishing in bed, all captioned with rubrics in which he is referred to as "li malade" (the sick man); it is only natural to assume that the patient whose urine is examined is the same "malade." The combined effect of the miniature, juxtaposed with the detailed discussion of the ink with which the text is penned and the later allusion to the text as a means of instructing the physician-lady just as the urine sample instructs the physician, is to suggest an analogy—albeit somewhat unexpected—between the inked words that flow from the narrator's heart and the urine that flows from his body. Ink and urine alike figure the lover and provide a text from which an informed reader can learn about his emotional or physical health.

In his final request for healing, the narrator explains that there are actually three ointments of which he has need. The first is his ink; the second is that his lady take the message that he has written her to heart and think of it often; the third is that she accept him into her service, "que cis escris ne soit mie peris" (in order that this writing not perish [fol. 4v]). Clearly, the "ointment" has become entirely figurative by this point. It is interesting that a plea for requital in love should focus almost exclusively on the fate of the written text; again, if this text is understood in erotic and procreative terms, then it is clearly essential that the lady read it and keep it from "perishing."

The motifs of sickness, of urine sample, and of sending a written plea for healing return in the untitled rejoinder to the *Response du Bestiaire*, which is introduced by the rubric "Ici respont amis a amee apriés la Response de la dame" (Here [male] friend replies to [female] beloved after the response of the lady [fol. 41v]). The lover's response takes the form of a narrative about Galen's efforts to cure Cleopatra and her husband—who, in this compilation so full of surprises, turns out to be Alexander, king of Greece—and the counterefforts of the court physicians to thwart him by switching the urine samples. In the course of the resulting intrigue, Cleopatra writes a letter to Galen, begging him to come to her and to save her life; again, the healer reads both a written text and a urine sample. Although this curious narrative does not seem to have much bearing on the *Bestiaire*—it is not even about love—the motif of reading and healing is used to establish its relevance to Richard's arriere ban. The outcome of the tale of Cleopatra, Alexander, and Galen is that the doctor must administer a cure the exact opposite of what the false urine samples had originally led him to prescribe. Even so, says the narrator, since his bestiary failed to elicit the cure he needed, "si me puist aidier et valoir li contraires" (may its opposite be of aid and value to me [fol. 43v]). Although this formulation does not have quite the suggestive richness of the *Medecine*, it does certainly support the analogy between urine sample and text. Since this image is not present in the *Bestiaire d'amours*, it would seem quite possible that the author of this piece drew on both the *Bestiaire d'amours* and the *Medecine*, and indeed may well have composed it specifically to follow the *Medecine-Bestiaire* progression.

The lady's second reply, finally, is a scholastic treatise on the categories and subcategories of love. Here, the text is figured as a *sop*, a chunk of bread soaked in wine; and again, the written text is the representative of its writer. The lady, who is evidently relenting to the lover's pleas, states that her treatise will keep him company in her absence, providing him with a source of "delight." This text, she explains, will help to stay his appetite: "Vous proi jou que . . . vous desjeunés de ceste soupe en vin, en esperance d'avoir miex au disner" (I pray you that . . . you break-fast on this sop, in hopes of having something better at dinner [fol. 44v]). And the text closes with the promise that the lover will eventually enjoy the lady's favors, which she will provide "selonc le vostre arriere ban" (according to your arriere ban [fol. 52v]).

We see here the indefinite expansion of the lyric configuration put into writing as the basis for conjoining the two original texts. The written text really does, it seems, have a tendency to increase and multiply, exemplifying the procreative principle of the love that it celebrates. As the prologue of the *Medecine* reminds us, God established love between man and woman not only for pleasure, but also "pour cou que d'eaus issist fruit qui a cent doubles montepliast" (in order that from them there issue fruit that would multiply two hundredfold [fol. 1]). In the *Medecine*, as in the *Bestiaire d'amours*, lyrical writing is an erotic and creative act, one that engenders an entire succession of responses.

The compilation that we have seen here is certainly heterogeneous; but the format of written dialogue, using love as the point of departure for metaphorical, allegorical, or philosophical discourse, can serve to unify almost any assortment of texts. Continuity within the compilation is assured through rubrics that identify each text as a response to the last, as well as by miniatures that represent the lovers in dialogue. One is reminded once again of Jean de Meun's *Rose*, where the original format of lyrical quest serves to generate seemingly unlimited material, as virtually everything is brought to bear on the general topic of love. And once again the movement from song to book entails a self-conscious lyrico-writerly poetics, essential to which are, in varying combinations and to varying degrees, the representation of writing as an act of love, an identification of writer and text, an exploitation of the anthology format, and a sense of the written text as a space within which writer and reader can interact.

A somewhat different use of compilation to create a context for the *Bestiaire* is found in the late-thirteenth-century Dijon MS Bibl. Mun. 526. The manuscript contains two short prose treatises on the stages and signs of love (fols. 1–3v): *Li Commens d'amours*, a prose treatise advising how a lover should comport himself and how he should address his lady, which includes narrative *exempla* and two short lyric citations with space for music, and is dedicated to the narrator's own lady (fols. 4–10v); *Le Poissance d'amours*, a prose dialogue between master and disciple about the nature of love, attributed to Richard de Fournival (fols. 10v–20v); the *Bestiaire d'amours*, also attributed in the explicit to Richard de Four-nival (fols. 20v–31); the *Response* (fols. 31–38); the *Roman de la rose* (fols.

38v–157); and some brief verse dits without titles or attributions (fols. 157v–160): an antifeminist poem, the last 130 lines of Baudouin de Condé's *Prison d'amours* and his *Conte de la rose*. On the final page of the last gathering is the *Turris sapientiae* of Johannes de Sancto Maxentio, a diagram of the virtues as elements of a fortified tower.[10] On an extra leaf bound in at the end of the book is a *Prière Nostre Dame*, attributed here to Richard de Fournival though elsewhere to Thibaut d'Amiens.

The last few pieces echo themes and motifs of the *Rose* and were probably chosen on this basis to finish out the final gathering; the prière, in a different hand from the rest of the manuscript, was probably added at a later time because of its association with Richard de Fournival. What is important here is the progression of prose works at the beginning, the *Rose*, and the relationship between these two parts of the codex. The corpus of prose texts defines a progression leading from the opening account of the stages of love through an exemplary love experience: the declaration of love is followed by a discussion of love comportment and the ways of causing a lady to yield; this body of texts is in turn followed by the arriere ban, as it is called here, a text that identifies itself as a final resort coming after an indeterminate number of other songs and declarations of love; and the sequence culminates finally in the lady's response, suggesting that she has begun to acquiesce. The lack of a clear break between the *Commens* and the *Poissance* implies a continuity of voice throughout the progression from "beginning" (commens) to "last resort" (arriere ban).

The poetics of the *Commens* is in keeping with that of the *Bestiaire d'amours* as I have described it above. The speaker adopts a lyric stance of love inspiration, invoking the God of Love and his lady, yet identifies his text as book (*livre*) rather than song. And once again the book is the representative of the speaker, sharing his quality of being illuminated (*enluminés*) by the grace of love.

The passage to the *Poissance* is marked only by a miniature representing a man sorrowfully reading a book, head in hand. This signals the movement from a discourse of love to one of love teaching, as is indicated by the opening lines:

Ki veut savoir et entendre le verité et la raison par coi ne de coi ne comment corages de femme est par force de nature esmeüs en amour, si mete diliganment l'entendement de son cuer a mon livre entendre.

[Whoever wishes to know and understand the truth and the reason why and how the heart of a woman is moved in love by force of nature, let him apply his heart diligently to the understanding of my book.] [Speroni ed., p. 30]

10. On the *Turris sapientiae*, see Evans, pp. 40–41 and fig. 12.

The pensive demeanor of the reader suggests, however, that his authority is founded not only on book learning but also on the experience of the pains of love; this is further suggested by the subsequent identification, in the explicit, of the author of the *Poissance* with Richard de Fournival, lover-author of the *Bestiaire d'amours*. Like the narrator of the *Bestiaire d'amours*, the master (*maistres*) of the *Poissance* combines lyric and learned authority.

The *Poissance* also shares with the *Bestiaire d'amours* the quality of seeming at once written and oral in its presentation. The narrator repeatedly refers to the project as a book; yet the format of dialogue is clearly oral in character. The disciple poses questions that are answered by the master, who in turn "drills" his pupil to test his understanding. Following the disciple's recapitulation of the argument, the master states, "Biaus fieus, bien m'avés entendu . . . et saciés, j'ai moustré et enseigné toute le Poissance et le verité de boine amour; et *Poissance d'amours* a mes livres a non" (Fair son, you have understood me well . . . and rest assured, I have taught the entire Power and the truth of good love; and my book is entitled *The Power of Love* [p. 77]). It is as though master and disciple are engaged in a conversation that takes place orally and is simultaneously recorded in the pages of the book. This instance of oral instruction is further juxtaposed with the lyric citations of the *Commens;* in these opening pages of the book, different kinds of orality and writing are played off one another. Again, lyric performance and learned dialogue fuse in the diction of lyrical writing.

This prose sequence, then, presents love teaching within an implied narrative of love experience; it contrasts and conflates clerkly and lyrical discourse, and juxtaposes different kinds of orality—musical, instructional—within a written format. As such it forms a whole comparable in many ways to the *Rose*, which follows. The parallelism of structure between the prose sequence and the *Rose* is underscored by the rubric appearing between the two parts of the *Rose:*

> A ches .ii. dairrains vers chi deseure fine li commencemens de le Rose ke Maistres Guillaumes de Lorris fist. Et a ches .ii. premiers [6ov] vers qui s'ensiwent le commencha a parfaire Maistres Jehans Chopinaus de Meun.

> [With these last two verses above ends the beginning of the Rose, which Master Guillaume de Lorris made. And with the next two verses that follow, Master Jean Chopinel de Meun began to complete it.] [Fol. 6o–6ov]

The movement from the "beginning of the Rose" to its conclusion by a different poet echoes the movement from the *Commens d'amours* to the *Poissance d'amours* and the bestiary texts, a movement that may also involve a change of author.[11] This parallel is further implied by the mini-

11. In her edition of the *Commens*, Saly argues that it is the work of Richard de Fournival.

atures at the beginning of the *Commens* and the *Poissance,* respectively. The former opens with an image of the God of Love shooting arrows at a man and a lady who kneel before him (fol. 4); a second miniature on the same page shows the man praying to the God of Love. The *Poissance,* however, opens with an image of a man reading a book. The iconography of love experience, and in particular of the powerful role of the God of Love, links the *Commens,* a predominantly lyrical text, to Guillaume de Lorris's lyrical romance. The iconography of clergie, on the other hand, links the *Poissance* to Jean de Meun's continuation, so frequently illustrated by the image of Jean as reader or writer. The arts of love with which the prose sequence opens further link this first half of the compilation to Guillaume's *Rose,* where "the art of love is all enclosed"; the greater emphasis on means of persuasion in the *Poissance* links this text to Jean de Meun's *Rose,* with its long discussions of seduction, persuasion, and assault. The *Bestiaire d'amours,* with its prologue motif of arriere ban—the text aids the lover in his conquest of the lady as a king's reserves aid in the capture of a city—corresponds to the battles waged in Jean's poem, whereas the *Response* suggests a similarly favorable ending: the lover does "get through" to his lady.[12]

The correspondence between the prose sequence and the *Rose* is naturally not absolute. But it is close enough to suggest a conscious act of compiling that responds to the affinities between the *Rose* and the *Bestiaire d'amours.* The arrangement of texts highlights the similarities between scribal compilational techniques and Jean de Meun's compilational poetics, pointing up, again, the quality of the *Rose* as a compendium, an anthology in narrative format. And it demonstrates the importance of Richard de Fournival, central figure of the prose sequence. Identified as author of both the *Poissance* and the *Bestiaire d'amours,* he

---

It is not actually attributed to him in the manuscript, however, and Saly's arguments do not strike me as conclusive. Although the compiler may certainly have believed that the *Commens* was the work of Richard, it seems equally likely that it was used as a preface to Richard's texts without any implication of authorship, just as Jean's poem could be the continuation of a poem by Guillaume de Lorris. The authorship of the *Poissance* is equally open to question, and my remarks are not meant to suggest that Richard must actually have written this treatise. Within the context of Dijon MS 526, however, the persona "Richard de Fournival" emerges as chancellor of Amiens and author of the *Poissance* and the *Bestiaire d'amours.*

12. In the prologue to his translation of Boethius's *De consolatione,* Jean de Meun himself described his contribution to the *Rose* entirely in terms of the storming of the castle and the plucking of the rose: "Je Jehans de Meun qui jadis ou Rommans de la Rose, puis que Jalousie ot mis en prison Bel Acueil, enseignai la maniere du chastel prendre et de la rose cueillir" (I Jean de Meun, who long ago in the *Romance of the Rose,* when Jealousy had put Bel Acueil in prison, taught how to take the castle and pluck the rose [quotation taken from MS Bibl. Nat. lat. 18424, fol. 2]). Although this is a somewhat offhand and probably humorous manner of designating a poem that describes a great deal more than the gathering of the Rose, it does indicate that this closing imagery could be used to stand for Jean's entire continuation.

figures as both teacher and lover, clerkly authority and lyric persona. Indeed, the two voices contrasted in the *Commens* and the *Poissance* fuse in the "I" of the *Bestiaire d'amours,* whose persona, as we have seen, comprises both lyricism and clerkliness. The latter aspect of Richard's identity is stressed by the explicit of the *Bestiaire d'amours,* which identifies him as "Master Richard de Fournival, Chancellor of Amiens" (fol. 31), whereas the former is at stake in the *Response,* where he is addressed as lover. The three poets named in Dijon MS 526—Richard de Fournival, Guillaume de Lorris, Jean de Meun—constitute a poetic trio in whose work the issues and problematics of lyrical writing find a strong, and profoundly influential, expression.

The nature of the compilation constructed around the *Bestiaire d'amours* in both the Dijon and the Vienna manuscripts is similar to the ways in which it is used in other manuscripts that are less tightly organized. I have already discussed two such manuscripts in the opening chapters: Bibl. Nat. fr. MSS 12786 and 25566. As we have seen, both of these codices present a mixture of lyrical and didactic texts and can be characterized by an overall movement from the lyrico-narrative or lyrico-dramatic to didactic dits and prose treatises. Within this context, the *Bestiaire d'amours*—lyrical prose, a didactic treatise functioning as a declaration of love—provides an important locus of mediation between the generic poles of the compilation, just as in Dijon MS 526 it effected a fusion of the voices established in the two preceding texts. An examination of the *Bestiaire d'amours* manuscripts yields a number of other examples as well: in the fourteenth-century MS Bibl. Nat. fr. 24406, for example, it is placed between the didactic prose *Traité des quatre nécessaires* and a series of twenty-nine musically notated songs to the Virgin; a manuscript now lost, described in a 1373 inventory of the Bibliothèque du Louvre, contained the *Bestiaire d'amours,* the *Compost de la lune,* the *Image du monde,* the *Tournoiement Antechrist,* and "pluseurs chançons notées" (many musically notated songs).[13]

A particularly rich example of this kind of compilation is Arras, Bibl. Mun. 657, dated 1278 in a colophon; it contains a large number of clerkly and didactic treatises in prose and verse, such as Alard de Cambrai's *Dits des sages,* a series of saints' lives, and a fragment of the *Roman des sept sages.* Its contents also include a sizable collection of trouvère lyric (chansonnier *A*). Interestingly, as we saw in Chapter 2, this happens to be the only surviving trouvère chansonnier in which trouvères are represented as writers; and one of the trouvères so represented is Richard de Fournival

13. MS Bibl. Nat. fr. 24406 also contains trouvère chansonnier *V.* This part of the manuscript, however, was copied by an earlier hand than the part containing the *Bestiaire d'amours:* I do not know if it was bound together with the *Bestiaire d'amours* during the Middle Ages or at a later time. See Segre's edition of the *Bestiaire d'amours,* p. lxiv, for a citation of the 1373 inventory.

himself. The contrast between chivalric and clerkly trouvères in the chansonnier section of the codex is similar in spirit to the poetics of the *Bestiaire d'amours*. Some of the more explicitly clerkly texts, in turn, are constructed as the presentation of oral discourse: the *Roman des sept sages* is a frame narrative within which a series of characters tell stories; the *Dits des sages* is rubricated as a series of oral presentations (see Chapter 3). Even the *Ave Nostre Dame* is a prayer meant to be spoken; and it appears as spoken word a couple of pages later in the miracle story, "Del povre clerc qui disoit Ave Maria adés, et pour coi fu il saus" (Of the poor clerk who constantly said the "Ave Maria," and thus he was saved [fol. 127v]). The interplay of lyrical and clerkly diction, oral and written textuality, is a widespread phenomenon of the thirteenth and fourteenth centuries, certainly not limited to the *Bestiaire d'amours* and its manuscripts; nonetheless, it is interesting that this text in which the issues are so explicitly focused should so often appear in a "mixed" context.

We must look not only to compilers for textual responses to the *Bestiaire d'amours*. The *Bestiaire d'amours* itself is expanded and brought to narrative conclusion through an anonymous continuation that appears in two Italian-made manuscripts of the fourteenth century and could be said to take the place of the *Response*. This continuation also responds to the affinities between the *Bestiaire d'amours* and the *Rose*. The continuator begins by extending the series of bestiary images; the new examples are added on to the original text with no indication of a break between text and continuation. This series of beasts leads into the narrator's lament, which turns into a reproach addressed to his heart, cause of his suffering. As the narrative picks up, the narrator's heart replies, urging him to take action by visiting the castle where his lady resides and obtaining an audience with her. The narrator accordingly rides off for the castle, accompanied by Humility, Mercy, and Good Chivalry. Upon arrival he prays for help to the God of Love; the latter, announcing that it is time for the lover to receive his reward, leads forth the lady, who gives him a red rose that she has been saving just for him. The narrative action is illustrated in both manuscripts. In the Pierpont Morgan Library MS M 459 the text ends with an image of the lady handing her lover the rose. In the Laurentian Library MS Ashb. 123 it ends with a representation of the lover, the God of Love, and the lady mounted on horses; the God of Love is in the center and holds the hands of the lover and of the lady, who has the rose in her other hand.

The continuator, though neither particularly gifted nor original in his work, does bear witness to a reading of the erotic discourse of the *Bestiaire d'amours*. As stated above, Richard compared the lady's pattern of response to her lover's words to an act of conception and birth. In manuscripts containing the *Response*, there is an implication that the lady has indeed "conceived" as a result of her lover's message and given birth to a text of her own; the relationship between the masculine persona of the *Bestiaire d'amours* and the feminine persona of the *Response* is one of metaphoric sexual intercourse. Perceiving this, the author of the continuation collapsed the format of the compilation into a single integrated text and replaced the image of textual coupling with an equally famous and even more audacious image for poetic and sexual consummation: Jean de Meun's plucking of the rose. The motif of the castle picks up and fulfills the arriere-ban motif of the prologue and suggests the same association between Richard's arriere ban and Jean's assault on the tower that we saw in Dijon MS 526.

A textual response to the continuation, finally, appears in the Morgan MS M 459 (which contains the continuation) in the form of an anonymous preface placed at the beginning of the *Bestiaire d'amours*.[14] Written in red ink, like a troubadour vida, this preface has a similar function of responding to, and rendering explicit, the implied narrative context for a lyrical text. The author of the preface informs us that the *Bestiaire d'amours* was written by a man both learned and a lover—a Jacobin "philosopher" who had long wooed his lady with all manner of lyric compositions. Finding himself in this hopeless situation the man, who by now had renounced his Holy Orders for love of his lady, decided to put all his efforts into making one final book to win her heart. And upon reading the arriere ban, the lady approached and conversed with the man; her heart softened, and she became favorably disposed toward his desires, "com uos orois a la fin" (as you will hear at the end [Segre ed., p. lix]).

This preface, illustrated at the beginning by an image of the lady (fol. 1) and then by an image of the man kneeling before the lady (fol. 1v), establishes the relationship between the composition of the *Bestiaire d'amours* and the seduction that, in this version, is recounted within the text itself. It is as though there has been an invisible chronological leap, in the course of the text, from the moment of writing—recorded in the prologue announcement of the intention to make an arriere ban and in the various supplicating words addressed throughout to the lady—to an indeterminate moment following the act of reading, when the lady allows herself to be persuaded. Here, the chronological progression suggested in other manuscripts by the succession of individual texts, each supposedly composed after the reading of the preceding piece, has been collapsed to take place within the single text.

## Lyricization of *Li Bestiaire d'amours*: *Le Bestiaire d'amour rimé*

The above examples are all instances in which the text of the *Bestiaire d'amours*, itself preserved, was amplified by one or more additional texts

14. This preface is printed in the Segre edition, pp. lvii–lix.

in a compilational format or by a continuation that served to extend the original text. An interesting response of a different sort is the *Bestiaire d'amour rimé*, a reworking in rhymed couplets of Richard de Fournival's *Bestiaire d'amours* believed not to be the work of Richard himself but of a contemporary.[15] The author of the *Bestiaire rimé* inserted numerous echoes of the *Rose*, once again making explicit the analogous poetics of the two texts. He also gave the whole a more lyrical cast than it had in its prose version. He added a prologue addressing the lady, who is compared to a red rose, before the discussion of memory; the aspect of lyric address to the lady is privileged over that of the didactic scientific treatise. Moreover, the addition of this prologue contributes to an association of Lady Memory and the poet's lady. In the single surviving manuscript of the *Bestiaire rimé* (Bibl. Nat. fr. 1951, copied about 1300), the poem is headed by a picture of a lady holding a palm branch and standing between two doors, one marked with an eye and one with an ear (fig. 9). The whole would seem to represent Memory, who is reached through the paths of veïr and oïr; similar images appear in some thirteenth-century manuscripts of the *Bestiaire d'amours*, as will be discussed below.[16] Since the opening lines of the text address the lady, however, it is equally tempting to see this image as a representation of her; and after all, she too is being addressed by parole and painture. Indeed, it is her memory that the narrator hopes to reach, securing a place there for himself. Thus the presentation of the text in its rhymed version strengthens the associations, already implied by Richard, between the transmission of love and the transmission of knowledge.

The rhymed version also modifies Richard's claim to have substituted writing for singing. Although the poet includes the discussion of parole and painture, clearly stating that his text will reach the lady in the form of illustrated writing, he nonetheless seems to consider himself as singing. As I suggested in the discussion of Guillaume de Lorris, the poet appears to be effecting a special sort of lyrical transcription: he is singing in written form. As a result, the dangers that Richard claimed to have avoided come back to haunt him. The nightingale and swan that sing themselves to death now function as models of the dangers of lyricism faced by the poet himself, who fears that he may die as a result of this work that so engages him, or that he may never finish it:

15. A fragment of yet another rhymed version appears in MS Bibl. Nat. fr. 25545; it is possible that this one is by Richard de Fournival. The poem opens, "Maistre Richars ha pour miex plaire / Mis en rime le bestiaire . . ." (Master Richard has put the bestiary into rhyme, the better to please [fol. 89v]). Unlike the other rhymed version, which modifies the statements about writing and singing and introduces significant additions into the prologue, this version adheres faithfully to the original for as far as it goes.

16. MS Bibl. Nat. fr. 412 opens with an image of two doors, one marked with an eye and one with an ear, but there is no lady in the miniature. MS Bibl. Nat. fr. 12469 opens with an image of a lady between two doors but without the eye or ear.

*Figure 9.* Eye and ear as gates to Memory, *Bestiaire rimé,* B.N. fr. 1951, fol. 1. (Photograph: Bibliothèque Nationale, Paris)

La mort dou roxignol m'effree,
Car je crieng que il ne meschee
De ceste oevre que j'ai emprise,
Pour ce que tant me plaist l'emprise

. . . . .

Certes, se sera grant merveille,
Se je puis finer cest ditié.

[The nightingale's death terrifies me, for I fear lest some ill luck come of this work that I have undertaken, so much does it please me. . . . Certainly, it will be a great wonder if I am able to complete this poem.] [Thordstein ed., vv. 213–16, 244–45]

The reference to not being able to finish the work is a particularly telling allusion to Guillaume's *Rose:* the poet is acknowledging the paradox of attempting to write a finished treatise in a lyric mode, that is, in a mode normally considered ephemeral and open-ended.

The *Bestiaire rimé* contains no hint of a response from the lady, but it does suggest a different sort of escape from the self-reflexivity of lyricism, the contact between performer and audience. As the narrator holds forth about the ups and downs of his love, a second voice enters the picture (v. 3089). At once he is engaged in dialogue with an unnamed interlocutor, possibly the "friend" to whom he had referred earlier (v. 3086). This voice from the audience questions the lover's claims and forces him to explain and justify his feelings. The dialogue, in "tu," can be distinguished from the lover's monologues, which remain in the first person.

The verse *Bestiaire* and the conjoined prose *Bestiaire* and *Response* each inscribe a communicative exchange into the text. In the prose *Bestiaire* and *Response,* however, the communication that takes place is a private one, effected through writing. Lover and lady are equivalent to author and reader, with each role played by each in turn. Within the confines of the text, writing is presented as a private means of communication. Our role as readers or observers of the exchange is not inscribed in the text.

In the verse *Bestiaire,* however, the poetic voice defines itself as oral; although he addresses the lady, the implied performance is evidently not a private communication to her but a public communication to some third party (or parties) about her. Our role as hearers-spectators of the lover's discourse is mirrored in the interlocutor, with whom we can identify precisely because his identity is not specified, and he is not a part of the love relationship. Paradoxically, Richard's insistence on a written voice produces a more private, and in that sense more lyrical, construct: the anonymous poet's insistence on an oral voice in turn results in a more public statement.

We saw a similar sense of writing as a more private mode of communication than speech or song in the *Roman du castelain de Couci;* there, too, writing had the effect of fixing the referents of lyric discourse, inscribing it in a specific context. Even though the *Bestiaire d'amours* could be copied many times over, the fiction is still that of an original act of writing executed by Richard de Fournival and addressed to a particular lady—specifically, the one who articulates the *Response.* Even if we hear it read aloud, the textual voice remains distinct from that of the performer, since it is so explicitly a written and not an oral voice. The verse *Bestiaire,* on the other hand, lends itself like a song to oral performance in which the performer takes on the voice of the lover and is assimilated to his persona.

Indeed, it is very possible that the versification of the *Bestiaire d'amours* was motivated, at least in part, by a desire to render the text more suitable for oral presentation. The anonymous poet replaces the written prose voice with one oral and poetic, making the necessary changes in the application of certain animal metaphors and allowing monologue to develop into dialogue through a poeticization of the performance situation. For someone receiving the poem solely through oral presentation, it might seem perfectly logical that the performer would adopt such a stance; the paradox of "singing in writing" would not necessarily strike all members of the medieval audience in the same way. At the very least, though, we can say that the author of the *Bestiaire rimé* had noted the movement from sung to written discourse in the prose bestiary and had recognized the need to adapt the text to its new format. It could be argued that he was merely making the best of a difficult situation, wanting to preserve the original prologue discussion about memory, text, and illustration while at the same time needing to transpose the text into a language appropriate for declamation. In this case, his work would still be interesting in the context of lyrical writing in that it reflects a certain hesitation to accept a purely written lyric voice. Although this may have been a factor, however, I believe that at least the poet, and probably some members of his audience, must have taken pleasure in the playful way the text vacillates between song and script. For the poet does not concentrate solely on oral communication; he also works out an elaborate puzzle of initials and anagrams.

First, the lover announces in the prologue that the lady's name begins with the initial of his surname, and ends with the initial of his first name (see vv. 124–53). Since, he says, the initial may be taken as representing the entire name, there results a visual sign that expresses a fusion of lover and lady: her name contains his but also is framed by and so in a sense contained by his. The lover expresses the wish that this conjoining of names could be realized in a conjoining of hearts as well. In the prose *Bestiaire-Response,* lover and lady are conjoined through a shared system of metaphors, expressed as visual signs; here, again, the visual sign expresses both lover and lady simultaneously.

An even more elaborate anagram appears at the end of the poem (vv. 3667–3718). Here, the narrator states that the words *dous regart* are an anagram containing both his and his lady's names, in both French and Latin. In order to arrive at these names it is necessary to turn one letter upside down and also to split it in half; presumably, the "u" is thereby transformed into an "n" and two "i's." The complexity of the instructions are such that the anagram remains unsolved today.[17] The point, however, is that again lover and lady are fused in a visual sign that simultaneously refers to both. The juggling of letters that are turned or dismantled further stresses the visual, concrete quality of the written sign. The fact that the names appear in both French and Latin may represent a conflation of speech and writing: the names as they are uttered and the names as they are written.

Equally important, this visual sign itself has the primary significance of "sight." Dous regart is the means by which lovers communicate, each providing a visual text to be read by the other; in a text of which painture forms an integral part, dous regart can even refer to the act of reading the book. Through an identification of the object of desire as a text—the association, I repeat, so central to Jean de Meun's *Rose*—the act of reading is equated with the act of gazing upon the beloved. In the final analysis it is still by means of visual communication, by an act of mutual reading, that lover and lady commune and fuse.

The effect in the verse *Bestiaire* is to polarize the dual functions of veïr and oïr identified by Richard. The prose *Bestiaire* as crafted by its author is entirely visual; writing becomes oral only when read. In the verse *Bestiaire* the poet plays with both the oral and the visual aspects of writing. On the one hand, it is the representation of his speaking voice; on the other, it is purely visual, a concrete object to be manipulated at will. Again, the poet exploits a paradox inherent in Richard's statement that writing itself appeals to both ear and eye:

toute escripture si est faite pour parole monstrer et pour che ke on le lise; et quant on le list, si revient elle a nature de parole. Et d'autre part, k'il ait painture si est en apert par chu ke lettre n'est mie, s'on ne le paint.

[All writing is made to show forth speech and in order to be read; and when it is read it reverts to the nature of speech. And on the other hand, it is

---

17. Thordstein offers one possible solution, ingeniously worked out, that would produce a lady's name and a man's first name in French and Latin; but even he is unable to formulate a surname from the designated letters. Since the text is missing a line during the instructions for solving the anagram, it is unlikely that we will ever be able to solve it. See Thordstein's edition of the *Bestiaire rimé*, pp. xciv–xcvi.

obvious that (the written text) entails *painture*, because there is no letter unless it is depicted visually (that is, through writing).] [Segre ed., pp. 6–7]

If the poet of the *Bestiaire rimé* was responding exclusively to the needs of a nonliterate audience that wanted the *Bestiaire d'amours* divested of its writerly diction, he would hardly have gone to such pains to devise puzzles accessible only to an audience that is at least semiliterate. Surely these fanciful spelling games, which turn up more and more frequently in the late thirteenth and fourteenth centuries, reflect a delight in the phenomenon of writing not only on the part of the poet but also on the part of the audience for which he wrote. Although some medieval readers or hearers of the prose or verse *Bestiaire* may have attended only to the play of animal imagery or the psychology of love, the subtlety of treatment that the motifs of song and script are given and the insistence on these themes in literary and iconographic programs testify both to a growing self-consciousness of the poet as writer and to an audience appreciation of the poet's playful manipulation of his craft.

## The Iconography of *Parole* and *Painture*

The importance of the themes of *parole* and *painture*, writing and performance, is clear not only from textual analysis of the *Bestiaire d'amours* and its descendents but also from the programs of illumination in *Bestiaire d'amours* manuscripts. As stated above, the manuscript tradition variously treats the *Bestiaire d'amours* as a lyrical or as a clerkly text, reflecting its polymorphous quality. Two examples of a lyrical treatment are MSS Bibl. Nat. fr. 12786 and 25566, discussed in Chapters 1 and 2. Although the miniatures in MS 12786 were never executed, the rubrics indicate what would have been represented. In addition to the series of animals and the arriere-ban image (usually a king and his knights) common to all manuscripts, this one would have featured representations of Lady Memory and the two lovers on the first page (fol. 31); the two lovers during the midpoint discussion of seduction as a progression through the five senses (fol. 36); and the God of Love at the end (fol. 42v). These images would provide an explicit lyrical framework for the text; the image of the God of Love further establishes a link with the *Rose,* which begins on the facing page.

In MS 25566 the *Bestiaire d'amours* and *Response* appear in the first half of the manuscript, the part devoted to lyric and dramatic works; it is not surprising to find that here too it is illustrated according to lyric iconography. The *Bestiaire d'amours* is framed by a representation of the God of Love shooting the two lovers with his arrows at the beginning (fol. 83), and the lover on his knees before the lady a few lines from the end (fol. 97v). The pure lyric quality of this latter miniature is tempered by the rubric, "Si comme li maistres prie a la dame" (How the master prays to the lady). The term *maistres* distinguishes this particular lover as a learned figure, as of course Richard de Fournival was; his identity as cleric is further established, here and in other manuscripts, by the representation of the lover as tonsured. The single miniature accompanying the *Response*, in turn, picks up the "bookish" aspect of the *Response* as a written reply: it represents a man reading from a book while another man kneels and holds a corner of the book (fol. 98). It does seem rather inappropriate that the two figures being conjoined here by means of the book should both be men; possibly the artist misunderstood his instructions here. In any case, the image balances the representation of lyric *prière* on the facing page; since the man is reading aloud from the book, as opposed to writing in it, the image captures the quality of *escriture* as a representation of voice.

Vienna MS 2609, another Artesian manuscript, also stresses the aspect of oral communication, making of the series of texts a lyric *débat*. This is appropriate to the presentation of the *Bestiaire d'amours* in this manuscript, where the addition of other texts before and after the *Bestiaire* builds from the initial declaration of love into an extended dialogue. The *Medecine* is headed with the image of a clerk holding an unfurled scroll, the emblem of discourse, whereas the *Response del onguement* is headed with the image of a lady addressing a clerk (fols. 1, 6). Similarly, the last two texts in the sequence are headed with images of a man and woman in dialogue (fols. 41v, 44).

The *Bestiaire d'amours* itself opens with an image suggesting the arriere-ban motif (itself illustrated explicitly on the following page): a tonsured cleric addresses a man armed with a spear, and hands him a sealed document (fol. 11v). This image, juxtaposed with the numerous images of direct address heading the other texts in the collection, establishes the metaphoric nexus of learned and seductive discourse and military assault. The function of the *Bestiaire d'amours* as a locus for interaction is further stressed by the image of the fool false-heartedly supplicating the lady (fol. 25v), contrasted with the image on the facing page of "Li maistres parlans a genous en humeliant a la Dame" (The master speaking on his knees, humbly, to the lady [fol. 26]); again, the term *maistres* identifies this lover with the author of the treatise. The images with which the *Bestiaire d'amours* ends and the (first) *Response* begins employ the same iconography as MS 25566. At the close of the *Bestiaire d'amours* is "The master begging the lady's mercy" (fol. 31v); directly following, on the same page, is the image of a woman writing in a book, looking into the eyes of a cleric standing before her. Again, lyric and clerkly modes of discourse are juxtaposed.

Finally, the lyrical aspect of the *Bestiaire d'amours* is further stressed in the Vienna manuscript by the series of three miniatures illustrating the discussion of song (*chant*) near the midpoint (Segre ed., pp. 38–39), during the discourse on the sense of sound. The discussion of the powerful effects of music that ushers in the account of the five senses is illustrated, as usual, by the image of someone beating a drum (fol. 19). At the line "Dont puisque ordenance de cant . . ." is the image of a mournful woman, a viellist, and three men singing from a scroll, identified as "The viellist of love, and the mourner, and several singers of love" (fol. 19v). A few lines later, at the passage "Par cesti raison . . ." (which describes the effects of music on bees), is a second miniature of a man beating a drum. This series of images at the midpoint suggest a kind of lyric core around which the *Bestiaire d'amours* is constructed. The central image recalls the famous (and very frequently illustrated) carol of Guillaume's *Rose* and may provide yet another echo of the thematic relationship of these two texts.

The two manuscripts containing the narrative continuation include illustrations of this narrative action, as stated above. In addition, the Morgan MS M 459 in particular has numerous images of the lover beseeching his lady (without identifying rubrics) scattered throughout the text. This emphasis throughout on the lover's plea, his direct confrontation of the lady, is of course appropriate to the reading imposed by the continuation, which turns the *Bestiaire d'amours* into a successful act of seduction; the narrative movement is reflected in the pictures, which move from the lover supplicating the lady to their union. That this narrative reading of the *Bestiaire d'amours* was especially important to the maker (or commissioner) of the Morgan manuscript is suggested by the preface, discussed above, that is attached to the text in this manuscript.

In other manuscripts, the *Bestiaire d'amours* is transmitted in a more learned context. In many cases the illustrations in these cases are limited to Lady Memory, the arriere ban, and the series of animals. In some, however, the illustrations do pick up the themes of *veïr* and *oïr*, performance and book. In the thirteenth-century MS Bibl. Nat. fr. 412, the *Bestiaire d'amours* and *Response* follow a large collection of saints' lives. There are no representations of the God of Love here; the text is presented as a didactic treatise. The opening miniature depicts the two doors leading to memory, one marked with an eye and one with an ear (fol. 228). This image is repeated for the *Response,* after the introductory section about Adam and Eve (fol. 237v). Thus the audiovisual aspect of the text is stressed; and the repeated image further strengthens the tie between the *Bestiaire d'amours* and its reworking, a tie intensified still more by the repetition of the images of the animals throughout the *Response,* which is not illustrated beyond the opening miniature in any other surviving manuscript.

166

An additional miniature in MS 412 gives an interesting twist to the importance of veïr and oïr. At the beginning of the *Response* is a miniature representing the two lovers seated side by side (fig. 10). The lady lectures the man and gestures to indicate speech; he not only turns his eyes toward her but also has turned an unusually large ear in her direction. Here, seeing and hearing are associated not with reading books but with performance as a combination of oral voice and visual gesture. There is certainly no indication in the text that the lady has ever addressed her lover in person. But as is implied in Richard's prologue, the written text is itself an embodiment of performance, and this representation of the lady's speech is stressed here. The equivocal nature of the written text, which "reverts to the nature of speech" through the reading process, is clear even from the rubric, which announces the *Response* and adds, in a conventional rubric formulation, "Si come vous porrés oïr ci aprés" (As you will be able to hear after this [fol. 236v]). Again, the orality of instruction fuses with the orality of lyricism to support the status of the lyrico-didactic text as at once performance and document.

The emphasis on performance and orality in so many thirteenth-century responses to the *Bestiaire d'amours,* both the verse redaction and the illustrative programs, can be contrasted with an emphasis on reading and writing in several fourteenth-century manuscripts. In MS Bibl. Nat. fr. 15213 the *Bestiaire d'amours* is bound with the *Fables d'Ysopet*. The *Bestiaire d'amours* is headed by a nearly full-page miniature in two parts (fol. 57; fig. 11). In the top half, a scribe at the left hands his written copy to a man at the right while a lady watches at the extreme right. Below, a man at the left hands the book to a lady on the right; the man and lady portrayed in the upper register watch, standing at the extreme left and extreme right, respectively.[18]

It is difficult to be sure of precisely who these many figures are. I would suggest tentatively that the man and lady from the top register are the author and Lady Memory: he has the book made under her auspices. Below, a messenger delivers the book to the lady. This act of transmission serves in a larger sense as a transmission from the author, standing behind the messenger, to the memory of the lady, represented by Lady Memory standing behind her. In any case, it is plain that the *Bestiaire d'amours* is here presented as a written work, the representative of its author, and that the activity of writing, the process of communication by means of books, is the governing context for the work.

In the London MS Brit. Libr. Harley 273, also of the fourteenth century, the *Bestiaire d'amours* appears in a context of religious and didac-

18. I base my identification of the figures in the lower register with those in the upper register on the fact that they are wearing identical clothing and have the same appearance (for example, hair). Admittedly, medieval artists did not always concern themselves with such identifying features.

*Figure 10.* The lady lectures her lover, *Response du bestiaire*, B.N. fr. 412, fol. 236v. (Photograph: Bibliothèque Nationale, Paris)

168

*Figure 11.* Opening page, *Bestiaire d'amours,* B.N. fr. 15213, fol. 57. (Photograph: Bibliothèque Nationale, Paris)

tic texts. Although the opening miniature depicts the two lovers conversing, two more miniatures follow on the same page (fol. 70); they illustrate the discussion of memory, represented by men in the activities of reading aloud and writing—the transcription of the written word as a visual sign and its translation into oral signs through the act of reading. The final prologue miniature, also on the same page, depicts the man handing his book to the lady. The placement of these four miniatures in such close proximity suggests a continuous progression from one to the next: before our very eyes, direct address is replaced by communication through the medium of writing. Indeed, the image of the book was so essential to this rendition of the *Bestiaire d'amours* that even the siren (fol. 73) is represented as singing from a book.

The most interesting iconographic program, from the perspective of parole and painture, appears in the Oxford MS Bodleian Libr. Douce 308, copied in Metz during the first half of the fourteenth century. The illustrations here provided for the *Bestiaire d'amours* pick up the thematics of parole and painture in a fascinating manner. The text is headed with a double miniature of the scribe at work and of the book being presented to a group of people. There is no hint here of the two lovers: this opening miniature illustrates the more general theme of the transmission of knowledge by means of books. The lovers appear at the top of the next page, engaged in conversation—the direct discourse that the text is meant to re-create. On this page Richard discusses the power of the book to re-create the presence of events distant in time or space, using the example of the story of Troy (cited above). The passage is graphically illustrated: a man reading a book looks up from the page to see a group of soldiers looking him in the eye and gesturing (fig. 12). The characters of the romance seem literally to have leapt off the page and materialized before the reader's eyes (and ears, if the gestures can be taken to indicate speech). The preceding miniature can be understood in a similar fashion: as the lady reads the text, her lover will seem to appear before her to speak to her directly.

The ensuing discussion of parole and painture is framed by two miniatures (figs. 13, 14). The first depicts two men holding up a scroll: a representation of parole and its power to conjoin speaker and hearer (or writer and reader). The second is in two parts. On the left is a collection of little birds and animals scattered over an ornamental background, framed by curtains: a representation of painture. The illustration of parole and painture as abstract concepts is a remarkable feature and reflects the importance of these elements in the fourteenth-century conceptualization of the book. The right half of this final miniature before the *Bestiaire d'amours* proper is, as usual, the arriere ban: a king leading his army to battle. Here, this picture echoes the representation of sol-

*Figure 12.* Representation of reading, *Bestiaire d'amours,* Bodleian Libr., Douce 308, fol. 86dv. (Photograph courtesy of the Bodleian Library, Oxford)

diers on the facing page; again, the illustrations visually express the power of the text to create the lover-author's presence. According to the military metaphor, the author is the king, summoning his forces for one final assault on the lady's defenses. The image of soldiers materializing out of a book and into the room with the reader suggests that, as warrior, the author too will come riding right off the page and into his lady's life. Although there is no evidence linking this iconographic program with the narrative continuations found in the Italian manuscripts, they are plainly based on a similar reading of the *arriere-ban* metaphor and of the act of writing as an act of seduction.

MS Douce 308 has one further unique feature. Many of the miniatures representing animals also show the two lovers, who view or dis-

*Figure 13.* Representation of *parole, Bestiaire d'amours,* Bodleian Libr., Douce 308, fol. 86dv. (Photograph courtesy of the Bodleian Library, Oxford)

cuss the animal in question. This manuscript does not include the *Response,* but the same idea of the book as a means of concretizing communication is clear. The illuminated text of lyrical writing provides a privileged space within which lover and lady, author and reader, come together in the presence of, and through the means of, the allegorical material.

The foregoing discussion has established the *Bestiaire d'amours* as a seminal text, one that gave rise to an extremely varied series of responses from writers in both verse and prose, compilers, and artists. Its nature is such that it could serve as either initiator or conclusion of a textual sequence; it was felt to be now lyric, now narrative, now didactic; often it mediated between these various literary types. What makes it such an

*Figure 14.* Representation of *painture, Bestiaire d'amours,* Bodleian Libr., Douce 308, fol. 87. (Photograph courtesy of the Bodleian Library, Oxford)

important text for the thirteenth and fourteenth centuries is that it embodies so perfectly the tension between song and book, between text as theatrical performance and text as material artifact. As with Guillaume de Lorris's *Rose,* this tension tantalizes, inviting resolution in one direction or another. The *Bestiaire d'amours* focuses many of the issues of both parts of the *Rose* and, indeed, occupies a middle ground between them; Jean de Meun's brilliant appropriation and reinterpretation of the *Rose* may well have been inspired in part by his reading of the *Bestiaire d'amours* as an initial response to Guillaume's poem. Other poets, too, responded to the mysterious and open-ended works of Guillaume de Lorris and Richard de Fournival and to the affinities between the two. In the following chapter, we will examine two such texts.

Chapter 6

# Lyrical Writing and Compilation
# in *Le Roman de la poire*
# and *Le Dit de la panthère d'amours*

The *Roman de la poire* and the *Dit de la panthère d'amours* combine two major aspects of lyrical writing as we have seen it in the preceding chapters: first-person narrative discourse and the use of lyric insertions. And each exploits compilatio as a poetic principle, using the central love experience as the focal point around which an assortment of other textual material can be grouped. Both poems are thus excellent illustrations of the extremely rich possibilities generated by the innovative poetics of such writers as Jean Renart, Guillaume de Lorris, Richard de Fournival, and Jean de Meun. In addition, examination of the differences between these two poems, separated by some fifty years, brings into focus certain developments that took place during the second half of the thirteenth century and that we have already noted in the comparison of Jakemes and Jean de Meun to earlier poets.

## Tibaut's Lyrical Romance: From Book to Nightingale
## and Back Again

The *Roman de la poire,* composed about 1250 by an unknown poet who identifies himself as Tibaut, survives today in two complete texts: the MS Bibl. Nat. fr. 2186, probably copied about 1275, and the early fourteenth-century MS Bibl. Nat. fr. 12786, discussed in previous chapters.[1] In addition, large portions of the text are preserved in the fourteenth-century MS Bibl. Nat. fr. 24431; and a further fourteenth-century fragment of one folio was recently discovered.[2] The two complete manu-

1. Portions of this discussion of the *Poire* were presented at the Ninth Conference on Manuscript Studies at the University of St. Louis; see the abstract, "Book as a Literary Form."
2. For descriptions of the manuscripts, see Marchello-Nizia's introduction to her edition of *Le Roman de la Poire.* On the newly discovered fragment, see O'Gorman.

scripts are the most important for the purposes of the present study. MS 2186, a beautifully illustrated volume devoted exclusively to the *Poire*, may postdate the composition of the poem by as little as twenty years and as such offers a nearly contemporary rendition. MS 12786 contains spaces for illumination and musical notation and places the *Poire* in an interesting context of lyrico-didactic works, as has been outlined in preceding chapters. I will return to the consideration of the role of the *Poire* in this manuscript at a later point, after an examination of the poem as it exists in the earliest manuscript.

The *Poire* opens with a twenty-line prologue in octosyllabic couplets in which the narrator announces his intention to compose poetry for his lady. A historiated initial "A" at the beginning depicts him in a gesture of vasselage before the lady, on his knees with his hands clasped in hers. The body of the text is in two consecutive parts, which for the sake of clarity I will refer to as part 1 and part 2, although there is no such explicit designation in the manuscripts. Part 1 is a sequence of first-person monologues composed in stanzas of four twelve-syllable lines each with internal and end rhyme.[3] The speakers are, in order: the God of Love; Lady Fortune; Cligès, who recounts the story of Fenice and the doctors; the *Poire* narrator, who receives a ring from his lady and vows to serve her; Tristan, who tells the story of King Mark's discovery of the two lovers sleeping with the sword between them in the forest; Pyramus, who explains how he and Thisbe communicate through the wall; the *Poire* narrator in dialogue with his lady, concerning a tournament that he attends; Paris, and the narrator with reference to Paris, concerning the sufferings of Paris and Helen; the narrator, who presents his book to the lady. The narrator's final monologue includes a twenty-three-line passage of octosyllabic verses in the rhyme scheme $a\ a\ b\ a\ a\ b$ with a lyric refrain at its center; the usual quatrains follow this interlude. The monologues are arranged in units of five stanzas to the page. Each begins on the recto side of the folio and faces a full-page illumination portraying the speaker of the piece and the narrative event to which he alludes. Most of the monologues are one page long, but that of Tristan is three pages, and the discussion of the tournament, as well as the narrator's final monologue, are each two pages.[4]

---

3. The one exception to this format is the first stanza spoken by Cligès, which is in sixteen-syllable lines (vv. 61–64). A short interlude near the end of part 1 appears in a different versification (vv. 241–63), as noted below.

4. In MS 2186, there is some confusion regarding the disposition of the tournament sequence and that of Paris and Helen. The first tournament passage (the narrator's preparation, during which the lady gives him her sleeve) appears on fol. 9, facing the miniature on fol. 8v. On fol. 9v is the miniature of Paris and Helen. The page that should have followed here is missing; the page now facing fol. 9v bears the second tournament passage, in which the narrator returns victorious. It would seem that the missing page must have held the text of Paris and Helen and a second miniature to go with the return from the

Part 2, which begins with v. 284 (Marchello-Nizia ed.), opens with a lyric refrain and then returns to the octosyllabic couplets of romance narrative. It is headed with a historiated initial "A" depicting the narrator with his hand on his heart. After a second prologue of about one hundred lines, the narrative proper begins. This transition is marked with a historiated initial "C" portraying the pear-tree incident from which the poem draws its name, recounted immediately following the initial: the lady picks a pear, takes a bite out of it, and hands it to the protagonist; upon biting into it, he is overcome with love for her. The narrative itself revolves largely around three series of refrains sung by allegorical personifications within the text; each refrain is decorated with a historiated initial depicting the encounter at which it was sung, and as with the refrains of part 1, space was left for musical notation that was never filled in.[5] The historiated initials in turn provide more than just running representation of the narrative: as is pointed out within the text, they form acrostics spelling out the name of the lady (ANNES—the narrator states that one letter is omitted to preserve her anonymity), the name of the narrator-protagonist (TIBAUT), and the word AMORS.[6] The lady and the lover, respectively, initiate the last two series of refrains explicitly for the purpose of forming these acrostics.

The interaction between text and image is of central importance in this earliest rendition of the *Poire*.[7] On fol. 1v, for example, the God of Love is shown exactly as he describes himself in the first two stanzas of his text, as a six-winged being with bow and arrows. In the next three stanzas, he tells us that Lady Fortune always does his bidding, keeping loyal lovers at the top of her wheel and casting down the false-hearted. This prepares us for the image of Fortune's wheel on fol. 2v and ex-

---

tournament. But in the only other manuscript to contain this part of the text, MS 12786, the two tournament passages are treated as a single unit, followed by the Paris and Helen text. Since the layout of MS 12786 is completely different—the text is illustrated with historiated initials rather than full-page miniatures, and the individual monologues no longer correspond to page divisions—this does not necessarily tell us how the text was disposed, or meant to be disposed, in MS 2186. But whether the Paris and Helen passage was supposed to be framed by the two tournament passages or was to follow them, the principle of interlaced episodes and the close interplay of text and illustration are the same.

5. On the refrains, see Bartsch; Marchello-Nizia ed., pp. xxxiv–xlviii.

6. For a discussion of the acrostics and speculation about the possible identity of "Tibaut" and "Annes," see Cramer-Peeters.

7. In her edition, Marchello-Nizia describes the illustration of MS 2186 on pp. xlix–lvi and publishes the miniatures and the acrostic initials. Vitzthum von Eckstädt used the manuscript as the basis for his identification of a non-Parisian miniature style, identifying a body of codices that he termed "the *Roman de la Poire* group," in *Pariser Miniaturmalerei*, pp. 88–113. Vitzthum's findings were revised by Branner, who assigned MS 2186 to a Parisian workshop that he called the Bari Atelier in *Manuscript Painting in Paris*, pp. 102–6, figs. 287, 289. The interplay of miniatures and text was noted by Serper, who calls attention to the dramatic quality of the *Poire*. The audiovisual quality of the manuscript is also stressed by Curschmann, pp. 237–38.

plains the peculiar quality of this particular representation, the only one I know of in which it is suggested that two people can occupy the same position simultaneously: the narrator's lady sits at the top and extends her hand to help him climb up beside her (fig. 15). This graphically portrays the notion, implied by the text, that Fortune's wheel has stopped turning and that the rising and falling of the humans attached to it is less a function of the wheel itself than of their faults and merits.

An even more important detail supplied by this series of miniatures is the explicit association of this portion of the text with the story of the *Poire* couple. The God of Love states only that he strikes lovers with his arrows; Fortune states that a certain unnamed pair of lovers has just risen to the top of the wheel. In the texts concerning the gift of the ring, the tournament, and the presentation of the book, the speakers are never identified. But the illustrations clearly show the *Poire* couple. First represented in the prologue initial, they are always recognizable by the heraldic pattern on their clothing: gold fleur-de-lis on a blue field charged with a red cross. This purely visual detail, never mentioned in the text, allows us to follow the *Poire* couple through the stages of their love and clarifies the relevance of such passages as Fortune's monologue to their story.

The layout of the first twelve folios, with nearly every two-page spread consisting of a new image and its accompanying text, encourages the reader to take each as a unit. Each opening corresponds to a theatrical moment: the appearance of a new character who makes his speech or acts out his story in the progression of exemplary love experiences. In effect, the Old French courtly romance tradition is recast as a series of tableaux vivants. Two vernacular figures, one explicitly modeled on the other, and two figures from classical tradition (though also vernacularized in other texts) are symmetrically disposed throughout the narrator's own performance. Tibaut exploits the potentials of lyrical romance, no doubt derived from Guillaume de Lorris's *Rose:* the voice of lover-narrator can be that either of the poet who makes himself a protagonist or of the protagonist who tells his own tale. In Tibaut's series of monologues, medieval court poet and heroes of vernacular and classical legend alike become first-person narrators of love stories. The illuminated book provides the space within which this series of lover-narrators comes to life. In this way the protagonist couple can enter the tradition of literary lovers and become themselves characters in a romance. The presentation of the book at the end of part 1 is the culmination of the initial series of performances, which function as a colorful prelude to the story itself.

The choice of figures and their disposition in and around the events in the story of the *Poire* couple are a skillful exploitation of compilatio as a poetic principle. The series begins with the God of Love and Fortune,

*Figure 15.* Lady Fortune, *Roman de la poire*, B.N. fr. 2186, fol. 2v. (Photograph: Bibliothèque Nationale, Paris)

announcing the initiation of the *Poire* love affair and the extremely optimistic outlook for its continuation. The third speaker is Cligès. The story of Cligès and Fenice is an explicit avoidance of unhappy outcomes: through artifice and contrivance on the part of characters and narrator alike, Cligès and Fenice are brought through various near calamities to a happy ending. The scene chosen for inclusion in the *Poire* is one such instance. The feigned death of Fenice exposed her to a series of trials that nearly brought about not only her actual death but the suicide of Cligès as well. Both tragedies are averted, however, enabling the lovers to enter upon the next phase of their story.

Specifically, the tragedy averted in the episode of Cligès is that which befell the next two exemplary couples: Tristan and Iseut, and Pyramus and Thisbe. The sequence of events most closely parallels that of Pyramus and Thisbe: a man, imagining that his beloved has died, commits suicide, as a result of which her death soon follows. And the death of Pyramus and Thisbe is portrayed in the miniature, even though it is not recounted until considerably later in the poem. The motif of death brought about by treachery and misunderstanding also recalls the death of Tristan and Iseut: imagining that Iseut has abandoned him, Tristan dies, causing Iseut in turn to die of grief. *Cligès* is an explicit reworking of the Tristan material, and the feigned death of Fenice is the means by which the lovers escape the adulterous life suffered by Tristan and Iseut. The appearance of Cligès, then, offers a narrative "undoing" of the negative aspects of the next two figures, and contributes significantly to the overall optimistic tone of the poem.

The scene chosen to represent Tristan and Iseut, in turn, is one of the more optimistic moments of their story. It refers to their life in the cave of lovers, an idyllic interlude in which they lived a pure lyric fantasy, with no outside intrusions. They are shown in the moment of discovery by the prime representative of that outside world, Iseut's husband; but in this case, due to the ruse of the sword, the love of Tristan and Iseut can be observed by King Mark without problems arising. Indeed, as a result of seeing Tristan and Iseut in this manner, Mark decides to pardon them and invites them back to court. In this rare moment, Tristan and Iseut are both united in their private world and, at the same time, linked in a positive way to the world of the court.

The appearance of this scene at the midpoint of part 1 casts a favorable light on the whole book. Moreover, this scene provides the iconographic "antidote" to the negative example of Pyramus and Thisbe that follows. There we find the first (and only) representation of a truly tragic event. An interesting correspondence exists between this scene and the Tristan scene. Both treat the potential danger posed by the outside world to the love couple. For Pyramus and Thisbe, this danger is represented by the lion, agent of the misunderstanding that leads to their double suicide; the actual instrument of death is the sword, which quite literally conjoins them by piercing both at once. In the Tristan miniature, King Mark, the symbol of the outside world, appears as a nonthreatening and even benevolent figure, blocking the sun to protect Iseut. And the sword appears not as the agent of death but as the agent of salvation, separating the two lovers physically but paradoxically allowing them to continue as a couple as a result of this deception. Thus, through the juxtaposition of narrative moments and images, the one tragic image is largely neutralized by the preceding two. Similarly, the rhetoric about the trials and tribulations of lovers is counterbalanced by the examples of lovers who seem, in fact, quite successful at overcoming these obstacles.

The episode chosen for Paris and Helen corresponds again to a happy moment in their story, the successful elopement. They are shown on the boat and then riding toward Troy. We know, though, that the story of Paris and Helen ended not only with the death of Paris and the return of Helen to her husband but, more important, with the ruinous ten-year war and, ultimately, the complete destruction of Troy. Again, this potentially threatening example is offset by the figure of Cligès at the beginning of the sequence. There we know that the story ended with the death of the husband and the triumphant reinstatement of the elopers as emperor and empress.

The neutralization of malevolent forces is also suggested in the tournament sequence, which may have framed the Paris and Helen text originally. Here the lover fighting in the name of his lady emerges victorious from a battle waged against the allegorical enemies of love. The series of narrative exempla thus serves to represent both the obstacles that confront lovers and the means by which true love can overcome such obstacles. The principle of compilatio allows this whole first part to function as a kind of lyricized anthology, the extraction of charged moments from a series of romances. One is reminded, indeed, of the series of summaries at the beginning of MS 375 (see Chapter 1), where the entire collection is reduced to a series of encapsulated narratives. In the *Poire*, the compilation is evoked to create a composite picture of love experience, its dangers and its victories. The interplay among the various elements creates a whole larger than the sum of its parts, able to express something that remains unstated. This sense of having created a unified oeuvre is expressed in the final image of part 1, in which the lover presents the book to the lady. The book, as a literary entity, rather than any specific passage within it, embodies the full poetic representation of love.

In part 2 the events of the narrator's love affair, having by now become romance material, are presented in more or less continuous narrative progression, in the course of which various episodes of part 1 are alluded to. Our move from part 1 to the narrative proper is marked by the change in versification and illumination; we return to the format of octosyllabic couplets and historiated initials used for the prologue. The collection of characters, narrative moments, and motifs first presented in simple juxtaposition provide the raw material that in part 2 is reordered, expanded, and combined with new material to form the narrative. Events in the history of the *Poire* couple are placed in temporal perspective, whereas the stories of other exemplary figures assume the subordinate role of gloss. For example, the story of Pyramus and Thisbe is told as an exemplum in which the narrator finds an image of his own feelings (vv. 717–41); Franchise refers to the story of Paris and Helen as an example (admittedly a somewhat oddly chosen one) of the joys that the narrator may expect to win if he follows the dictates of love (vv. 1067–72). Loyalty alludes to the lady's gift of her kerchief at the time of the tournament (vv. 2471–74), situating this event in a time previous to the lyric exchange that forms the acrostics.

Through this juxtaposition of elements, the format of the book provides a dramatization of the processes of compilation and conjointure by which the romance is produced. Such an interpretation is supported by the closing lines of part 1, "Il *m'a fette* tel plaie dont ne me puis esbatre, / qu'en ce livre *dirai, q'ai fet* por vos esbatre" (He *has dealt* me such a wound that I can have no relief from it, as I *will tell* in this book, which I *have made* to entertain you [vv. 282–83, emphasis mine]). The birth of love and the making of the book are in the past; this, indeed, is what we have just witnessed. What lies in the future is the actual *telling* of the story, the narrator's presentation to his audience. It is as though, having passed through the processes of textual creation, we can now experience the text itself.

Part 2 offers its own example of compilation and integration of elements in its use of refrains to create acrostics. Here a new body of material, representing a lyric rather than a narrative tradition, contributes to the formation of a miniature, nonnarrative text within the text. Analysis within the text of these three names attributes considerable significance to the configuration of letters that each presents. The narrator points out that "Annes" and "Amors" both begin and end with the same letters, proving the lady's worthiness as an object of love (vv. 2790–92); the lady assures her lover that he should not doubt the strength of their love, since, after all, both of their names contain six letters and two syllables (vv. 2732–35). Furthermore, she says, if "Tibaut" is spelled backward and the "b" flipped upside down (forming a Gothic "s"), one gets two Latin words—presumably "Tua sit" (let her be yours)—that tell him she truly belongs to him (vv. 2736–43).

If the acrostics exemplify the expressive power of the written word as an assemblage of letters to be manipulated as such, the refrains themselves introduce a new lyric impulse. They are sung by the allegorical personifications acting as messengers between the God of Love and the narrator, or between him and his lady, and are presented in the text as spontaneous oral performance; in the illuminations, the communicative act is stressed by the gestures of the characters (fig. 16). This performative quality is especially marked in the first series, where the succession of songs builds into a crescendo of musical and theatrical intensity. The first singer, Beauty, accosts the narrator through song and speech, "Sanz chartre seëllee en cire, / sanz parchemin" (without a charter sealed with wax, without parchment [vv. 839–40]). The second, Courtesy, sings a refrain that is "cler et seri, a longue aleine" (clear and harmonious, full voiced [v. 886]); the third, Nobility, accompanies her song by dance steps. This lyricism reaches its peak in the arrival of the God of Love, who is surrounded by an entourage of singing birds and jongleurs; the catalogue of birds, musical instruments, and performers takes up a full thirty lines of text. Later, in the final exchange of songs, the narrator sends his lady a nightingale, the lyric symbol par excellence, and the last two historiated initials portray the couple in the presence of the bird. This final image can be read in juxtaposition with the book portrayed at the close of part 1. The contrast between book and nightingale reflects not only the contrast between the written literary tradition portrayed in part 1 and the popular oral tradition represented by the refrains of part 2 but also the more general fusion of lyric and narrative, oral and written modes at every level of the *Poire*.

The *Poire* exemplifies perfectly the theatrical quality of the illuminated manuscript, which reproduces a performance of the text. The story of the acrostics is the story of the creation, through oral performance, of a written text. The same can be said of the *Poire* as a whole. A narrative drawing on romance tradition, relying for its effect on illuminations, acrostics, and anagrams, it is fully realizable only in book form. Yet the narrator recounts his tale in the form of a dialogue with an unnamed personage, who, like the interlocutor of the narrator of the *Bestiaire rimé*, functions as representative of a live audience. At every step, the development of the narrative is motivated by the questions and assertions of this interlocutor, who presses the narrator for more details and challenges his hyperbolic or allegorical statements. For example, when the narrator claims that Love attacked him with "hundreds and thousands of sergeants and knights," his interlocutor demands to know what sort of men an abstract concept like love could possibly have and insinuates that the narrator is the victim of drunken hallucinations. The narrator responds with an initial account of the three singing messengers; the interlocutor at once requests a description of the songs. Thus the composition of the text mimics oral exchange, declamation, song; but the end result is a book.

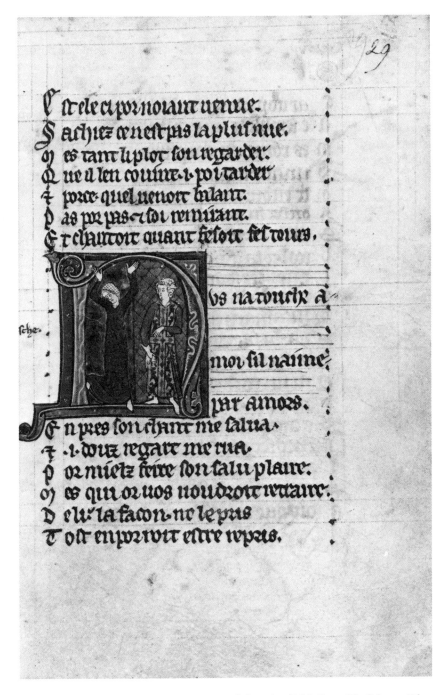

Et ele ci por noiant venue.
Sachiez ce n'est pas la plus nue.
Qes tant li plot son regarder.
Que il len covient .i. poi tarder.
Et porce quel venoit enfant.
Pas por pas et soi remuant.
Et chantoit quant fesoit ses tours.

Vos ne trouchez a
moi fil na ivne
par amors.

En pres son chant me salua.
Et .i. douz regart me rua.
Por miex feire son salu plaire.
Qes qui or vos voudroit retraire.
De lu' la façon ne le pris.
Tost en porroit estre repris.

*Figure 16.* Nobility and the lover, *Roman de la poire*, B.N. fr. 2186, fol. 29. (Photograph: Bibliothèque Nationale, Paris)

We are also told that the text is destined for oral performance before the lady and that it is meant to bring her a personal message of love and desire such as that normally associated with chanson courtoise. This oral delivery, though, is to be of a specific type. The two passages in which the narrator and his lady discuss the promised performance of the poem are replete with forms of the verb *lire* (to read), stressing that this performance is to be one intimately tied to a written text. For example, the narrator states:

> car cist romanz que ge ci voi
> savra molt bien parler por moi
> et mostrer pleinement a l'ueill
> que ge demant et que ge veill.
>
> .   .   .   .   .
>
> qui c'onques ce romanz li lisse,
> qu'il soit leüz a sa devise;
> et quant el verra toz les leus,
> ja ses cuers n'iert si orgueilleus.

[For this romance that I see here will know very well how to speak for me and how to show plainly to the eye what I am asking and what I want. . . . Whoever reads this romance to her, let it be read at her pleasure, and when she has seen all the places, her heart will not be so proud.] [Vv. 2221–24, 2235–38]

These descriptions of reading and showing the text to its intended audience contrast with the spontaneous performance represented by the refrains; this pure lyricism, through its incorporation into the romance, is subordinated to the formation of the written word. The book, as an artifact, is an embodiment of textual performance. It reproduces an "original" oral delivery and generates new oral delivery in the future.

The acrostics, built out of historiated initials of refrains, are the focal point for this interpenetration of lyric and romance, song and written word. As acrostics, they are a written text; as refrain initials, they are sung. As a sequence of visual images, they spell out the narrative; the words themselves form a nonnarrative text emblematic of the love relationship. Just as the nightingale contrasts with the book to express the interplay of romance and lyricism, so the construction of the acrostics contrasts with the entire first part of the poem. The lyricization of romance is followed by the transformation of lyricism into writing.

## Romance as Book: Codicological Analogues
## for the *Poire*

As a compilation, the *Poire* offers the following elements: romance of antiquity (Pyramus, Paris); courtly romance (Cligès, Tristan); lyricism (refrains); allegorical personification; and the French aristocracy (the protagonist couple wear the fleur-de-lis). This assemblage of material bears a certain resemblance to some of the anthologies described in Chapter 1. The *Poire* poet, for example, has employed a technique somewhat analogous to that of the compiler of MS 1450, the insertion of well-known narratives, in an abridged form, into a larger narrative structure. In the case of MS 1450, a historical and not a lyrical compilation, there is a stronger narrative link between Wace's text and Chrétien's romances, which are presented as taking place within the chronological framework of *Brut.* In the *Poire,* the link is not narrative but thematic. Nonetheless, the principle is similar, and the comparison serves to underline again the similarities between scribal and poetic practices.

The thematics of the *Poire* bears a certain resemblance to MS 375 as well. MS 375, too, combines the story of Troy, the story of Cligès, and other romance material ranging from ancient to contemporary settings, and the collection manifests an interest in the themes of false death and the combat for the lady. MS 375 lacks the strong lyric flavor of the *Poire,* as well as the allegorical presence; but again, it bears witness to practices in the making of books that are analogous in spirit to the synthesis effected in the *Poire.*

A compilation thematically closer to the *Poire* is the Bodleian MS Douce 308. Since each text is a separate codicological unit and there are three different hands, each corresponding to a different illuminator, we cannot assume that the codex as it stands today represents a medieval compilation. Three of the texts are copied in the same hand, however, and these, at least, must originally have formed a single collection: the *Voeux du paon,* chansonnier *I* (without space for musical notation), and Jacques Bretel's *Tournois de Chauvency.* This combination of texts offers a thematics very similar to that of the *Poire.* The *Voeux,* which narrates a portion of the legend of Alexander, offers heroes of antiquity, placed in a courtly setting in which battles alternate with festive activities, courtly pastimes, and amorous interludes. The *Tournois* transposes this thematics into a contemporary setting, presenting lyricism and chivalric prowess in a more purely decorative mode. A group of French aristocrats, historically verifiable figures, assembles for a series of tournaments, punctuated by evenings spent in song, dance, and general merriment. These latter scenes feature a large number of refrains sung by members of the company (although the manuscript gives no musical notation) as well as an amorous conversation overheard by the narrator and a discourse on love that he recites for the banqueters. Finally, the spectators at the tournament include a number of allegorical personifications. The *Tournois* itself, then, is thematically similar to the *Poire,* in that a contemporary setting provides the framework for lyric performance, tournaments, allegorical personification, and discourse on love. It is bound together with pure lyricism on the one hand and an epic tale on the other. Like the tale of the *Poire* couple, the *Tournois* provides a nucleus around which other texts can be gathered. Again, the comparison serves to illustrate the affinities between poetics and compilational practices—the *Poire* presents a complete anthology in abbreviated form.

The layout of the *Poire* in MS 2186, with its opening series of miniatures, suggests an imitation of the *Rose*. As I have argued elsewhere, the progression of exemplary images, which introduces the thematics of the narrative and warns of the forces that threaten lovers, bears a structural resemblance to the series of exemplary and admonitory images, nearly always represented in miniatures, that the *Rose* protagonist examines before his encounter with the carol of love.[8] The entire *Roman de la poire* is a response to the *Rose*, and reestablishes the function of the written text as a means of communication between lover and lady. The lyricization of the opening images (instead of static wall decorations, we find a series of figures who address the reader directly) goes along with the increased emphasis on communication in the *Poire*, a poem in which even the narrative takes the form of a dialogue.

Interestingly, a similar (and most likely unrelated) response to the *Rose* can be found in the fourteenth-century British Library MS Royal 19 B XIII. Here a bifolio leaf has been bound in the front of the manuscript, directly preceding the *Roman de la rose*, and decorated on the inside (fols. 3v–4) with two full-page miniatures. The God of Love sits on his throne, holding an arrow, while a man kneels before him (fol. 3v, top); in the lower half of the page and on the facing page are the ranks of his followers, both male and female, disposed in rows of four figures each and including both aristocrats and religious. Except for the God of Love, each figure holds an unfurled scroll inscribed with an amorous refrain, some joyous and some sorrowful. They include such phrases as "Jolietement me maintiendray" (I will keep myself in gaiety); "Ay! Ay! Nus ne doit amer" (Alas! Alas! No one should love); "Ma dame, je vous aim" (My lady, I love you); "Lasse, j'ai failli a joie" (Alas, I have lost out on joy). Since the scroll was conventionally used to indicate speech, the *Rose* is in effect preceded by a series of figures associated with lyric utterances: an elegant "carol" ushers in the narrative, itself in turn initiated by the series of wall images that must be penetrated before we can arrive at the main carol. The *Rose* is thus endowed with a further layer of theatrical images. There is no reason to assume that this treatment of the *Rose* was inspired by the *Poire*, which does not appear to have had a really wide circulation. Rather, it indicates a similar fascination with the *Rose* as a

---

8. See Huot, "From *Roman de la Rose* to *Roman de la Poire*." On the relationship of *Rose* and *Poire*, see Marchello-Nizia, pp. lix–lxv. The *Poire*'s participation in the tradition of vernacular love allegory is noted by Serper and by Jung, *Etudes sur le poème allégorique*, pp. 310–17.

narrative structured around sequences of images and an analogous construction of lyrical tableaux as the prelude to a lyrical romance.

The format of MS 2186 offers another interesting codicological analogy, already pointed out in art historical discussions of the manuscript:
the series of full-page miniatures disposed in two parts and the use of
historiated initials within the romance proper resemble the layout of
Psalters in the thirteenth century.[9] A Psalter commonly began with a
calendar, followed by a series of miniatures representing scenes from
the Old Testament, the life of Christ, or both. The Psalms, in turn, were
conventionally ornamented with historiated initials placed at regular
intervals. The analogy between the *Poire* manuscript and a Psalter is
strengthened by the iconography of the God of Love as an angel and by
the representation of the two lovers at the pear tree in the iconography
of Adam and Eve. And like a Psalter, MS 2186 is a small book that seems
designed for private reading and contemplation.

Why the *Roman de la poire* should resemble a Psalter is a question that
must be answered with care. A person wishing to design a book for
private reading or perusal had few models. In particular, full-page miniatures were extremely rare in vernacular literature of this period. A
Psalter offered the model of a book with full-page miniatures, one that
might be used for private devotional purposes. For this reason alone, the
artisans who planned and executed the manuscript might have borrowed motifs familiar from their own work as scribes and illuminators of
Psalters.

Beyond that, a Psalter does offer certain points of analogy with the
*Roman de la poire*. A Psalter too is a lyric compilation. The full-page
miniatures at the beginning of a Psalter set up a narrative context within
which the Psalms can be read as the record of Jewish history and as a text
prefiguring the life of Christ. This narrative is not that recounted literally by the Psalms but rather one that is thematically and metaphorically
related. The relation of the Psalms to this opening narrative is somewhat
similar to that which Guillaume le Clerc claimed for his *Bestiaire divin*:
the Psalms contain, in fragmented and reordered fashion, the story of
sacred history, which is also the story of Christ in allegorical form. In this
sense the narrative cycle of pictures mirrors the lyric cycle of Psalms. A
similar principle governs the relationship between the various elements
of the *Poire*: the illustrated cycle at the beginning thematically mirrors
the narrative that follows, whereas the series of lyric insertions, owing to
the historiated initials, likewise figures the sequence of narrative events.
The format of MS 2186 does not reflect an intention to design a ver-

---

9. MS 2186 was termed a "Psalter of Love" by Loomis, p. 90. The relationship of the
*Poire* illuminations to Psalter decoration is also discussed by Stones. On Psalter decoration
in France, see Leroquais, pp. lxxxvi–cxxxvi.

nacular Psalter of courtly love but rather a perception of the Psalter as a book with certain structural affinities to the poem in question, and therefore a useful model in planning the format through which the poem would become a book.

Ultimately, examination of the role played by sacred iconography and by the use of textual or codicological motifs associated with devotional literature raises extremely complex questions, touched upon in the previous chapter, which lead beyond the scope of the present study. Just as the *Poire* brings about an interpenetration of lyric and narrative modes, so also it moves between the registers of courtly and sacred poetics. We are given two narrative accounts of the onset of love. In one version, the narrator bit into a pear given him by his lady; in the other he was besieged by the forces of Love, and his heart was stolen away. In the first case the narrative suggests a replay of the Fall; in the second, we are reminded of Bel Acueil and the rose locked up in the tower "qu'Amors prist puis par ses esforz" (which Love then took with his troops [*Rose*, v. 3486]). Even the acrostics representing the lovers' names have affinities both with the acrostics and anagrams of courtly poetry and with poems built on the letters in the name MARIA, or on the correspondence AVE and EVA, composed in the vernacular by such poets as Gautier de Coinci and Thibaut de Navarre.[10]

For the purposes of the present study, it is sufficient to locate the *Poire* as one of numerous thirteenth-century texts that experiment with an interplay of courtly and sacred poetics. The *Poire* poet is less explicit in this regard than others we have seen. Richard de Fournival adopts a literary genre with strong sacred connotations; Jean de Meun explicitly introduces discussion of such topics as the Incarnation and the divine creation of the world into his continuation of the *Rose*. As we have seen, there are certain thematic, poetic, and linguistic principles that support the movement between the registers of courtly, sexual, and sacred discourse and that contribute to the authorization of the lyrical text of love as a written literary document. Such principles are not addressed in the *Poire* with the same clarity or depth as in the other works that we have examined in this light. The *Poire* does, however, contribute to the background against which these more complex texts were written—it indicates the pervasive nature of such issues during the thirteenth century and exemplifies the configuration of poetic possibilities to which a writer like Richard de Fournival or Jean de Meun was responding.

10. This association is raised by Deroy in the response to Serper's "Thèmes et allégorie," p. 403. Gautier de Coinci plays on the letters of the name Maria in his *Miracles de Nostre Dame*, Book 2, "Salus Nostre Dame," vv. 12–56. Thibaut de Navarre devotes a full stanza to the symbolic significance of each letter of the name Maria in "Du tres douz non a la Virge Marie," *Chansons*, no. 57; see Wallensköld's notes in his edition of *Chansons de Thibaut de Champagne*, pp. 201–3, for further references to poetry based on the name Maria.

## Le Roman de la poire and the Evolution of Lyrical Writing

With its playful treatment of the tension between song and written sign, the *Poire* participates in the general context of early and middle thirteenth-century lyrico-narrative composition while distinguishing itself from such later compositions as the *Roman du castelain de Couci* or Jean de Meun's *Rose*. The *Poire* is based on a concept, familiar from other thirteenth-century examples we have seen, of the book as a space in which to project performance. It shares with the *Bestiaire rimé* the format of declamation and dialogue with an unidentified interlocutor, coupled with the writerly devices of acrostics and anagrams. In its preservation of the oral quality of the lyric insertions, the *Poire* remains in the tradition of Jean Renart's *Rose*. And, as in Renart's poem, the written format allows the lyric anthology to mediate between lover and lady, both of whom contribute to its formation. In Renart's *Rose* this is brought about through the conflation of opposing lyric types: Liénor's chanson de toile tempers Conrad's chanson courtoise. Tibaut employs a somewhat similar technique in part 1 of the *Poire,* where the juxtaposition of positive and negative exempla suggest a means of resolution of the dangers inherent in "courtly love." His treatment of the lyric insertions is somewhat different, however. Although they are presented as purely oral performances, it is through their implied status as written documents that the songs can conjoin lover and lady as coauthors and coreaders of the acrostic text. In this respect, Tibaut is closer to such mid-century writers as Richard de Fournival and his continuators.

In its insistence on the communicative value of the poetic text as mediator between lover and lady, the *Poire* resembles the other early responses to Guillaume de Lorris's *Rose*. Like the *Bestiaire rimé*, the *Poire* contains numerous verbal echoes of the *Rose;* it also calls attention to itself as a completed text. The *Poire* recuperates the narrative "failure" of the *Rose* by placing emphasis on the production of the written romance rather than on the narrative consummation of the love affair. As with the *Bestiaire d'amours* and its *Response,* the love relationship is projected into the poetic space of the book, where lover and lady collaborate in the production of the text.

In the play of songs and acrostics in the *Poire,* we can see various latent poetic principles that are rendered more explicit and developed more fully by such writers as Richard de Fournival and Jean de Meun. For example, it is only after the formation of the acrostic ANNES that the lady comes into focus as a character and responds by forming the acrostic TIBAUT. Although the first acrostic results from refrains sung by the messengers of love, its creation is credited to the narrator: the lady wishes to name her lover because ".II. foiz oit nomé mon non" (he named my name twice [v. 2354]). We recall too that it is through the correspondence, among these acrostics, of letters and syllables that the lady's qualities as love object are revealed and that the validity of the love relationship is established. In effect, the narrator first creates the image of the lady as object of desire; as a result of this, she comes to life and responds by creating him as her *ami* (lover). Finally, in their collaborative formation of the third acrostic, lover and lady literally "make love." The erotic implications of poetic language, so richly explored in the *Rose,* are evoked here in a lighthearted manner, in keeping with the playful tone of the poem as a whole. In the mutual creation of lover and lady, one is reminded of the *Bestiaire d'amours,* where the lady "gives birth" to her lover as a result of his pleas.

I have distinguished the *Poire* from the texts of the later thirteenth century on the basis of its greater emphasis on the book as a re-creation of performance; the quality of the text as representative of a lyric persona who uses it as a means of making contact with the object of his desire; and the concept of the lyric text as a "freely floating" performance piece available for appropriation by anyone who wishes to take on the role of lyric persona. In the *Roman du castelain de Couci,* songs do sometimes serve to bear a message from the castelain to his lady, and of course the poem as a whole is a lyrico-narrative offering from the poet to his lady. As discussed in Chapter 4, this story is informed by a nostalgia for the trouvère ideal and takes as its hero a representative of the early lyric tradition. In spite of these archaizing tendencies, however, the poem bears certain more modern features that will prove important in the fourteenth century. In its focus on lyric composition rather than performance, it departs from the earlier tradition of lyric insertions: the castelain composes his songs in private moments and never sings them publicly. The songs are presented as the record of specific experiences and as such have a value as historical documents; as composed pieces, they have a history themselves.

Jean de Meun, in turn, does not even claim to be writing for the sake of making contact with anyone in particular; his apology to the reader assumes a general audience. For him, the poetic enterprise has become an end in itself and not a step toward consummation of an amorous quest; indeed, the conquest of the rose is itself a necessary step toward the consummation of the poetic project. Through the assimilation of the poetic text with the love object, the central focus of the poem is the act of writing, and the central relationship is that of the poet and his creation. Although the *Poire* valorizes the production of the textual artifact, the love relationship remains the necessary context within which, and for which, poetic activity takes place; and although the status of the text as a written sign is certainly important, its reference to oral performance is equally so. It would be a mistake to posit a monolithic and unwavering progression throughout the thirteenth century; for example, the *Tournois de Chauvency,* composed in 1285, postdates Jean de Meun's *Rose* yet must be classed with Jean Renart's *Rose* in its use of lyric insertions purely as performance pieces. The *Chastelaine de Vergi* in turn, though composed in the early thirteenth century, cites a song by the châtelain de Couci as an authoritative text rather than a performance piece.[11] Nonetheless, it is clear from the texts that we have examined here that, overall, there is a movement toward a more writerly poetics and toward a celebration of the book as a product of writing and compilation rather than a record of performance.

In this regard, it is interesting to compare the treatment of the *Poire* in MS 2186 to its treatment in MS 12786, perhaps fifty years later. As stated earlier, the illuminations of MS 12786 were never executed; but the spaces left for historiated initials give us an idea of the intended iconography. With only two exceptions, the location of the spaces left here corresponds to that of the miniatures and historiated initials of MS 2186, and there is no reason to believe that the images would have been appreciably different had the artist done his work. Of the two spaces left in MS 12786 that do not correspond to any image of MS 2186, one is located at the passage where the narrator recounts the death of Pyramus and Thisbe (fol. 6v; v. 720). It seems most likely that this initial would have featured the death scene, whereas the initial corresponding to Pyramus's monologue would have represented Pyramus and Thisbe at the wall. The two scenes of the miniature in MS 2186, which would have been difficult to fit into a single initial, could logically be divided and placed each at the appropriate passage.

The other extra historiated initial in MS 12786 is the initial of the refrain sung by the lady following the construction of the acrostic TIBAUT (fol. 21v). This produces an "E" at the end of TIBAUT, which was completed on the preceding page (fol. 21), making the full sequence of historiated letters TIBAUTE. One wonders whether this could be an intentional play on words, allowed to remain implicit, whereby the narrator's name assumes a feminized form, as if to suggest a fusion of masculine and feminine personae. The device is one used by Villon some two hundred years later, with the acrostic VILLONE formed in "La Ballade de la grosse Margot" and "La Ballade pour prier Nostre Dame";[12] considering the intricacy of the *Poire* acrostics as they are explicitly announced by the text, it seems entirely possible that further intricacies could lie just beneath the surface. As it happens, the word TIBAUTE is also an anagram for BIAUTET (beauty); and Beauty, as the first of the singing messengers encountered by the protagonist in his tower, may be considered the prime representative of the lady as love object.

These additional associations would increase the signifying powers of

---

11. See Zumthor, "De la chanson au récit." Zumthor calls the citation of the châtelain de Couci "une sorte de *citation d'autorité*, peut-être comparable à celles que l'on rencontre dans la poésie latine du même temps" (p. 79, emphasis his).
12. See Uitti, "Note on Villon's Poetics."

TIBAUT[E] as the middle term in the acrostic text, mediating between ANNES and AMORS—names whose common first and last initials, as stressed by the narrator in his discussion of the acrostics, result in a certain equivalence. Through the anagram TUA SIT, TIBAUT already represents not only the narrator-lover but also his relationship to the lady, coauthor of the acrostic text and reader of the romance. If TIBAUT becomes TIBAUTE-BIAUTET, then this image of the masculine narrator-lover becomes in fact an image of the lady, as feminine reflection of her lover, and the entire acrostic text is a representation of and series of comments upon her. Such a construct would be in keeping with the narcissistic quality of much lyrical poetry in the thirteenth century, in which the lady exists primarily as a projection from the lover's imagination, a poetic construct that he has created. Guillaume de Lorris's Amant, gazing at the image of the rose, is but one step removed from Narcissus, gazing at the image of himself; Pygmalion devotes himself to the product of his own fantasy. The narrator of the *Bestiaire rimé* states that his lady's name contains his name as well and that the same set of letters can represent him, her, and the loving glances exchanged between them. It does not seem impossible, therefore, that the extra "E" was marked out in MS 12786 in recognition of its power to add this further dimension to the acrostic text.[13]

Overall, the treatment of the *Poire* is less performative in MS 12786, and more oriented toward the principle of compilatio. The replacement of the full-page miniatures with historiated initials and the changed page layout (no longer does a monologue correspond to a page) diminishes considerably the theatrical effects of MS 2186, in which the book functioned as a "stage," a framed space in which the monologues and dialogues of part 1 could be played out. The historiated initials of MS 12786 preserve the visual quality of the text and explicitly map out the interlacing of episodes in part 1 and the acrostics of part 2. The techniques of compilation and conjointure and the juggling of written signs are highlighted; the two representations of Pyramus and Thisbe, as noted above, would further underline the disposition of the narrative and the relationship between parts 1 and 2. As such, the *Poire* is an important element of the overall composition of the codex, which, as has

13. It is not certain that the effect on the acrostics was noticed by the scribe of MS 12786, who did not take particular care in the execution of the acrostic initials: in several places he made the historiated initial be not that of the refrain but that of the line immediately following the refrain, so that the acrostic is destroyed. It is possible, therefore, that the historiation of this extra initial is due to a failure to perceive the integrity of the acrostics; the scribe of MS 12786 does seem to have been primarily concerned with marking the disposition of lyric insertions and narrative exempla. Nonetheless, in a poem such as this, one must ask why the original poet, who certainly understood very well the acrostic function of the refrains, would have inserted an extra refrain if it was not meant to participate in some manner in this program.

been seen in previous discussions, is a well-integrated collection. The integration of lyric insertions into the narrative of the *Poire* exemplifies the use, at the level of the individual text, of a technique operating at the level of the codex as well. The "Poitevin song" between the *Bestiaire d'amours* and the *Rose* acts as a lyric insertion between these two first-person, lyrical texts; the series of motets is a large-scale lyric insertion within the context of the codex as a whole. The movement within the *Poire*, from a series of textual motifs and narrative moments to the ordering of these motifs within a single narrative framework, mirrors the juxtaposition of the *Rose* and the series of texts that represent elements contained by the *Rose*. Whether or not the *Poire* was originally planned as the opening text of the collection, it is at least an appropriate choice for this position providing the codex with a prologue in which the essential principles of lyrico-narrative and lyrico-didactic compilation are exemplified.[14]

This contrast between the thirteenth- and fourteenth-century treatments of the *Poire* not only fits into the larger picture of literary history during this period but also parallels the contrast between thirteenth- and fourteenth-century manuscripts of the *Bestiaire d'amours*. There are a great many more manuscripts of the *Bestiaire d'amours*, and the contrast in this case is not absolute. The representations of dialogue in the fourteenth-century Vienna MS Nationalbibl. 2609 and the projection of the two lovers into the poetic space of the bestiary image in the fourteenth-century Bodleian MS Douce 308 are in keeping with the thirteenth-century emphasis on oral discourse and performance and, indeed, recall the performative qualities of *Poire* MS 2186. As the discussion in the preceding chapter showed, however, it is primarily in the fourteenth-century manuscripts, including the Vienna and Douce manuscripts, that the representation of reading, writing, or the presentation of the book appears and, in some cases, takes on a central importance.

The more writerly quality of lyric and lyrico-narrative poetry in the late thirteenth century and the increased focus on poetic composition and compilation rather than performance are evident in the *Dit de la panthère d'amours*. The *Panthère*, composed sometime between 1290 and 1328, has strong affinities not only with the *Poire* but also with the *Bestiaire d'amours* and the *Rose;* it is an important statement about these texts and the relationships among them and can help us to assess the ways in which the poetic innovations of the thirteenth century were received and reinterpreted by fourteenth-century poets.

---

14. Walters, "Chrétien de Troyes and the *Romance of the Rose*," argues that the *Poire* was chosen as a prologue to the book as a whole (p. 374). Since no original pagination or numeration of gatherings survives, however, it is impossible to be certain that the current order is the original one; see the discussion in Chapter 1. Unfortunately, the placement of the *Poire* in prologue position must remain a hypothesis.

## Le Dit de la panthère d'amours as a Literary Compilation

The *Panthère* represents a varied blend of literary material; and, interestingly, this blend is remarkably similar, thematically and generically, to the contents of MS 12786. The allegorical dream format of the *Panthère* is modeled on that of the *Rose;* and the God of Love explicitly advises the *Panthère* protagonist to read the *Rose* in order to learn about love. Venus in turn recommends Drouart La Vache's translation of Andreas Capellanus's *Art of Love* and cites an otherwise unknown poem—possibly a lapidary, or at any rate a poem with lapidary material—attributed to Jehan L'Espicier, which explains the virtues and allegorical properties of a gold ring set with jewels. Both Venus and the protagonist cite lyric poetry by Adam de la Halle, and both additionally compose short dits d'amour; the protagonist composes a lyric cycle at the end of the poem. Richard's *Bestiaire d'amours* is a powerful implicit presence; dreams, and the allegorical significance of dreams, are an important theme.

I have suggested that the compilation of texts in MS 12786 functions as a response to Guillaume's *Rose,* which is continued and fulfilled through its placement at the nexus of this poetic system. The *Rose* is also identified as a seminal text in the *Panthère.* The God of Love states that when it comes to the question of how to succeed in love, "Dedens le rommant de la Rose / Trouveras la semence[15] enclose" (Within the *Romance of the Rose* you will find the seed enclosed [Todd ed., vv. 1033–34]). Here, too, the *Rose* provides an underlying narrative construct that contributes to the coherence of the composite whole; and it is probably Guillaume de Lorris's part of the poem that is at issue. The lover's behavior and the indeterminate ending suggest Guillaume but not Jean de Meun: the *Panthère* protagonist refuses to make any overt attempts at winning his lady's favor, preferring to await good fortune. The *Panthère,* like the *Poire,* offers an alternative development of Guillaume's system, as elements of the *Rose* are appropriated and expanded or exploited as points of contact with other texts. Let us examine a few examples.

The central image of Nicole's poem is of course the panther. The God of Love explains to the protagonist the allegorical significance of the panther, image for his lady, and of her enemy the dragon, symbol of the

---

15. In his edition of the *Panthère*, Todd gives the reading *science* from the fifteenth-century Leningrad manuscript, but I see no reason to reject a perfectly good fourteenth-century reading. The term *semence* (seed, sowing) recalls Guillaume's statement about the fountain that "Cupido, li filz Venus, / sema d'amours ici la graine" (Cupid, the son of Venus, sowed here the seed of love [vv. 1587–88]) and supports the *Rose* narrator's assertion that although many romances and books have spoken of the Fountain of Love, "ja mes n'oroiz mielz descrivre / la verité de la matere" (you will never hear the truth of the matter described better [vv. 1598–99]).

envious and covetous enemies of love; thus the poem does contain an abbreviated *Bestiaire d'amours.* The use of allegory was already an essential, and innovative, feature of Guillaume's romance, where the protagonist falls in love with a rose. Nicole has transformed Guillaume's flower into an animal. In fact, a more general association of flowers and animals is suggested by Nicole's emphasis on the spectacular colors of the beasts and particularly the panther, as well as on the sweet odor of the panther's breath. The beasts of the forest where his dream takes place, for example, are:

> Verdes, jaunes, bleues et perses,
> Sores, fauves, indes les unes,
> Blanches et noires, rouges, brunes.

[Green, yellow, different shades of blue, sorrel, tawny, some violet, white and black, red, brown.] [Vv. 62–64]

The panther in turn contains all colors, as the medieval etymologists felt her name implied;[16] and of course it was for her sweet breath that the panther was primarily known in medieval bestiaries. This description of multiple colors and sweet odors echoes Guillaume's extended description of the Garden of Delight, colorfully blanketed "de flors de diverses colors / dont mout estoit bone l'odors" (with flowers of diverse colors, whose odor was very good [*Rose,* vv. 1407–8]). The kaleidoscopically colored panther with its alluring breath also recalls l'Amant's vision of the rose, formed from the "colors plus de cent" (more than a hundred colors) generated by the crystals, illuminated with a brilliant *vermeille* (red), and exuding an intoxicating odor that "tote la place replenist" (filled the entire place) (*Rose,* vv. 1544, 1657–58, 1668). A final echo of the botanical image appears in the concluding section of the *Panthère,* where the lady has become "la bone herbe" (the good herb [v. 2446]) that heals the lover's eyes.

The passage from flowers to animals is in fact suggested by an important passage of the *Rose:* the description of the God of Love's robe. Guillaume tells us that Love wore a "robe de floreites" (robe of flowers [v. 877]) made out of flowers of every kind and color, including purple, black, white, yellow, and various shades of blue. These flowers are woven together in such a way as to create a mosaic pattern of animals and geometric design:

> A losenges, a escuciaus,
> a oiselez, a lionciaus

16. On the panther in medieval bestiary tradition, see Todd's edition of the *Panthère,* pp. xvii–xxiii.

195

et a betes et a liparz
fu sa robe de toutes parz
portrete, et ovree de flors
par diverseté de colors.

[With losenges, escutcheons, birds, lions, and beasts and leopards, his robe was decorated all over, and worked in flowers through their diverse colors.] [Vv. 879–84]

The God of Love's robe, in other words, is a visual *Bestiaire d'amours*.[17] Nicole echoes this passage—hinting, perhaps, at one of the keys to the decoding of his own poetic system—in his description of the God of Love. Nicole's God of Love is ornamented with gold and jewels of all colors; his robe is decorated with pearls "a bestes et a oysiaus" (in a design of beasts and birds [v. 255]). Guillaume's bestiary of flowers is answered by an analogous bestiary of jewels; latent in both passages is an allusion to the "flowers" and "colors" of rhetoric.

Guillaume's robe of love provides an important image of compilatio. The conjoining of diverse elements creates a new order of units, a new poetic language; and it is this textual fabric, with its two levels of signification, that encloses the personification of love. Similarly, Guillaume's poem encloses the art of love, and it too signifies at two (or more) levels; the visual imagery of the dream recombines to form an image of the love experience that the dream prophesizes. The process is repeated, at an even more fundamental level, in the vision at the fountain. Here, rather than colored flowers creating a pattern of animals, pure colors combine to create a vision of, among other things, flowers, including the particular flower upon which the protagonist fixes his desire. Nicole in turn has taken Guillaume's imagery of compilatio and artifice and made it a poetic principle in his reworking of the *Rose*. Guillaume's text of flowers and colors, constructed around a rose, and Richard de Fournival's explicitly visual text of beasts, come together and fuse in the fabric of Nicole's poem.

This network of associations linking vegetal, lapidary, and linguistic artifice may not be entirely arbitrary. According to the medieval lapidary tradition, "nus sages homs ne doit douter que Diex n'ait mis vertuz en pierres et en herbes et en paroles" (no wise man should doubt that God placed power in stones and in herbs and in words [MS 12786, fol.

---

17. These descriptions of the God of Love's vestments recall the miniature in Douce 308 representing the bestiary figures scattered across an ornamental field. This miniature and Nicole's description are similar visual responses to Richard's text.

24v]).[18] In MS 12786 the lapidary that states this association in its prologue is followed by the *Bestiaire d'amours* with its prologue about parole
and painture, and the *Rose*.[19] In the lapidary, the colors, ornamental
qualities, powers, and allegorical significance of stones are described; the
bestiary combines visual representation and verbal explication of animals and their allegorical significance; in the *Rose,* flowers have both an
ornamental and a signifying function. The anthology codex effects a
juxtaposition of different allegorical registers, different ornamental and
signifying systems. In the *Panthère,* the implied association of three bestiaries—one of flowers, one of jewels, and one of parole and painture—
effects an even more tightly woven fusion of the multifaceted language
of allegory.

Why did Nicole choose the panther as the particular animal to represent his lady? He may have been motivated in part by the strategic
location of the panther at the midpoint of the *Bestiaire d'amours.* The
panther is the culmination of Richard's discussion of the five senses:
following seduction by sight and sound, the panther with its sweet breath
signifies seduction by the "flaire de la virginité" (scent of virginity). The
progression of love through the five senses is represented in the *Rose* as
well: following his fascination with birdsong and music and his examination of the visual beauties of the garden, the protagonist finally suc-
cumbs to the sight and odor of the rose, and eventually advances to the
sense of taste with the kiss. Although the motif of seduction through the
senses is hardly unique to the *Rose* and the *Bestiaire d'amours,* Richard's
construct does allow for a reading of the rose and the panther as analogous: the substitution of the panther for the rose enables Nicole in turn
to effect a conflation of these two important texts.[20]

Beyond that, the particular qualities of the panther make it especially
effective as a means of evoking what I have called the "audiovisual
poetics" of the *Bestiaire d'amours.* The panther, too, has this "audiovisual"
quality. She is a visual spectacle, containing "de chascune beste / La

18. "Fragments du Lapidaire de Philippe," in Pannier's edition of *Lapidaires français,* p.
292. This idea appears in both verse and prose lapidaries of both the Christian allegorical
and the pagan "Marbode" traditions; for example, the prologue of an early thirteenth-
century verse lapidary of the Marbode tradition, explaining that God distributed special
powers among stones, plants, and words, concludes: "En cestes trois choses habunde /
Tote la force de cest monde" (In these three things abounds all the power of this world
[Pannier ed., "Lapidaire de Berne," vv. 19–20]).

19. Pannier notes that the Christian allegorical lapidary often appears in conjunction
with the *Bestiaire divin* and raises the possibility that both might be the work of Guillaume le
Clerc; see Pannier's edition of *Lapidaires français,* pp. 231–34.

20. Richard de Fournival's narrator states that it was his excessive pride that induced the
God of Love to hunt him down (Segre ed., pp. 43–44); this detail, although conventional,
does also recall both the pride of Narcissus and the stalking of l'Amant by the God of Love
in the *Rose.*

colour" (the color of every beast [vv. 483–84]); according to the God of Love, this signifies "l'abondance / Des vertus" (the abundance of virtues [vv. 474–75]) in the protagonist's lady, who contains all the qualities that are distributed among the other ladies.[21] The panther's breath, in turn, represents the lady's wise speech, "Car parole si est alaine" (for speech is breath [v. 508]). The panther, in other words, embodies parole and painture, the two necessary components of Richard's text. She is a visual compendium of colors representing the qualities of the love object, just as the *Bestiaire* is a compendium of images of animals representing qualities of the love experience; and she is the source of parole, just as writing reverts to speech when it is read aloud. We could even say that the protagonist's experience of gazing upon the colors of the panther and marveling at her sweet breath figures the experience that Richard's narrator offered to his lady, whom he hoped would gaze at the pictures, listen to the words, and so fall in love with him. By transposing these qualities into the figure of the lady, Nicole suggests, like Jean de Meun, an association of text and lady. The ramifications of this association, and Nicole's contribution to the evolution of lyrical writing, will become apparent as we continue to examine the poem.

We have seen a possible allusion to Guillaume de Lorris's fountain sequence in Nicole's emphasis on colors. A stronger allusion to this passage of the *Rose* appears a little later on, during the protagonist's conversation with Venus (vv. 1039–1629). Here Venus presents the protagonist with a dit declaring his love along with an emerald ring that is to be wrapped inside the dit and presented to the lady. Venus takes this opportunity to cite Jehan L'Espicier and to explain the allegory of ring, gold, emerald, and also diamond (although there is no diamond). The protagonist is initially enthusiastic, but upon receiving the poem and ring he falls asleep (within the frame dream) and dreams that he offers the gift to his lady, who angrily refuses him. He awakes in anguish (back to the frame dream) and vows never to approach the lady directly, so great is his fear of rejection. In the course of the conversation with Venus, both before and after the internal dream, he and Venus quote from songs by Adam de la Halle.

This passage has several points in common with the fountain passage of the *Rose*. At the most literal level, both draw on the lapidary tradition. Guillaume does not cite any authority for his account of the crystals, to which he ascribes special powers of mirroring that are probably of his own invention.[22] His description of the action of the sun's rays on the

21. The word *panthère* even echoes Richard's *painture;* possibly this was intended as a subliminal reference to the poetics of the *Bestiaire d'amours*.

22. Guillaume's crystals are described in terms reminiscent of medieval accounts of the role of the eyes in love psychology. For a review of the scholarship on this subject, see Hillman.

crystal, however, may have been motivated by the lapidary tradition that crystal would catch on fire if struck by the sun.[23] The *electre*, an alloy of gold and silver, may have been another source. This stone, like Guillaume's crystals, had aphrodisiac powers, and in one lapidary of the early thirteenth century is described as follows:

> Et si est samblant a la greve
> De fontaine qui bien resplant,
> Et samble cristal qui espant
> Sa blanchour quant solas i fiert.

[Thus it is similar to the sand in a fountain, which sparkles, and it resembles crystal, which casts a white light when the sun strikes it.] [Pannier ed., "Lapidaire de Berne," vv. 198–201]

The crystals were considered important enough that some illuminators of the *Rose* took the trouble to draw them in representations of the Fountain of Love. It is quite possible, then, that Nicole's insertion of lapidary material would have appeared to medieval readers as a reworking and rendering explicit of one aspect of this celebrated passage.

That the jeweled ring is enclosed within the written text of the dit is an interesting detail and further echoes the location of the crystals within the Fountain of Love. Guillaume's fountain is a literary construct, marked by the written reference to Narcissus's death, and it occasions the narrator's recapitulation of the Narcissus story. This narrative within the larger narrative mirrors l'Amant's own story, just as the crystals themselves mirror the Garden of Delight. The mise-en-abyme is reconstructed by Nicole in the ring, which allegorically figures the qualities of the love experience, and the dit, which mirrors the feelings the protagonist had expressed in his own earlier dit:

> Dedens ce dit moult bien escript
> Avoit la deesse descript
> De mon dit[24] toute la matiere.

[Within this very well written dit, the goddess had described all the material of my dit.] [Todd ed., vv. 1148–50]

The association of the emerald ring with Guillaume's crystals may be further heightened by the lapidary emphasis on the reflective powers of

23. One early thirteenth-century lapidary says of crystal, "Nunlz ne doubtoit que feu ne faice / Qui au rais dou solest le met" (No one who put it into the sun's ray doubted that it would produce fire [Pannier ed., "Lapidaire de Berne," vv. 1050–51]).

24. In his edition of the *Panthère* Todd here gives the reading *cuer* from the fifteenth-century manuscript. Again, I feel that the fourteenth-century reading is equally plausible and that it should not be ignored.

the emerald; its mirrorlike quality is sometimes compared to that of water:

> Ki bien l'esguarde par desure
> Puet l'en veeir tut ensement
> Cum en clere eve sun semblant.

[Whoever looks at it from above can see his face there, just as in clear water.]
[Pannier ed., "Lapidaire de Cambridge," vv. 222–24]

The emerald was even said to reveal future or distant events; lapidary tradition tells of an emerald mirror that enabled Nero to monitor the affairs of the Roman Empire.[25] The movement from the mirrorlike crystals that afford l'Amant his first vision of the rose to the emerald that inspires the *Panthère* protagonist's admonitory vision of his lady is authorized by lapidary tradition.

The dream inspired by the ring serves as a warning to the protagonist of the despair that may await him if he is not careful; in that respect, too, it is analogous to the story of Narcissus in the *Rose*. The content of this warning, however, is entirely different. The danger represented in the *Rose* is that of lyric isolation and solipsism, to be avoided through making contact with a reciprocating "other," object of desire. That in the *Panthère* is refusal, unfavorable reception; and it is precisely through avoidance of direct contact with the object of desire that this danger is to be circumvented. Rejection and loss of contact with the beloved is in fact the fate that befalls Guillaume's Lover. The dream experience of Nicole's protagonist is an encapsulation of Guillaume's *Rose*, divested of its allegorical trappings.[26] By holding this narrative sequence up as a negative example, Nicole identifies his poem as a surpassing of Guillaume's *Rose*.

In certain respects, Nicole's rewriting of the original *Rose* resembles that of Jean de Meun. In content and tone, the two poems are admittedly very different. But both poets take the basic structure of Guillaume's poem as a point of departure, expanding the original poetic system and incorporating other literary material. Nicole, as we have seen, develops intertextual links between the *Rose* and other allegorical literature while also intensifying the lyricism of the *Rose;* Jean drew

25. Nero's mirror appears in both the Marbode and the Christian lapidaries. MS 12786 states that "moult est bone esmeraude a esgarder et a mirer. Noirons en ot un mireor ou il se miroit, et savoit par la force de ceste pierre ce qu'il voloit enquerre" (emerald is very good for seeing and gazing. Nero had an emerald mirror that he looked into, and he knew by the power of this stone whatever he wanted to find out [Pannier ed., p. 294]).

26. It is interesting to note that, as the narrative moves from one dream level to the next, it passes into and out of the allegorical register; in the internal dream, the lady is evidently no longer a panther.

largely on the Latin tradition. Both, however, made Guillaume's poem the nucleus for a literary compilation, as did the author of the *Roman de la poire* and the compiler of MS 12786. Different though these four works are, the processes of writing and anthologizing are fundamental to each. We must turn now to an examination of writing in the *Panthère*. What perspective does this poem offer on lyricism and lyrical writing?

## Performance and Book: From Carol to Lyric Compendium

Writing is an explicit aspect of the exchange between the protagonist and Venus: Guillaume's visual mirroring is replaced by the verbal mirroring of poetry, made visual through writing. Although the explication of the ring is given orally, Venus presents this material as the citation of a written text, which she tells the protagonist to read. Even more striking is the treatment of the lyric insertions: Adam's songs are authoritative texts about love. The pieces are clearly songs and they would normally be experienced through oral performance. The protagonist says of Adam at one point, "En son chant ainsi le chanta" (In his song he sang it thus [v. 1071]); and again, "D'Adam ay je oÿ retraire / .I. ver encor" (I have heard recited another verse of [or about] Adam [vv. 1082–83]). Within the *Panthère,* however, these songs are not so much performed as cited. The narrator introduces one song, for example, with the words, "Ainsi com j'ay oy chanter / En ce chant d'Adam que je dire / Vous veil" (Just as I have heard sung in this song of Adam which I want to tell you [vv. 1587–89]). The word *dire* could mean "to sing" in Old French. But in contrast to *chanter* it has distinctly nonmusical connotations. The derivatives *dit* and *chant* were often used to distinguish the words and the tune of a song, respectively. The opposition of *chanter* and *dire* appears in the *Bestiaire d'amours*, where *dire* refers to the discourse adopted by the narrator as a replacement for song; commenting that he has yet to obtain mercy, the narrator exerts himself "ne mie a forment canter, mais a forment et atangnamment dire" (not at all to sing boldly, but to discourse boldly and aggressively [Segre ed., p. 10]). The *Panthère* protagonist's formulation similarly implies a nonperformative rendition: song here passes from song to document. This status is further implied in the protagonist's designation of Adam, in his address to Venus, as "vostre clerc Adams" (your clerk, Adam [v. 1069]. Adam is a clerk of love; and his works are at once song and written text.[27]

It is hardly an accident that Adam should be the trouvère so chosen by Nicole: as we saw in Chapter 2, Adam's works form a literary compen-

27. On *clergie* in the works of Adam de la Halle, see Zaganelli.

dium unto themselves in MS 25566, whereas in chansonnier *A*, Adam and Richard de Fournival are the two trouvères represented as writers. Both the portrait and the compilation date from the late thirteenth century and are thus more or less contemporary with the *Panthère*. Poetic, codicological, and iconographic evidence converges to highlight the pivotal role played by Adam de la Halle in the history of lyrical writing. When we consider additionally that Nicole sets the action of the *Panthère* in Soissons, domicile of Richard de Fournival; that both MS 25566 and chansonnier *A* contain the *Bestiaire;* that MS 12786 conjoins the *Poire,* the *Bestiaire,* the *Rose,* lyric pieces, and other allegorical material; and that the scribe of the Bibl. Nat. MS fr. 24432, the only surviving fourteenth-century manuscript of the *Panthère,* perceived such affinities between the *Bestiaire* and the *Panthère* that he attributed the latter to "Mestre Richart de Fournival, Chanoine de Soissons," we can begin to appreciate something of the context within which the *Panthère* must be read. It is a work profoundly informed by the poetic and codicological phenomena that we have examined throughout this book.

The more writerly treatment of lyricism is clear if we compare the *Panthère* to the *Rose* or to the *Poire.* The profusion of songs surrounding the dream might suggest a replay of the carol that the *Rose* protagonist encountered on his way to the Fountain of Love. And the *Panthère* protagonist's initial encounter with the God of Love is in the context of musical celebration that recalls the God of Love's first appearance among the carolers of the Garden of Delight. Similarly, the God of Love makes his appearance in the narrative portion of the *Poire* surrounded by an entourage of singers and musicians, and the vision of the lady and of the love relationship is provided by the refrain acrostics. These acrostics effect a mise-en-abyme of the *Poire* narrative comparable to that produced by Guillaume's Narcissus passage or Nicole's dit and dream. But the visual acrostics are generated from a series of musical performances and thus differ markedly from Nicole's written dit or his evocation of Adam's clerkly lyrics. The second "carol" of the *Panthère* has become a series of textual citations, aimed not at dramatizing a particular love experience but at codifying love experience in general. Indeed, the differences between the *Panthère* and the *Poire* parallel the differences between the more performative thirteenth-century treatment of the *Poire* in MS 2186 and the more writerly fourteenth-century treatment in MS 12786.

In the lyric cycle at the end of the poem, lyric discourse has been even more fully integrated into the narrative voice of the *Dit de la panthère d'amours* as a written text. The narrator explains that after awakening he reflected upon his dream and saw that the only "lie" in it was the panther's favorable response at the end—he has had, as yet, no such response from his lady. He then proceeds to reiterate his love for her and to narrate the course of this love by citing a series of lyric pieces that he has composed at various stages of the love affair. The dual nature of this sequence was noted by Ernest Hoepffner, who terms it "a sort of epilogue" and finds that, in comparison with the didactic dream narrative, this section has a more personal and more intimate character. At the same time, Hoepffner remarks that this concluding section contains an example, complete with generic designation, of each of the principal formes fixes (except the lay), so that it becomes as well "a sort of *Canzoniere*."[28] At once lyrical autobiography and ars poetica, the concluding section of the *Panthère* embraces literariness and lyricism.[29]

The formes fixes were musical as well as literary forms, and the poems of this final sequence could easily be set to music and performed. Here, however, they are incorporated into the narrative and cited as documents that record the protagonist's feelings at different stages of the love experience. Describing the carefree early period of his love, for example, the narrator states that he sang frequently during this time and that, inspired by love, he composed his first lyric piece, a ballade. Upon quoting the song, he reiterates its accuracy as a representation of his behavior at a certain point in the past: "Au commencier me maintenoie / Ainsi" (In the beginning I behaved in this way [vv. 2317–18]). At times the continuity of voice between narrative and lyric passages is virtually seamless, as the narrator appears to be composing the song "on the spot." Announcing his undying love, for example, he states:

> S'en di ceste chançon jolie,
> Qu'Amors de nouvel me fait faire,
> Pour ce que mon cuer y declaire:
>
> Pour ennuy ne por contraire
>   Ne pour mal souffrir
> Ne me puis d'amer tenir.

[I tell of it in this pretty song, which Love causes me to make anew, because he declares my heart in it: Not for sorrow or contrarity, nor for having suffered pain, can I keep myself from loving.] [Vv. 2223–28]

The distinction between lyric and narrative discourse here is one of versification, rather than one of performance versus writing. Both the octosyllabic couplets of narrative and the lyric formes fixes are available to a writer who wishes to record a love story. Both can be used to address

---

28. Hoepffner, "Poésies lyriques du *Dit de la panthère*," pp. 214, 227.
29. The more accurate term would be "pseudoautobiography"; I do not mean to suggest that the narrative should be read as a factual account of events that befell the real Nicole de Margival.

either a general audience or the particular audience of the lady: after a lyrico-narrative recapitulation of his love experiences, the narrator finally addresses the lady herself, first in octosyllabic couplets and then in a rondeau. At the end, he reiterates that the work as a whole has been produced through the combined process of introspection and writing:

> Que ceste oevre est toute accomplie,
> Quant est de rimer et d'escrire,
> Et de tout mon estat descrire.

[For this work is all completed, in terms of rhyming and writing and of describing my entire condition.] [Vv. 2627–29]

This interpenetration of lyric and narrative discourse in a medium at once lyrical and writerly is an important consequence of the poetic and codicological innovations of the thirteenth century as we have examined them here. The passage from chanter to dire reflects the passage from chanson to dit, from performance to book.

## Lyrical Writing in Le Dit de la panthère d'amours

The nature of the *Panthère* as a piece of lyrical writing is established in the prologue and epilogue. In the prologue, the narrator states he has composed the work especially for his lady but does not dare send it directly to her for fear of arousing envious gossip or, perhaps, offending her (vv. 1–18). Instead, he plans to disseminate it widely, sending copies to all loyal lovers in the hope that it will eventually be seen by "Cele por qui fu commencie" (she for whom it was begun [v. 25]). We recognize here a writerly transformation of the trouvère topos of dissemination of the song, articulated, among others, by Conon de Béthune:

> Chançon legiere a entendre
> Ferai, car bien m'est mestiers
> Ke chascuns le puist aprendre
> Et c'on le chant volentiers;
> Ne par autres messaigiers
> N'iert ja ma dolors mostree
> A la millor ki soit nee.

[I will make a song easy to understand, for I greatly need everyone to be able to learn it and sing it willingly; nor will my sorrow ever be revealed by any other messenger to the best lady ever born.] [Wallensköld ed., no. 1, vv. 1–7]

The same process was represented in the *Roman du castelain de Couci*, where the châtelain depended on the popularity of his songs and their performance by minstrels for his sentiments to be revealed to his lady. In the *Panthère*, however, it is no longer through performance of song that the lover's message will reach his lady, but rather through the copying and reading of his dit. And the hidden clue that lets the lady know that the poem is dedicated to her is not the lyric *senhal* or a suggestive *envoi*, but rather the anagram by which the writer signs his work.

As a result of this setup, the poem has a kind of double focus, addressing itself at once to the lady and to a general readership. The narrator expresses his hopes that the poem will find favor with his lady, stating in the prologue, "Si li pri qu'ele en gré reçoive, / Que por li l'ai empris a faire" (Thus I beg of her to receive [it] in good will, for I undertook to make it for her [vv. 36–37]). In the epilogue he reiterates that love inspired his work, "Que a ma dame peüst plaire" (That it might please my lady [v. 2623]). At the same time, although the lady is addressed in the lyric insertions and in the dits, the frame narrative is addressed to a general audience. Directly following the prologue, the narrative begins with the line, "Seignor, j'ai oÿ des m'enfance . . ." (Lords, I have heard since my childhood . . . [v. 41]). And in the epilogue, the narrator expresses the hope that his future audience will effect any textual emendations that it deems necessary to improve upon his work:

> Si pri trestous ceulz qui l'orront
> Et qui amender y savront
> Ou corrigier s'il y a point,
> Por Dieu, qu'il le mettent a point.

[Thus I beg all those who will hear it, and who will know how to amend it, or make corrections if there are any, for God's sake, that they put it right.] [Vv. 2612–15]

The confluence of lyric and narrative voices here resembles that of the conjoined *Rose* and may well be Nicole's response to that composite text.[30] An allegorical dream of love, versified in honor of the lady figured by the dream, and a body of lyric discourse addressed to this lady are inscribed in a written context that addresses itself to a larger readership. Nicole's prologue dedication echoes that of Guillaume de Lorris,

---

30. It is not certain that Nicole knew Jean de Meun's continuation, nor is it necessary to postulate that he did; he could have derived his treatment of lyrico-narrative discourse from the general body of thirteenth-century texts such as those we have examined here. It is possible, however, that he did know Jean's continuation, especially if the *Panthère* was composed toward 1328 (Todd's terminus ad quem), and chose to compose the *Panthère* as an alternative response to Guillaume de Lorris without verbal echoes of Jean de Meun but with certain poetological borrowings.

"or doint Dex qu'en gré le receve / cele por qui je l'ai empris" (Now may God grant that she for whom I have undertaken it, receive it in good will [*Rose*, vv. 40–41]). Nicole's appeal to a general audience—"tous ceus . . . Qui aimment bien et loiaument" (all those . . . who love well and loyally [vv. 21–22]), "trestous ceulz qui l'orront" (all those who will hear it [v. 2612])—in turn corresponds to Jean de Meun's apology: "Or antandez leal amant . . ." (Now listen, loyal lovers . . . [*Rose*, v. 15105]). We saw a somewhat similar construct in the *Roman du castelain de Couci:* Jakemes's appropriation and incorporation of the châtelain's lyric corpus into a written narrative format resembles Jean's appropriation of Guillaume's poem and its incorporation into the new romance. As was pointed out by David Hult, the effect at the conjoining of Guillaume and Jean is to bracket the whole of Guillaume's poem in quotation marks, making of it a kind of lyric monologue for which Jean's poem provides the narrative context and continuation.[31] What is innovative about the *Panthère* is that a single author figure generates the diversity of voices, bracketing, as it were, his own lyric discourse in quotation marks. Songs and dits are clearly cited as independently composed texts incorporated into the larger narrative structure.[32] And the concluding section of the final lyric sequence, in which the narrator does finally address the lady directly, is also set apart as a dramatic monologue performed for the benefit of the general audience:

> Pour ce veil, sans plus sejourner,
> Devers ma dame retourner,
> En qui j'ai m'entencion mise,
> Et li proier en ceste guise:
>
> Douce dame, courtoise et bele . . .

[And so I wish, without further ado, to return to my lady, to whom I have turned all my thoughts, and entreat her in this way: Sweet lady, courteous and beautiful . . .] [Vv. 2477–81]

This multiplicity of voice within a single authorial identity, at once lyric persona, lyric poet, narrator, and writer, is of profound importance for the poets of the fourteenth century, as will be seen in Part 3 of this book.

31. Hult, "Closed Quotations." A similar technique is used by the anonymous continuator of the *Bestiaire d'amours*, who in effect turns the entire work into the protagonist's lament and address to his heart: this in turn makes it possible to continue the narrative by having the heart reply and suggest a course of action, which the protagonist then follows (see Chapter 5).

32. Hoepffner, "Poésies lyriques," feels that these lyric insertions really were composed in the author's youth and compares the *Panthère* to the *Vita nuova* (pp. 215–16). All that is important for my purposes, however, is the chronology set up within the text, where the poems are presented as records of past experience and of past poetic activity.

A similar interpenetration of lyrical and writerly modes governs the two-part structure of the poem and the figure of the lady as she appears in the dream and in the lyric sequence, respectively. The closing section recasts the dream narrative in lyric terms: the lover declares his devotion to his lady; is initially optimistic and then, at apparent rejection, crestfallen; rallies with a new profession of love; and finally imagines a favorable response from the lady and his own joyful reply. But the treatment of the basic material is very different. In the dream narrative, the lady appears as the panther, an image drawn from the clerkly bestiary tradition and a figure of textuality. In the concluding section, she is first the reference point for the lover's lyric discourse and then, in the rondeau that he conceives for her, a lyric voice generated from this discourse.[33] The entire first part is grounded in a series of written texts, anterior to the protagonist's experience, that serve to explicate and give form to this experience; even Venus's dit is said, in the fourteenth-century manuscript, to reflect not the protagonist's feelings as such but his own previous poeticization of these feelings. In the second part, lyric texts are presented as having derived from unmediated sentiments of love. The relationship between dreamer and lady is, to a large extent, governed by the model of text and reader: with the God of Love's help, he reads the panther as an image of his lady; in his dream, she reads the dit that Venus has provided. In the second part, their interaction is that of lyric dialogue. This dialogue, however, takes place within the narrator's imagination; it is made possible by the construction of the lyric compendium, itself a function of writing.

Lyricization of a literary tradition, application of writing to lyricism, the *Panthère* combines techniques that we have seen in the texts previously examined. Again, the written text provides a space where lover and lady can interact as readers of one another. Yet even this interaction is strangely hypothetical. The narrator states his refusal to send the poem directly to the lady, addressing it rather to an audience at large. He admits that the one falsehood in his dream is the favorable outcome of his suit, while the panther is glossed within the dream itself as a metaphor. Even the lyric exchange at the end is presented as the narrator's wish, not as a reality. The entire relationship, it would seem, is a figment of the poet's imagination. What is represented in the dit is the writer's relationship with his own textual creation, with which he interacts variously as clerkly narrator, lyric poet, and protagonist.

To make such a statement is not to discount the content of the *Panthère* as a love poem. It is rather to remark on the integration of the self-

---

33. The dual representation of the lady as panther and as lyric persona may derive from the *Rose*. Here, the lady appears both as a rose, a symbolic image laden with erotic and sacred connotations, and as allegorical personifications of qualities familiar from the courtly tradition.

reflexive quality of lyricism and the writerly intertextuality of the romance tradition in the new model of lyric poet as writer. The written voice does not fade away; it reaches an audience widely dispersed through space and time. But the written text that allows the contact between writer and reader is at the same time a barrier that prevents the live interaction possible between singer and audience. Like Pygmalion, the writer can create a new reality, but also like Pygmalion, he may find that this textually constituted reality serves to isolate him. While a number of thirteenth-century poets held up writing as the means of breaking the lyric circle of isolation, we have also seen that there was a current, perhaps especially pronounced in Jean de Meun, that led toward a privileging of the relationship of writer and text and an eroticization of the activity of writing itself. In this fashion the writer becomes once more a performer, one whose "performance" takes place in the privacy of his study and reaches its audience in the form of a visual record.

# PART THREE

# LYRICISM AND THE BOOK
# IN THE FOURTEENTH CENTURY

Or veult l'amant faire dis et balades,
Lettres closes, segrectes ambaxades;
Et se retrait
Et s'enfermë en chambre ou en retrait
Pour escripre plus a l'aise et a trait.

[Now the lover wants to make dits, ballades, closed letters,
secret dispatches; and he withdraws, and shuts himself up in
his room or in a retreat, in order to write more comfortably
and leisurely.]
        Alain Chartier, "Débat de deux fortunés d'amour"

Chapter 7

# The Vernacular Poet as Compiler:
# The Rise of the Single-Author Codex
# in the Fourteenth Century

As we move from thirteenth- to fourteenth-century poets, we encounter significant innovations in both poetic and codicological practices. Not only is there a new self-consciousness in the manipulation of lyric and narrative, in performative and writerly modes, and in the concept of poetic identity, but also the works of these later poets appear in anthology codices devoted entirely to a single author. Guillaume de Machaut and Jean Froissart, and after them such writers as Christine de Pizan and Charles d'Orléans, evidence an involvement with the process of compilation and book production that was not apparent in the poets of the thirteenth century. The codices of Machaut and Froissart were almost certainly organized by the authors themselves; Machaut may well also have designed, or at least influenced, programs of illumination for his works.[1] A given poem appears in the context of other poems by the same author; the sequence of texts defines a particular poetic personality and the development of his career. That the composer of lyric and lyrical narrative poetry is also identified as the author of a book is of great significance, reflecting both a new consciousness on the part of poets and also an audience interest in possessing a given poet's complete works. Before analyzing individual texts, it is well to examine the overall

1. There is little question that both Machaut and Froissart supervised the preparation of codices, although of course we do not know precisely the extent of their involvement. Machaut's role in manuscript preparation is discussed by Avril, "Manuscrits enluminés"; Byrne; and Williams. Poirion refers to the innovative quality of Machaut's carefully ordered manuscripts during his discussion of Machaut in *Poète et le prince*, pp. 192–205; Brownlee discusses the literary significance of Machaut's compilations in "Transformations of the Lyric 'Je'". Froissart refers to the preparation of codices in his Chronicles, as will be seen below. In the introduction to his edition of the *Espinette*, Fourrier suggests that both of the surviving anthology manuscripts of Froissart's poetry (Bibl. Nat. fr. MSS 830, 831) could have been copied from an autograph original (p. 16).

organization of the codices themselves and the precedents for this kind of manuscript production.

In the opening chapters we saw that the middle and late thirteenth century witnessed some tendency toward the compilation of texts by a single author. Trouvère songs, perhaps because of the identification of author and protagonist and the centrality of the lyric "I," are nearly always grouped by author; evidence suggests that Thibaut de Navarre had his works compiled, and a complete compilation of the works of Adam de la Halle survives, though not necessarily from within the poet's lifetime. Among narrative texts, the romances of Chrétien de Troyes are treated as an author corpus in MS Bibl. Nat. fr. 1450, and they frequently appear elsewhere in pairs or groups. In manuscripts other than MS 1450 nothing (such as rubrics or author portraits) explicitly indicates that they are to be read as an integrated corpus or that common authorship is the basis for their association. But Chrétien's system of intertextual allusions, such as the connections between *Yvain* and the *Charrette* or the reference to *Erec et Enide* in the prologue to *Cligès,* would authorize such a reading. The works of Adenet le Roi likewise tend to be transmitted in pairs or groups; and we saw that authorship is an organizational principle in Arsenal MS 3142.

MS 3142 is interesting not only for its association of narrative poems by the same author but also for its collections of dits. The dit, like the song, was a genre that lent itself to transmission in author corpora, perhaps again because of the centrality of the poetic "I" as authority figure. The romance narrator grounds his authority in the real or fictional written source(s) of his story, whereas the persona of song or dit is himself the authorizer of poetic truth; he speaks from his own experience, be it of love, of political intrigue, or of life in general. Rather than citing a previous written work, the dit poet is more likely to cite a dream or an event witnessed in the world. Since the narrative dit figures so prominently in the oeuvres of both Machaut and Froissart, it is important to consider both the nature of the dit as a literary genre and the relationship between dit poetics and the organization of single-author codices.

In a discussion of Machaut's *Livre du voir dit,* Jacqueline Cerquiglini offers two hypotheses concerning the dit as a genre: that it is a genre marked by a principle of discontinuity and that it is a type of discourse in which an "I" is always represented.[2] Cerquiglini further associates the first characteristic with the dit as an explicitly written genre; the principle of discontinuity, of a compositional structure that is extrinsic rather

2. Cerquiglini, "Clerc et l'écriture," pp. 158 and 160. I do not take these characteristics of the dit as fixed generic requirements, but they do provide a useful insight into the affinities between poetics and compilation practice during this period.

than intrinsic to the material, is a function of writing.[3] The "I" of the dit in turn is a voice projected into writing. According to Cerquiglini, the voice of the dit is neither the universal "I" of trouvére lyric nor that of the romance author who writes himself into his text in the third person to distinguish himself from the first-person voice of the live narrator who will read aloud or recite his works. The voice of the dit may mimic oral declamation, and dit poets such as Watriquet de Couvin undoubtedly recited their works at court; but the written text is primary.

These two hypotheses concerning the generic distinction of the dit are useful for an understanding of the relationship between the dit as a literary form and the phenomenon of single-author codices. First of all, as I have said, the centrality of the poetic "I" clearly lends itself to an association of poems by the same author. Moreover, if the dit is to be associated with a principle of discontinuity, with ordering principles extrinsic to the material, then it is logical that the dit would lend itself to compilation: the series of individual dits is marked by the rhythm of closure and reopening, as one text ends and the next begins. The organizational principles peculiar to single-author compilations—authorship, patronage, circumstances of composition—are associated with the extratextual act of poetic composition rather than, as in romance compilations, with the fictional or didactic world within the text (although in many cases the process of composition may be represented within the text). In other words, this manner of compilation itself can be associated with what Cerquiglini has identified as a typical feature of dit poetics.

It is a difficult and perhaps fruitless endeavor to determine whether the evolution of the dit influenced or was influenced by habits of manuscript production; most likely the process worked in both directions. For the present, it is enough to say that the dit and the single-author codex are related phenomena. Our investigation of the single-author codex must therefore include not only such poets as Adam de la Halle, Thibaut de Navarre, Chrétien de Troyes, and Adenet le Roi but also the masters of the thirteenth- and early fourteenth-century dit; I will focus here on Rutebeuf, Baudouin de Condé, his son Jean de Condé, and Watriquet de Couvin.

## "Rustebuef, qui rudement oevre": A Thirteenth-Century Author Corpus

The poetry associated with the figure Rutebeuf must have enjoyed an immediate and fairly widespread popularity, for it is transmitted in

3. Ibid., pp. 159–60. In the same passage Cerquiglini cites Zumthor's statement in *Essai de poétique médiévale*, p. 41, that "oralité et écriture s'opposent comme le continu au discontinu."

twelve manuscripts. Three large compilations of his works survive from the late thirteenth century, though none can be dated with certainty from within his lifetime, and his poems additionally turn up in anthologies of didactic and allegorical verse, sometimes in pairs or small groups of three or four. About Rutebeuf himself, nothing is known except what can be deduced from his works. The persona that emerges is in the tradition of the Latin Goliards: he laments his poverty and sings of life in the taverns. To what extent his works can be taken as autobiographically accurate is unclear. What can be said is that Rutebeuf spent most of his adult life in Paris; that he was educated and evidently made his living through his verse; and that he was deeply involved in the disputes between the University of Paris and the mendicant orders.[4]

There is no evidence to suggest that Rutebeuf himself ever undertook the preparation of codices of his collected works. The order of pieces is completely different in each of the three major collections and, as we will see below, only one of them shows even the most rudimentary signs of deliberate arrangement: if there was ever an authoritative arrangement of Rutebeuf's complete works, it has left no trace in the manuscript tradition.[5] Rutebeuf never directly identifies himself as a writer, although he hints at the possibility of such an identity in three of his poems, commenting that if he was "bons escrivains" (a good writer) he would still be unable to exhaust even half of his chosen topic (*La Vie de Sainte Elysabel*, vv. 985–90; *Le Sacristain et la femme au chevalier*, vv. 97–102; *Le Dit de Nostre Dame*, vv. 19–23). That Rutebeuf should think of himself as writer is especially appropriate to the *Vie de Sainte Elysabel* and the *Sacristain*, which he presents as translations from the Latin and which, as hagiographic works, can be regarded as authoritative treatises. But to posit the condition "If I was a writer" is not to state that one is a writer. The only terms that Rutebeuf unambiguously uses to designate his literary activity, even in other hagiographic and religious poetry, are the more neutral terms commonly employed by vernacular authors: *rimer* (to rhyme), *mettre en rime* (to set in rhyme), *conter* (to narrate), *faire* (to make). In the *Mort Rutebeuf* he even suggests that he has led the life of a performer, stating, "J'ai fet rimes et s'ai chanté" (I have made rhymes and also I have sung [v. 38]). The term *chanter* does not necessarily refer to an oral performance of musical material, however; it can also refer

---

4. On Rutebeuf manuscripts, see Faral and Bastin's introduction to their edition of the *Oeuvres complètes de Rutebeuf*, vol. 1, pp. 11–31, 224–25; for a discussion of Rutebeuf, his milieu, and his literary context, see pp. 32–93. For a literary analysis of Rutebeuf's work and its polemical content, see Regalado, *Poetic Patterns*. Rutebeuf MS *A* (Bibl. Nat. fr. 837) has been published in a facsimile edition by Omont.

5. This is a telling difference between Rutebeuf and Thibaut de Navarre, for example; the latter is said to have compiled his songs, which appear in virtually the same order in numerous manuscripts. See Chapter 2.

more generally to literary discourse, as is shown by Rutebeuf's statement in the *Sainte Elysabel,* "Si com l'escripture le chante" (Just as the Scriptures sing of it [v. 126]). Given this fluidity of the terms *chanter* and *escrire* and the variety of words employed by Rutebeuf to refer to his poetic activity, we cannot say to what extent he may have concerned himself with the preparation of manuscripts for presentation or sale, to what extent he would have recited or read his works aloud, or how he expected others to receive them. The lack of clear indicators may be a sign that the mode of transmission was less important for Rutebeuf than the content and social function of his works, produced variously for polemical purposes, for devotional use, or for entertainment.

Nonetheless, it is a tribute to Rutebeuf's strong poetic personality that his works were gathered together by his contemporaries, and an examination of these three collections contributes to our understanding of the status of the author corpus in the late thirteenth century. Of the three, the most complete is Bibl. Nat. fr. MS 1635, compiled after 1285 in southeastern Champagne or western Lorraine; the most thematically uniform is Bibl. Nat. fr. MS 1593, written in a hand of the Ile-de-France but in a language that suggests Champagne; the third, which is the only one explicitly marked as an author corpus, is Bibl. Nat. fr. MS 837, compiled after 1276 in the Ile-de-France.[6]

MS 1635 shows virtually no concern for the arrangement of texts. Neither thematic nor generic categories have been respected. Satiric pieces, religious works, and fabliaux; narrative and nonnarrative works in a variety of verse forms; all are intermingled in no discernible order. In certain cases poems that are closely related are paired: the *Ordres de Paris* is followed by the *Chanson des ordres,* and the *Dit de Pouille* by the *Chanson de Pouille.* The *Mariage Rutebeuf* is followed by the *Complainte Rutebeuf,* and the *Griesche d'hiver* by the *Griesche d'esté,* as indeed is the case in MSS 837 and 1593 as well. On the other hand, the two poems about Guillaume de St. Amour are not paired, nor are the various poems in honor of the Virgin. The fact that certain poems are appropriately linked may be due simply to a process of compilation that gathered together single poems, pairs or small groups of thematically linked poems, and other small groups that may not have been thematically unified.

A particularly clear indication that the compiler was not interested in creating a meaningful sequence of texts is the placement of the *Mort Rutebeuf* (here titled *Repentance Rutebuef),* in which the protagonist reflects on his career as a poet and announces that this will be his last poem, near the beginning of the collection (the third of the fifty-one

6. Faral and Bastin ed., p. 60.

pieces). Although it could possibly be argued that this piece might be used as a sort of prologue, presenting the figure of the poet to whom these various works are due, such an arrangement would surely demand that the piece in question occupy first place. Similarly, three other poems focused on Rutebeuf's persona, the *Pauvreté Rutebeuf, Mariage Rutebeuf,* and *Complainte Rutebeuf,* appear at the approximate midpoint of the collection.[7] These could be seen as providing the name and social standing of the author-protagonist of the collection, appropriately placed at the midpoint as the conventional locus of naming and otherwise identifying the author or protagonist of a romance or a compilation. In Chapter 2, I discussed the importance of the naming of Adam de la Halle at the midpoint of his compilation in MS 25566 and related this structural principle to the naming of Guillaume de Lorris and Jean de Meun at the midpoint of the *Rose.* But again, if such were the intended function of these poems, it is hard to explain why the polemical *Vie du monde* would have been inserted between the *Pauvreté* and the *Mariage.* It seems most likely that the suggestive placement of these poems is simply coincidence. Perhaps it is due to an original collection, more carefully arranged, to which the compiler of MS 1635 added material drawn from other sources; if he had copied from such a collection over a period of time, inserting other individual pieces whenever he happened to come across them, the result could be a collection in which traces of the original architectonics survive. In the lack of more compelling evidence, however, the existence of such an original must remain strictly a hypothesis.

We are on even less sure ground as regards the arrangement of MS 1593, for the original manuscript was dismembered and rebound with other material in the fifteenth century, and it is impossible to determine how much of the original may be missing. Three gatherings of Rutebeuf's poems remain; these are now preceded by *Renart le Nouvel,* and the *Fables d'Ysopet* of Marie de France and the *Evangile des femmes* have been inserted between the second and third gathering. The final four gatherings, evidently not from the original manuscript, contain the *Dit dou soucretain* of Jean le Chapelain, the *Mariage* and *Complainte Rutebeuf,* and the *Lai du conseil.* According to Faral and Bastin, the third gathering of Rutebeuf could not originally have followed directly from the second; the most likely supposition is that there was originally at least one more gathering of his poems in this position.

Since we do not know the original extent of the collection, it is impossible to say what may once have been the opening or midpoint texts. There is some evidence, however, that the *Priere Rutebeuf* was the last

7. These pieces are nos. 25, 27, and 28 out of a total of fifty-one; calculating in terms of pages, the *Pauvreté* begins on fol. 44v out of a total of eighty-four folios.

piece.[8] If the collection was originally packaged as an author corpus, this "personal" lament may have been selected as the author's final reflections on the social woes with which his poetry is concerned. The Rutebeuf corpus in MS 1593 consists almost entirely of pieces relating to the disputes between the university and the mendicant orders, together with three Crusade pieces and two poems in honor of the Virgin. Although these have not been arranged in any discernible order, they do reflect a concern with social and political polemics, to which the devotional pieces are not inappropriate. The two *Griesche* poems are somewhat less appropriate to the collection as it stands but do participate in the general field of poetry relating to life in Paris and the social context of the students and scholars who were involved in the clash with the friars. The inclusion of two fabliaux, however, is less easily explained. It is possible that the original, larger collection included a much greater diversity of pieces and that the fifteenth-century compiler who created the current volume discarded all but the three gatherings most appropriate to his plan for a collection of didactic and satirical poetry.

It is in MS 837, finally, that we find the only explicit designation of the poems as a unit, defined as such by their common authorship. The collection is framed by the rubrics, "Ci commencent li dit Rustebuef" (Here begin Rutebeuf's dits [fol. 283v]), and "Expliciunt tuit li dit Rustebuef" (Here end all Rutebeuf's dits [fol. 332v]). This much at least allows us to examine the collection as an author corpus; and although its arrangement is, for the most part, as lacking in order as that of MSS 1593 and 1635, certain features may reflect an attempt at meaningful organization.

The collection opens with the *Vie de Sainte Elysabel*. Although it would be stretching things to say that this piece fully introduces the collection that follows, the prologue does state certain themes that will remain important. The opening lines cite a biblical passage (2 Thess. 3:10) commonly used in diatribes against the mendicant friars, "Ne doit mengier qui ne labeure" (He who does not labor should not eat [v. 2]). A few lines later, requesting the Virgin's aid in the production and dissemination of his work, the narrator comments that this literary activity constitutes his form of labor, "Quar autre labor ne sai fere" (For I don't know how to do any other labor [v. 14]). The voice that is established at the beginning of the collection is thus defined at once as a poet by profession, and one who sets himself (as one who works for his living) against the mendicants. Although Rutebeuf certainly did not compose this prologue with

---

8. The *Prière* comes at the end of a gathering, ending in the left column of fol. 111, of which the right column has been cut away. The verso side of the page is blank and, unlike the other gatherings that appear to be from this same manuscript, has no catchword. See Faral and Bastin ed., pp. 12–16.

the intention of introducing his other works, a compiler looking for an appropriate piece to begin the collection might well select this one. *Sainte Elysabel* also contains Rutebeuf's longest discourse on his name (vv. 2155–68), so the collection begins with a strong statement not only of the author's predilections but also of his name and his self-caricature. In this regard, it is noteworthy that the second longest discourse on the name "Rutebeuf" occurs in the epilogue of the *Sacristain,* the second piece in the collection.

The invocation of the Virgin in the opening lines is equally appropriate: the two works that follow *Sainte Elysabel* are the *Sacristain* and *Theophile,* both miracles of the Virgin; the collection also includes the *Ave Maria Rutebeuf,* and ends with the *Mort Rutebeuf,* in which the poet-protagonist again invokes the Virgin as his special protector. In addition to his polemical stand against the mendicants and his profession as versifier, then, the persona "Rutebeuf" can also be defined by his devotion to the Virgin. Indeed, Rutebeuf's cult of the Virgin contributes to the unification of his corpus through the references that link one poem to another. In the *Ave Maria,* he recounts the story of Theophilus at some length, and in the *Mort* he recalls Saint Mary the Egyptian, saved through the intervention of the Virgin. Saint Mary and Theophilus, both celebrated earlier by Rutebeuf in his capacity as author, now recur in his meditations as exemplary figures in whose salvation he finds hope for himself.

The collection is framed both by prayers to the Virgin and by the poet's statement of his craft. In the opening prologue he announces versifying as his profession, and in the closing poem he reflects on his career. The final poem, which announces itself as the author's last composition, is certainly an appropriate piece to end on. That it is titled here *La Mort Rustebeuf* (Rutebeuf's death) rather than *La Repentance Rutebuef* (Rutebeuf's repentance) as in the two other manuscripts that give it a title indicates further that it was chosen to mark the close of Rutebeuf's poetic corpus and of his life. Since the persona "Rutebeuf" is known only as a poetic persona, defined by his works, this equation of corpus and person is in keeping with the conventions of his poetry. One is reminded here of the compilation of Adam de la Halle's works in MS 25566, which similarly ended with a reference to death and an equation of the author with the protagonist of the collection.

Finally, it is worth noting that the midpoint of the collection is occupied by the *Mariage* and the *Complainte Rutebeuf.* We saw that in MS 1635 the suggestive placement of these poems near the midpoint was difficult to reconcile with other features of the compilation. Here, the location of these two poems can more easily be read as a deliberate evocation of the author-protagonist at the center of his collected works, although this must still remain a conjecture. The poems of MS 837 do not otherwise reflect a conscious ordering; they are as disordered as those of MSS 1593 and 1635. Still, it is possible that the compiler took care to locate appropriate pieces at the beginning, midpoint, and end of the collection, stressing at each point the identity of the author, without concerning himself with the order of the pieces beyond that.

The evidence that emerges from the Rutebeuf manuscripts, then, is mixed. His poems did clearly circulate in author corpora, apparently from the very beginning. But in only one case can it be said, and even then without complete certainty, that the identity of the author was elevated to an organizational principle, or that the collection of poems as a whole was perceived as having a poetic structure. There is no sign that Rutebeuf, or anyone else, undertook the thematic or generic organization of his works; insofar as the collection has a structure, it is an extremely rudimentary one. No attempt was made to codify his poetic achievement. And the number of manuscripts containing individual poems, often without even indicating authorship, indicates that his poems also circulated independently; the bond of common authorship was not such as to prevent the fragmentation of the corpus. For all that, the existence of the Rutebeuf compilations is significant. His personality as author was powerful enough that generically diverse texts were gathered together on the basis of this authorship, and these collections stood as models on which fourteenth-century poets who wished to compile their works could build.

## Transformations of *Le Roman de la rose:* Baudouin and Jean de Condé

In addition to the collections found in various anthology manuscripts, the dits of Baudouin and Jean de Condé are gathered together in a fourteenth-century codex, Arsenal MS 3524, devoted entirely to the works of these two poets.[9] The manuscript surely postdates the death of Baudouin, who is not believed to have lived into the fourteenth century, but it may date from within the lifetime of Jean.[10] It is not known, however, whether Jean was responsible for this arrangement of texts. Whoever may have undertaken the task of compiling the manuscript,

9. On the manuscripts containing the works of Baudouin de Condé, see vol. 1 of Scheler's edition of *Dits et contes*, pp. ix–xviii; on the manuscripts of Jean de Condé, see Scheler's vol. 3, pp. xii–xv. For information regarding a further manuscript containing three poems by Jean de Condé, see Ribard, "Contribution à la connaissance." For general background and discussion of Jean de Condé, see Ribard, *Un ménestrel du XIVe siècle.*

10. Scheler locates Baudouin's poetic activity between about 1240 and 1280 in his introduction to vol. 1 of his edition (p. xiii). In the introduction to vol. 3 he modifies these dates slightly to arrive at the period of about 1245–90 for Baudouin's poetic activity and places Jean's poetic activity at about 1305–45 (p. xxi, n. 1).

though, it is clear that, in addition to the aspect of the book as a didactic work aimed at the edification of the reader or hearer, the collection represents a conscious effort to present the works of two particular poets, whose presence as authors is an important unifying factor.

The book begins with Baudouin's dits, initiated by a miniature of an old man conversing with a pilgrim beside a cross, and the rubric, "Ci commence aucun des dis Bauduin de Condeit. Premerement la voie de paradis" (Here begin some of Baudouin de Condé's dits. First the *Road to Paradise* [fol. 1]). The miniature is specifically appropriate to the *Voie de paradis,* a dream vision in which the protagonist makes a pilgrimage to Heaven and receives advice along the way from an old man that he meets at a roadside cross. It also announces the didactic character of the collection as a whole and suggests that Baudouin's poetic authority is grounded in an attitude of penance and an experience of the world; the pilgrim, a little like the minstrel, is one who has traveled widely, always remaining somewhat at the margins of society but able to move freely within it and to observe human behavior in a variety of contexts. The protagonist, indeed, comments on the crowds of people that he encounters lingering outside the entrance to the "straight and narrow" path to Paradise, who include "gent laie et lettrée . . . les plus grans singnors . . . prinches et prelas" (lay and educated people . . . the highest nobility . . . princes and prelates [Scheler ed., vv. 92–94]). These figures can be identified with the society that the minstrel has observed throughout his lifetime and to whom he offers the fruits of his experience in the form of versified teachings.

The old man, in turn, functions as a doubling of the voice of Baudouin de Condé, who, as poet, is of course the author of his words of admonition as well as of the protagonist's dream narrative; and since the codex includes the works of Baudouin's son as well, it is logical that the former would be portrayed as an elder. Insofar as the pilgrim corresponds to the narrator, he can be taken as the representative of Baudouin de Condé; but insofar as he acts as audience for the old man's sermon, he can be seen as the representative of the reader, reminding us that we, too, are engaged in a pilgrimage toward Heaven or Hell. While not a conventional author portrait, the miniature at the head of the collection nonetheless gives visual representation to the poetic identity that lies behind the series of dits: that of an old and wise man, one who has been around and seen much of the world and who imparts moral teachings, relevant to every reader, about the pilgrimage of life. The *Voie de paradis* in turn is an appropriate piece with which to begin. As the longest of Baudouin's dits here preserved and his only dream narrative, it provides a conceptual framework within which the shorter and mostly nonnarrative pieces that follow can be read.

The passage from the works of Baudouin to those of Jean is marked by the rubric, "Ci finent le dit Bauduin de Condeit. & commencent aprés li Jehan son fil" (Here end Baudouin de Condé's dits. And next begin those by his son Jean [fol. 50v]). A second rubric announces Jean's first poem:

Ci commencent aucun des dis Jehan de Condeit, qui sont bon & profitables a oïr. Car molt y a de bons exemples pour le gouvernement de touz ceulz qui a bien voldroient venir. C'est la messe des oisiaus & li ples des chanonesses, et des grises nonnains.

[Here begin some of Jean de Condé's dits, which are good and profitable to hear. For there are many good examples for the comportment of all those who want to come to good. This is the *Mass of the Birds and the Suit of the Canonnesses and the Grey Nuns.*] [Fol. 51]

The *Messe des oisiaus* is illustrated with a miniature of a tree covered with birds who, together with a garland-bedecked figure, perhaps Venus, attend a mass performed by three other birds, a representation of the event with which the poem, another dream vision, opens. The dreamer-narrator of the *Messe des oisiaus* is a less active participant in the narrative than that of the *Voie de paradis* and acts mainly as witness of the events. Perhaps for this reason he has not been included in the miniature. The rubric stresses Jean's presence as author of the entire collection, however, as well as the didactic nature of the poetry. What was expressed for Baudouin by the opening miniature is here expressed by the rubrication.

The miniature is nonetheless important in suggesting what kind of poetry we have here and how it is to be read. The representation of birds, the landscape setting, and the courtly figure decked with a garland of flowers, together with the dream format, evoke the tradition of courtly lyric and lyrical narrative, of which the outstanding example is of course the *Roman de la rose*. The opening section of the *Messe des oisiaus* is closely modeled on the *Rose*. The dream takes place in the month of May; it opens with a description of the multitude of birds that the narrator finds in a garden, which is replete with the usual fountains, flowers, and trees; the gathering is presided over by Venus, goddess of love. The detailed description of the mass that soon follows, however, adds an interesting twist: lyric carol has become liturgical *kyriele,* in this didactic appropriation of courtly lyricism. A moralistic reworking of the *Rose* material is apparent throughout the poem.[11] The scene that follows the mass, a picnic led by Venus that soon turns into something very much like a drunken orgy, is glossed by the narrator as a representation of the divine frenzy enjoyed by the lovers of God. And the amorous

11. On Jean's use of allegory, see Lepage, "Dislocation de la vision."

debate with which the remainder of the poem is concerned—whether nuns and canonnesses should all be allowed to take lovers, a question that Venus settles in the affirmative—is glossed with reference to the dispute for primacy among the disciples of Christ and leads ultimately to the narrator's praise of conventual chastity.

The transformation of the *Rose* material is continued in Jean's second poem, the *Dit d'entendement,* which presents a dream set in the month of December. The progressive change is indicated not only by the movement from springtime to winter but also by the narrator's recognition of Entendement (the term *entendement* combines "intention," "intellect," and "understanding"), whom he meets in a garden. Entendement, it turns out, is already known to the protagonist; and he is, in fact, the very embodiment of a transition from a lyrical poetics of frustrated desire to a didactic poetics of image and exegesis. The narrator gratefully recalls Entendement's "strong assaults and clamors" at the Castle of Love,

> Là où ière si entrepris,
> Que Desirs m'ot lacié et pris,
> Mais de ses mains me delivrastes,
> Maintes merveilles me monstrastes.

[There where I was so overwhelmed, that Desire had captured and bound me; but you delivered me from his hands, you showed me many marvels.] [Scheler ed., *Dits et contes*, vv. 43–46]

In an inversion of the *Rose* material, we have here not an assault led by Love on behalf of the protagonist against the Castle of Jealousy but rather one led by Entendement to free the protagonist from the Castle of Love. Jean de Condé's protagonist is evidently an Amant who decided to take Reason's advice, both with regard to the renunciation of desire and with regard to the glossing of texts. He is not, as is the *Rose* protagonist, dazzled by sensual appearances. As the dit proceeds, the protagonist and Entendement encounter a series of allegorical beings; each is immediately glossed for its moral significance by Entendement at the protagonist's request. The method is fundamental to the didactic dit as a genre; such poems are very often constructed around a central figure or image that is exploited for its moral significance or as a springboard for sermonizing. It is from these central images that the poems draw their titles and, in more heavily illuminated manuscripts, the miniature with which each opens.[12]

12. For example, in Arsenal MS 3142, each of Baudouin's dits is headed with a miniature representing the central image (rose, cloak, and so on). The experience of reading the illuminated manuscript—encountering first the image in miniature and rubric, then the textual explication of the image—duplicates the protagonist's experience of witnessing "marvels" and receiving the explication from his guide.

Both portions of the codex, then, that of Baudouin and that of Jean, begin with allegorical dream narratives, marked by a didactic appropriation of the *Rose* in particular and of courtly lyricism in general. The *Voie de paradis* moves quickly away from the lyrical format, but its prologue strongly evokes the lyrico-narrative tradition. Its opening lines are a reworking of Bernart de Ventadorn's famous song, "Can vei la lauzeta mover / de joi sas alas contral rai" (When I see the lark move with joy his wings against the sunbeam [Nichols ed., vv. 1–2]). Baudouin's narrator invokes the song of the lark, which, singing in praise of springtime, "Tent ses eles contre le ray / Du soleil et dist: 'or le ray'" (Holds his wings out against the sunbeam and says, "Now I have it back" [Scheler ed., vv. 5–6]). The song goes on to describe the lark's fall, as, overcome by "sweetness," it "forgets itself." The lark's ecstasy in turn is contrasted with the singer's painfully frustrated desire, itself mirrored in the third stanza in the image of Narcissus, who "lost himself" in the fountain. This progression would certainly be appropriate to the *Rose*, in which the protagonist does arrive at the fountain of Narcissus and is soon on the brink of despair. Baudouin, however, envisions a different progression. His protagonist is Heaven bound, and his lark accordingly does not fall but rather "monte à tour / Et rent grasses au creatour" (keeps climbing and renders thanks to the Creator [vv. 11–12]). This transformation of a well-known song exemplifies the general system of transformations engaged in the movement from song or lyrical romance to didactic dit. The network of allusions is continued throughout the narrative. After a description of earth's "mantle of flowers" (v. 38) strongly reminiscent of the opening passage of the *Rose*,[13] the narrator reveals that he set out in his dream, not for pleasure but on a pilgrimage to Paradise; the narrow path, difficult to enter, recalls the narrow and nearly hidden gateway to the Garden of Delight; the assembly of people gathered outside it, refusing to enter, suggests the anticourtly images on the wall, those excluded from the garden. The process, indeed, is that rendered more explicit by Jean de Condé in the *Messe des oisiaus*, where the narrator guides us through a point-by-point reading of the scene of courtly celebration as spiritual allegory.

This is not the place to argue whether Baudouin and Jean were rendering explicit what they took to be the allegorical significance of the *Rose* or reinterpreting its imagery in a creative adaptation of secular material to spiritual purposes. In either case it is clear that the *Rose* is a major presence at the basis of each author's work; the location of the dream-vision poems at the beginning of each corpus stresses the importance of the *Rose* as the point of departure for such a compilation. In the

---

13. Scheler identifies verbal echoes of the *Rose* in his notes to the *Voie de paradis* (vol. 1, p. 484).

*Rose*, song is adapted to romance; lyrical themes appear in a written form, fused with material drawn from both vernacular and Latin written traditions. The dit is the logical extension of this process. The strategic location of these allusions to the *Rose* reflects its important role as a model for the adaptation of vernacular lyricism to writing and for the vernacular book in general.

In such works as the *Roman de la poire* and the *Dit de la panthère d'amours*, we saw that the *Rose* was appropriated as the basis for a literary compilation; and Jean de Meun, of course, used Guillaume's *Rose* as the basis for his continuation-compilation of material. Scribal editors, in turn, sometimes used the *Rose* as the nucleus for an anthology, as in MS 12786, or as the counterpoint to a series of texts, as in the Dijon MS 526 of the *Bestiaire d'amours*. We see a similar phenomenon in the Arsenal Condé anthology. Each section of this codex is unified through the ongoing presence of its author; the whole is unified through the relationship of parentage between the two. The passage from the first poet to his son is reminiscent of the passage from the first *Rose* poet to his continuator, whose birth is seemingly generated from the death of his predecessor. Baudouin's poems end on a note of mortality with the *Dit des trois morts et des trois vis*, but the father's voice is renewed in that of his son. The association of poetic continuation with the continuation of lineage recalls the *Rose*. The powerful presence of the *Rose* at the beginning of the book and at the juncture of the two authors—at the moment of renewal—strengthens this association as well as contributing to the overall unity of the whole; as I have said, Jean's *Messe des oisiaus* helps render explicit certain aspects of Baudouin's poetics. The son is in this sense not only the biological but also the poetic heir to his father, continuing and expanding the former's poetic enterprise, just as both ultimately continue and expand the *Rose*.

## Watriquet's *diz en escrit*: The Minstrel as Compiler

Watriquet de Couvin, identified as "minstrel to the count of Blois," composed his dits during the first half of the fourteenth century.[14] Collections of his works survive today in five fourteenth-century manuscripts.[15] Watriquet's presence is especially strong in the illumi-

---

14. Watriquet is identified as such in the opening rubric of Arsenal MS 3525 (fol. 1), an illuminated collection of his works very similar to the one discussed below. He also identifies himself this way in the *Trois Chanoinesses de Cologne*, vv. 80–82.

15. On the manuscripts containing Watriquet's works, see Scheler's edition of *Dits de Watriquet de Couvin*, pp. xvii–xxiii. Scheler identifies seven Watriquet manuscripts in the 1373 inventory of the library of Charles V (pp. xxii–xxiii). For an edition of the *Dit des .vii. vertus* and a description of the single manuscript that contains it, see Livingston. Watriquet

nated manuscripts, where he appears at the head of nearly every poem; since he always wears a distinctive tunic, half yellow and half green, his identity is unmistakable.[16] The most persuasive evidence for Watriquet's active role in the preparation of codices is the presentation page in the Bibl. Nat. MS fr. 14968 (fig. 17). The miniature represents a gathering of people on the left, including Watriquet, whose gesture indicates speech. In the center, Watriquet (represented a second time) kneels and offers a book to a seated nobleman; a group of courtiers watches from the right. The rubric reads:

Veschi comment Watriqués sires de Verjoli baille et presente touz ses meilleurs diz en escrit a monseigneur de Blois son maistre. Premierement le mireor aus dames.

[See here how Watriquet, sire of Prettyverse, offers and presents all his best dits in writing to my lord of Blois his master. First the *Mirror of Ladies*.] [Fol. 1v]

On the facing page is a rubric announcing the *Mireoir as dames*, together with a miniature representing Watriquet, in his usual attire, on horse-back in a forest, talking to a woman whose entire body is half white and half black:

Ci commence li mireoir as dames que Watriquet commença a faire le pre-mier jour d'esté, en l'an .xxiiii. Et chevauchoit parmi grant forest a une matinee. Et pensoit moult a la bonté & la biauté de pleuseurs dames et damoiseles, & devint en ce penser aussi comme touz ravis. Et encontra une dame partie a moitié de blanc & de noir qui Aventure estoit apelee.

[Here begins the *Mirror of Ladies* that Watriquet began to make the first day of summer in the year 1324. And he was riding through a great forest one morning. And he was thinking greatly about the goodness and beauty of many ladies and maidens, and in these thoughts he was as if completely ravished away. And he met a lady, divided half white and half black, who was called Adventure.] [Fol. 2]

---

provides dates in the prologues of thirteen of his dits; these fall during the period 1319–29. It is not known how much earlier than this he may have begun to compose poetry, or how much later he may have continued to do so. I am grateful to Kumiko Maekawa of the Gunma Prefectural Women's College, Tokyo, for alerting me to the importance of the Watriquet manuscripts. Maekawa has studied the Watriquet manuscripts in connection with her doctoral thesis, "Recherches iconographiques sur les manuscrits des poésies de Guillaume de Machaut."

16. I have seen this type of illumination in two manuscripts: Bibl. Nat. fr. MS 14968 and Arsenal MS 3525. There is no illumination in Bibl. Nat. fr. MS 2183. I have not been able to examine other Watriquet manuscripts.

*Figure 17.* Watriquet presents book to patron, B.N. fr. 14968, fol. 1v. (Photograph: Bibliothèque Nationale, Paris)

The dit begins on the following page; it is decorated with further internal miniatures representing Watriquet's arrival at the Castle of Beauty and the events that take place there.

The presentation page certainly suggests strongly that Watriquet undertook the preparation of the volume, although it is impossible to know just how much control he would have had over such matters as iconography, rubrication, or even the ordering of texts. The book is inscribed in the context of a relationship between poet and patron, as is appropriate to the didactic dit; Watriquet is an instructor who directs his lessons to the count. Numerous references in the dits that follow tell us that this was Watriquet's normal role; in the *Tournoi des dames,* for example, he portrays himself reciting *contes, biaus examples,* and *dis* (stories, beautiful exempla, and dits) for the count. The presentation miniature evokes oral recitation in the image of Watriquet speaking, but here the oral delivery is doubled in the presentation of the written artifact. The dual representation of Watriquet and the specification "in writing" to distinguish this particular presentation of dits from previous oral presentations reflect the importance of this movement from oral to written delivery: the minstrel has become the author of a book.

The rubric on the facing page focuses attention on the act of poetic composition, specifying the day on which Watriquet began to "make" the dit. As we have seen, a general shift of focus from performance to composition is apparent in lyrico-narrative texts of the later thirteenth century, and this concern with composition is to be associated with a more writerly concept of the song as specifically referential, documenting a particular experience. Clearly, a similar writerly attitude toward the dit is at issue here; it is noteworthy that many of the dits are dated and thus anchored to a specific moment in the poet's life.

Indeed, a comparison of the rubric to the dit itself reveals that the rubric, the voice of the book, intensifies this writerly concept of the poetic text. The first day of summer is mentioned in the prologue as well, not, however, in connection with the making of the poem but with the adventure that it recounts. On the first day of summer, explains the narrator, he became absorbed in thought, "Et ou penser me fu avis / Que fusse en une grant forest" (And in the thought it seemed to me that I was in a great forest [Scheler ed., *Dits,* vv. 40–41]). The poem, in other words, describes a sort of vision that the poet claims to have experienced on the first day of summer and which he put into writing at some indeterminate later time:

> Por ce est mes cuers assentiz
> A ce c'un dit vous conte et die,
> A oïr plaisant melodie,
> De la plus très bele aventure
> C'onques meïsse en escripture.

[For this reason my heart assents that I narrate and tell you a dit, harmonious to hear, of the most beautiful adventure that I have ever put in writing.] [Vv. 10–14]

In the rubric this sequence of events is recast. The implication of the rubric is that the experience that the poet had on the first day of summer and that he casts in the form of an allegorical vision was in fact that of writing a poem. The progression "began to make . . . and he was riding along" mirrors that within the text from the meditation on beauty to the imagined adventure that this meditation inspired, suggesting that it was the act of writing itself that generated the scenario.

The rubrics also identify the narrator-protagonist of the poem as Watriquet, its author. This identity of author and protagonist, stated in the opening rubric, is repeated in the rubrics, beginning "Vesci comment Watriquet . . ." (see here how Watriquet . . .), accompanying some of the miniatures within the poem. Watriquet is, of course, also recognizable throughout by his attire. The combination of rubrics and miniatures stresses the single identity of protagonist, narrator, poet, and author of the entire collection. This, indeed, is written into the poem itself, in a reference to the normally first-person protagonist by his name: " 'Dame, vos diz forment m'agrée,' / Dist Watriqués" ("Lady, your words greatly please me," said Watriquet [vv. 490–91]). The collection is at once a series of adventures experienced by Watriquet and a series of poems written, performed, and compiled by Watriquet.

Watriquet's role as court poet is reiterated in the miniature and rubrics introducing the second poem in the collection, the *Dit du connestable de France*, a eulogy of Gaucher de Châtillon, count of Crecy and Porcean, constable of France, who died in May 1329.[17] A miniature at the end of the *Mireoir as dames* represents Watriquet standing before a row of four seated men; all five figures gesture in speech. The accompanying rubric reads: "Coment li dus de Bourbon commande a faire le dit du connestable" (How the duke of Bourbon commands the *Dit of the constable* to be made [vol. 26v]).[18] The poem begins on the facing page; it is headed by a miniature of a coffin surrounded by candles, incense, heraldic emblems, and four mourners and by a rubric identifying the "dit du conestable de France, Conte de Porchiens, nommez Gauchier de Chastillon; fais par Watriquet" (dit of the constable of France, count of Porcean, named Gaucher de Châtillon; made by Watriquet [fol. 27]). The miniatures and rubrication contribute, once again, to a decoding of

17. Scheler ed., *Dits*, identifies the historical figures in question in his notes to the *Dit du connestable* (pp. 423–24).
18. The rubric on fol. 26v is in a different hand from the others, but the miniature seems to be the work of the artist who executed the other miniatures. Perhaps the rubric was accidentally omitted when the manuscript was first made and added shortly thereafter.

the allegory of the poem. Much of the panegyric is placed in the mouth of Prowess, who mourns the death of his "father" and refers to the grief that he and his three sisters, Generosity, Courtesy, and Loyalty, feel over the constable's death. These four figures not only correspond to the four mourners in the second miniature but also recall the four figures (aside from Watriquet) in the first miniature. Thus the duke of Bourbon, who commissions the poem, is associated with the figure of Prowess, the central voice of the poem. This correlation of text and miniatures has the social function of paying a compliment to one of Watriquet's more prominent patrons. But within the poetic economy of the book, it reminds us once again that the allegory is a metaphoric representation of Watriquet's position as court minstrel: he divines the sentiments of his patron and casts them in poetic form.

This scene of poetic commission bridges the potential rupture between the statement of closure at the end of the *Mireoir* and the announcement of a new poem at the beginning of the *Connestable*. We see that Watriquet has simply turned from one particular poetic purpose to another. The *Mireoir* is, as its title indicates, addressed to ladies; the queen that Watriquet encounters in the Castle of Beauty is identified, though heraldic references, as Jeanne d'Évreux, queen of France.[19] The opening rubric states that in this mirror "toutes dames se doivent mirer & prendre garde" (all ladies should behold themselves and take note), and the poem closes with a dedication to all ladies "grans et petites" (great and small [v. 1291]). In the miniature that immediately follows, we see that Watriquet is now asked to compose a poem addressed to men; and the dit accordingly opens, "A sage preudomme obeïr / Se doit on d'ounneur pourveïr (One should procure oneself honor by obeying a wise and noble man [vv. 1–2]). The ordering of the poems does not, in fact, correspond to the chronological order of composition; several of the poems that follow the *Connestable* bear dates that would place their composition between the *Connestable* and the *Mireoir*. For the purposes of the compilation, however, a fictional sequence can be evoked. It is appropriate to the social conventions of the fourteenth century that the collection should open with a poem in honor of feminine beauty and, in particular, the queen of France and that this is then followed by a poem in honor of an exemplary male figure. The series of miniatures and rubrics at the beginning of the collection firmly establishes the context of Watriquet's career as court minstrel, within which the remainder of the poems can be read.

19. Scheler ed., *Dits*, identifies the queen in the poem as Jeanne d'Evreux on the basis of the heraldic emblem described on her clothing. Since Jeanne did not become queen of France until 1325, and Watriquet claims to have written the poem in 1324, Scheler suggests that the passage in question may be a later interpolation (notes to the *Mireoir*, pp. 411–12).

If Watriquet's role as poet is particularly stressed at the beginning of the collection, his role as performer emerges strongly at the end, with the *Fastrasie*. This parody of courtly lyric, which so distressed Auguste Scheler, is clearly a performance medium, in which the minstrel improvises humorous verses that take a refrain as their point of departure and transform its courtly sentiments into something much more down to earth.[20] The miniature (fol. 161v) accordingly represents Watriquet and a fellow minstrel standing before the king and his attendants, and the rubric states, "Ci commence li fastras de quoi Rainmondin et Watriquet desputerent le jour de Pasques, devant le Roy Phelippe de France" (Here begins the fastrasie of which Rainmondin and Watriquet disputed on Easter day, before King Philip of France [fol. 162]).

The book, then, provides a space within which Watriquet can put himself on stage. At one level, the written transcription of texts is a representation of the speaking voice of the minstrel. We have seen already that in the opening miniature Watriquet is doubled, appearing both as performer and as the author of a book; that in the prologue to the *Mireoir as dames,* the narrator refers to the text both as written and as "harmonious to hear"; and that he elsewhere portrays himself as performing before the count. Some dits close with reference to an implied speaking voice: "Si m'en tais, plus n'en iert moustrez" (and so I fall silent, nothing more will be revealed), states the narrator at the end of the *Dis de l'arbre royal* (v. 548); the *Dis de l'ortie* closes, "Si s'en tait Watriqués atant; / Sages est qui des bons s'escole" (and so Watriquet falls silent now; he is wise who learns from good people [vv. 479–80]). The book records the words of the minstrel, preserving their quality as speech.

One is reminded here of other vernacular didactic compendia, such as Alard de Cambrai's *Livre de philosophie et de moralité;* as we saw in Chapter 3, this anthology of material drawn from the auctores is rubricated in such a way as to suggest a series of oral presentations by the various poets and philosophers, although Alard himself is the writer responsible for the compilation. The iconography of MS 3142 supports this reading, by representing Alard as a scribe, whereas the auctores are shown holding the scrolls associated with oral declamation. Watriquet in turn implicitly identifies himself as an authority, if not quite an auctor, in that he plays both roles: he is the one who composes the dits and whose voice speaks through them and who compiles them to make a book. The comparison with Alard is not fortuitous; as Jean-Charles Payen has shown, Watriquet's *Dit des .vii. vertus* is built almost entirely of material

20. In his notes to the *Fastrasie,* Scheler ed., *Dits,* expresses his regret that the task of editing Watriquet's complete works should entail the publication of a poem that he finds meaningless and vulgar (p. 491). The *Fastrasie* is certainly of a different tone from the rest of Watriquet's works, providing a sort of comic relief after the long series of moralizations and revealing a different side of his function as court minstrel.

drawn more or less verbatim from Alard's compilation.[21] Watriquet may have used one of the abridgments of Alard's work rather than the original,[22] but nonetheless this shows his familiarity with the written corpus of vernacular didactic literature, and we may suppose that he would have taken codices of this sort as models in deciding to compile his own works.

At another level, the narratives themselves are a mise-en-scène of poetic composition and of Watriquet's privileged status as a poet. In these poems Watriquet, like Jean and Baudouin de Condé, portrays himself entering an explicitly literary space inhabited by allegorical personifications who impart wisdom to him and in which all that takes place has a moral or spiritual significance. The poet is one who has access to intellectual abstractions, one who can confront the true essences of things. As the narrator states in the prologue of the *Mireoir as dames*, "tout le voir y ai apris / De savoir cognoistre biauté" (there I learned the whole truth of knowing how to recognize beauty [vv. 16–17]). He assures us that he is not like the many who claim undue knowledge of feminine beauty without actually knowing how to judge it (vv. 20–21). Through his imaginative powers he generates meaningful images; his intellectual powers in turn enable him to read these images and draw from them a lesson. Most of the dits begin with a miniature representing Watriquet and the object or creature that will provide the focus for this poem's teaching; often he is accompanied by the allegorical personification who will explain to him the significance of the central image or event. This teaching is never directed at Watriquet personally; his are not the lyrical dream visions of such texts as the *Rose* or the *Panthère*. It is, rather, of large political, social, or spiritual scope. Watriquet mediates between his court audience and the body of wisdom to which he as poet has access. Such, as he tells us, is his business: "D'autre mestier ne sai user / Que de conter biaus dis et faire" (I don't know how to practice any profession other than making and recounting beautiful dits [*Tournois des dames*, vv. 436–37]).

As was hinted at in the opening rubric of the *Mireoir*, the narrative setup is a metaphor for Watriquet's own imaginative and intellectual process. The book, then, is the mise-en-scène of the minstrel's performance; the individual dit is the mise-en-scène of the mental process that resulted in its formation. Although the content of the poems is aimed at the audience, the poet is a powerful presence within each text and within the book as a whole. He is a major source of continuity in the collec-

21. Payen, "Le *Dit des .vii. vertus*." According to Payen, Watriquet simply transcribed passages from Alard, inserting them into a work of which he composed only the introduction, the conclusion, and the transitional passages between citations.

22. Payen finds it more likely that Watriquet had access to a florilegium or *remaniement*, of which there were evidently a great many; see "Le *Dit des .vii. vertus*," p. 392.

tion—the continuity of voice in the implied series of performances and the narrative continuity of the poetic career of Watriquet de Couvin. Both principles are embraced in the relationship of Watriquet and the count of Blois, principle exemplar of Watriquet's aristocratic patronage: it is for the count that Watriquet performs, for his edification that the poems are written, and to him that the book is presented.

## Machaut's Books: The Conjoining of Song and Dit

In the anthology manuscripts of Guillaume de Machaut, produced throughout the second half of the fourteenth century and into the fifteenth century, we encounter something different from those of Watriquet or the Condés.[23] Machaut's anthologies are characterized by a much greater diversity, including narrative dits d'amour, short nonnarrative dits, lyric poetry without musical setting, courtly lyric set to music, sacred music (the *Messe Nostre Dame*), and even historical material (the *Prise d'Alexandrie*). As in many large miscellaneous codices compiled by scribes, the works are arranged according to genre and versification; the narrative poetry forms one large subdivision, the nonmusical lyric poetry another, the musical compositions yet another. The lyric formes fixes are distinguished as categories of compilation, and where they are intermingled, as in the nonmusical lyric anthology titled the *Louange des dames,* individual poems are labeled accordingly. The diversity of verse form, of music and poetry, is thus stressed by the manuscript format. Yet it is clear that Machaut regarded his codices as unified works; his celebrated *Prologue*, which serves to introduce not just a particular work but the entire collection, stresses the overall unity of the whole. Before proceeding to an examination of individual codices or individual poems, we must establish the background for collections of this kind. What sort of precedents can we find for Machaut's anthologies?

In the compilations of Watriquet and the Condés, as well as in those of Thibaut de Navarre, Adenet le Roi, or Chrétien de Troyes, the continuing presence of the author contributes significantly to the unification of the poetic corpus, albeit to a varying extent for different poets. In these collections, though, author identity is not the only source of coherence; there is also a generic uniformity—be it dit, song, chanson de geste, or romance—and a thematic consistency—morality, love, matière de France, or matière de Bretagne. These factors are not necessarily absolute. Thibaut's corpus does include pastourelles, jeux-partis, lays, re-

23. For descriptions of Machaut's manuscripts and their contents, see Chichmaref's edition of *Poésies lyriques*, pp. lxxiii–cxvi. Some of Chichmaref's dates must be revised. Most important for our purposes, Bibl. Nat. fr. 1586, long regarded as a fifteenth-century manuscript, is now recognized as the earliest surviving manuscript, dating from 1350–55; see, for example, Avril, "Manuscrits enluminés."

ligious lyric, and Crusade songs in addition to chansons courtoises; Jean de Condé's three principal collections include fabliaux, allegorical narrative, moral tales, and nonnarrative didactic dits;[24] Adenet's *Cléomadès* does not participate in the same historical arena as his poems concerning the family history and political alliances of Charlemagne. Still, Thibaut's works are all musical; Jean's are all didactic to one extent or another, whereas none is musical; Adenet's are all narrative, set in the past. The diversity is not stressed in any of the surviving manuscripts: neither Jean's poems nor Thibaut's songs are categorized according to poetic type.[25]

Although a given anthology codex may exhibit considerable generic diversity, it is, as we have seen, difficult to find manuscripts in which generically diverse works by a single twelfth-, thirteenth-, or early fourteenth-century author are associated. Wace's hagiographic works are never associated with his romances, nor Chrétien's songs with his; Richard de Fournival's songs are never associated with the *Bestiaire*.[26] Jean de Meun's *Testament*, sometimes with the *Codicille*, is frequently paired with the *Rose*, but such pairing may be due, at least in part, to the first-person voice common to these texts. Indeed, it could be said that the *Testament* continues the story of the *Rose* poets by complementing the account of Guillaume de Lorris's death at the midpoint with the voice of Jean de Meun just before his death. In any case, it is noteworthy that whereas the *Testament* and *Codicille* are found in a significant number of *Rose* manuscripts, Jean de Meun's translations almost never are; and not one of the mansucripts cataloged by Langlois gathers together his complete works.[27] This is somewhat surprising, considering Jean's formidable

24. Ribard comments on the diversity of Jean de Condé's oeuvre in "Des lais au XIVᵉ siècle?" especially p. 946. Although all three of the principal collections—Arsenal MS 3524, Bibl. Nat. fr. MS 1446, and the MS B, III, 18 of the Casanatensis, Rome—are characterized by this diversity, it is interesting that Jean's two longest narratives, the *Lais du blanc chevalier* and the *Chevalier à la mance*, are excluded from these collections and appear only in the Turin MS L. I.13, which does not contain any other poems by Jean de Condé.

25. Thibaut's songs do actually reflect a certain tendency toward generic ordering, with most of the jeux-partis grouped together. This is far from completely systematic, however, and no surviving manuscript rubricates Thibaut's different lyric corpora as such. His songs of all types are simply treated as one codicological entry, "Les chansons le roi de Navarre." See Chapter 2.

26. MS 657 of the Bibl. Mun. of Arras does contain both the *Bestiaire d'amours* and Richard de Fournival's songs, but the latter are in the chansonnier section. The codex, a large anthology, also contains a number of other diverse texts; and there is no indication that the compiler of the manuscript considered it particularly significant that the author of the *Bestiaire* was also represented among the series of trouvères.

27. See Ernest Langlois, pp. 213–18. The manuscript distribution of the works attributed to Jean de Meun is described by Badel, *"Roman de la Rose" au XIVe siècle*, pp. 63–66. For the fourteenth century, Badel shows fifteen manuscripts with the *Rose* and the *Testament;* seven with these texts plus the *Codicille;* one with the two former texts plus the *Trésor;* and two with all four texts. The tendency toward complete compilations of Jean de Meun's poetic works is even greater in the fifteenth and sixteenth centuries: Badel lists

reputation. The prologue to the translation of Boethius, in which Jean lists his other works of poetry and translation, would even seem to invite such a compilation; and it is, of course, possible that a collection of Jean's works did once exist. But the evidence of the nearly three hundred surviving *Rose* manuscripts shows that such would have been the exception rather than the rule and offers an important indicator of just how unusual the compilation of an author's "oeuvres complètes" really was.

It is, therefore, extremely significant when we do find examples of generically diverse author corpora. In these, a new principle of compilation is evident: the personality of the author is deemed central enough to inspire the conjoining of texts that would not ordinarily be associated. The pairing of Jean Bodel's *Congé* with his *Chanson des Saisnes* in MS 3142 suggests that Bodel's authorship of the *Saisnes* is of special significance. It is not only that the name Jean Bodel conjures up an assurance of clerkly authority, literary excellence, or historical accuracy. There is an implication, subliminal but nonetheless important, that our reading of the *Saisnes* could be enhanced by some knowledge of Bodel's life and his position as poet of Arras. The compilations of Rutebeuf's poems, in which hagiographic narrative, fabliau, political diatribe, and personal poetry in the goliardic tradition are gathered together, similarly suggest that the fact of authorship by Rutebeuf transcends these generic differences. And, as we saw in Chapter 2, the compilation of Adam de la Halle's works in MS 25566 suggests that we can learn something from observing the unfolding of Adam's poetic career through the progression of songs, plays, and dits; the inclusion of Watriquet's *Fastrasie* in his collection of dits indicates a similar desire for a complete author corpus.

We must place the anthology manuscripts of Guillaume de Machaut in the latter context; yet the diversity of his manuscripts, coupled with their careful organization, is approached only by the Adam de la Halle collection in MS 25566. Both the chansonniers and the collections of dits are important precedents for his compilations. But the notion of combining the lyric and narrative compositions of a single poet could not have derived from either of these sources. The idea is new and seems to have been born about the turn of the fourteenth century, an outgrowth of numerous factors that we have seen in the preceding chapters: the active role of the scribe in literary tradition and the analogies between scribal practice and poetic process, the consciousness of the vernacular lyric or

---

fourteen manuscripts from this period with all four texts, and a total of eight that contain the *Rose* along with only one or two of the others. In contrast, only two manuscripts cataloged by Langlois contain Jean's translation of Boethius in its entirety; one combines Jean's translation with the anonymous translation in verse and prose, and an additional five contain other translations of Boethius. Only one contains his translation of Vegetius; none contains the translation of the Epistles of Abelard and Heloise, although the Dijon, Bibl. Mun. MS 525 did originally contain these epistles in Latin.

lyrico-narrative poet as a writer, the attention to the act of poetic composition and the primacy of composition over performance, the important unifying function of authorial presence in a pluralistic work like the *Roman de la rose* or in a diverse poetic corpus like that of Rutebeuf or Adam.

If the vernacular poet is a writer, he can also be a producer of books; and if he is to write a book, it can theoretically be any sort of book he wants. Machaut seems to have realized this or to have seen its importance in a way that his predecessors did not. When an author's poems were compiled and treated as a single codicological unit, as with Thibaut de Navarre, Rutebeuf, and the Condés, then somehow the individual pieces were no longer subject to further codification. It was as though the division of Rutebeuf's works into saint's lives, crusade poems, and so on, would have fragmented the corpus: it would no longer be a self-contained item. Similarly, the division of Thibaut's songs into jeux-partis, pastourelles, and so forth, would have meant their dispersal among the various subdivisions of the chansonnier itself. Prior to Machaut, only in the case of Adam de la Halle do we find an author corpus treated as a small book unto itself, with generic division, yet also as a self-contained whole subject to poetic organization and provided with an explicit. This concept of the author corpus is central to Machaut's poetic career: he is the author of books, and these books are at once carefully articulated anthologies and poetically unified wholes.

We have seen that Nicole de Margival used the implied subtext of the *Rose* as a vehicle for the compilation of diverse poetic material, all of which was brought to bear on the experience of the central poetic "I"; in the Arsenal manuscript of Baudouin and Jean de Condé, as in the Dijon manuscript of the *Bestiaire,* the narrative structure of the *Rose* is imitated in certain aspects of the textual arrangement, so, again, the implicit or explicit presence of the *Rose* contributes to the unification of a body of otherwise atomized texts. The *Rose* is the thematic nexus of an anthology like MS 12786 or, even more explicitly, Dijon, Bibl. Mun. MS 525. Here the *Rose* is followed by a large body of texts, including the *Testament* and *Codicille* of Jean de Meun, the *Chaton en français,* the *Roman de Fauvel,* the *Jeu des Echecs,* the epistles of Abelard and Heloise, and a French verse translation of the *Consolation of Philosophy.* An elaborate system of marginal notations, evidently the work of the scribe, maps out the various points of contact among these texts, in particular between the *Rose* and the other texts in the anthology. In all these cases, the *Rose* in some way contributes to the unification of disparate material. Nicole de Margival, however, like Tibaut in the *Poire,* subsumes the variety of textual material under the narrative unity of his poem; he does incorporate individual songs and dits into this system but does not attempt to account for a continuity that would bridge the gap from one discrete poem to another without the device of a frame narrative. In the case of the Condés, in turn, it is far from certain that either of the poets was conscious of evoking the *Rose* as a principle of textual compilation; it may have been a later compiler who capitalized on the presence of the *Rose* in certain of their dits. In MS 12786 and the Dijon manuscripts, it was certainly the idea of the compiler to bring together a group of texts that would play off the *Rose* in one way or another.[28] Although all these examples can help us to understand the background for Machaut's books, none of them is precisely what he produced.

Machaut likewise used the *Rose* as a point of departure; as a central presence in his works, it does contribute to the unity of the oeuvre as a whole. But Machaut's use of the *Rose,* and his use of the anthology format, combine the practices of scribal compilation and editing with those of poetic conjointure. Machaut both wrote the poems and gathered them together into a single poetic system; he created a series of texts that although generically diverse would form a coherent ensemble. His presence as both author and protagonist not only unifies a composite text like the *Remede de Fortune;* it also allows for a sense of continuity across textual boundaries, across rubricated "explicits," even from one literary genre to another. Because Machaut projects himself into his narrative works as lover, poet and writer, the anthology is unified both externally, through the historical fact of common authorship, and internally, through the continuing poetic and amorous adventures of a particular protagonist. But there is no overall narrative framework to the anthology; the implied narrative of Machaut's poetic career is sufficient.[29]

The unification of Machaut's compilation and the importance of authorship in effecting this unity are expressed in the *Prologue* that precedes the collection in the later manuscripts.[30] The *Prologue* presents Machaut's election as poet, through the intervention of Nature and Love, and includes a long technical account of poetic and musical forms and the process of composition. That Nature and Love are the two

28. Dijon MS 525 does have a particularly high concentration of works by or attributed to Jean de Meun, including some short, spurious pieces. The compiler, however, chose to include the Epistles of Abelard and Heloise in Latin rather than in Jean's translation, and he used his translation of Boethius only for the closing section of the text; the prologue to this translation, in which Jean reviews his literary achievements, is therefore not included. It is unclear to what extent a consciousness of Jean's corpus influenced the choice of texts in this collection. The transition to Jean's translation of Boethius is marked by a rubric but without any reference to the fact that the codex contains other works by this author; the marginal notes refer only to thematic relationships among texts and make no explicit mention of authorship. For a description of this manuscript, see Ernest Langlois, pp. 122–25.

29. In *Poetic Identity,* Brownlee discusses the importance of Machaut's mise-en-scène of poetic process and of his treatment of the codex as a literary artifact.

30. Machaut's *Prologue* is published by Chichmaref, *Poésies lyriques,* and by Hoepffner in his edition of Machaut, *Oeuvres.*

authorities presiding over Machaut's poetic career recalls the *Roman de la rose:* under the conjoined auspices of Nature and Love the poetic-amorous quest is fulfilled. Machaut's election further echoes Jean de Meun's poetic election at the midpoint of the conjoined *Rose:* the God of Love promises to nourish and inspire the young Jean and also prays to Lucina, goddess of childbirth, to preside over his birth, implying that the creation of a poet is a function both of natural processes and of a poeticized love psychology. Machaut thus presents himself as the heir to Jean de Meun and thereby implicitly writes himself into the tradition leading from Tibullus, Gallus, and Catullus through Ovid to Guillaume de Lorris and his continuer.

While Machaut does not adopt Jean's analogy between writing and procreation, his *Prologue* does stress the affinities between natural and poetic creation. The first *Prologue* ballade, spoken by Nature, emphasizes the importance of form in the creative process:

> Je, Nature, par qui tout est *fourmé*
> Quanqu'a ça jus et seur terre et en mer,
> Vien ci a toy, Guillaume, qui *fourmé*
> T'ay a part, pour faire par toy *fourmer*
> Nouviaus dis amoureus plaisans. . .

[I, Nature, by whom all is *formed,* whatever there is below and on land and sea, come here to you, Guillaume, I who have *formed* you apart, in order to cause you to *form* new pleasant amorous dits.] [Hoepffner ed., st. 1, vv. 1–5; emphasis mine]

Guillaume's reply in turn stresses the importance of order in the work of both Nature and the poet: "Dont drois est, quant vous m'*ordenez* / A faire dis amoureus *ordenez*" (so it is right, when you *order* me to make amorous, *ordered* dits [Hoepffner ed., st. 2, vv. 5–6, emphasis mine]). The ballade spoken by Love, finally, echoes the opening analogy in its use of *faire* (make) for both natural and poetic creation (Hoepffner ed., st. 3, vv. 4–8). Machaut's is a rarefied love poetry. Within the *Prologue* love does not inflame the poet with desire, as in *Amores* 1.i, but provides him with pleasant thoughts and hopeful spirits. In this presentation, the poetic text is a general celebration of the positive effects of love on the human psyche, not a seductive message sent by the poet to his heart's desire. Machaut's sublimation of love—what we might call "love for love's sake"—is an essential quality of his poetic oeuvre and is related to the primacy of writing in Machaut's concept of poetic process.

Poetic creation, then, results from a combination of technical expertise and inspiration; it is a process of ordering and giving form, both musical and rhetorical, to love sentiment. The emphasis on *ordenance* in turn can extend to the ordering of the oeuvre, and verse form is an important ordering principle at this level. In his emphasis on book production and his focus on the poet as writer rather than performer, Machaut differs from the trouvères, even Adam de la Halle, and from a minstrel like Watriquet. We have seen that Watriquet remained a performer even as he was also identified as author of a book. Although oral performance is sometimes a factor in Machaut's persona, it is increasingly superseded by writing as his career progresses. Watriquet's anthology has the dual aspect of being a series of adventures of the persona "Watriquet" and a series of oral performances by this persona. We will see that the performative aspect is still important in Machaut's earlier dits and in the illumination of his earliest surviving anthology, MS Bibl. Nat. fr. 1586, produced in the early 1350s. But the activity of writing is equally so; and in later manuscripts, as in Machaut's later dits, the figure of the writer, identified with Machaut, is separated from that of the performer altogether. Machaut went farther than any previous French poet in establishing his identity as a writer, author, and compiler and in exploring the poetic implications of this stance; it is no doubt partly for this reason that Eustache Deschamps honored him as "noble poet" in the first known application of the term *poete* to a vernacular author.[31]

## The Compilations of Jean Froissart

It is well known that Froissart was heavily influenced by Machaut; this influence extends not only to individual dits but to the anthology codices themselves, of which two survive, both dating from within Froissart's lifetime.[32] Like Machaut, Froissart compiled his poetic works in large collections, with lyric texts categorized according to verse form; the principal difference is that Froissart's codices have no musical compositions and, except for the author portrait at the beginning of MS Bibl. Nat. fr. 831, are not illuminated. They are, however, beautifully written manuscripts that give an ordered picture of his poetic career. Of the poetic works, only *Meliador* is omitted from both codices, probably because of its unwieldy length within the context of an anthology.

The overall unity of Froissart's codices is stressed by the rubrics, virtually identical in the two manuscripts, that appear at beginning and end of the collection. In MS 831, these read:

> Vous devés sçavoir que dedens ce livre sont contenu pluisour dittié et traitié amourous et de moralité, les quels sire Jehans Froissars, prestres, en

31. See Brownlee, "Poetic *Oeuvre* of Guillaume de Machaut."
32. For descriptions of Froissart's anthology manuscripts, see Fourrier's introduction to his edition of *Espinette*, pp. 7–17.

ce temps tresoriers et canonnes de Cymai, et de nation de la conté de Haynnau et de la ville de Valenchienes, a fais, dittés et ordonnés à l'aÿde de Dieu et d'Amours, et a le contemplation et plaisance de pluisours haus et nobles signours et de pluisours nobles et vaillans dames; et les commencha a faire sus l'an de grasce Nostre Signour mil. CCC..lxij. et les cloÿ sus l'an de grasce mil trois cens Quatre vins et quatorze; et vous ensagnera ceste table comment il sont escript ou dit livre par ordenance.

[You should know that within this book are contained many amorous and moral poems and treatises that Sir Jean Froissart, priest, at this time trea-surer and canon of Chimay, of the nation and the county of Hainaut and the city of Valenciennes, made, versified, and ordered, with the help of God and love, for the contemplation and enjoyment of many high and noble lords, and many noble and worthy ladies; and he began to make them in the year of grace of Our Lord 1362 and concluded them in the year of grace 1394; and this table will teach you in what order they are written in the said book.] [Fol. 1v]

   Explicit dittiers et traitiers amoureus et de moralité fais, dittés et or-donnés par discret et venerable homme sire Jehan Froissart, priestre, a che tamps tresorier et chanonne de Cymai et cloÿ che dit livre en l'an de grasce Nostre Seigneur mil. CCC. iiijˣˣ & .xiiij., le .xijᵉ. jour dou mois de may.

[Here end the amorous and moral poems and treatises, versified and or-dered by the discreet and venerable man Sir Jean Froissart, priest, at this time treasurer and canon of Chimay; and he concluded this aforesaid book in the year of the grace of Our Lord 1394, the 12th day of the month of May.] [Fol. 200v]

These frame rubrics stress the nature of the collection as a self-contained and unified whole; the specification of the dates of composition and the details concerning the historical identity of Jean Froissart again remind us of the importance of the author and of the circumstances of composi-tion; what unfolds before us in this manuscript is the drama of poetic creation. In the acknowledgment of God and love as the two sources of poetic inspiration, Froissart's "preface" echoes Machaut's *Prologue,* with its portrayal of Nature and Love as the deities of poetry. Also like Ma-chaut's *Prologue,* Froissart's statement stresses poetic composition as an act of creation (*fais*), versification (*dittiés*) and ordering (*ordonnés*). An analogy between poetic composition and the compilation of the oeuvre is suggested by the use of the word *ordonner* for the former, and *ordenance* for the arrangement of the anthology.[33] Finally, Froissart resembles

---

33. *Ordonner* is one of the words used most frequently by Froissart to indicate poetic composition, which he evidently conceived as a process of arranging words according to formal structures. See Lucien Foulet's study of Froissart's use of this word. Foulet concen-trates exclusively on the Chronicles, but his findings are relevant for Froissart's poetry as well.

Machaut in that the avowed motivation for his poetic activity is not the wooing of a lady but the entertainment of aristocratic patrons. This motivation distinguishes Froissart the poet, a priest and the author of the entire anthology, from his various amorous narrator-protagonists. The prefatory statement all but acknowledges that the poet adopts the role of love-struck youth for dramatic or didactic purposes, and that the first-person voice of the dits amoureux reflects at least as much self-caricature as autobiography.

Although MS 831 contains fewer texts than MS 830, the order in which they appear is nearly identical in the two manuscripts. As we will see in our examination of Froissart's poetry, the sequence of texts is informed by the implied narrative progression of the poetic career, moving from the *Paradis d'amour* at the beginning to the *Plaidoirie de la rose et de la violette* at the end. At the center of the collection in each manuscript is the *Prison amoureuse,* where Froissart portrays himself writing poetry and compiling it into a book for his patron "Rose," identified by various allusions to historical events as Wenceslas de Brabant. This is the most heterogenous of the dits: it comprises prose letters narrating Rose's love affair; prose letters providing commentary on Froissart's poetic compositions; short verse narratives, themselves containing still other short narratives; numerous lyric texts; and, of course, the frame narrative itself. It is also the text in which Froissart most explicitly focuses on his role as poet and maker of books. Located at the midpoint of the collection, it mirrors Froissart's role in the preparation of the codex itself. As is the case with Machaut, Froissart's self-presentation in prologues and his mise-en-scène of the process of text production permit a progressive redefinition of his role as poet through the course of his works. The continuity is heightened through his recurring use of the motif of dream and of Ovidian and pseudo-Ovidian mythology. I will examine this series of dreams and mythological exempla and the ordering principles of the collection as a whole in Chapter 10.

Given that these two manuscripts date from within Froissart's lifetime and provide such detailed information about Froissart's background and his role as author, it is most likely that he was responsible for their production. Certainly, it would not be surprising if Froissart, whose dits reflect an intimate familiarity with the works of Machaut, chose to follow his celebrated predecessor in this respect as well. Froissart's role in the preparation of manuscripts is attested in a passage from his Chronicles, where he describes the book that he presented to Richard II:

> J'avoie de pourveance fait escripre, grosser et enluminer et recoeiller tous les traités amoureux et de moralité que au terme de trente quatre ans je avoie par la grasce de Dieu et d'Amour fais et compilés.

[Through foresight I had caused to be written, copied and illuminated, and gathered together all the amorous and moral treatises that, in the course of thirty-four years, I had made and compiled by the grace of God and love.] [Buchon ed., vol. 3, p. 198]

It is possible that MS 831 could, in fact, be the manuscript that Froissart presented to King Richard. It is known to have been in England by the early fifteenth century; more important, the texts omitted from this collection include precisely those that might be politically offensive to the English king during this delicate moment in history—that is, those expressing pro-French sentiment, flattering the accomplishments of the French court, or alluding to Froissart's relations with Richard II's political adversaries. Finally, MS 831 contains a ballade, not found in MS 830, pertaining to the legendary English King Brut.[34] This evidence of political editing is most interesting, for, even if it does not prove conclusively that MS 831 was the very one copied for Richard II, it does demonstrate the care with which Froissart's collections were prepared; the omission of texts is by design and not by accident.

Although Froissart most commonly represents himself as a writer (and never as a singer), he does make some references to a particular kind of oral performance that he engaged in: reading his works out loud. In the *Dit dou florin,* he states that Gaston Phébus, count of Foix and viscount of Béarn, paid him eighty florins to read *Meliador* aloud during the winter of 1388–89 in installments of seven pages a night. The opening miniature of MS 831, which appears at the head of the opening rubric, similarly represents a man seated in an ornamental chair, reading aloud from a book before an audience of a man and two ladies. The association of this miniature with the rubric in which Jean Froissart is named as author of the book, and in which it is specified that he wrote the poems it contains for an audience of courtly men and ladies, certainly invites identification of this public reader with Froissart, since his is the voice that speaks to us through the book. In this image of the poet reading aloud from his book we see a vestige of the performative aspect of courtly poetry. Froissart's works are presented as written texts, to be read in a book as part of an ordered whole; yet the written word does still mirror the spoken voice, and even the late fourteenth-century audience experiences a book as something that may give rise to oral performance.

34. On the selection of texts in MS 831 and the evidence that it may have been prepared for an English patron, see Dembowski's introduction to his edition of the *Paradis d'amour,* pp. 3–4, 6–12.

Chapter 8

# From Song to Book in an Early Redaction of the Oeuvre of Guillaume de Machaut: The Codex Bibl. Nat. fr. 1586

Guillaume de Machaut was a prolific and a very popular poet. He was praised by Eustache Deschamps, as noted in the previous chapter; cited in treatises on the Second Rhetoric; held up as the French counterpart to Ovid in René d'Anjou's *Livre du cuer d'amours espris;* lovingly imitated by Jean Froissart and Christine de Pizan.[1] Nine fourteenth-century and three fifteenth-century manuscripts of his collected works survive today, and others are known from library inventories.[2] Interestingly, though, his works are rarely found outside these manuscripts of his collected works. It would seem that, even from an early point in his career, Machaut was perceived as the author of anthologies: his works formed a coherent whole that was not likely to be tampered with.

Given this integrity of Machaut's poetic oeuvre, it has seemed appropriate here to organize the investigation of his work in terms of the books that he produced. I will focus, in this chapter and the next, on two manuscripts that date from within Machaut's lifetime and that were most likely made under his supervision: MSS Bibl. Nat. fr. 1586 and 1584. In each case a general description of the manuscript and the evidence for Machaut's role in its production will be followed by a discussion of texts

1. Machaut is cited, for example, by Deschamps in his *Art de dictier* (composed 1392), in Saint-Hilaire and Raynaud's edition of Deschamps's *Oeuvres*, vol. 7, pp. 266–92, as well as in fifteenth-century treatises on the second rhetoric and in treatises on the Ars Nova. See Earp, pp. 45–46. The influence of Machaut on Froissart and Christine de Pizan is well known; see, for example, the various discussions by Poirion, *Poète et le prince.* In *Le Livre du cuer d'amours espris*, René d'Anjou ranks Machaut next to Ovid in his description of the tombs of the six exemplary poets, Ovid, Machaut, Petrarch, Boccaccio, Jean de Meun, and Alain Chartier (Wharton ed., pp. 141–43).

2. See Earp's detailed discussion of the Machaut manuscript tradition. A complete chart indicating the order of pieces in each manuscript appears in the introduction to Chichmaref's edition, vol. 1, pp. lxxvi–c. It should be noted, however, that Chichmaref uses a different set of sigla and that some of his dates must be revised in the light of modern research.

that exemplify Machaut's poetic stance at the time the manuscript was made. Through these discussions we can examine the ways in which Machaut exploited miniatures, rubrics, and other textual and paratextual elements in an all-encompassing poetic system. There can be little doubt that Machaut was deeply concerned with the orderly arrangement and visual effect of his books; the iconographic programs of MSS 1586 and 1584 reflect his manipulation of poetic voice and of the roles of lover, writer, and performer. An attentive reading of these codices, as poetic and visual constructs, brings us to the heart of Machaut's poetics.

## The MS Bibl. Nat. fr. 1586: General Description and Background

MS Bibl. Nat. fr. 1586, long thought to be a fifteenth-century copy, is now recognized as the earliest surviving Machaut manuscript, probably begun in the late 1340s and completed by 1355. It has been suggested that the manuscript was begun for presentation to Bonne of Luxembourg; after her death in 1349, the work was presumably completed for some other wealthy patron.[3] The manuscript is divided into three sections: the narrative dits, the lyric texts without music, and the lyric texts with musical notation. There are five dits: *Le Temps Pascour* (identified in other manuscripts and in modern times as *Le Jugement dou roy de Behaingne*, probably because of its relationship with the *Jugement dou roy de Navarre*, which does not appear in MS 1586); *Le Remede de Fortune; Le Dit des quatre oisiaus* (otherwise known as the *Dit de l'alerion*); *Le Dit dou vergier;* and *Le Dit dou lyon.* Since each dit is copied as a separate fascicle unit, we cannot be certain that this order corresponds to the original one or that there were not once other dits subsequently removed. If the manuscript was indeed intended for Bonne, it is logical that the poem written in honor of her father, John of Luxembourg and King of Bohemia, would have occupied first place; and that the *Jugement Navarre*, which overturns the judgment ascribed to her father, would be omitted. But this tells us nothing about the order of the remaining pieces, and the association of the manuscript with Bonne is in any case only a hypothesis. Unless further evidence is uncovered, we must treat each dit in MS 1586 as an independent unit, without making arguments based on their order.[4]

3. The art historical evidence for the early date of MS 1586 is discussed by Avril, "Manuscrits enluminés." See also "Chef-d'oeuvre de l'enluminure," especially pp. 112–14. The chronological placement of MS 1586, its possible association with Bonne of Luxembourg, and certain peculiarities of its construction are also discussed by Günther.

4. Keitel has remarked on the foliation signs on certain leaves, which may indicate a different original order. The signs in question are a series of letters indicating the relative order of gatherings. From these we know that the *Vergier* did originally follow the *Alerion;*

All of the dits are profusely illustrated with miniatures one column in width and about ten lines of text in height. The *Remede* additionally contains several half-page or three-quarter-page miniatures; and each dit is headed with a three-quarter-page frontispiece. Four of these represent springtime landscapes, the particulars of which identify the dit in question. The *Jugement Behaingne* (*Temps Pascour*) opens with a representation of the knight and lady debating, observed by the protagonist at one side, in a landscape of trees and flowers (fol. 1). This announces the role that the narrator-protagonist is to play in the poem: he is the witness through whose eyes we see the events of the narrative, but these events revolve around the other two characters.[5] The *Alerion* (*Quatre oisiaus*) opens with a similar landscape containing four youths: one sits beside a nest of birds, with a bird on his finger and one at his side; one gazes up into a tree, holding a sling and presumably bird hunting; two chase butterflies with a net (fol. 59). Although the four figures do not correspond directly to characters within the poem, they do signal the four divisions of the text. Their activity focuses attention on the birds and butterflies, as is appropriate to the theme of the dit. The *Vergier* opens with the protagonist in a garden, gazing at a rose-covered bower (fol. 93). The lack of other figures necessarily focuses attention on the protagonist and on the garden itself as the locus and substance of his experience; in particular, we see him in relation to the rosebush and the small enclosure that it creates. This subtle but unmistakable allusion to the *Rose* reflects the nature of the *Vergier*, which is closest of all the dits to Guillaume de Lorris's poem. The *Lyon* is headed by a landscape teeming with birds and animals, with a castle just visible at one side, and a river in the foreground (fol. 103). The absence of human figures is striking (according to François Avril, this is one of the earliest known purely landscape paintings of the postclassical period) and identifies the place as the enchanted isle of animals discovered by the protagonist of the *Lyon*.[6] The *Remede*, finally, is headed not with a landscape but with an image of the protagonist and his lady gazing at one another in front of her castle, a huge and elaborately executed structure that dominates the scene (fol. 23).

The manuscript's lyric section, which begins with the *Louange des dames*, is marked by a small miniature (fig. 18) that represents the lyric

---

but according to these signs the *Alerion* would have been the first piece in the collection. Earp, however, points out that these signs could have been for the use of the illuminator. In Earp's opinion, the system of foliation currently found at the tops of the pages is the original one, and the manuscript has therefore not been reordered (p. 136). Earp's arguments are plausible, though not conclusive.

5. For a detailed study of Machaut's manipulation of narrative voice and his concept of poetic identity, see Brownlee, *Poetic Identity*. For a general study of Machaut's dits, see Calin, *Poet at the Fountain*.

6. Avril, *Manuscript Painting*, p. 90. The miniature is reproduced as plate 26.

*Figure 18.* Author portrait, *Louange des dames*, B.N. fr. 1586, fol. 121. (Photograph: Bibliothèque Nationale, Paris)

poet in the same flowery landscape. He is writing on a scroll, and four other scrolls lie on the ground beside him (fol. 121). The plethora of scrolls no doubt represents the large number of short lyric texts here assembled; recalling the associations of the scroll with oral performance, we may say that the texts are being represented as a series of utterances. The passage from narrative to lyric poetry represents a potential discontinuity; the miniature serves to remind us at this juncture that it is the continuing presence of the poet-compiler that serves to unify the collection of disparate texts.

The four large landscape scenes and the numerous smaller miniatures, most of which also figure a garden setting, impart a lushness, an aura of courtly luxury and lyricism, to the codex. They also contribute to the unification of the texts by presenting a series of variations on a theme. It is as though the poems are all set in the same landscape; the *Remede* and *Lyon* miniatures show us the castle to which these gardens belong. The motif continues in the musical section of the codex, where each of the lays begins with a miniature. These, too, represent figures in a garden setting, suggesting that the series of lays may be read as analogous to the carol in the *Roman de la rose*.

Was MS 1586 made under Machaut's direct supervision? Is he the designer of the illustrative program? There is no hard and fast evidence to prove or disprove Machaut's involvement with the production of this manuscript. I believe, however, that there is sufficient circumstantial evidence to say that Machaut's supervision of its arrangement and illumination is very probable. First, it is important to establish the early date of the manuscript; not only a fifteenth-century dating but even a later fourteenth-century dating would cast doubt on Machaut's control over the process of compilation, since it omits works written after 1355.[7] If the manuscript is late, it is certainly a copy of an early manuscript, and this copy and its decoration could have been undertaken without Machaut's even being aware of it. The arguments adduced by François Avril for the placement of the manuscript about 1350 are based both on the general style of the miniatures and on the identification of the Master of the *Remede de Fortune* with an artist whose other work can be dated. This is compelling evidence, not to be dismissed. Equally important, the iconographic evidence also points to an early date for the manuscript. The figure of the poet is always represented in a garden setting, writing on or reading from a scroll, and images of writing alternate with images of oral performance. Iconographically, MS 1586 is reminiscent of

7. Although it is impossible to determine whether the codex might once have contained additional dits, the same is not true of the lyric and musical works, as the end of a section in this part of the manuscript does not necessarily correspond to the end of a gathering. The consistent exclusion of later works of all sorts leaves little doubt about the early date of the collection.

trouvère chansonniers *a*, *M*, and especially *O*, where the poetic "I" appears in a variety of poses that encompass private meditation, making songs, performing them, and interacting with the lady. Although lyric composition is separated from lyric performance, the former is still conceived in a "lyric" mode—that is, as taking place outdoors or in a nondescript setting, with the motif of the scroll representing the written text, and never in a study, at a writing desk, or in conjunction with a book. Among Machaut's manuscripts, MS 1586 is the only one that maintains this trouvère iconography; as will be seen, later manuscripts increasingly employ such motifs as the book and the author at his writing desk, and in one way or another effect a separation of the poet from the lover or performer. On these grounds, then, it is reasonable to argue that MS 1586 represents an early codification of Machaut's oeuvre, one for which late thirteenth- and early fourteenth-century books provided the models.

Given that MS 1586 was made in the 1350s, Machaut's role in its production is possible but still not certain. Here, we cannot escape from the realm of hypothesis; nonetheless, important arguments do exist to link Machaut to the manuscript. First, we know that by this time, Machaut had come to view his extant corpus as a poetic whole, subject to internal organization, that reflected his moral biases and poetic personality. This much is clear from a reading of the *Jugement Navarre*, written in the late 1340s, which would have been Machaut's newest work at the time MS 1586 was compiled. It may even have been composed simultaneously with the initial work on MS 1586; perhaps its absence from the collection is due to the book's having been commissioned and its contents specified before the *Jugement Navarre* was completed. If the manuscript really does reflect Machaut's concept of his oeuvre, then we would expect to find parallels between the book and the poem. In fact, the *Jugement Navarre* is a key text in the codification of Machaut's oeuvre, for Machaut here forges a poetic identity that transcends the boundaries of this particular poem. In the *Jugement Navarre*, the narrator, identified as "Guillaume de Machaut," is accosted by a group of ladies who accuse him of slighting women in his *Jugement Behaingne*. The king of Bohemia's judgment is reversed, and Guillaume is required to compose a lay, a chanson, and a ballade in penance. By presenting himself as an established poet, author of the *Jugement Behaingne* and composer of lyric pieces, Machaut uses the *Jugement Navarre* to conjoin the two divisions, lyric and narrative, of his poetic work.

Even more important, the *Jugement Navarre* contains an explicit statement of Machaut's oeuvre as a collection of written texts that the poet needs to put into order. The ladies' spokeswoman accuses Guillaume of having maligned women in one of his works, telling him that he will see what she means if he checks through his writings. He replies somewhat pompously that he has written many things, of different types ("de pluseurs manieres," v. 885) and treating different topics ("de diverses matieres," v. 886), no two of which are alike. To sort through all this material would be a nearly impossible task:

> Se tout voloie regarder
> —Dont je me vorray bien garder—
> Trop longuement y metteroie.

[If I wanted to look at all of it—which I would really like to avoid doing—it would take too long.] [Vv. 893–95]

Behind the humor of this passage we can clearly see Machaut's pride in the number and diversity of his poetic works. At the same time, the entire discussion stresses that these disparate works are united as the work of a single individual. Properly arranged, they would create a coherent composite picture of his poetic craft and his doctrine of love. MS 1586 in turn is the result of just this careful reading and ordering by the poet of his own works.[8]

If we accept that MS 1586 does date from about 1350, contains everything that Machaut had written up until this time—with the exception of the *Jugement Navarre*, which, as we saw, could well have been omitted for political reasons if the manuscript was intended for Bonne of Luxembourg—and corresponds to a moment in his career when he explicitly voiced the desire to put his works in order as the various manifestations of a particular poetic ego, then the probability of Machaut's involvement with the production of the manuscript is very strong. In the lack of unambiguous documentary evidence, it remains only to ask whether the arrangement and iconography of the manuscript correspond to what we know of Machaut's concept of his poetic oeuvre and of his own poetic identity during this period. We have already seen that the narrative and lyric sections of the manuscript are conjoined through the image of the lyric writer-compiler, an iconographic detail that corresponds to the poet-centered view of the oeuvre in the *Jugement Navarre* and is therefore consonant with a reading of the illustrative program as Machaut's work. Still, an independent iconographer could have come up with this device; an author portrait is frequently used to conjoin the two portions of the *Rose*, for example, and the image in MS 1586 could represent an artist's adaptation of this well-known motif to the context of lyric compilation. In order to judge the likelihood of Machaut's involvement with the iconographic program, we must look more closely at the relationship between text and image. Since a detailed examination of the entire

8. See Brownlee, *Poetic Identity*, pp. 15, 21.

manuscript goes beyond the scope of the present study, I will focus here on two key programs within the codex: the illuminations of the *Remede de Fortune,* within the narrative corpus, and the illuminated series of lays in the lyric section.

## *Le Remede de Fortune:* A Poetic and Iconographic Analysis

The *Remede de Fortune* is the first-person account of the narrator's youthful initiation into love; it describes his infatuation with a certain lady, for whom he composes lyric poetry. At one point, when his fear of declaring himself to the lady has caused him to withdraw in despair to a secluded garden, he is visited by Hope, who delivers a long discourse on love comportment and on the importance of an optimistic outlook on love: by being satisfied with the condition of love as an end in itself, the lover is invulnerable to the ravages of Fortune. The narrator's success with the lady is never clear-cut; although he does eventually declare himself to her, she vacillates between encouraging him and ignoring him. He takes Hope's words to heart, however, and continues to compose poetry and to love faithfully, regardless of the lady's reaction.

The *Remede* is celebrated today largely for the lyric pieces—one of each of the formes fixes with musical notation, and a nonnotated *prière*— which the narrator-protagonist represents himself as writing or singing or, in two cases, as receiving from Hope. At once art of poetry and art of love, the *Remede* is a key text for Machaut's presentation of himself as love poet. Its importance in Machaut's eyes can be gauged from the quality of its illumination; the skilled Master of the *Remede de Fortune,* whose work in MS 1586 is limited to this text, was evidently commissioned specially to illustrate this important piece.[9] The *Remede* is the most profusely illustrated of the dits in MS 1586, with at least one miniature for almost every two-page spread (see the table of miniatures in Appendix B). Even where the scenes are extremely similar, as in the numerous miniatures illustrating the conversation between the lover and Hope, care has been taken to avoid monotony by varying the poses of the figures, so no two miniatures are quite alike. As throughout the codex, the graceful, stylized gestures of the figures resemble the movements of a dance, which is played out step by step through the pages of the book.

---

9. Avril identifies the three artists of MS 1586 in "Manuscrits enluminés," pp. 123–24. See also Avril's brief discussion of the Master of the *Remede de Fortune* in *Manuscript Painting,* pp. 25–28 and 84–89. Avril reproduces the opening miniature (pl. 23), the representation of the carol where l'Amant sings his virelay (pl. 24), and the banquet scene (pl. 25).

The importance of the *Remede* is also reflected in the rubrication that articulates the text into its episodes and identifies the speakers of dialogue passages. This latter technique surely derives from the *Rose*, the only prior example, to my knowledge, of vernacular courtly narrative rubricated in this manner. The designation of the protagonist as "l'Amant" identifies him with the protagonist of the *Rose;* the impact of these rubrics is such that the *Remede* evokes the *Rose* not only poetically but also visually as a written document.[10] Following in the footsteps of Nicole de Margival, Machaut integrates different branches of the lyrico-narrative tradition through the use of lyric insertions, the use of first-person narrative, and the centrality of the act of lyric composition and the figure of the poet.[11] My reading of the *Remede* will focus largely on the lyric pieces and the miniatures that accompany them. The lyrico-narrative poetics of the *Remede* are an important crystallization of the large-scale poetics of Machaut's oeuvre; their reflection in the illuminations of the *Remede* provides a visual mapping out of poetic process. Clearly, the miniatures were planned by someone who knew the text well. An intelligent scribe or artist could certainly have acquired such knowledge. Still, the close relationship between text and image does lend support to the hypothesis that Machaut himself designed, or helped to design, the iconographic program.

The opening miniature, a classic representation of dous regart, sets the stage for the love story. Standing at one side with his manservant, l'Amant is separated from his lady. She in turn stands in the doorway of her castle, set off by the architectural framework and rendered inaccessible by a bar across the gateway. Three ladies-in-waiting also stand between her and the lover. Yet the eyes of the two lovers clearly meet, and she points in his direction. The miniature thus skillfully establishes the tension of a love relationship to which is granted a psychic but not a physical consummation—the lady seems to respond, yet she remains out of reach. Such, indeed, is the quality of the love experienced by the *Remede* protagonist, who by the end of the dit has succeeded in writing songs and poetry but is not quite sure whether he has succeeded in winning the affections of his lady.[12]

The first poem written by l'Amant is the lay; it is framed by a miniature at each end. At the head, the poet sits in a landscape of trees and flowers writing on a long scroll (fig. 19); the rubric states, "Comment

10. Brownlee has further pointed out that in MSS Bibl. Nat. fr. 1584 and 22545 the rubric "l'Amant" does not appear until after the protagonist has heard Hope's chanson royal; that is, the point where he begins to be a properly educated lover (*Poetic Identity*, p. 230, n. 19).

11. The connection between Nicole's *Panthère* and the *Remede* was first suggested by Hoepffner, "Poésies lyriques du *Dit de la Panthère*."

12. The sublimation of love in the *Remede* is discussed by Kelly in *Medieval Imagination*, pp. 100–105, 130–37.

*Figure 19.* Lover writing lay, *Remede de Fortune,* B.N. fr. 1586, fol. 26. (Photograph: Bibliothèque Nationale, Paris)

l'amant fait un lay de son sentement" (How the lover makes a lay about his sentiment [fol. 26]). At the end, he stands before his lady in another garden landscape, holding his scroll; the rubric states, "Comment la dame fait lire a l'amant le lay qu'il a fait" (How the lady has the lover read the lay he has made [fol. 28v]). The motif of the scroll, first, deserves mention. Lyric poetry, in the context of the *Remede,* is sung, and it is consistently represented by a scroll, as will be seen. It is still an oral performative medium. But at the same time, Machaut presents himself as a poet, a writer and maker of texts. His depiction of the lyric poem evokes the same fusion of oral and written modes that we have seen in the *Rose* and the texts that it inspired, and in chansonnier illuminations: the written text is an artifact that embodies a performance. The repetition of the word *lire* (to read) in both rubric and text stresses the fact that this lay is indeed written, whereas the use of the scroll suggests in turn that it was written in order to be read aloud or sung.

The written text is presented as the link between the two moments of solitary inspired composition and public performance. The scroll visually represents the written text in each miniature, and the actual text of the lay lies in between, forming a bridge. As a performance piece within the context of the narrative, the lay allows l'Amant to give social expression to his private sentiment—that is, to create and assume a role in courtly society. The conjoined text of lay and narrative, written and illuminated and presented to us in the book, enables Machaut to create and assume *his* role in courtly society: that of poet.

251

The hero of the *Remede* is just a young man, however, and he is not yet ready to take public responsibility for his lay and its amorous implications. Accordingly, upon being asked to reveal the authorship of his lay, he flees the society of his lady and her circle to take refuge in an enclosed garden. Here an important series of events takes place: l'Amant first writes a complainte, then is comforted by a long discourse and two songs from Hope, by the end of which he has advanced to the point where he can reenter society. The composition of the complainte and the interlude with Hope are linked as complementary poetic experiences, for the discussion and songs of the latter are presented as explicit antidotes to the problems posed by the complainte. The miniature showing the arrival of Hope, with the rubric announcing her arrival to comfort the lover, appears immediately after the end of the complainte (fol. 35), even though there is actually a twenty-line passage describing the protagonist's sufferings before Hope shows up. The placement of the miniature creates a continuity between the complainte and the following episode. It is as though Hope is generated by the complainte; the act of lyric composition has created the space within which she can appear.

Let us look more closely at the complainte itself. It is illustrated with five miniatures; the series of images offers a successive crystallization of the protagonist's experience. The first, which takes up nearly a full page (fol. 30v), is in two parts. In the upper register, we see l'Amant in the garden, a mournful expression on his face, writing musical notes on another long scroll; the rubric states, "Comment l'amant fait une complainte de Fortune et de sa roe" (How the lover makes a complainte about Fortune and her wheel). Below is a representation of what he is writing about: Lady Fortune turning her wheel. Here, then, we are given the first image for the experience of the unhappy lover, explicitly presented as a poetic formulation. We recognize this, of course, as a conventional image from literary and iconographic tradition, here appropriated by the lyric poet in the upper register and imparting a learned, clerkly atmosphere at the beginning of his complainte. The mixture of lyricism and clerkliness is further stressed by the juxtaposition of the didactic image with the lyrical image of the lover in the garden with his sheet of music.

The rubric for the next miniature appears at the bottom of the facing page: "Comment Nabugodonosor songa qu'il veoit une figure qui se claime statua" (How Nebuchadnezzar dreamed that he saw a figure that is called a statue [fol. 31]). At the top of the next page is a miniature showing a king asleep in bed next to a large statue with a gold head, dark body, and brown feet (fig. 20). This next visual metaphor for the ravages of fortune is therefore also presented as the product of someone's imagination: Nebuchadnezzar is in a sense the counterpart of l'Amant as the source of the image. There is a difference, though. L'Amant is shown as

252

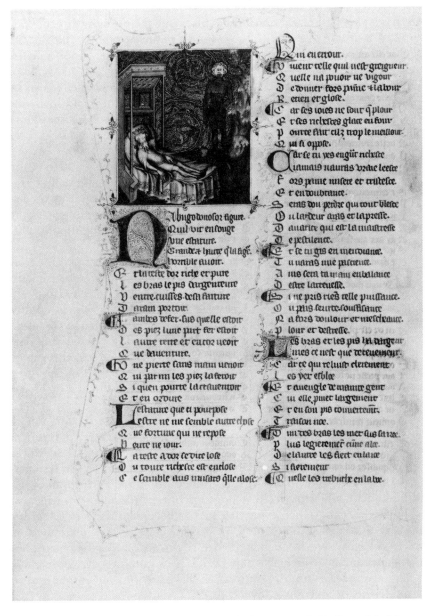

*Figure 20.* Nebuchadnezzar's dream, *Remede de Fortune*, B.N. fr. 1586, fol. 31v. (Photograph: Bibliothèque Nationale, Paris)

a writer, who evokes and explicates his image through poetic craft, whereas Nebuchadnezzar encounters his image through the direct experience of a dream vision and, as we know, required others—indeed, in the present context, l'Amant himself—to interpret the vision and to write it down.

In the next miniature and corresponding text the poetic focus turns to l'Amant's own experience. Here we see him, downcast, head in hand, pointing at a blindfolded lady (fol. 32v). The rubric explains that he is complaining of Fortune, and in the accompanying text he begins to apply the foregoing explication to his own situation. In this image, l'Amant does not write; he confronts the allegorical representation of his woes face to face. The author figure of the first miniature and the dreamer-protagonist of the second are fused. We are witnessing a conjoining of courtly lyricism and clerkly didacticism, as these images from the written tradition begin to be integrated into the formulation of private affective experience.

The succeeding miniature presents an even more direct formulation of l'Amant's feelings of despair: as he watches from one side, his lady passes through a doorway into her castle (fol. 33v). Between him and her is an attendant; her face is hidden by the arch of the door. She is literally in the act of vanishing from before his eyes, an elusive image of desire that seems ever unattainable. In the last miniature (fol. 34v), finally, we see l'Amant alone, dejected and without further resources; the rubric explains that he is complaining to himself. These two final images give us the literal referent for the metaphoric images: this is what it means to l'Amant to be at the bottom of Fortune's wheel.

The function of the complainte as poetic text is different from that of the lay. The latter was a performance piece; it served to define the protagonist as lover-performer and provided him with a social voice. The complainte, on the other hand, is never performed within the narrative; it serves rather to define the protagonist as lover-writer and provides him with a literary voice, a language of text and image in which to formulate his experience. Now that he has become a bona fide literary persona, the victim of Fortune, he can advance to the next stage of experience available to such personae, that of comfort from an allegorical personage. Since the experience is essentially lyric, Machaut's protagonist receives not the consolation of Philosophy but rather that of Hope, friend of all courtly lovers.

Hope gives l'Amant a moral framework within which to situate himself, thereby giving him a foundation on which he can depend: the code of the *fin amant*. She too presents an emblematic image, the "shield of true love" (fig. 21), whose colors and insignia inform l'Amant how to conduct himself and what to expect. This shield is represented as hanging on a tree between l'Amant and Hope, who look at it (fol. 38). Just as

*Figure 21.* The shield of love, *Remede de Fortune*, B.N. fr. 1586, fol. 38. (Photograph: Bibliothèque Nationale, Paris)

the images of Fortune were presented as the product of poetic discourse and dream imagination, respectively, so here the image of true love is generated by the discourse of Hope. Hope also sings two songs that express this moral code in lyric terms; again, we see a progression from a more didactic to a more lyrical mode of expression. The first, l'Amant tells us, lulled him into a sort of trance in which he heard the song but was conscious of nothing else; the miniature accordingly shows Hope singing (with the ubiquitous scroll) while l'Amant sleeps (fol. 38v). This scene provides a subtle echo of the sleeping Nebuchadnezzar; the negative image of the visual dream is answered by the positive image of the aural dream. In the miniature directly following the song (fol. 39v), l'Amant wakes up, emblematic of his improved spiritual condition; and from this point on he is an active participant, conversing with Hope rather than passively listening.

The next lyric piece is the balladelle that Hope gives l'Amant. She informs him that he is to keep this song and sing it whenever in need of comfort. In other words, she provides l'Amant with an optimistic lyric voice to replace the despairing voice of the complainte. His role as poet-lover has been somewhat redefined to allow him a constructive means of participating in courtly society. This endowment of the lover with a new lyric voice is visually represented by the miniatures at beginning and end of the song: in the first, Hope hands a scroll to l'Amant (fol. 45v); in the second, he holds the scroll and watches as she departs through the trees (fol. 46v).

Following this, l'Amant loses no time in exercising his new lyric voice and making his way back to society. First, he composes a ballade, illustrated with the by now familiar image of l'Amant writing on a scroll in a garden (fol. 47v): once again, poetic composition is the first stage of the poet-lover's entrance into society. The motif is repeated for the prière, where l'Amant kneels before his lady's castle and writes on a scroll (fol. 49). This is the second stage: he does not yet dare approach the lady, but the castle into which we last saw her disappearing, and in front of which we first saw her, figures her by metonymy. In the next miniature, finally, he joins the carol next to his lady and sings a virelay (fol. 51). Here, at last, he is able to assume a social role. This is the third oversized miniature of the *Remede*, and appropriately so, since it represents a milestone in the poet-lover's development.[13]

---

13. This is the only instance in the illustration of the *Remede* in MS 1586 in which there is no scroll to indicate the lyric text. Perhaps the absence is due to the constraints of realism: since the lover is participating in a circle dance and holding hands with the ladies on either side of him, he has no free hand in which to hold a scroll. The lack of scroll is appropriate, though, to the spontaneous oral performance, contrasting with the earlier scene where the lover read his lay aloud. The *Remede* as a whole encompasses the different possibilities of lyric production and transmission.

In the succeeding passage, l'Amant manages to address his lady, as represented in three miniatures. He tells her about his love, his adventure with Hope, and his poetic compositions, the series of events we have just read about. L'Amant thus becomes not only lyric poet but also narrator of his own story. Interestingly, the fusion of orality and writing associated with lyric texts also applies to the dit, though in reversed order. Where the former are first written and then sung, the narrative is evidently first recounted orally and only later written down, reflecting the complementary nature of lyric and narrative poetry. The lyric, though preserved and embellished in written form, finds its true fulfillment in the spectacle of musical performance, whereas the narrative dit, though explicitly rooted in an essentially lyric formulation of experience, finds its true fulfillment in writing.

The stages of l'Amant's education as lover and poet are expressed in the five oversized miniatures. In the first we see the initial tension of the love experience fraught with obstacles. The second portrays the lyric poet writing in a philosophical mode; this represents not only a stage in l'Amant's growth but also the conflation of lyricism and clerkliness so crucial to the poetic genius of Machaut, the great composer of courtly polyphony and writer of lyrical books. The third large miniature shows l'Amant's successful adoption of the role of singer. The fourth is the banquet scene: l'Amant is at one end of the room and his lady at the other, and they exchange meaningful glances across the musicians, guests, and architectural forms in between. Given the associations between the lady and the castle, the fact that l'Amant finds himself inside it, in visual contact with the lady, is expressive of their new intimacy, as well as of his integration into courtly celebration. The fifth large miniature, finally, accompanies the rondeau whereby l'Amant bids farewell to his lady. It shows a tournament scene; l'Amant, scroll in hand, rides off, looking back at the audience of ladies.[14] This scene, too, is of courtly entertainment; the ritualization of chivalry here corresponds to the stylization of social intercourse represented in the carol scene. L'Amant, of course, does not participate in the tournament; he maintains the role he has established for himself, that of court poet and singer.

This tournament miniature has a peculiar detail. Throughout the poem, l'Amant's lady has been identified by a pink hat that she wears in every miniature, including the one that follows this one.[15] In the tourna-

---

14. Interestingly, the lover is shown with a scroll here; someone riding on horseback would be most unlikely to sing from sheet music. Here the scroll is surely an iconographic device to indicate "song."

15. At times, l'Amant himself wears the pink hat. He has it in the banquet scene, for example, perhaps in indication of the bond between him and the lady; and the same pink hat is worn by the protagonist of the *Jugement Behaingne* in the opening miniature of this poem, perhaps to suggest the common identity of the protagonists of the two poems.

ment miniature, though, none of the ladies toward whom l'Amant gazes wears a hat. This may seem a small detail, yet it creates a vaguely disturbing sensation in the reader. Just where is l'Amant's lady? Is she not the basis of his newfound social identity—certainly of his identity as l'Amant? The meaningful gaze of the other two miniatures is gone, as several ladies, all of identical appearance, look off in the general direction of the departing singer.

The uncertainty generated by this visual detail (or lack thereof) is, I believe, significant. In the concluding passage of the poem, l'Amant is far from sure of his lady's feelings, and his attempt to question her produces no decisive result. The extent to which l'Amant has succeeded in establishing an actual relationship with her is not at all clear; in the end the relationship is not in fact what determines his identity. Rather, it is devotion to the ideal of love and his career as poet-singer: he is the protégé of Hope, lecturer and singer herself, and the epitome of devotion without need for experiential fulfillment. Like Jean de Meun or Nicole de Margival, Machaut creates a persona whose identity as lover is subsumed by his identity as poet.

Brownlee has pointed out that the attribution of chanson royal and balladelle to Hope contributes to the distinction between l'Amant, fictional lyric poet and hero of the dit, and Machaut, author of the whole.[16] I would add that Machaut as author, though never explicitly named— not even by means of an "aucteur" rubric—is implicitly evoked through a series of constructs that, like this one, are ultimately rooted in the *Rose* as a model of poetic continuation. L'Amant, first of all, has several points in common with his predecessor in the *Rose*. Besides the general fact of being a more or less frustrated lover, he moves around the periphery of a castle, longing to approach the lady inside; he participates in a carol; he experiences a dreamlike allegorical episode in a garden. His complainte recalls the closing passages of Guillaume de Lorris's *Rose*, frequently rubricated "La complainte a l'amant" (The lover's complaint) or "Comment l'amant se complaint" (How the lover complains) in manuscripts of the late thirteenth and fourteenth centuries.

Machaut's Amant, however, does more than merely articulate his own woes. We have seen that, in the complainte episode, l'Amant codifies the dream vision of Nebuchadnezzar. The image of the sleeping Nebuchadnezzar and his ominous vision is, to be sure, based on the biblical text; but in its present context of courtly lyricism, it additionally recalls the miniature at the head of so many manuscripts of the *Rose:* the dreamer asleep in bed, with the menacing figure of Dangier standing beside him. Dangier, indeed, has much in common with Nebuchadnezzar's statue as it is interpreted in the complainte: the statue is an image for Fortune,

16. *Poetic Identity*, p. 47.

and misfortune in turn is defined as rejection, or fear of rejection, by the lady. This implicit association of Nebuchadnezzar and the dreamer of the *Rose* implies an association of l'Amant, the poet who casts Nebuchadnezzar's dream in poetic form and explicates it, with Jean de Meun, the poet who performed a similar service for Guillaume de Lorris.

L'Amant himself needs to have his experience explicated by Hope, who in turn provides him with a poeticization of love sentiment appropriate to the new vision she has taught him. This, then, is a second model for poetic continuation, one that contains the first; and, as we have seen, l'Amant assumes the role of dreamer during part of this episode. Following Hope's departure, l'Amant, renewed, assumes control once again of his own story; and the entire episode of complainte and Hope thus becomes a narrative that he presents to his lady. Finally, the entire series of dreams and poeticizations is cast in the form of a lyrico-narrative dit by the invisible, but strongly implied, author figure.

Within the poetic economy of the *Remede*, then, l'Amant incarnates a remarkable variety of roles. He is alternately writer, composer, reader, singer, and narrator; learned and lyrical poet, codifier of his own experience and that of others; subject of Hope's poetic discourse, audience for her lyric and didactic performance, and recipient of her written text. Machaut responds to the composite *Rose;* the processes of textual conjoining and continuation and the generation of different poetic voices from a central lyrico-narrative "I" can be contained within the work of a single author. As is stressed by the illuminations, the poem as a whole provides a model for the complex and varied processes of poetic creation and transmission.

The author who orchestrates this series of tellings, retellings, continuations, and reinterpretations of the woes and remedies of Fortune is analogous to the *aucteur-acteur* of the *Roman de la rose*. Although sharing the first-person pronoun with his protagonist, he speaks from outside the fictional world. His role, indeed, corresponds to that attributed to l'Aucteur in the rubric introducing Jean de Meun's continuation in MS 1569 (cited in full above, Chapter 3): "Ci dit l'aucteur comment Mestre Jehan de Meun parfist cest romans" (Here the author tells how Master Jean de Meun completed this romance [fol. 28]). L'Aucteur is bigger than any of his characters and narrators; he contains them all, generates their voices from his, orchestrates their various performances and acts of narration or exposition. Similarly, the author of the *Remede* arranges and presents to us a compilation of material derived from various sources and filtered through the perspectives of his different poet-protagonists. The repeated generation of this author figure, throughout the codex, contributes to the unification of the whole: the ultimate author-compiler, origin of diverse poetic voices and locus of textual conjoining, is of course Machaut himself.

# The Iconography of the Lays in MS 1586:
## Carol or Compilation?

As stated above, the lays are the only musical texts outside the *Remede de Fortune* to be illustrated in MS 1586. This is appropriate enough; of all the formes fixes, the lay was technically the most difficult, and Machaut clearly wanted to give these striking examples of poetic virtuosity an important place in his book.[17] The presence of the miniatures adds an important theatrical dimension to the written text; in the absence of the performer, they provide a visual representation of the voice speaking each piece. An examination of the relationship between text and image shows that, although the miniatures are simple and largely formulaic, they nonetheless respond to elements within the texts; by suggesting a particular interpretation of the text, they contribute in turn to the codification of the series of lays as a unified poetic construct.

The illustration for the first lay (fig. 22) is based on the opening lines of the poem:

> Loyauté, que point ne delay,
> Vuet sans delay
> Que face un lay;
> Et pour ce l'ay
> Commencié seur ce qu'il me lie
> En amours . . .

(Loyalty, in which I don't delay, wants me to make a lay without delay; and so I have begun it on how it (that is, the lay) binds me in love.] [Chichmaref ed., Lay 1, vv. 1–6]

This poem occupies first place among the lays in all seven major collections and serves to introduce the lays as a special collection within the codex.[18] The generic designation is given in the third line and emphasized by the series of four rhymes on the syllable *-lay*. This rhyme is modified in line 5 to *lie*, stressing the binding relationship between poetic composition and love. Participating in the same alliterative field is the first word of the poem, *Loyauté*, identified as the primary motivation for the poet's activity. From the word chain *loyauté-lay-lie-amours* developed in the opening lines, there emerges an image of the poetic "I" as the

---

17. In all the other manuscripts that contain music, the lays open the musical section. Location in first place is a somewhat different way of highlighting the lays, one more oriented toward compilatio and the architectonics of the book than is the technique of illustrating each one individually.

18. "Loyauté" is the first lay in the seven manuscripts that contain it. The only two that do not include it are the closely related MSS Arsenal 5203 and Berne, Bibl. Mun. 218; these contain only four lays and no music.

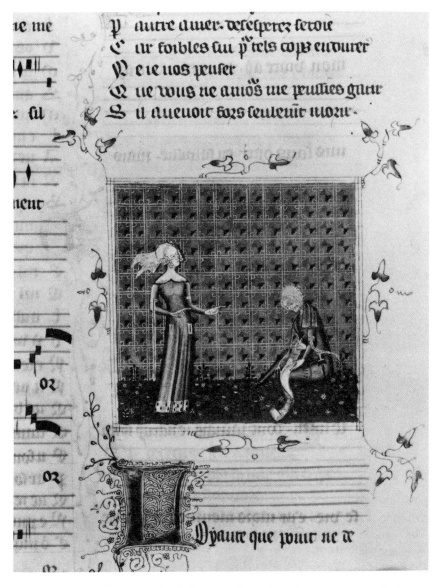

*Figure 22.* Machaut, Lay 1, B.N. fr. 1586, fol. 165. (Photograph: Bibliothèque Nationale, Paris)

*Figure 23.* Machaut, Lay 2, B.N. fr. 1586, fol. 168v. (Photograph: Bibliothèque Nationale, Paris)

persona in whom the parallel activities of love and poetic activity are conjoined in exemplary fashion, through his loyal commitment to each. The complete fusion of poem and persona is achieved in the closing line, "Car ma vie et mon lay define" (For I terminate my life and my lay [v. 432]). The illumination depicts the "I" as he is defined by the text, in the act of writing his lay on the usual scroll; the personification of loyalty, instigator of poetic activity, gestures her encouragement (fol. 165). At the same time, the male-female couple suggests the love relationship, source of poetic inspiration. Thus text and image together serve to establish the voice of poet-lover and so provide a fitting opening for the lays as a whole.

The next three poems, by virtue of their illumination, offer a kind of extended prologue to the series of lays. The miniatures (figs. 23–25) represent, respectively, the three phases of the poetic act familiar from the *Remede* iconography: private meditation (fol. 168v), written composition (fol. 170), and oral performance (fol. 173). "J'aim la flour," the first, is a classic declaration of love, for which the illustration of solitary meditation in the garden is certainly appropriate. The next lay, "Pour ce qu'on puist miex retraire," announces the speaker's intention to make a lay explaining his condition: "Je vueil faire avant ma mort / Un lay dou mal qui me mort" (Before my death I want to make a lay about the ill that pains me [Lay 3, vv. 3–4]). After telling his story, the speaker returns in the closing lines to the audience for whom the poem is composed: "Si pri Dieu que ciaus confort / Qui y penront exemplaire" (Thus I pray God that he comfort those who will follow my example [vv. 239–40]).

The audience and the presentation of the lay to an audience comprise the opening theme of the lay that follows: "Aus amans pour exemplaire / Vueil .j. lay retraire" (To lovers, as an example, I wish to recount a lay [Lay 4, vv. 1–2]). The placement of "Aus amans pour exemplaire" is noteworthy, for it is the only exception to the division of the lays into those with music (the first ten, aside from this one) and those without (the last five). It seems unlikely that Machaut, for whom the careful ordering of his works was so important, would have overlooked such a detail. Perhaps "Aus amans" has been associated with "Pour ce qu'on puist miex retraire" on the basis of their complementary rhyme schemes: "Pour ce qu'on" uses the rhymes -*aire* and -*ort,* in the order *a b b b b a,* in its opening and closing stanzas, whereas "Aus amans" opens with the same rhymes, in the order *a a a a a b.* The opening line of the latter also echoes the closing line of "Pour ce qu'on." These verbal associations have been exploited in the manuscript arrangement so that the two poems form a nearly continuous pair.

We need not assume that these first four lays were actually composed for the purpose of providing an introduction to the other lays. Each stands on its own as a performance piece and was no doubt regarded by contemporary audiences as an independent unit. The order of the opening lays, however, is the same in six of the seven major collections, suggesting that Machaut considered this arrangement an effective one.[19] The selection, ordering, and illumination of the lays within the codex create for them a context quite different from that of musical performance. Because of the simultaneous presence of all lays in the book, we are encouraged to look upon each individual piece as part of an ordered whole. Within this textual space, independently composed

19. The order of the first seven lays is the same in all of the principal manuscripts except MS Bibl. Nat. fr. 9221, which opens with "Loyauté" but then follows a completely different order. Following the seventh lay, the other manuscripts agree fairly closely among themselves, but differ from MS 1586.

*Figure 24.* Machaut, Lay 3, B.N. fr. 1586, fol. 170. (Photograph: Bibliothèque Nationale, Paris)

poems can function together to create a model of poetic inspiration, composition, and performance; just as, in other anthology manuscripts that we have seen, independently composed poems can create a model of translatio studii and imperii, of genealogical continuity, or of the movement from the natural world to its spiritual implications.

The next four lays are accompanied by miniatures that simply portray the "I" of the poem in a springtime setting. Like "J'aim la flour," they are essentially declarations of love and offer the illuminator little possibility for visual interpretation. The miniature does, however, indicate whether the "I" of the poem is a man or a woman and therefore serves as a marker to distinguish one lay from another. It is in itself significant that the poems would have been illustrated even when there was, so to speak, nothing to illustrate except the voice itself. The idea of having the lays illuminated, rather than any visually suggestive aspect of the poems themselves, clearly motivated the work.

The ordering of the lays is, again, suggestive. Following the introductory group are two lays in which the lyric persona speaks not as one who is preparing to make a lay but as one who has already established a reputation as a maker of lays and has an extant corpus. "Nus ne doit" and "De trois raisons" both open with discussions of the tone present in the lays, explaining why the poet has chosen an attitude of lament and how this should be understood. These are appropriately placed at a point where the lyric persona has indeed been established as lover and poet. They contribute to the equation of these two identities by explaining the content of the poems as a function of the poet's experience and serve to explain how the remaining lays should be read. Like the *Jugement Navarre,* with its references to the previously written *Jugement Behaingne* and the soon to be written lyric pieces, these two lays elaborate a poetic "I" that transcends the individual poem and draws together the entire collection. Following these two is a return to the pure articulation of love, here presented from both sides: first a man's declaration then that of a woman. This series culminates in the despairing language of the *lay mortel* (mortal lay), in which the lover declares himself on the verge of death. This poem is illustrated with the image of the male protagonist shying away from a bush on which a profile face appears (fol. 184). Most likely this face, spying on the lover through the leaves, represents Mesdis (Slander), identified within the poem as the cause of his woes; the first reference to Mesdis occurs within the first double strophe (v. 9), next to the miniature, inviting such a reading.

The lay mortel ends in the middle of the last page of the gathering. The gathering that follows contains more lays, followed by other musical pieces. But the lay mortel is directly followed by a ballade that fills the space left on the page after the lay was completed, as though this may at one time have been the end of the lay collection. It has been suggested that the transcription of the remaining pieces may have occurred after a short hiatus, during which these pieces were completed and gathered together.[20] In this case the lay mortel would originally have been a way

---

20. The possible break in the copying of MS 1586 is located between the lay mortel, which closes one gathering, and the *lay de plour* (lay of tears), which begins a new gathering. It is seen as a break because of the ballade, "Amours me fait desirer," which follows the lay mortel on the last page of that gathering. The supposed break has generated considerable controversy among musicologists. See Keitel; Günther. If there was a break, it cannot have been too major, for the same two scribes that copied the manuscript up to this point also completed it. Moreover, "Amours me fait desirer" continues the theme of impending death. Possibly the ballade was placed there deliberately, as part of the quasi-narrative progression at this point; or perhaps it was selected on the basis of thematic continuity to

of closing the lays as a self-contained corpus within the codex by announcing, more insistently than in any previous lay, the death of the poet-lover: the mark of closure at the end of the first piece would thus be repeated, on a grand scale, for the series as a whole.[21]

Following the lay mortel and the ballade copied at its close is "Qui bien aimme a tart oublie," the lay de plour, also a poem about death in which a lady laments the death of her lover. Although it might be imposing too much narrative continuity on the lays to identify this as an explicit response to the death of the lay mortel protagonist, the theme of death was probably intended to provide a link between these two lays. Such a link would be especially important given the need to bridge the disrupting effect of the ballade that follows the lay mortel. The relation between these poems is all the more intriguing in light of the association of the lay de plour with the *Jugement Navarre;* there Machaut is commanded to write a lay in order to atone for having wronged the lady of the *Jugement Behaingne.* In some manuscripts the lay de plour is appended to the *Jugement Navarre;* since the lady of the *Jugement Behaingne* was mourning her dead lover, the lay de plour would fulfill the task assigned in the *Jugement Navarre.* The juxtaposition of the male protagonist of the lay mortel, grief-stricken over the failure of his love, and the female protagonist of the lay de plour, mourning her dead lover, does recall the debate of the *Jugement Behaingne,* as does the illustration for the lay de plour, which depicts a man and woman conversing (fol. 187). In fact, it is difficult otherwise to explain the choice of this image for the lay de plour. Since MS 1586 does not contain the *Jugement Navarre,* there is no explicit textual support for this reading; but since the *Jugement Navarre* was Machaut's newest work when MS 1586 was copied, it may have influenced the disposition of lays.[22]

The alternation of male and female voices and the use of this device to

---

fill a space accidentally left in the transition from one gathering to the next.

21. Cf. in this regard the Adam de la Halle compilation in MS 25566, which ends with the evocation of Adam's death; and the Rutebeuf compilation in MS 837, which ends with the *Mort Rutebeuf.* It seems to have been a convention that a compilation of lyric or "personal" poetry could end with the death of its author-protagonist. Also relevant in this regard is Jean de Meun's statement that Guillaume de Lorris's portion of the *Rose* breaks off because of the death of its author. This principle reflects the lyric identification of singer and song, extended to the lyrical writer and his corpus.

22. It is interesting that according to the table of MS 1584 the lay mortel and the lay de plour were meant to be paired here, also; scribal oversight is probably responsible for the misplacement of the lay de plour at the end of the lays. The only other manuscript that includes the lay de plour among the lays (as opposed to placing it directly after the *Jugement Navarre*) is the fifteenth-century MS Bibl. Nat. fr. 843; although the order of the lays is somewhat different here from that found in either 1586 or 1584, the lay mortel and the lay de plour remain together. It should also be noted that other pairs and triplets of lays and of ballades appear in the later manuscripts. Evidently Machaut maintained a certain interest in composing such lyric dialogues, early versions of what would become fully developed lyric sequences in the hands of Christine de Pizan.

*Figure* 25. Machaut, Lay 4, B.N. fr. 1586, fol. 173. (Photograph: Bibliothèque Nationale, Paris)

create pairs of lays are even more explicit in "Ne say comment commencier," a man's declaration of love (fol. 189) and the following poem, "Se quanque Diex en monde a fait," a woman's declaration of love (fol. 191). The illumination singles out these lays in several ways. First, they are the only lays, and indeed the only texts in the manuscript, with marginal images in addition to the framed miniature. Second, these miniatures are the only ones among the lays that do not portray the poetic "I"; the lyric protagonist has been displaced to the margin, and the miniature shows the beloved of whom the poem speaks. Finally, the blue flower held by the man in the margin of "Ne say comment" and in the miniature of "Se quanque Diex" endows him with a distinctive identity: we cannot help but feel that it is the same man in both cases and hence the same couple. The two lays are thus linked as reciprocal expressions of love in a mutual relationship. The subordination of the "I" in the margin to the beloved in the miniature stresses in each case that the poem is not merely a private, ego-centered meditation on love but an expression of love aimed at a specific external object. The dual representation of man and woman, in reversed positions, underscores the symmetry of the love relationship and of the poems that portray it.

Again, the arrangement and illumination of these lays in the context of the book influence our reading. There is no discernible intrinsic relation between these two lays: both are typical formulations of fin'amours and could be performed in conjunction with other pieces. But within the textual space of the book, they are given a particular rendition that allows them to function as a unit. As with the third and fourth lays, this represents the conjoining of a musical lay to one without music; in this case, the close connection helps to effect the transition from the musical lays as a group to those without music. In this way the nonmusical pieces are integrated into the collection of lays. Since they are the only nonmusical texts in this section of the codex, Machaut may have been particularly concerned with establishing a continuity and textual integrity to the series of lays as a whole.

The last three lays, finally, are of a more didactic character, as is expressed in the illumination. "Maintes foys oy recorder" and "Amours se plus demandoie," like "Aus amans," are illustrated with images of the lyric persona before an audience (fols. 192v, 196). This indicates a distinction in tone. Those lays illustrated with single individuals open with a direct enunciation of the love or grief experienced by the "I," sometimes with reference to the composition of the lay; those illustrated with group scenes have a more didactic tone, offering generalized discourse on proper love comportment. This is not to say, of course, that those pieces identified as "private" would not have been performed, but the miniature represents the stance adopted by the voice, which may be one that identifies itself as lecturing an audience or one that creates the fiction of solitary meditation or private communication.

"Amours se plus," whose miniature depicts a lady addressing three other ladies, is more oriented toward personal experience than "Maintes foys," but the speaker still presents herself as an exemplary figure who dutifully fulfills her obligation to Amours. The illumination indicates that it concerns a woman's experience, and the inclusion of an audience distinguishes it from "Amis, t'amours me contrainte." The latter is a private declaration of love, addressed directly to the beloved; "Amours, se plus demandoie," which has no address to the beloved and elaborates a model of love behavior, is a more public piece. "Maintes foys" is an even more generalized discourse on love comportment. Although the "I" is at least identified as a woman, the love experience in question remains hypothetical: the protagonist states that if she ever knows that she has a true lover, "Einsois feray / Ce que devray" (Then I will do what I must [Lay 13, vv. 85–86]). Possibly for this reason it was not considered important even to identify the text as a woman's voice. Also, of course, the parallel images of man and woman addressing an audience continue the juxtaposition of male and female personae.

Framed by these two lays, finally, is "On parle de richeces et de grant signorie," in which the conjoining of male and female roles is thematized by both text and miniature in a most interesting way. The miniature (fig. 26) represents a man seated on the ground and writing while a woman watches from a nearby castle tower (fol. 194v). The couple represented in the miniature corresponds to the two voices represented within the text, which falls into two sections, divided precisely at the midpoint. The first half (vv. 1–88) is an exposition of love comportment. Its opening seems unusually grandiose for a lay, with a sober didactic tone and a versification reminiscent of the Alexandrine *laisse:* "On parle de richeces et de grant signorie, / D'avoir sens, los, puissance, biauté, noble lingnie. . ." (One speaks of wealth and of great lordship, of having sense, worth, power, beauty, noble lineage [Lay 8, vv. 1–2]). As the poem continues, the lines of verse do become gradually shorter; we find twelve-syllable lines in the first three double strophes, decasyllabic lines in the fourth and fifth, and octosyllabic lines in the sixth and seventh. This versification is unique—among Machaut's other lays, decasyllabic lines occur only very rarely (certainly not for an entire strophe) and twelve-syllable lines not at all—and contributes to the atypically weighty feeling of this lay.

In the second half of the poem (vv. 89–178), a woman announces her intention to conform to the foregoing model of behavior and declares her love for her "friend." This marks a change in the poetic "I" from the codifier of love to the participant and results in an increased specification of the "I," which cannot declare itself a lover without being identified as male or female. Corresponding to this is a shift in the versification, which is now based on an odd number of syllables: seven-syllable lines in the eighth double strophe, five-syllable lines in the ninth and tenth. The syllable count continues to decrease, resulting ultimately in lines of two and three syllables; the original twelve-syllable lines reappear in the final double strophe, in accordance with the circular structure required of the lay.

The first half of the poem thus has a very serious, clerkly aspect; the second half is more typical of courtly lyric. This duality of voice and tone—the division of the poem into equal sections, supported by the versification—is not matched in any other lay. This unique structural

*Figure 26.* Machaut, Lay 8, B.N. fr. 1586, fol. 194v. (Photograph: Bibliothèque Nationale, Paris)

feature of "On parle de richeces" is expressed in the miniature, which depicts the two voices of the poem: the male poet, whose clerkly identity is stressed by the fact that he is writing, and the courtly lady in her castle.

The series of illuminations causes the lays to stand out among the other lyric collections of MS 1586; they are the lyric counterpart of the *Remede de Fortune*, the most profusely illustrated of the dits. The lay miniatures, like the narrative commentary of the *Remede*, serve to establish a three-fold poetic identity of lover, writer, and performer and point toward the emergence of an author figure whose authority lies behind the various lyric personae. The lyric "I" is identified at the beginning and end of the lays as writer, poet, and codifier of love, more so than as lover; although in both cases he is shown with a female personage, his role in relation to this lady is strictly that of poet.

Although love and the vicissitudes of love experience are certainly presented along the way as the source of poetic inspiration, no single lover persona emerges from the collection, which encompasses both male and female voices. What does emerge as a constant is the persona of poet, able to cast his own experience and that of others in poetic language. The use of the female voice in the last three lays stresses the withdrawal of the poet as lover from the picture, giving way instead to lover and poet as distinct personae. Indeed, the very idea of love experience as the immediate substance of poetry seems to be on the point of vanishing. The eleventh and twelfth lays still stress the love relationship as the immediate context for poetic exchange. In the thirteenth, however, the man appears not as lover but as performer; and, as is revealed in the text, he does not even perform his own story. In the fourteenth, the man is no longer a performer but a writer; the lover has assumed a separate identity. In the fifteenth, finally, the man has disappeared entirely, and even the lady has become a sermonizer. This redefinition of the lyric persona from lover to poet and codifier of love remained one of Machaut's central preoccupations throughout his career.

We have seen, too, that the arrangement of the lays creates a series of pairings in which the second poem continues or directly responds to the first; we have also observed that in two cases the voice of the lay is identified generally with the author of the entire collection. These phenomena can be associated both with the role of the *Jugement Navarre* in Machaut's larger corpus and with the poetics of the *Remede de Fortune*, in which the lyric pieces correspond to a narrative sequence and which is constructed on various models of poetic continuation and response. The relationships among the lays are clarified by the miniatures. The parallels between this iconographic and compilational program and the poetic techniques central to these two dits—the one contemporary with the preparation of the manuscript, the other singled out as being of central importance through its illumination—argue strongly for Machaut's close involvement with the production of the manuscript.

One further detail supports the association of the lays with the *Remede*. In the illustration for the first lay, Loyalty wears a scarf that flutters in the air and is exactly like the scarf worn by both Fortune and Hope in the *Remede* illustrations. This scarf is the mark by which Hope in particular can be identified, just as the lady can be identified by her pink hat, and would seem to be the mark of an allegorical personification. There is thus a subtle connection between the two allegorical figures who, in different texts, provide inspiration in love and poetry. This connection in turn stresses the unity of the codex as a whole. Although the lays were not illuminated by the *Remede* master, it is quite possible that the illuminator of the lays could have had access to other sections of the codex; and Machaut, as supervisor of the entire project, could have been responsible for various details of the illumination. Since Hope, complete with scarf, appears in seventeen of the thirty-four *Remede* miniatures, including several that involve the composition or performance of lyric texts, the motif is well established; its recurrence at the opening of the lays is surely not mere coincidence.


## Conclusion

The role played by miniatures in this codification of Machaut's oeuvre is, as these examples demonstrate, considerable. The illuminations reflect the diversity of poetic material and voice; they also serve a purpose of textual identification similar to that of the rubric. At the same time, through the associations evoked between lay and dit and the repeated representations of the poet in his various manifestations, they contribute materially to the overall unity of the oeuvre: the book becomes not just a repository of texts, but a visual rendering of an integrated poetic system.

MS 1586 presents a theatrical, lyrical rendering of Machaut's compositions; even writing takes place in a garden, on long graceful scrolls, and the lover of the *Remede* must reach the important milestone of singing before his lady. The alternation of male and female voices in the progression of lays imitates the format of the carol. The carol in the *Rose* is normally illustrated with a line or a circle in which men and ladies alternate, and a similar image is used in MS 1586 for the carol of the *Remede*. In literary depictions of carols, such as Jean Renart's *Roman de la rose* or Jacques Bretel's *Tournois de Chauvency*, it is standard for men and ladies to answer one another with refrains or rondeaux. During the middle section of the lays, then, the carol is evoked; and the images of singers in a garden setting contribute to the aura of courtly celebration. The combination of miniature and marginalia for the two lays "Ne say comment" and "Se quanque Diex" suggests the format of the carol even more strongly, as the two figures, one in the miniature and one in the margin, literally gaze at one another over the space in which the song is executed. One wonders indeed whether this configuration might reflect a technique of staging, in which a male and a female singer could perform a pair of songs, each alternately standing to one side to sing while the one on whom the song focused assumed "center stage," perhaps executing some simple dance steps.

At the same time, the introductory lays, by stressing the figure of the poet, set the sequence of texts as a literary compilation, an author corpus; and the closing poems look toward a different pairing of male and female, one corresponding not to lover and lady but to poet and protagonist. The careful conjoining of musical and nonmusical pieces further reminds us that the principles of arrangement are more literary than performative. The equivocal nature of the series of lays is analogous to that of the *Remede:* seemingly a love story about a trouvère figure, it turns out on closer examination to present a complex model of poetic composition and literary compilation to which the love story is, if anything, secondary.

Machaut's MS 1586, as a literary, musical, and visual work of art, captures with extraordinary sensitivity the creative tension between song and book. Machaut explores the dynamics by which singing is replaced with writing as the lyric activity: the carol is projected into the book, the trouvère becomes an author. We have seen a precedent in the *Panthère,* where the lyrical dream vision becomes the skeleton of an anthology and the carol a series of citations; an earlier stage of the process is represented by the *Poire,* where the book is a space for performance. Machaut has created not merely a lyrical narrative but a lyrical codex. His redefinition of lyricism and the lyric poet, which leads him increasingly to affirm the role of writer over that of singer or lover, also results in an adaptation of the "theatrical" function of the book; rather than a stage for oral performance, the illuminated codex becomes a stage for the execution of writing and compilation. In order to follow out the consequences of this concept, we must turn to later works and a later manuscript.

Chapter 9

# A Late Redaction of Machaut's Oeuvre:
# The Codex Bibl. Nat. fr. 1584

In MS Bibl. Nat. fr. 1584, we encounter Machaut's oeuvre in a form that it assumed some twenty years after the production of MS 1586. The division of texts into narrative, lyric, and musical pieces remains unchanged; the addition of the *Prologue,* announcing the author of the book as a whole, renders more explicit the authorial voice and poetic unity of the collection. Again, we have only circumstantial evidence for Machaut's personal role in the preparation of the manuscript. François Avril believes that the miniatures were executed during the 1370s by a provincial artist, whom he locates in Reims, working under Machaut's supervision.[1] Avril further notes that some of the illuminations of the *Voir Dit* bear Latin inscriptions, which in his opinion must be due not to the artist but to the author himself.[2]

To these arguments may be added the evidence of the much-quoted opening rubric, placed at the head of the table of contents: "Vezci l'ordenance que G de Machaut vuet qu'il ait en son livre" (Behold the order that G. de Machaut wants there to be in his book [fol. A]). There is nothing unusual about a table of contents at the beginning of a large anthology manuscript; but if the book was the work of an independent compiler, it seems unlikely that the table would have such a rubric. That the order is attributed specifically to Machaut identifies him as the author of the whole, and indicates that the compilation and ordering of the codex are an integral part of the poet's work. The rubric suggests that the table is no mere aid to the reader but rather the author's plan for his book, which is hereby presented explicitly as the systematically ordered works of a particular poet. Given, then, that the manuscript was apparently made in Reims, during Machaut's lifetime, and that it so explicitly

1. Avril, "Manuscrits enluminés," p. 126.
2. Ibid., pp. 131–32.

attributes the plan of the codex to Machaut himself, it is most likely that he did supervise the project. Again, the evidence of date and suggestive rubrication is complemented by the iconographic evidence. To what extent do the miniatures of MS 1584 reflect Machaut's poetic stance during this later stage of his career?

Like MS 1586, MS 1584 is profusely illustrated, and in most cases its iconography is very similar to that of MS 1586. The *Dit dou vergier* is headed by an image of the protagonist entering an enclosed garden; at the head of the *Jugement Behaingne*, he stands in a garden, and on the next page watches the debate from behind the bushes; the *Dit dou lyon* opens with the image of the protagonist and the enchanted isle. The other miniatures in these texts, though fewer in number, generally correspond to those found in MS 1586. The notable exceptions are the *Remede de Fortune* and the *Dit de l'alerion*. The latter has only the single miniature at its head, which illustrates the title: a man with a hunting bird. The *Remede* is headed with an image of an old man addressing a boy (fol. 49v) and has a program of illumination very different from that of MS 1586 (see Appendix B).

## Le Remede de Fortune in MS 1584

A comparison of the *Remede* iconography in MSS 1586 and 1584 reveals that differences obtain not only in the choice of subjects for illustration but even in the treatment of subjects common to the two codices. The change is apparent, for example, in the treatment of the two central emblems of the poem: Nebuchadnezzar's statue and the shield of love (figs. 27, 28). These images appear in both MS 1586 and MS 1584 but with a significant difference. In MS 1586, these images were shown as the product of dream and oral discourse respectively. In the representation of Nebuchadnezzar's statue, the sleeping king and his bed take up more than half of the miniature; the bed is in the foreground, separating us from the statue in the background (fig. 20). The image is depicted and rubricated as the experience of Nebuchadnezzar, and his mediating presence is a necessary dimension of our reception of the image. Similarly, the shield hangs on a tree while Hope and l'Amant discuss it (fig. 21). It is explicitly located within the space defined by their interaction; it is by virtue of Hope's oral presentation that we come to know the emblem and its meaning. The book, as we have seen, re-creates the experiential context of dream or oral declamation.

In MS 1584 these mediating characters are not represented. Instead, the emblematic images are generated directly from the written text itself; the book itself provides the context for the image. The immediacy of these images is heightened by the play on the miniature frame as a

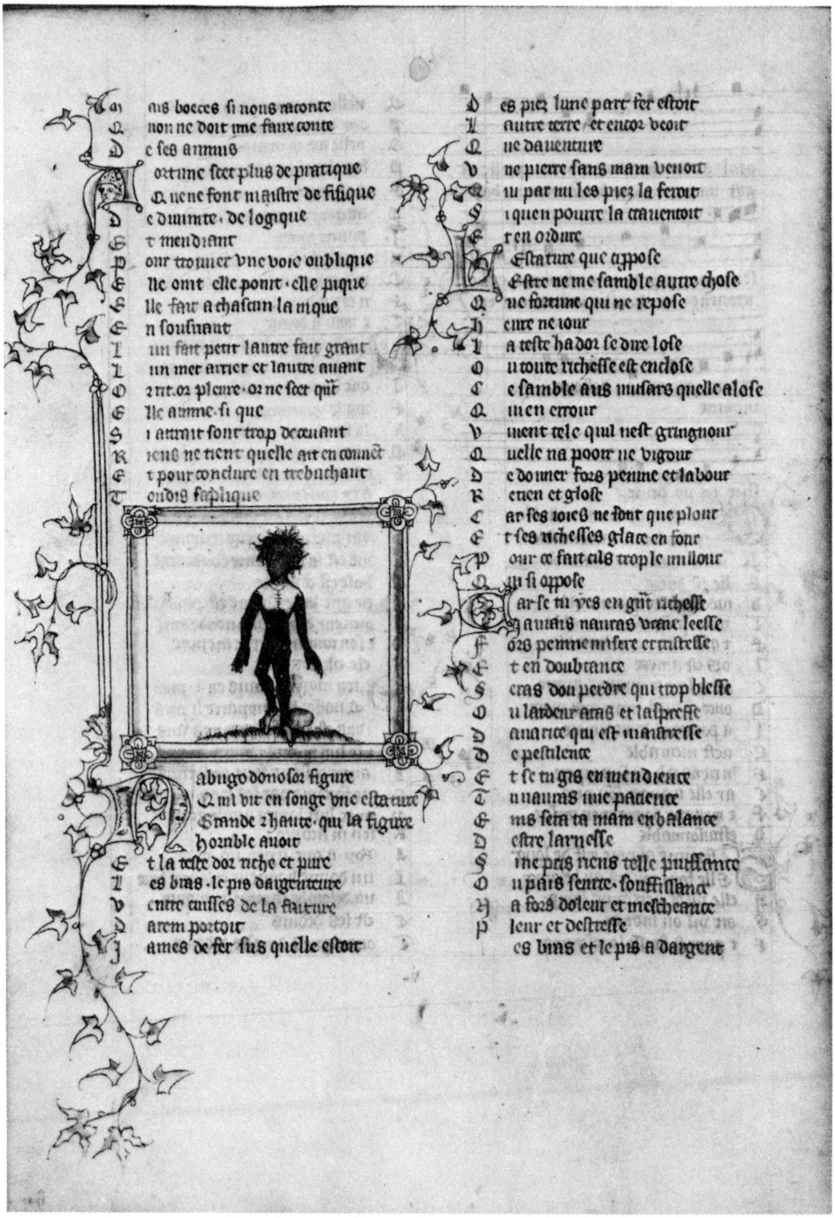

*Figure 27.* Nebuchadnezzar's statue, *Remede de Fortune*, B.N. fr. 1584, fol. 56v. (Photograph: Bibliothèque Nationale, Paris)

designator of space: Nebuchadnezzar's statue, with one foot raised and the other protruding over the frame, seems on the verge of toppling out of the frame altogether (fol. 56v). The shield of love hangs from the picture frame (fol. 62). In both cases the elements of the page determine the space in which the image exists; there is no sense of a separate, pictorial space. The images are like diagrams, directly attached to the written words that describe and explicate them.

The songs have been treated in a similar manner. The *Remede* is presented as a lyric anthology: the songs are even listed separately at the end of the opening table of contents under the rubric, "Ces choses qui s'ensievent trouverez en Remede de fortune" (You will find these things that follow in the *Remede de Fortune* [fol. Bv]). As with the emblematic images, these songs for the most part are not illustrated as the product of a performance or as an act of lyric creation.[3] The mediating persona whose experience is reproduced in the songs is de-emphasized; instead, the songs are generated from the written text of the book. They can be read as musical interludes in the narrative text or consulted individually as distinct lyric pieces. In either case, they are conceived as written texts to be encountered in the context of the book, product of the poetic authority that is responsible for everything else in the book.

Finally, the love story itself, stressed in MS 1586 as the narrative context within which lyric composition and performance take place, is also de-emphasized and retains a largely symbolic value. The lady appears in the miniatures as a sort of focal point around which the lover revolves: we see him leaving her, returning to her, leaving her again. And we see him praying to the castle, her emblem. But we do not see their conversations, the exchange of rings, the songs performed in her presence, the meaningful glances. The lady is a referent point, a component of the lyric configuration; beyond that, she is not important. Indeed, there are more miniatures showing l'Amant with Hope, a mere allegorical abstraction, than with the lady who was presumably the occasion for the entire amorous and poetic experience.

This, I believe, is no accident. As the experiential and performative aspects of the dit are de-emphasized by the illumination, so the didactic and writerly aspects are highlighted. We know from the *Prologue* that the poet whose works we are reading is a writer, aided in his enterprise by "sense, rhetoric, and music," and that he serves love less through amorous behavior than as an abstract poetic and intellectual ideal. Thus

---

3. There is an image of l'Amant listening while Hope sings her balladelle (fol. 69v); a picture of him kneeling before the castle at the head of the prière (fol. 72); and a picture of him taking his leave of the lady (without a scroll) at the end of the rondeau, itself an expression of farewell (fol. 78v). None of the songs is illustrated with images of composition or writing, and only one is illustrated with an image of communication between lover and lady.

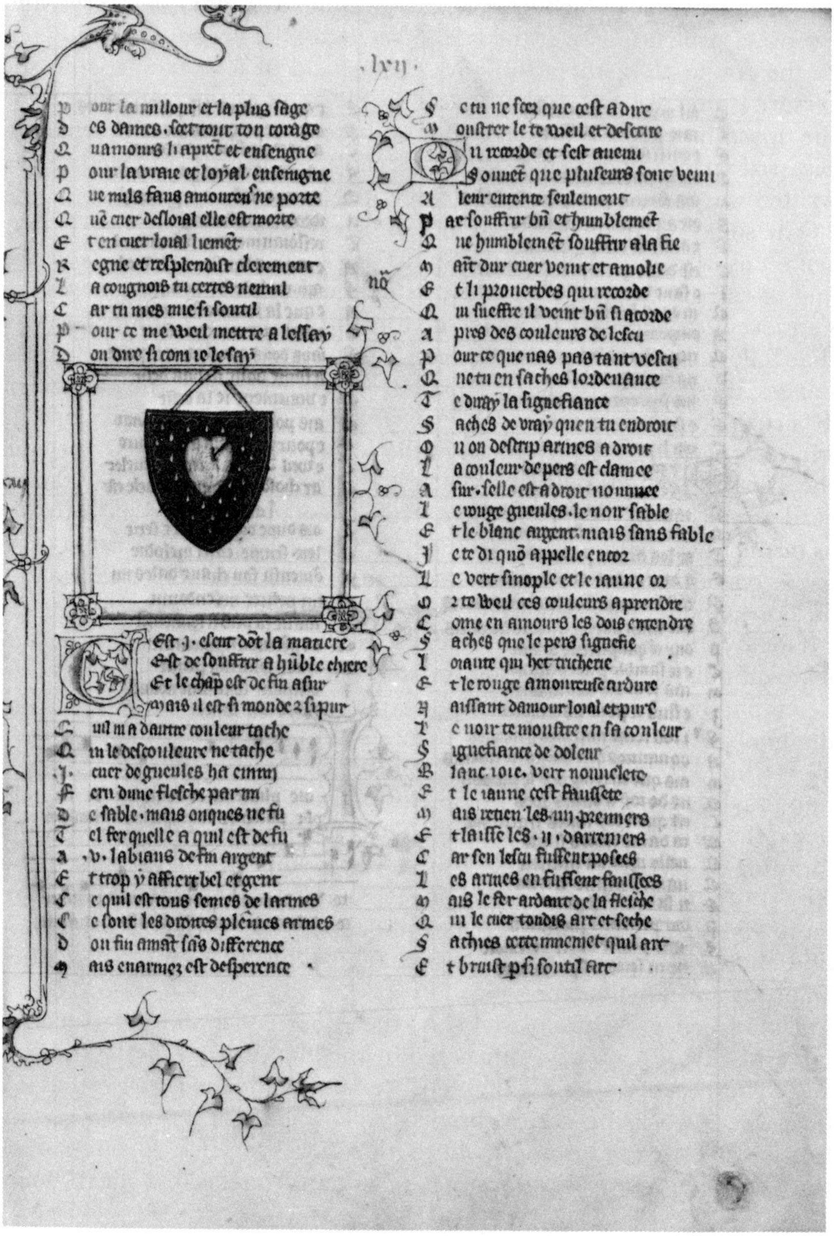

*Figure 28.* The shield of love, *Remede de Fortune*, B.N. fr. 1584, fol. 62. (Photograph: Bibliothèque Nationale, Paris)

Hope, abstraction of the mental attitude that enables l'Amant to write poetry without necessarily receiving encouragement from the lady, really is more important than the lady herself. Similarly, the emblems, statue and shield, are more important for their didactic value as poetic images than as the product of a particular experience. This view of the *Remede* is stressed by the opening and closing miniatures. At the head, we see the elderly man and his young pupil. These figures do not correspond to any personages within the dit: they illustrate the prologue discussion of the process of learning and maturation and announce the overall didactic character of the poem. The old man could easily represent Machaut himself, the aging poet who does not appear as such in the dit but who crafted it and speaks to us through it, addressing issues of youth.

In the final miniature, we see l'Amant praying to the God of Love. This is likewise not a scene from the narrative, for the God of Love never appears as a character in the *Remede*. The miniature illustrates the epilogue, literalizing the narrator's statement of homage and service to love. We are left with the image of the persona as one who serves the image of love as an abstract ideal and a poetic icon. The lover's pose recalls the miniature at the head of the *prière*: there he worshiped the symbol of the lady; here he worships the symbol of love. The *prière* itself, moreover, is addressed not to the lady but to the personification of love. In both cases we are removed from any particular love experience. The image of l'Amant before the God of Love is, in fact, the same as the final miniature for the *Vergier*; it is as though the persona is worshiping his own former poetic creation. In MS 1586, the love experience, ambiguous though it might be, still provided the overall context for the *Remede,* and an experience of contemplation, composition, and/or performance governed each individual lyric text. In MS 1584 the miniatures locate the *Remede* in a context of didacticism and devotion to love as a literary abstraction.

The illustration of the *Remede* in MS 1584 suggests a significantly different perspective from that implied by the overall design of MS 1586 and even by the poetics of the *Remede* itself. Does this difference reflect the ideas of an iconographer other than Machaut, or did Machaut himself change his ideas in the course of the approximately twenty years separating the two manuscripts? This question can be broached through an examination of Machaut's later dits, those written during the 1360s. In these we can see the evolution in Machaut's thought, in his concept of himself as poet and writer and in his treatment of lyricism, lyrical narrative, and the book. The separation between performer, lover, and writer, and Machaut's identification of himself in the latter role, is strengthened in these later works. In the *Voir Dit* in particular, Machaut focuses on the writerly process more closely than in any of his other works and explores the poetic implications and the paradoxes of the role of lover-writer. In so doing, he revises not only his own earlier poetics but also those of Jean de Meun, his most important model. These changes within Machaut's poetics do correspond to those effected in the iconography of the *Remede*. The collective evidence strongly suggests that the new program of illustration was designed to "update" this important early work, bringing it into line with such later works as the *Fonteinne amoureuse* and the *Voir Dit*.

## *Le Livre du voir dit:* A Mise-en-Scène of Lyrical Writing and Compilation

The *Voir Dit*, which can be dated 1363–65, is one of Machaut's last major compositions.[4] Within the body of his dits it is most closely related to the *Remede de Fortune:* these two dits are the only ones in which Machaut presents himself in the role of lover, composing lyric poetry in honor of his lady. The *Voir Dit* additionally takes up the important themes of the *Remede*. Once again Machaut has an encounter with Hope that results in the composition of lyric poetry; he is treated to the explication of an emblematic image representing "true love"; and there are two contrasting images of Fortune, both of which are explicated in detail. The *Voir Dit* can be seen as an elaborate reworking of the *Remede* material and as such allows us to gauge the ways in which Machaut's thinking may have changed during the intervening years. What is important in the present context is to examine points of contact between the two texts and to analyze the representation of poetic composition and compilation in the *Voir Dit*. By so doing we can determine the ways in which the poetics of the *Voir Dit* reflect the rereading of the *Remede* implied by its new iconographic program.

We can begin, once again, with the images emblematic of love and fortune. We have seen that in the *Remede*, these images were generated through lyric composition, visionary experience, and oral declamation. In MS 1586, they are represented as such; our reading of the image in each case is mediated by the presence of the figure responsible for its creation. In MS 1584, however, we saw that the images of shield and statue were treated as diagrams, generated directly from the written text. In the *Voir Dit*, the corresponding images are presented within the text explicitly as diagrams: schematic images, designed by the "ancients,"

---

4. I have used the only edition available to me, *Livre du voir dit*, ed. Paulin Paris. It is greatly to be hoped that the edition long promised by Paul Imbs will soon appear. The only book-length discussion of the *Voir Dit* is Cerquiglini's excellent study, "*Un engin si soutil*," which should be consulted by all students of Machaut's poetry.

combining not only symbolic colors and attributes but also short inscriptions (fig. 29).

The first such image, the "image of love," is described to Guillaume as an artifact by "a lord" (Paris ed., pp. 297–301); the lord states that he will explain, "Comment li ancien entailloient / L'image d'Amour, ou paignoient" (How the ancients sculpted or painted the image of love [vv. 7300–1]). The description proceeds in terms of the artistry with which this "image" was made—the materials used and the arrangement of visual elements. They would make a youth "with chisel or paintbrush," as beautiful a figure as could be produced by a skilled artist's hand ("main de subtil," v. 7305). This youth would then be decked out with a green wreath and various inscriptions in gold or silver. The illustration that accompanies this speech is based not on the oral account given within the narrative but rather on the ancient "original" artifact in question, for in the illustration the inscriptions are not in French (as in the textual account) but in Latin. Thus, rather than a miniature that dramatically visualizes the narrative situation, we find that text and image together serve to re-create and explicate a classical (albeit fictional) document. This combination focuses our attention less on the interaction between two fictional characters than on the didactic content of their conversation and on the visual text to which their conversation refers.

The second image (pp. 333–35), the first of two figuring fortune, is even more explicitly presented as a text, for the narrator tells us that he found it in a book "called Fulgentius" (v. 8235) and that it was devised by Titus Livius. Again the description proceeds in terms of an artifact, a visual representation endowed with multiple inscriptions that was supposed to have been crafted "long ago" by "the matrons of Rome" (v. 8239). This time the voice that describes the artifact is not even an oral one but that of a book. And once again, although the text quotes the inscriptions in French translation, the illustration (fig. 29) presents them in Latin. The image in the *Voir Dit* re-creates for us the image in the book that Guillaume was reading, itself a re-creation of an earlier image. In both cases attention is focused not on the narrative action of the dit but on the dual significance of the illustrated text: on the one hand, the didactic content, a series of teachings about love or fortune; on the other hand, a referential series of verbal and visual texts figuring antecedent texts.

This manner of representation is appropriate to the *Voir Dit,* a poem in which the central narrative action is the reading and writing of poems and letters, their compilation into a book, and the writing of the frame narrative that contains them. Although Guillaume does see Toute Belle a few times during the first half of the dit, his primary experience of her is through her portrait and her letters: she is, for him, another illustrated text. Songs, although sometimes provided with musical notation

*Figure 29.* Fortune, *Voir Dit,* B.N. fr. 1584, fol. 297. (Photograph: Bibliothèque Nationale, Paris)

and evidently destined for performance by Toute Belle, are treated within the scope of the narrative as written documents, folded up in letters: a vivid representation of the status of the narrative with lyric insertions, now treated entirely as a written document and not as the recreation of a performance.

The primacy of the written and visual over the oral is established in numerous details of the narrative that surrounds the letters, the poems, and the interactions between Guillaume and Toute Belle. The narrator stresses, for example, the silence of his reply to Toute Belle's first letter, written "Celéement, à pou de cry" (Secretly, with little noise [v. 445]). He similarly insists on his silent reading of her second letter; not wanting to reveal its contents to those around him, he read "entre mes dents" (between my teeth [v. 676]). These indications at the beginning establish the framework for the work that follows, a systematic exploration of lyrical writing taken to its logical extreme.

The process of writing and compilation is repeatedly stressed throughout the narrative, as other readers of the *Voir Dit* have pointed out. The narrator frequently includes details relating to the preparation of the letters—whether he writes himself, for example, or dictates to his secretary. The making of the book itself is a recurring theme; and the jumbling of the letters, which the narrator attributes to his inability to discern the proper order of those that are undated, foregrounds the process of compilation. That the letters, as they appear in the manuscripts, are rather clearly not in the chronological order required by the narrative, has been taken by some to mean that they are genuine love letters exchanged between Machaut and a young girl named Peronne d'Armentières and that the aging poet really did find himself unable to put them in the proper order.[5] It seems, however, quite unlikely that Machaut, who was so profoundly concerned with the architectonics of the book and the orderly presentation of his oeuvre, would falter so notably with regard to his own private correspondence or that modern readers and editors would prove more successful than he at reconstructing his own love affair. It is far more likely that this confusion was deliberately written into the *Voir Dit* as a means of highlighting the compilational process and perhaps even as a means of playfully figuring the problematics of any attempt to transpose the experience of love into writing.

It has often been remarked that Machaut habitually portrayed himself in comic terms, juxtaposing his success as poet with his failure as lover.[6]

---

5. Paris, noting the apparent disorder of the letters, attempted to "restore" them to their "original" order. The problem, together with a brief summary of the relevant scholarship, is addressed by Brownlee, *Poetic Identity*, pp. 235–36 (n. 8) and 237–38 (n. 12).

6. For example, see Brownlee, *Poetic Identity*; Kelly, *Medieval Imagination*; Calin, "Problèmes de technique narrative."

The protagonist of the *Remede,* we recall, was a shy and awkward young man who composed beautiful poetry and music but who had difficulty pursuing even a casual conversation with his lady. He did, however, manage to sing at least one song in her presence, in addition to reading her his lay; to speak with her on a few occasions; often to gaze at her from afar; and even to exchange rings with her. These milestones of the love relationship, however, while illustrated prominently in MS 1586, are downplayed or omitted altogether in the illustration of MS 1584. And when we read the *Voir Dit,* we can see why Machaut may have modified the iconographic program of the *Remede* in this manner. Within the *Voir Dit,* Guillaume's difficulties as lover are associated not only—perhaps not even primarily—with his old age and his nonnoble status but with his identity as writer.

Toute Belle is associated with the traditional qualities of lyricism: she is young, beautiful, and seductive; and she repeatedly asks for music so that she can sing Guillaume's pieces. The poet's access to this world of youth, beauty, desire, and musical performance is, however, severely limited by his reliance on the vehicle of writing. As I have stated, his experience of Toute Belle is largely a silent one, mediated by documents and artifacts and by the person of the secretary-scribe. Even when Guillaume visits Toute Belle, their lyrical encounter in the garden, which starts out with an exchange of sung refrains and rondeaux and culminates in the kiss under the tree (pp. 91–97), also includes the composition of a ballade and its transcription by the ever-present secretary. After praising Guillaume's ballade, Toute Belle requests a written copy so that she can read it and learn it more easily. Toute Belle's request suggests that Guillaume's oral delivery of his ballade is insufficient. He is not in fact a lover singing for his lady but a poet-composer producing a literary work that needs to be written down so that it can be properly read, studied, and learned. The attention to the technical details of written transmission is reflected in the accompanying miniature (fol. 242). Here we do not find the somewhat fanciful image of the lyrical writer reclining on the grass, a fluttering scroll spread across his lap, which was used throughout MS 1586. Instead, the writer is portrayed here, as elsewhere in MS 1584, seated on a bench with inkwell and pen case.[7] The *Voir Dit* is a mise-en-scène not only of lyric composition but of compilation and written transmission.

The constant intervention of scribe and written document between the lovers further attenuates the already equivocal nature of their rela-

___

7. For example, a writer seated at a desk writing in a book appears at the head of the *Prologue* (fol. Fv) and again at the head of the *Fonteinne amoureuse* (fol. 154). In the latter text the narrator is shown writing down l'Amant's complainte as well (fol. 155v); in the latter image, pen case and inkwell are portrayed.

tionship. Rather than being drawn into intimate contact by Guillaume's rendition of the ballade, Toute Belle turns her attention to its transcription: "endementiers / Que mes escrivains l'escrisoit, / Ma douce dame la lisoit" (while my copyist was writing it, my sweet lady was reading it [vv. 2218–20]). Although the written document may enable distant lovers to communicate, it also, and necessarily, serves to preserve that distance in that what the reader encounters is not the author but the written record of his words mediated by the scribe. The lover as writer recedes from the empirical world of music and declamation, of face-to-face encounters and emotional interaction—in short, from those aspects of experience normally associated with lyricism. Isolated in his study, hidden behind the written word, the lover as writer is forced at last to confront the profound differences between the role of trouvère and that of author. He may dream of the miracle of Pygmalion, of a successful transposition of the trouvère equation of singing and loving into a poetic equation of writing and lovemaking.[8] But any attempt to realize this miracle is at best problematic. What Guillaume discovers is that writing does not reenact or enable lovemaking but, rather, replaces it entirely.

Even within the scented cloud of Venus, by far the most erotic moment in any of Machaut's writings, Guillaume's primary action, as far as one can tell from the narrative, is the composition of a virelay. The virelay does hint at erotic fulfillment when it describes in some detail the death of Dangier at the hands of Venus. As any reader of the *Rose* knows, the death of Dangier and the intervention of Venus are likely to be followed by an act of sexual consummation. And the virelay does appropriate the language of procreation, stating that "onques villeine pensée / Ne fu engendrée, / Ne née entre moy & li" (Never was any base thought engendered or born between me and her [vv. 3823–25]). If not "base thoughts," what then was engendered inside the cloud of Venus? Presumably, the virelay. But is a virelay produced through sexual coupling? Do we not rather see that, as love and eroticism are transposed into the language of poetry, poetic activity comes to replace sexual activity? Such a reading would seem to be borne out by the narrator's statement that after the cloud lifted, Guillaume, who had just composed a poem, was rather more moved by the experience than Toute Belle,

---

8. There is an obvious allusion to Pygmalion in the intense devotion Guillaume pays to the "ymage" of Toute Belle; his comment after one of his dreams, that no "ymage" has ever been known to speak, further recalls the representation of Pygmalion in the *Rose*, for there it was only when Galatea spoke that Pygmalion realized he was not dreaming and that the miracle was a reality. Guillaume's dismissal of the speaking image and his attribution of the entire episode to the artifice of Morpheus (pp. 330–31) constitutes the tacit admission that the power of Pygmalion, that of creating the presence of the beloved through art and passing from signifier to signified and from writing-sculpting to lovemaking, is nothing but a textual fiction.

who had merely acted as audience for the act of poetic composition; he was "tous estahis" (totally ecstatic [v. 3847]), whereas she was "un petitet estahie" (a little bit ecstatic [v. 3849]).

The distinction between written text and empirical reality, finally, is central to the crisis that unfolds during the second half of the *Voir Dit*. As Guillaume struggles with his attempts to reconcile Toute Belle's idealized portrait and affectionate letters with the oral reports of her infidelity and insincerity, he is in effect forced to make a choice between the primacy of writing and that of the lyric world of experience. Toute Belle's confessor chastises Guillaume for having chosen to believe the oral reports, which he characterizes as "Une chanson qui n'est pas belle" (A song that is not beautiful [v. 8767]), and he produces yet another pagan image of fortune with which to figure Guillaume's behavior. Both oral and written accounts, of course, can lie. The confessor's report conflicts with the other five that Guillaume has heard, indicating that one or the other must be false; and we know that Guillaume has written at least one insincere letter. But writing, precisely because of its detachment from the empirical world, affords the opportunity for an idealization of love: the written text has the peculiar quality of mediating between the lovers while at the same time shielding one from the other.

By accepting his identity as author and his association with the written word, Guillaume relinquishes his desire for a truly lyrical mode of writing, one embedded within and dependent upon an amorous engagement. We may read this as a subtle acknowledgment of the fictionality of the *Voir Dit;* what is definitely "true" is that Machaut wrote a series of poems and letters and compiled them within a frame narrative and not necessarily that he had a love affair with Peronne d'Armentières. As was suggested by the MS 1584 rendition of the *Remede,* the love relationship is generated from the poetic text, and not vice versa.

## Performance and Book in *Le Dit de la harpe*

The preoccupations that we have noted in the *Voir Dit* can be identified in Machaut's other late works as well. A particularly interesting piece in this context, which bears the further advantage of being short enough to allow for a fairly detailed analysis, is the *Dit de la harpe.*

The *Dit de la harpe* is one of Machaut's later works and also one of his least well known. It is a short piece of about 350 lines in which the poet compares his lady to a harp by identifying each string of the harp with a moral or courtly virtue that his lady possesses. The twentieth-century distaste for this kind of methodical, nonnarrative allegory is no doubt responsible for the lack of attention paid to this poem. Machaut, however, seems to have considered it an important piece: in MS 1584, this poem of only two and one-half folios (five pages) is decorated with no fewer than fourteen miniatures, making it the most densely illustrated text in this or any other extant Machaut manuscript. The *Harpe*, in fact, can be read as a statement, in microcosm, of Machaut's view of himself as love poet at this later stage of his career.

In the prologue of the *Harpe*, Machaut seems to offer us a musical performance of love lyric. He announces that, as one dedicated to love, ".i. dous lay que i'ay fait harperay" (I will play on the harp a sweet lay that I have made [Young ed., v. 13]). He places himself in a tradition of performers: Orpheus, poet and musician of love; Phoebus, god of music and poetry; David, singer of Psalms. And, having established this context, he moves on to the harp itself, selecting strings in groups of two, three, four, and five, perhaps meant to suggest chords. As he does this he comments on the beauty of the harp and the sweetness of its notes; the third and fourth strings, for example, allegorically identified as Gentility and Humility, "accroissent le doulz son de la harpe" (increase the sweet sound of the harp [v. 147]).

Yet for all this, no musical performance ever takes place. The *Dit de la harpe* is not set to music, nor could it be, since it is not a lyric form. And even within the text itself, although the narrator seems to have a harp, we realize as the poem progresses that no actual, tangible harp exists. Rather, the harp and the act of playing it are entirely conceptualized. The speaker "plays" the harp purely through language in that he names the strings. This act of naming effects a transformation from musical note to intellectual abstraction. Instead of music, we are given moral qualities; instead of an Orphic or Davidic performance, in which music calms the wrath of God or rearranges the order of this world and the next, we are given a lecture about social comportment.

A similar abstraction has taken place with regard to the lady and the entire love experience. The comparison of a lady to a harp, an instrument that the male harpist cradles in his arms and over which he runs his hands, is rich in erotic implications. Yet the *Harpe* is anything but an erotic poem. The portrait that is drawn of the lady is almost entirely limited to moral qualities. We do learn of the color of her face. Even this, however, is not held up as an object of delight but as an indication of inner virtue: her face changes color when she hears of misdeeds or bad words. Aside from that, the only indication of her physical appearance is the statement that she is endowed with beauty; and even this is rendered nonerotic through the comparison of her beauty to that of the Virgin Mary. We seem to have almost entirely left the empirical world of sight, sound, and touch and entered a conceptual world of moral and intellectual abstractions.

The *Dit de la harpe* as it comes down to us, however, does have a certain kind of materiality—the text itself. The musical setting that should have accompanied the text if it really were a lay is absent; but the intense flurry of illumination calls attention to the visual and material presence of the text in a very striking way.

The illuminations do contribute to the initial context of love and musical performance. The poem is headed by a picture of a crowned man playing the harp while a woman listens; the following miniature portrays Orpheus in the act of recalling Eurydice from Hell, whereas the next portrays King David with his harp. Thereafter, the miniatures illustrate the allegory of the harp strings. In some cases, there is a clear reference to the textual passage. For example, in the discussion of the first two strings, Loyalty and Perfect Goodness, the narrator alludes to the importance of these qualities in horses, stating that no horse, however beautifully decked out, would be worth anything at all without these qualities (vv. 129–34). The miniature accordingly shows a nobleman riding a horse with an ornamental saddle and bridle. The discussion of Charity and Sweet Pity (vv. 165–74) is illustrated by a picture of two women passing out food to the poor (fig. 30). Youth is, as the text dictates, holding Delight and Happiness by the fingers; Peace, Health, and Wealth are shown admiring Youth, in accordance with the narrator's statement that the latter is more important than the three former attributes (fig. 30). In other cases, where there is no explicit visual imagery in the text, the illuminations simply portray noble men or ladies, one for each string. In places where the text includes a reference to the sound of the harp, one of the figures may be shown holding a harp. Finally, the description of the narrator's lady is illustrated by a picture of an enthroned woman.

In the illuminations, then, the allegory of the harp strings as virtues finds expression. An important transformation has taken place here. There has been a movement of abstraction from harp strings to virtues; and then a reconcretization as these virtues in turn are personified. This two-part movement corresponds to a movement from something musical and performance oriented, to something purely visual and book oriented. It is as though musical performance is being turned into an illuminated book right before our very eyes.

The text itself is given a material quality through the anagram at the end. The names of the poet and his lady, we are told, can be found by rearranging these letters, minus an "r" and a "t": "Qu' esperance m'a fait riche d'amour: / Dame d'atour humble, clere de vis, / Sage d'un" (That hope has made me rich in love: Lady of humble bearing and bright face, a wise man from a [vv. 351–53]). This device calls explicit attention to the quality of the text as a written document, an assortment of letters that can be arranged at will. The anagram is a conventional way for a fourteenth-century author to sign his poems, employed by Machaut in nearly every one of his dits. This anagram, however, is a peculiarly diffi-

*Figure 30.* Allegorical personifications, *Dit de la harpe,* B.N. fr. 1584, fol. 175v.
(Photograph: Bibliothèque Nationale, Paris)

cult one and has baffled generations of Machaut scholars.[9] It is easy enough to extract the name "Guillaume de Machaut" from the lines indicated by the narrator. There then remains a host of letters, supposedly making up the name of the lady. As they stand, after Machaut's name has been extracted, they read: "Qu'esperance faire d'amour / Dame hbceredevs / sdn." Indeed, it seems that the beloved lady is just beneath the textual surface: we have hope, lovemaking, the lady, and some jumbled text. Certainly many names can be extracted from these lines. We can get, for example, "Dame Peronne," as readers of the *Voir Dit* have not failed to note. Or, alternatively, we can get "Ma douce dame de Navarre" (and it has been suggested that the poem may be dedicated to the wife of Charles le Mauvais de Navarre); "Duchesse de Berri"; or even "Roine de France." None of these, however, uses up all the letters available; therefore, none can be accepted as the final solution.

Previous readers of the *Harpe* have given up at this point, declaring the anagram unsolvable. Perhaps this fact is more significant than has been realized. Perhaps there is no single lady's name to be found here. After all, as we have seen, the love experience has become a highly abstract affair by the end of the poem. Maybe the lady in question is no one lady, but rather noble ladies in general—alternatively lady, duchess, or queen, of France, Navarre, or wherever. Beyond that, perhaps the lady is no flesh and blood lady at all but simply text—that other presence that, along with the presence of the poet, goes to make up the poem. In this respect, it is probably no accident that we can derive the names Orpheus and Erudice (as her name is spelled in the *Harpe*) from the anagram. The narrator has, after all, compared himself to Orpheus, and his lady is like Eurydice: she seems on the verge of emerging from the poetic text of love, but she never quite does. Each time we think we have found her, our expectations are frustrated, and we are left with nothing but a pile of letters. Indeed, as we manipulate these letters, other possibilities present themselves: words relating to the poeticization of the love experience—besides *esperance* and *amour,* we can make *dous pensers* (sweet thought) and *souvenirs* (memory)—and even words relating to poetic and musical craft—we can make, alternatively, *musique-harper-chanter* (music-harp-sing) or *sens-escrire-poeme* (sense-write-poem). Perhaps Machaut's "lady" is none other than the conflation of lyricism and writerly craft that makes up his poetic oeuvre.

Let us return to the figure of Orpheus. The parallelism of the narrator with Orpheus is stressed by the juxtaposition of miniatures on the opening page and supported by verbal echoes. The narrator promises to "harp a sweet lay" (v. 13); Orpheus "sweetly harps" a lay in his quest for

9. For a discussion of the various attempts to solve the anagram, see Young's notes to the *Harpe.*

Eurydice (vv. 48–49). The repeated rhymes in the prologue, on -*port* and -*porte*, are echoed in the statement that Orpheus goes to play at the *porte* (gate) of Hell (vv. 45, 49).

It is interesting, then, when several lines later the narrator tells us that trees, birds, and beasts were moved by Orpheus's playing, "En escoutant le doulz son de sa lire" (In listening to the sweet sound of his lyre [v. 69]); and continues in the next line, "Encor vueil ie plus grant merueille dire" (I want to tell you a still greater marvel [v. 70]). The juxtaposition in rhyme position of *lire* (lyre), relating to Orpheus, and *dire* (tell, speak), relating to the narrator, is significant: just as the lyre was Orpheus's instrument, so the instrument of this fourteenth-century "Orpheus" is language. The word *dire* recurs some thirty lines later: "Or m'es-coutés: .i. petit vous vueil dire" (Now listen to me: I want to speak to you for a bit [v. 99]). By the epilogue, the narrator is no longer referring to his poem as a "lay," but as a "dit" (v. 334). This progression from *lay/lire* to *dire/dit*, which parallels the contrast of *dire* and *chanter* noted above in the *Bestiaire d'amours* and the *Panthère*, is a reflection of the transformation of musical performance into illuminated book and of love experience into poetic text. Indeed, this transformation is already hinted at in the word *lire* itself, which means both "lyre" and "to read."

As part of this general progression, the narrator introduces a new model at the textual midpoint to replace the musician Orpheus: Saint Paul. He states that the seventh string is Charity,

> Que Saint Pol tint en si grant amité
> Qu'en ses escris l'auctorise et aprueue
> Plus que vertus que i'y sache ne trueue.

[Which Saint Paul was so fond of that he honored it and approved it in his writings more than any other virtue that I know of or find there.] [Vv. 166–68]

Like Orpheus, Saint Paul is an expert on love, author not only of the famous discourse on charity but also of discussions of marriage and the ideal woman. But Saint Paul is not a singer; he is a writer. Nor is he a lover; he is an *auctor*. The love he writes about is an intellectual and spiritual, not a sensual, love. As such Saint Paul provides a complementary model for the poet of the *Harpe*. And indeed the narrator seems to have adopted this authoritative stance about seventy-five lines later when he states that he is going to add an additional four strings to his harp "de mon auctorité" (on my authority [v. 245]). As a poet who writes with authority about music, love, and virtue, the *Harpe* narrator draws equally on Orpheus and Saint Paul, although creating something different from each.

The dual identity of the *Harpe* narrator is expressed in another way in the epilogue. Here he dedicates the dit to his lady, stating:

> Qu'en li pris ay le sens et la matiere,
> Et apris m'a dou faire la maniere.
> Car vraiement faire ne le peüsse
> Se son gent corps onques veü n'eüsse.

[For from her I got the sense and the material, and she taught me how to make it. For truly I would not have been able to make it, if I had never seen her noble person.] [Vv. 335–38]

We recognize here a clear allusion to Chrétien de Troyes's famous prologue to *Le Chevalier de la charrete*, in which the narrator dedicates his work to another noble lady, "ma dame de Champagne" and claims to have received the "sense" and the "material" of the poem from her (Roques ed., vv. 1, 26–27). Chrétien here suggests a conflation of the trouvère with the clerkly romance narrator; Machaut in turn sets himself up as heir to this dual vernacular tradition. The components of the vernacular model, lyricism and clerkliness, correspond to the previously established models of Orpheus and Saint Paul.

The dual nature of the poetic "I" is visually expressed, finally, in the movement from the first miniature to the last. In the first, he appears as harpist before his lady, juxtaposed with Orpheus; he is the lover-singer of the trouvère tradition and, the crown suggests, the "King of Minstrels." One is reminded of portraits of Adenet le Roi, for example, or of the portrait of Pierrekin de la Coupelle in chansonnier *M*. The crown, however, also associates him with David, shown on the next page playing before God—a spiritualization of the trouvère, who no longer sings out of love for any specific person but in praise of the embodiment of love itself. In the final miniature, heading the narrator's description of his lady, we see the lady herself, enthroned. There is no longer any mediating presence, no longer any lover or singer. The lady appears as an iconic image, directly linked to the written text that enumerates her virtues. We have just seen a whole progression of ladies who personify these virtues individually; here, we have the final lady, personification of all virtues collectively. The relation of love and performance has been completely abstracted; the lady has become a moral allegory, the trouvère has become the voice of a written text.[10] Interestingly, the

10. A similar progression is suggested in the opening and closing miniatures of the *Harpe* in MS Bibl. Nat. fr. 22545 (copied about 1390), which has essentially the same iconographic program as MS 1584 for this poem. At the beginning, MS 22545 figures a nobleman playing the harp for a lady; at the end a tonsured man kneels before the lady. Here, too, we have passed from the aristocratic trouvère figure, to the clerkly poet figure. The lady in turn may carry implicit Marian associations, given her iconic status, her enthronement, her quality as exemplar of all virtue, and, in MS 22545, her role as object of worship.

progression from the first miniature to the last is analogous to the progression noted earlier from the iconography of the *Remede* in MS 1586 to that of the *Remede* and the *Voir Dit* in MS 1584. The *Harpe* reflects Machaut's preoccupation with the movement from performance to book; its poetic and visual representation of this process again supports the reading of MS 1584 as Machaut's own codification and visual interpretation of his works.

## Writer, Lover, and Performer in
### *La Fonteinne amoureuse*

The *Fonteinne amoureuse*, composed 1360–61, is the poem in which Machaut most explicitly presents himself as poet in the service of an aristocratic patron. As such it complements such works as the *Voir Dit* and the *Dit de la harpe* by addressing the distinction between poet and lover in somewhat different terms. This poem is also important to our examination of MS 1584. Aside from the *Harpe* the most densely illustrated text in the manuscript is the complainte of the *Fonteinne amoureuse*, with nine miniatures in as many pages, seven of them concentrated in the three pages surrounding the midpoint of the complainte in illustration of the myth of Ceyx and Alcyone. The cluster of miniatures calls attention to the importance of this central myth for the frame narrative of the *Fonteinne amoureuse* and for Machaut's oeuvre in general.

The elaborate series of negotiations involved in staging the dream stresses its quality as a theatrical production. It is produced by a configuration of characters who represent a thorough dismantling of the lyric persona of lover-writer-performer that was still evoked, if tenuously, in MS 1586. Several characters are needed for the dream to take place. First, there is Alcyone, the lover whose experience the dream concerns and for whose benefit it is staged; she relies on her spiritual mentor, Juno, who in turn acts through her messenger, Iris. The god of sleep is director and scriptwriter: he receives his inspiration and material from Juno through Iris and determines the manner in which this will be cast as a dream. Morpheus, finally, is the actor whose performance, as ordered by the god of sleep, brings the dream to life.

This set of characters corresponds to that in the frame narrative. There again we have the lover, who prays to the God of Love just as Alcyone prayed to Juno; his pose, kneeling before the God of Love, echoes that of Alcyone a few pages earlier. The scriptwriter in this case is the poet-narrator, to whom l'Amant's prayer is transmitted as he lies in bed attempting to sleep. His correspondence with the god of sleep is stressed by the image of him lying in bed, just a few pages before the similar representation of the god. The poet takes the pure lyric lament,

293

orally expressed, and turns it into a written text. The importance of his role in turning voice into script is stressed by the image at the head of the complainte, in which l'Amant declaims and the narrator writes. And it is the presence of the poet—his participation, through writing, in l'Amant's experience—that makes it possible for l'Amant to have his dream. We are reminded that this dream is the combined efforts of a poet-writer and the actor Morpheus by the lines spoken by the lady, which are another lyric poem—the *confort de dame* (lady's consolation)—and by l'Amant's statement of gratitude, upon awakening, to Morpheus and to his poet companion.[11]

The image of the narrator writing while l'Amant declaims (fig. 31) is a striking transformation of a type of author portrait that was still current in the fourteenth century: the image of the author dictating his text while a scribe writes it down. In portraits of this type, the author may be marked as the more important figure, either through his larger size or through attributes of learning; he may wear a monk's habit while the scribe is a layman, for example, or he may hold an already inscribed book.[12] The written text is merely the record of the "living" text, the orally expressed voice of the author. Machaut's reworking of this motif preserves the idea of the written text as the record of an oral voice but with an important reversal of priorities: the voice of the chivalric lover reverberates in the complainte ("Douce dame, vueilliez oïr la vois / De ma clamour," [Sweet lady, please hear the voice of my lament (vv. 235–36)]) and therefore he would seem to be the author, whereas the learned poet is the scribe. This reassignment of roles relocates the authorial presence from dramatis persona to writer, associating the creative authorial act with book production. A more conventional portrait of the author as scribe appears at the head of the poem (fol. 154); this image has already served to place Machaut in the tradition of learned writer-poets such as Jean de Meun, Marie de France, and Benoît de Sainte-Maure. The second image reiterates and expands this notion of the

11. For an interesting discussion of the myth of Ceyx and Alcyone in the *Fonteinne amoureuse* and of the relationship of the latter to the *Voir Dit*, see Looze. Looze ignores the figure of the god of sleep, seeing Morpheus as the counterpart for the poet-narrator. This is not without justification, since the allusions to Morpheus in the *Voir Dit*, as well as in the poetry of Froissart, suggest that the god of sleep was eclipsed by the figure of Morpheus, who thus assumed the identity of "scriptwriter," *metteur-en-scène*, and actor. Thus Morpheus is indeed the counterpart of the poet; the former produces theatrical events—analogous, perhaps, to a minstrel like Watriquet—and the latter produces books.

12. See, for example, the representation of Gautier de Coinci dictating his *Miracles Nostre Dame* in the fourteenth-century MS Bibl. Nat. nouv. ac. fr. 25541, fol. 2, reproduced by Focillon, pl. 2. It is not difficult to find other cases; a similar image appears, for example, in a Parisian Moralized Bible produced about 1235 (Pierpont Morgan Library, MS M 240, fol. 8); and in a late thirteenth-century copy of Philippe de Beaumanoir's *Coustumes et usages de Beauvais* (Berlin DDR State Library, Hamilton MS 193, fol. 1v). The latter image is reproduced and discussed by Camille, "Seeing and Reading," pp. 37–38 and plate 8.

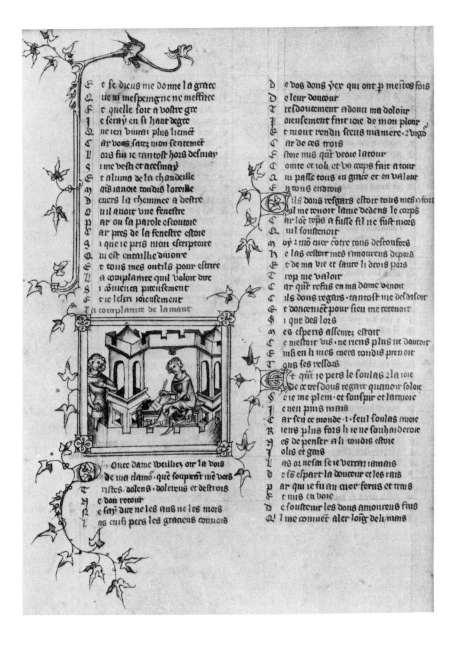

*Figure 31.* The lover and the writer, *Fonteinne amoureuse,* B.N. fr. 1584, fol. 155v.
(Photograph: Bibliothèque Nationale, Paris)

295

writer-poet, graphically reminding the reader of the innovative nature of Machaut's practice.

The complementary identities of l'Amant and the narrator are reflected in their respective participation in the dream that they share. The narrator is, after all, still a poet of love, and he is addressed specially by Venus, who, as he remarks, "parla longuement / De la pomme a moy seulement" (spoke at length about the apple to me alone [vv. 2637–38]). In keeping with his learned status, though, Venus does not address him about any particular love experience but rather about love itself. The text of her speech to him is narrative and recounts the judgment of Paris, an episode from classical literary tradition that is intended not for his emotional solace but for his edification. L'Amant, on the other hand, receives a lyric message dependent on the context of his love relationship. The privacy of this pure lyric moment is stressed by the absence of the narrator from the miniature in which the lady addresses l'Amant, even though both male figures appear in all the other miniatures following the complainte. It is as though the poet's presence has been absorbed by the written text of the confort de dame that accompanies the image of Venus, lady, and lover.

This relationship of lover and poet in turn reflects the relationship between the two authors of the *Rose*. Through the anagram giving his name and that of his patron, we learn that the extratextual, historical referents for the narrator and l'Amant are Guillaume de Machaut and Jean de Berry; through a fortunate coincidence, we have another Guillaume-Jean coupling, although here their roles are reversed. Once again the orally expressed, lyric lament of the lover-singer is transformed into a written text by the poet-writer, whose intervention allows for a fulfillment, at least poetically, of the lover's dilemma.

The presence of the *Rose* in the *Fonteinne amoureuse* is made all but explicit by the description of the fountain, with its numerous carved figures. The description of these figures as the prelude to the dream parallels the description of the wall images at the beginning of the *Rose*. And, just as most *Rose* manuscripts included visual representations of these images, so this passage, in MS 1584, has two miniatures showing the carved figures on the fountain. Admittedly the poses of the figures are too vague to allow for identification of specific characters; nonetheless, the prominent role of the visual artifact is stressed, and the reference to the *Rose* cannot be missed. Among the figures described on the fountain is Narcissus, who, we are told, looks as though he is about to come to life. And small wonder; this image was sculpted by Pygmalion himself, at the request of Venus. Here, the two complementary myths of the *Rose* are conflated in a most interesting way. Pygmalion serves the deity of love, and also the unfortunate lover Narcissus, by creating a work of art that perpetuates the image of Narcissus and, indeed, nearly brings him back to life. Considering the close association established in the *Rose* between Narcissus and l'Amant-Guillaume de Lorris, and between Pygmalion and Jean the poet, this fountain carving is emblematic of the poetic resuscitation of Guillaume's textual persona by Jean. Thus the *Fonteinne* evokes multiple versions of its essential underlying construct: Pygmalion and Narcissus; Jean de Meun and Guillaume de Lorris; the god of sleep-Morpheus and Alcyone; the narrator and l'Amant; Guillaume de Machaut and Jean de Berry. In each case the two members of the configuration are linked by their common relationship to a spiritual abstraction: Venus, love, or Juno. And they are equally linked through their complementary relationship to the work of art—visual, poetic, or theatrical—that is created by one member with reference to the experience of the other.

The importance of the opposition of writing and orality can be appreciated through comparison of the *Fonteinne amoureuse* to a passage in the fourteenth-century *Roman de Perceforest* (see Appendix C).[13] Here the knight Lyonnel, distraught, silently composes the words to a lay de la complainte. He then wishes aloud that this lay could be heard by lovers everywhere. No sooner said than done; at this moment a minstrel appears and offers to sing the lay wherever he goes. Lyonnel promptly teaches his poem to the minstrel, who composes a melody for it. Later, the minstrel is overheard singing and playing the lay on his harp by three maidens, one of whom happens to be Blanchette, Lyonnel's lost beloved. Her pity is aroused; she composes in turn a lay de confort and teaches it to the minstrel. He performs it everywhere until one night, by chance, he is overheard by Lyonnel, who is much comforted.

This episode again presents the composition and diffusion of the lyric text as a cooperative effort between the lover, who produces the words and raw material from his experience, and the figure who receives the lover's text and packages it for diffusion. But in this case the opposition is not that of the oral lament and the written poem. Rather, it is that of the verbal text—first silent, then spoken—and the musical performance. The minstrel does contribute his technical expertise in crafting the melody and playing it on his harp. But he also contributes himself, as

---

13. The *Roman de Perceforest* remains largely unedited; the portion to which I refer is not edited, and I have transcribed it from the fifteenth-century manuscript Bibl. Nat. fr. 346. I am grateful to Jane H. M. Taylor of the University of Manchester for bringing this passage to my attention. The lyric poems have been edited by Lods, *Pièces lyriques du "Roman de Perceforest."* Lods discusses the romance and its author in *"Roman de Perceforest";* on the lyric and other poetic insertions, see pp. 161–81. Taylor also discusses the work in the introduction to her edition, *Roman de Perceforest: première partie,* and offers several arguments for placing the composition of the romance between 1330 and 1350 (pp. 26–29). It is impossible to say whether or not Machaut actually knew *Perceforest,* but the *Perceforest* passage certainly exemplifies the more traditional consciousness of the lyric to which Machaut responds.

Lyonnel's representative and then as the lady's, supplying his own voice to breathe life into the lovers' words. The lyric text here cannot exist on its own; it is a function of Lyonnel's or the lady's thought processes, of the speaking voice, of the minstrel's singing voice. In the *Fonteinne amoureuse*, however, the lyric text can exist on its own as a written artifact. The lover is served, not by a singer, who will dramatically and musically express his sentiments to a listener, but by a writer, who provides him with a written record of his sentiments that can be sent or shown to whomever he wishes.

The construct in *Perceforest* is closer to that in Machaut's own earlier *Dit dou lyon* (1342). Here, the narrator-protagonist fills a role closer to that of the minstrel, in that he must articulate the mute lion's sentiments and solicit advice from the lady for him. There is no question of creating a written document for the lion. We might say that the *Dit dou lyon* is mid-way between the *Perceforest* episode and the *Fonteinne amoureuse,* for the narrator does not create a musical performance either, and he does refer to the finished text as a "book." By doing so he acknowledges that his real service is the written composition of the dit, no doubt for some patron who is, so to speak, the extratextual counterpart of the lion. Like Watriquet's eulogy for the constable of France, the *Lyon* contains the thinly veiled allegory of its own creation. It is telling, however, that this creation should be represented in 1342 as an act of oral delivery and that the poet-patron relationship is cast in the guise of the courtly adventurer and the lion. In the *Fonteinne,* nearly twenty years later, the poet-patron relationship is more explicit, and the act of writing is incorporated into the fictional world. The transition from the *Lyon* to the *Fonteinne* mirrors that from the *Remede,* where lyric compositions are performed musically and the author-compiler, though strongly implied, remains invisible, to the *Voir Dit,* where lyric poems are written down, frequently without musical notation, and the narrative focuses explicitly on the activity of writing and compiling.

Both the poet and the minstrel occupy a privileged position; but these two roles are differently defined. We saw in previous chapters that the minstrel is someone who travels, who moves through society and has access to a wide range of people and experience. He is a useful message-bearer for this reason; his performance abilities attract first Blanchette's and later Lyonnel's attention and enable him to enter the fairy kingdom. The poet of the *Fonteinne amoureuse* does not need to travel anywhere. His privileged access is to the world of imagination, to the poetically constituted dream world, the mythological persona of Venus, the lyric persona of the comforting lady. Rather than executing a series of performances widely separated in space and time, the poet creates a poetic construct that brings together lover and lady as textual personae. To say that lover and lady are each granted a poetic dream vision of the other stresses the simultaneity of this contact. As we have seen in previous chapters, the written format allows for a poetic consummation of the love relationship through its projection into the book. This consummation is realized empirically if lover and lady are each provided with a copy of their common text so that, though geographically separated, each has constant access to the words and image of the other. The poet mediates between the intellective and imaginative realm, where messages take poetic shape, and the material artifact in which they are embodied as successful communication. Within the world of the *Fonteinne*, the "truth" of dream and text is not called into question, or even really addressed. The narrative focus is on the role of the poet, on the mediation between experience and text rather than on that between lover and lady. Perhaps one of the points that emerges from the juxtaposition of the *Voir Dit* and the *Fonteinne amoureuse*—and the protagonist of the *Voir Dit* is explicitly identified more than once as the author of the *Fonteinne*—is that, with the separation of performance and writing, these two kinds of mediation have become increasingly distinct and cannot be collapsed into the single role of lover-writer.[14]

The image of the poet as one who has access to allegorical or mythical abstractions already appears in figures like Jean de Condé and Watriquet. With Machaut, however, the poetological construct is much more elaborately defined. We can take as a point of contrast Watriquet's *Fontainne d'amours*, a likely source for Machaut's *Fonteinne amoureuse*.[15] Watriquet's poem describes his visit to a fountain with elaborate ornamental basins. These basins, their chains, and the attendants that guard and maintain them all bear allegorical identities and collectively present a psychology of chivalric love; the basin of Prowess, for example, hangs from the chain of Belief, and is guarded by Opinion (vv. 87–148). To drink from this water induces a kind of love-madness. Upon drinking, Watriquet experiences a dream in which he attends a banquet presided over by the God of Love. The progression of dishes is again allegorical, mapping out the psychology of love travail: the meal begins with "un regart qui mort a / Maint cuer vrai" (a glance that has killed many a true heart [vv. 286–87]), and includes such things as sighs and complaints cooked in desire. Relief finally comes with the dessert, a "motet chantant" (singing motet) that promises pity and is served in a sauce of kisses (vv. 321–25); but at this point, Watriquet says, he woke up.

Machaut has borrowed the motif of the ornamental fountain that

---

14. Machaut cites the *Fonteinne* four times in the *Voir Dit:* Guillaume sends a copy of it to Toute Belle; he explains that her book will be three times as long as the *Fonteinne;* and he refers the reader to the *Fonteinne* for information about Morpheus. See Looze, p. 145.

15. Again, it is impossible to say for sure whether or not Machaut knew Watriquet's poem. Scheler's investigation of library inventories, however, turned up no less than seven Watriquet manuscripts in the library of the Louvre by the end of the fourteenth century (Scheler ed., *Dits*, pp. xxii–xxiii). Evidently Watriquet's works enjoyed a considerable popularity and prestige during the fourteenth century; it is likely that Machaut was aware of them.

induces lovesickness, not in those who look into its waters, but in those who drink them, and that is the occasion for a dream about love, beginning with a banquet and culminating in lyricism. But he has drastically altered the disposition and details of these elements so as to shape them into a construct that conforms to his model of poetic creation. Machaut's fountain, instead of simply representing the qualities of lovers, bears images rich with mythological and literary associations, including the classical tradition and its vernacularization; the epic of a love that destroyed a civilization; and the more lyrical image of Narcissus, destroyed by his own love. The dream comprises banquet and lyricism, but in Machaut these are distinct components: the banquet in question is the marriage banquet in which the golden apple appears, and this occasions the discourse, addressed to the poet, about the powers of Venus and the Trojan War. The lyric confort in turn is addressed to the lover. Watriquet suggests a distinction between himself, as poet, and the courtly lovers in attendance at the banquet when he states that he alone was single and that he awoke before he could partake of the lyrical "dessert." Machaut's treatment of the material heightens the richness of the literary allusions and renders more explicit the contrasting roles of poet and lover and the complex process of poetic creation.

The illumination of the *Fonteinne amoureuse* in MS 1584 contrasts with the treatment of the *Remede de Fortune*. There, the lyric texts were mostly unillustrated; here, both complainte and confort are headed with the image of their respective creation, as were the lyric texts of the *Remede* in MS 1586. As we have seen, the *Remede* corresponds to an earlier phase of Machaut's career. The roles of lover, poet, and performer are shown as complementary facets of a single poetic "I"—even if the role of poet is finally the overriding identity—and in MS 1586 the illumination for both the *Remede* and the lays explores the relationship among these roles. The combination of text and image exploits a tension between an integrated lyric construct, encompassing these three roles, and the fragmentation of the construct into separate personae. In the *Fonteinne amoureuse*, written about fifteen years later, the three roles of writer, lover, and performer have been polarized and defined as distinct entities, and the illumination contributes to the articulation of these separate personae.

The articulation of roles is reflected in the illustrations accompanying the lyric sections of MS 1584. The *Louange des dames*, the ballades, and the lays each open with the image of a man beseeching or embracing a woman. For these texts we are given the visual representation of the pure lyric voice of lover; there is no attempt, as in the lays of MS 1586, to identify this figure with the figure of the poet, whom we have seen in his capacity as writer in the miniatures of the *Prologue* and the *Fonteinne*. The motets, on the other hand, are illustrated with the image of a group of men singing around a wine barrel. This image of performance is appropriate to the motet. Although all of Machaut's musical pieces would of course have been performed, they can also be read as poems; still, the textual interplay of the motet in particular can be appreciated only through performance. Because of the multitude of singers, the performers are distinguished from both poet-composer and lover; we know that each of these characters cannot simultaneously be identified with the lyric "I" and that the harmony of parts is due to the guiding, if invisible, hand of the author. Similar iconography appears in two other Machaut manuscripts of the late fourteenth century. In MS Bibl. Nat. fr. 9221, both the rondeaux and the lays are illustrated by scenes of group performance, and each complainte is headed with an image of the lover. In MS Bibl. Nat. fr. 22545–46, the ballades, rondeaux, and virelays are illuminated with images of courtly couples, whereas the *Louange des dames* and the lays each open with the image of the poet writing in a book. Again, the roles of clerkly writer, lover, and singer are distinguished. The images in MS 22545–46 of the learned author, seated in a wooden stall and holding a book, are in striking contrast to the earlier images of the lyrical writer contemplating his scroll among the flowers, and they provide a visual counterpart to Deschamps's designation of Machaut as "poete."

The impact of Machaut's achievement is manifold, affecting not only formal and stylistic developments in vernacular lyric and secular polyphony but also the very nature of lyrical narrative, lyrical writing, and the concept of an author's oeuvre as constituting a book. The fourteenth-century appreciation of Machaut's poetry can be gauged from the works of his followers: such poets as Deschamps, Froissart, and Christine de Pizan. Froissart's poetic works are a particularly close imitation of those of Machaut and therefore also a particularly close reading of Machaut's innovations and their implications for vernacular lyrico-narrative poetry. Therefore let us now turn to the works of Froissart in order to examine the status of lyrical writing during the closing decades of the fourteenth century.

Chapter 10

# The Poetics of Lyrical Writing
# in the Works of Jean Froissart

The two surviving copies of Jean Froissart's lyrico-narrative anthology, MSS Bibl. Nat. fr. 830 and 831, were copied in 1393 and 1394,
respectively. The two manuscripts probably derive from a common
model. As we saw in Chapter 7, their production was almost certainly
overseen by Froissart himself, and there is some evidence that MS 831
was edited for political reasons, to render it a fit gift for King Richard II
or some other English patron. Aside from the omissions of MS 831, and
its possibly accidental placement of the *Espinette amoureuse* after rather
than before the *Prison amoureuse,* the two codices contain the same series
of pieces in the same order. Both begin with the dits, starting with the
*Paradis d'amour* and leading up to the *Prison amoureuse* at the midpoint;
following the *Prison,* the lyric poems are arranged according to verse
form; and the collection ends with the *Joli Buisson de jonece,* the *Dit dou
florin* (MS 830 only), and the *Plaidoirie de la rose et de la violette.*[1] The
careful division into lyric and narrative pieces and the overall chronological ordering of dits are clearly modeled on the anthologies of Machaut,
whose works are probably the single most important influence on
Froissart.[2]

Since Froissart's anthology is such a carefully ordered whole, I will

---

1. Froissart's two anthology manuscripts are described and their contents listed by
Fourrier in the introduction to his edition of the *Espinette,* pp. 9–14. The *Prison amoureuse*
occupies the midpoint in the sense that it is the seventh of fourteen entries in MS Bibl. Nat.
fr. 831 and the ninth of eighteen in MS Bibl. Nat. fr. 830 and also in that the central pages
of each manuscript fall within this text: in MS 831 the *Prison* occupies fols. 62–101, out of a
total of 200 folios; in MS 830, it occupies fols. 76–114v, out of a total of 220 folios.
Considering that Froissart was constrained by the actual length of his various poems and
that he did need to keep an orderly distinction between lyric and narrative works, this is
surely as close to the midpoint as one could ask for.

2. Poirion points out the similarities in organization between the anthologies of Machaut and those of Froissart in *Poète et le prince,* p. 206.

concentrate on its important structural points: the "prologue," the *Paradis d'amour;* the midpoint, the *Prison amoureuse;* and the "epilogue," the *Plaidoirie de la rose et de la violette.* In addition, I will examine Froissart's other two major dits, the *Espinette amoureuse* and the *Joli Buisson de jonece.* My reading will focus on the themes that have been important throughout this book: the concept of poetic identity, the treatment of lyricism, and the processes of writing and compilation.

## Froissart's Prologue: *Le Paradis d'amour*

*Le Paradis d'amour* is the first piece in both of Froissart's anthologies, and constitutes a prologue to the oeuvre that follows. It may be the first dit that Froissart ever wrote; it is clearly a work of youth, highly derivative of Machaut. Froissart intended in this poem to announce himself as a poet, and it was probably to this end that he incorporated the allusions to Machaut's *Prologue* scene of poetic election. We cannot, of course, rule out the possibility that some of these prologue allusions were added or elaborated at a later time, when Froissart first compiled his anthology and decided to place this piece in first place. In either case, it is a fitting opening to the collection that follows, providing an initial statement of the themes and the poetics of the whole.

The *Paradis* recounts a dream vision sent to the poet-protagonist by Morpheus and Juno in response to his prayers. In this dream, he finds himself in a beautiful wood, surrounded by birds and flowers. Overcome by lovesickness and despair, he utters a complainte. At once he is accosted by two ladies, who turn out to be Hope and Pleasance, outraged by his attack on their lord, the God of Love. After a long lecture about love comportment, they lead him to a meeting with the God of Love, whom he addresses in the form of a lay. In the course of his conversations with Hope and Pleasance, the lover additionally composes two rondeaux and a virelay. Toward the end of the dream, he encounters his lady, for whom he composes a ballade and from whom he receives a garland of daisies. Upon awakening, he gives thanks to Morpheus and Iris for the dream and to Orpheus for having taught him the art of the formes fixes.

The *Paradis* is a tissue of allusions to the French courtly tradition, most notably the *Rose* and the works of Machaut. Its introductory function as the first piece in an anthology is particularly marked through its allusions to Machaut's *Prologue* and his *Dit dou vergier.* The latter two poems open Machaut's MSS Bibl. Nat. fr. 1584 and 22545–46 and provide a conjoined introduction of poetic election and love doctrine; they are linked through the closing lines of the *Prologue,* "Et pour ce vueil, sans plus targier, / Commencier *le Dit dou Vergier*" (And so I wish, without further ado, to begin the *Poem of the garden* [vv. 183–84]). The *Paradis* picks up the *Vergier*'s allegorical dream of the lyric garden, its love teaching, and its meeting with the God of Love, which reaffirms rather than initiates love service. At the same time, the characters who guide the lover to the God of Love are Hope, Pleasance, and Sweet Thoughts, the same figures that the God of Love presents to Machaut in his *Prologue*. And Machaut's description of Nature's gifts of Sense, Rhetoric, and Music, which includes a discussion of Orpheus as the ideal musician and a technical description of the various metrical forms available to the love poet (vv. 135–59), is echoed in Froissart's closing statement of thanks to Orpheus, who, he says, taught him how to sing ballades, rondeaux, virelays, and lays (vv. 1712–16). These textual reminiscences underscore the prefatory function of the *Paradis* as the opening piece in a collection portraying the poetic career of an individual. The *Paradis* also draws on other works by Machaut: the progression of formes fixes recalls the *Remede de Fortune*, while the encounter with Hope and Pleasance recalls the similar encounters with Hope in the *Remede* and the *Voir Dit;* the references to Juno, Iris, and Morpheus clearly echo the *Fonteinne amoureuse*. Froissart responds to Machaut's works collectively, implying that for him Machaut is indeed the author of a unified anthology and not merely of isolated pieces.

The *Paradis* conflates the *Rose* and a principal set of responses to it: Froissart reads the *Rose,* as it were, through the medium of Machaut's reworkings. Indeed, by beginning with the lover's complainte, the end point of Guillaume de Lorris's *Rose,* and moving on from there to the reunion with the lady and her gift of flowers, the *Paradis* provides a continuation and resolution of the plight of the archetypal Amant. Froissart thus identifies himself as next in line for the legacy of Guillaume de Lorris, following after the first two great continuators, Jean de Meun and Guillaume de Machaut.

The closing references to Orpheus and Morpheus strengthen the sense of a tradition running from Guillaume de Lorris through Jean de Meun and Machaut to Froissart and remind us that this vernacular tradition is grounded in the Latin tradition, represented by Ovid. Ovid himself was the author of lyric collections, love teaching, and the *Metamorphoses,* one of the greatest narrative anthologies of all time; as such he provides an important model for a poet like Froissart, interested in establishing himself as lyric and narrative poet, writer, author of generically diverse books. As is well known, Jean de Meun identified Guillaume de Lorris and himself as heirs to Ovid and the classical tradition, and Guillaume, Jean, and Machaut all drew on the Ovidian narrative repertoire. Froissart is the next in line to tell the Ovidian tales. In fact, in his later dits Froissart treats the *Metamorphoses* in somewhat the same way that he treats the works of Machaut: he takes the collection of stories as a whole and pieces together composite narratives that draw on several different tales.

The figure of Orpheus in particular evokes both Jean de Meun and Machaut. Machaut compares himself to Orpheus in both the *Prologue* and the *Dit de la harpe*, whereas Jean, as we have seen, implicitly defines himself as a "corrected" Orpheus, one who writes and begets a rich literary heritage. The "Orpheus" who taught Froissart the art of composing in the *formes fixes* is most immediately Machaut, but behind Machaut the earlier vernacular "Orpheus" is also visible.

Morpheus, too, can be a coded way of referring to Machaut. The alternate title for the *Fonteinne amoureuse* is the *Livre de Morpheus,* and Morpheus as enactor of the dream is the counterpart of Machaut, its author. Froissart's assimilation of the actor Morpheus with the god of sleep, "director" of the dream, makes this even clearer. Orpheus taught him the art of lyric versification; Morpheus provided the narrative framework, the mise-en-scène of amorous and poetic process. Froissart here acknowledges the two dimensions of his poetry, both of which derive from a conjoined reading of Machaut and the *Rose:* lyric and narrative, song and dream.

Both Orpheus and Morpheus are performers; at this point, the young Froissart does not make a point of distinguishing himself (or his vernacular predecessors) as writers. The lyric poems that he composes during the dream are all performance pieces, for singing or recital. At this early stage of his career, Froissart would not yet have begun to produce books. In his later works, however, a consciousness of writerly process is manifest. In these later dits, the *Espinette amoureuse,* the *Prison amoureuse,* and the *Joli Buisson de jonece,* Froissart's manipulation of both courtly and mythological material bespeaks a fascination with the poetics of writing and compilation, as well as a sensitive reading of the treatment of these issues in the works of his predecessors.

## Dream, Image, and Poem: Froissart Responds to *La Fonteinne amoureuse*

Froissart was clearly impressed by Machaut's interweaving of dream, visual imagery, and poetic text in the *Fonteinne amoureuse* and by the use of multiple Ovidian myths to express processes of imaging and recording. We have already seen his use of Morpheus in the *Paradis.* A more complex response to the *Fonteinne* is formulated in the *Espinette amoureuse,* composed about 1369.[3] Here Froissart describes his initiation into love. The young lady of his affections, whom he meets over a reading of

---

3. On the date of the *Espinette,* see Fourrier's introduction, pp. 32–34.

*Cléomadès,* is largely unmoved by his ardent lyric compositions, and he eventually hears that she is to be married. This news causes him to fall ill; during his illness, the distraught lover composes a long complainte. Upon recovering, he goes to England, taking with him a mirror that was once his lady's. Sleeping with the mirror under his pillow, he dreams one night that she appears to him in the mirror and speaks a lyric confort, promising to love him faithfully. Heartened, he returns to France and renews his courtship. He meets with only marginal success but chooses to interpret her somewhat capricious behavior in the most favorable possible light. The poem ends with the relationship very much up in the air and the young lover enjoying his lyrical fantasies. Like Machaut in the *Fonteinne,* then, Froissart uses the structure of a complainte followed by a dream in which the lover receives a confort from his lady, and he glosses the events of the narrative with a clustering of Ovidian and pseudo-Ovidian exempla. Froissart's handling of the dream motif and his selection of mythological figures enable him to define his own identity as lyrical writer and poet of love.

We have seen that in the *Fonteinne* Machaut separates the roles of writer, performer, and lover. His own role as narrator is distinguished from that of the lover-protagonist, and Narcissus is the lover-protagonist of Pygmalion's fountain sculpture. This separation of roles is further reflected in his treatment of the judgment of Paris, recounted during Venus's address to the narrator at the beginning of the dream. In the twelfth-century *Roman d'Eneas,* the choice of Juno, Pallas, or Venus was portrayed as a choice between wealth, military prowess, and love.[4] Machaut, however, restores Pallas to her identity as goddess of wisdom, and he associates Venus, as goddess of love, with all the attributes of the aristocratic lover. Whereas the figure of Juno remains unchanged, the choice between Pallas and Venus is accordingly redefined as that between clergie and chevalerie.[5] This distinction corresponds to that between the narrator, learned poet and avowed coward, and l'Amant, a knight and lover. By associating love with the condition of knighthood and opposing these to clerkly learning, Machaut insists on his own more narrowly defined role as poet and writer, witness and codifier of chivalric and amorous adventures but not himself a participant. The narrator's claim that knightly courage would be unfitting in a clerk suggests

---

4. The *Eneas* identifies Pallas as "deesse de bataille" (goddess of battle [v. 147]) and describes the judgment of Paris as a choice among "la richece" of Juno, "la proece" of Pallas, and "la feme" promised by Venus (the wealth; the prowess; the wife [vv. 165–68]).

5. In Machaut's account, Paris announces his decision as follows: "Gardés vos tresors amassés, / Vostre scens et vostre clergie, / Car l'estat de chevalerie / Vueil, et me tieng a la promesse / De Venus" (Keep your stored up treasures, your sense, and your learning, for I want the state of chivalry, and cling to Venus's promise [*Fonteinne amoureuse,* vv. 2130–34]).

by implication that love, that other knightly activity, would be equally so, an assertion borne out in the *Voir Dit*.

Froissart, returning to the model of the *Eneas*, reopens the possibility for the composite role of lover-poet. His protagonist enthusiastically chooses to follow Venus, giving up not learning but worldly power as represented by wealth and force of arms. Indeed, Froissart specifies that his exemplary young man passes into the tutelage of Venus from that of Mercury, who has taught him to "parler par soutieueté" (speak subtly [v. 404]). Having acquired the skills of subtle discourse, Froissart's persona begins to learn about love: clearly, we have here the making of a love poet.

The complainte of the *Fonteinne amoureuse* contains the myth of Alcyone and Ceyx; this tale of dream-making as a theatrical production, staged at the request of the distraught lover, serves as a model for the actual dream that follows within the frame narrative and by implication for the construction of the dit itself. Froissart likewise encloses an informing mythological exemplum in his complainte but chooses a different myth, that of Apollo and Daphne; his protagonist wishes not for a dream but to see his lady transformed into a laurel. How is this wish comparable to that expressed by the lover of the *Fonteinne amoureuse?*

Neither Machaut's nor Froissart's lover wishes for a meeting with his lady. The former wishes for a medium of communication, whereby each can see the other's image and hear the other's voice—for a sort of presence-in-absence. This is provided first by the written transcription of the complainte and then by the dream, which can be understood as figuring what I have called the theatricality of the illustrated lyric text. As we have seen, the poem turns on the correlated distinction of clerk and knight, writer and performer, author and protagonist, and presents a kaleidoscopic series of vocal and silent, verbal and visual texts. Froissart's reworking is at once more lyrical, in his restoration of the common identity of narrator and protagonist, and more writerly, in that he wishes not for a dream but for his lady to become a laurel. He does not ask for a face-to-face encounter or an exchange of messages but, rather, for an artifact, whereby he can possess his lady in transmuted form. Whereas the dream evokes the theatrical quality of literature, the laurel evokes the writerly quality of the text that at once represents and eclipses its referent.

Like l'Amant in the *Fonteinne amoureuse*, Froissart's lover gets his wish, and the lady's image makes this wish fulfillment explicit, stating that she will always be a laurel for him. Her response covers fifteen strophes, the same number as were taken up in his complainte with the opening remarks and the Apollo myth. His poem has generated hers. By writing a poem he has created a textual representation of her.

Froissart's construct is, of course, reminiscent of the myth of Narcissus and its reworking in the *Rose,* since he sees his beloved in a mirror in a dream.[6] Because she is his textual creation, it also recalls Pygmalion, who longed to communicate with his *ymage* and was convinced of his miracle when he heard her voice address him. Froissart conflates Narcissus and Pygmalion, and in so doing reverses the progression of Pygmalion's miracle: rather than bringing a statue to life, he has transformed a real lady into an image. He collapses the distinction that was made in the *Rose,* where Pygmalion's love for a concrete, external image is contrasted with Narcissus's love for an image that is inseparable from himself: the writerly quality of the Pygmalion story is reinfused with the lyrical quality of the Narcissus story. Froissart suggests that the lyrical writer has not escaped the narcissism of the singer, for even the visual text emanates from his imagination, mirror and echo of his desire. The lady who appears in the poetic text speaks not with her own voice but with that of the lover-writer.

Froissart's dream recalls the *Voir Dit,* where Toute Belle's portrait speaks to Guillaume in a dream (pp. 315–30). Here, the portrait recounts at length the story of Apollo and Coronis, warning Guillaume not to "kill" Toute Belle through an overly hasty reaction to the tales of her indiscretion. A similar allusion appears in Froissart's dream, when the lady evokes the conflated myths of Acteon and Cephalus, vowing that she will never give him cause to kill her through her suspicions of his infidelity; the reference to Acteon in turn suggests that she will never kill him through anger or refusal. The allusion to this passage of the *Voir Dit* is telling, for it is here that Guillaume's original equation of the portrait and the lady is challenged, and he is told that he should think of them as two separate entities. Why, asks the portrait, should it be punished when he is angry with Toute Belle herself? Indeed, Guillaume is chastised for having fallen away from his original adoration of the portrait. This shift of focus from the real Toute Belle to her idealized image participates in the larger movement within the *Voir Dit,* where, as we have seen, Guillaume must ultimately settle for a relationship with image and texts rather than one in the flesh. Froissart reiterates this aspect of the *Voir Dit* as a fundamental quality of lyrical writing. The movement from lady to image, from Daphne to laurel, replays that from Toute Belle to her portrait and letters.

There is a qualitative difference between the Apollo-Daphne myth and those that figured so importantly in the *Rose*—Narcissus, Orpheus, and Pygmalion. Narcissus embodies desire in a pure state and the in-

---

6. The lady of the *Espinette* has already behaved like Echo, in that she returns the young lover's poem—his own words—rather than giving him a reply (vv. 957–72). Figuratively speaking, her entire confort is an echo of his earlier complainte.

ability of desire to do more than record itself; Orhpeus exemplifies the inability of song to create a lasting presence, one capable of meeting and measuring up to the force of desire that lies behind the song. Pygmalion in turn is the poet's fantasy: the miracle of creating a lasting, living presence through art, a true "other." The myth of Apollo and Daphne carries a different implication. Apollo does not suffer the loss of Narcissus or Orpheus, for he does come to possess the laurel; but neither does he enjoy the victory of Pygmalion, for he never possesses Daphne. The Apollo-Daphne myth is an encapsulation of the statement made by the *Voir Dit:* the writer's primary relationship is with texts, and although the text may be a medium of communication between the writer and his subject, or between writer and reader, it serves at the same time to displace this relationship. For Froissart's lady to proclaim herself a laurel is, in effect, a statement of her irreality. The dreamer sees before him only an image and not the real lady. However "realistic" the text may be, however detailed its visual imagery and however eloquent its language, it remains in the end a text.

The Apollo-Daphne myth is central to Froissart's poetics, and he incorporates allusions to it into his other major dits as well.[7] His choice of this myth represents an innovation within the French courtly tradition. One wonders whether Froissart might have known Petrarch's similar use of the Apollo-Daphne myth. It is not impossible that he did; Froissart was in Milan in 1368, on the occasion of the marriage of Lionel, duke of Clarence, and Violante Visconti, with whose family Petrarch maintained good relations. He had also traveled to Avignon, where Petrarch spent much of his life, about 1360.[8] Petrarch's powerful reputation was well established by the 1360s, and it would be hardly surprising if an up-and-coming French poet like Froissart, whose Chronicles testify to his undying curiosity and his energy for gathering information, took an interest in the works of the famous Italian. Not only the fascination with the

7. Froissart refers to Apollo's love of the laurel in the "Pynoteus" episode of the *Prison* (v. 1760), and it is through a laurel leaf that Apollo transmits life into the statue of Neptisphele (vv. 1739–40, 1914–25). In the *Buisson,* he refers again to the Apollo-Daphne myth (vv. 3154–63), and Orphane, heroine of one of Froissart's pseudo-Ovidian myths, is the sister of Daphne (v. 2111); in the myth of Hero and Cepheus, which Froissart invented to explain the origin of the daisy, Cepheus dies by falling from a laurel (vv. 3214–41). For further discussions of Froissart's use of Ovidian mythology, see Kelly, "Inventions ovidiennes de Froissart"; Picherit. Zink discusses Froissart's conflation of the myths of Acteon and Cephalus—in his opinion, an expression of the dual fear of the hunter, that of killing and that of being killed—in his article "Froissart et la nuit du chasseur," especially pp. 71–72. I join the above critics in seeing deliberate artistry in Froissart's modifications of Ovidian material rather than, as some would have it, numerous errors resulting from an imperfect knowledge of Ovid. The latter opinion is expressed by Fourrier in his introductions to the *Espinette* (p. 38) and the *Buisson* (p. 24) and is reiterated by Kibler, "Self-Delusion in Froissart's *Espinette amoureuse,*" p. 88, n. 1, and p. 92, n. 2.

8. On Froissart's trips to Avignon and Italy, see Fourrier's edition of the *Espinette amoureuse,* pp. 33–34. Froissart refers to his trips to Avignon in vv. 794–98.

myth of Daphne but also the movement from youthful folly to the responsibilities of adulthood in the *Joli Buisson de jonece* and the transition there from courtly love poetry to the *Lay de Nostre Dame* recall Petrarch's *Rime sparse*. Since Froissart does not mention other vernacular poets by name—not even Machaut, with whose works he was clearly intimately acquainted—it is difficult to ascertain just how widely he had read; it may well be that his response to Machaut and the *Roman de la rose* reflects at least a passing knowledge of Petrarch's poetics as well.

The myth used to authorize the dream of the *Espinette*, finally, is one invented by Froissart himself. The story of Papirus and Ydoree, communicating with one another by means of magic mirrors crafted by Papirus, is the lyrical writer's fantasy of communication over distance through art, as is the dream in the *Fonteinne amoureuse*. Froissart makes it more explicit that this communication takes place through technical expertise, capitalizing on the association of "mirror" or "speculum" and book. The very name "Papirus," evoking "papyrus" or "papier," associates this story with the process of writing; we recall, indeed, that the protagonist of the *Espinette* had earlier attempted to secure his lady's favor by sending her a "ballade written on paper" (v. 1278). The name "Ydoree" is placed in rhyme position with *doree* (golden), a quality of the story: "De Papirus et d'Ydoree / Est l'istore tres bien doree" (The story of Papirus and Ydoree is indeed golden [vv. 2681–82]). These associations suggest that the relationship of Papirus and Ydoree may be not only that of lover and beloved but also that of the story, an imaginative construct, an "ydee doree" (golden idea), and the paper on which it is written. To mediate between author and reader is also to mediate between the imaginative and material worlds—to make a book. The myths employed to inform the successful love relationship—Apollo and Daphne, Papirus and Ydoree—are myths of writing and textual reification. Froissart develops the self-reflexive quality of lyrical poetry, and the equation of poetry and love, into a rarefied poetics of the self as writer.

The motif of the magic mirror recalls the legend of Virgil's mirror, set up in Rome in order to reveal approaching enemies.[9] Since the story of Virgil's mirror is recounted briefly in Adenet le Roi's *Cléomadès* (Henry ed., vv. 1691–98), which Froissart and his lady read together at the beginning of the *Espinette amoureuse*, its relevance to this particular poem is easily established. In *Cléomadès*, the tales of Virgil's technical feats are used to demonstrate the powers possessed by clerks. Having identified Virgil as a great clerk, wise and subtle (v. 1817), Adenet adds that he has recounted Virgil's exploits as authorization for the exploits claimed for the kings in his story, "car clerc furent de grant afaire" (for they were clerks of great rank [v. 1830]). Froissart's lyricized version of this con-

9. Fourrier ed., *Espinette amoureuse*, p. 38.

struct, which he uses to authorize his own imaginative creation, implicitly associates him with the legendary figure of Virgil, clerk and lover, author of historical and lyrical poetry.

## Midpoint of Froissart's Book: *La Prison amoureuse*

The *Prison amoureuse* was composed about four years after the *Espinette amoureuse*, in 1372 or 1373.[10] Two narrative lines are interlaced in this dit: that of the narrator-protagonist, to whom I will refer by his pseudonym Flos, and that of his patron, who goes by the pseudonym Rose and who clearly represents Wenceslas de Brabant.[11] Rose's story unfolds by means of prose letters that he sends to Flos, narrating his experiences and requesting advice and poetry. At times he also sends Flos samples of his own poetry. Flos dutifully supplies Rose with both lyric and narrative compositions, as well as prose letters containing amorous advice, a commentary on the tale of Pynoteus that he composed for Rose, and a commentary on a dream narrated by Rose. At first, both Rose and Flos are involved in love intrigue, and their stories run in somewhat parallel tracks. Flos is troubled at his lady's choice of song in a carol, whereas Rose is burdened by his inability to communicate his love to his lady. In the second round of episodes, Flos passes a pleasant afternoon with his lady; Rose succeeds in communicating his love and has an initial conversation with the object of his affections.

Following this first series of letters and encounters, however, the focus of the narrative shifts. Flos does not see his lady any more after these two opening episodes, and indeed barely even mentions her for the duration of the poem. The process of writing poems and letters and reading those sent by Rose comes to occupy all of his time; in the course of the dit, he passes from the role of lover-poet to that of poet-compiler, reenacting within the abbreviated space of a single poem the evolution followed by Machaut over the course of his career. Rose in turn expresses an increasing interest in the poeticization of his love affair, and in the second half of the dit, although he continues to refer to the progress of his relationship with the lady, his letters are largely devoted to Flos's "Pynoteus" composition—his and his lady's reactions to it, requests for interpreta-

---

10. On the date of the *Prison amoureuse*, see pp. 28–29 in Fourrier's edition.

11. The historical allusions are explicated by Fourrier in his introduction to the *Prison amoureuse*, pp. 19–28. See also Thiry; Kibler, "Poet and Patron." Kibler's assertion that the exchange of letters was a real one and that Wenceslas actually wrote not only the lyric poetry attributed to Rose but also the entire dream narrative and complainte strikes me as quite unlikely. There is no concrete evidence that Wenceslas ever wrote anything other than forme-fixe compositions. One cannot stress too much the danger of taking a narrator at his word when he explains the genesis of his text.

tion, and the dream that "Pynoteus" inspired. Even Rose, in other words, is increasingly defined as subject, author, and reader of poetic texts; his final request is for his entire set of experiences in love and poetry to be made into a book, so that he and his lady can read about themselves. It can hardly be an accident that this explicit picture of the relationship between poet and patron, writer and reader, appears at the center of Froissart's books, where it enunciates the principles that serve to unite the collection as a whole.

The "Pynoteus" tale is in many ways central to the *Prison amoureuse;* it embodies the mythological constructs fundamental to Froissart's poetics, it generates Rose's dream narrative, and it is glossed by Flos as an allegory for Rose's love experiences. Before drawing further conclusions about the role of the *Prison amoureuse* within Froissart's anthology, therefore, I wish to examine the conflation of mythological figures in "Pynoteus," and the statement that this implies about the poetics of lyrical writing.

Several different myths have been brought together in the "Pynoteus": the stories of Pyramus and Thisbe, Orpheus and Eurydice, and Pygmalion and Galatea are the most obvious elements in the narrative, whereas the myth of Phaeton is explicitly recounted in Pynoteus's prayer. Additionally, Pynoteus alludes to Apollo's love for both Leucothoë and Daphne, and the latter is reiterated through the use of the laurel leaf as the medium by which life enters the statue. Finally, the presence of Apollo and the motif of death and resuscitation, later glossed by Flos an an allegory for the jealousy that sometimes came between Rose and his lady, subtly evokes the myth of Apollo and Coronis, recounted in the *Voir Dit* by Toute Belle's portrait as a warning against jealous reaction to the news of Toute Belle's indiscretions. The presence of Phaeton, whose story is glossed by Flos as the mirror of Pynoteus's own loss, further suggests that other son of Apollo, Aesculapius, born of Coronis in the wake of this similar tragedy.

Pynoteus appears as a Pyramus figure in the first part of the story. Neptisphele is devoured by a lion and Pynoteus finds only her blood-stained belt on the ground. But there are crucial differences between Pynoteus and Pyramus. For one thing, Pyramus is guilty of misreading the signs; Thisbe is not in fact dead. Also, although his suicide does result in the creation of a monument to their love—the blood-darkened mulberries—Pyramus himself is entirely unaware that he has produced it. He thus constitutes a purely negative model of the lover-reader or lover-writer and must be transcended.

Pynoteus transcends Pyramus by becoming an Orpheus figure. Where Pyramus had simply despaired, Orpheus decided to do something about it. He went to reclaim Eurydice from Hell. Pynoteus also decides to "do something." After the manner of an Orphic poet, he convenes all the wild beasts and demands that justice be meted out. After the lion has been discovered and killed, Pynoteus does begin to despair. He contemplates suicide, conjuring up a vision of his projected arrival in Hell that is reminiscent of Orpheus's journey. Orpheus, however, failed in his endeavor—the singer can evoke his beloved, but he cannot actually reconstitute her as a living presence. Pynoteus must surpass Orpheus also; this he does in the manner of Pygmalion. Unlike Orpheus, Pynoteus realizes and accepts that "Neptisphelé ne rarai mes" (I will never have Neptisphele back [v. 1689]). He decides that what he can do is to make "une tele" (one such) to replace her and accordingly constructs a statue that exactly resembles her. Apollo, god of poetry, brings the statue to life, and the love affair continues.

The conflation of Orpheus and Pygmalion is reminiscent of the passage from Narcissus to Pygmalion, and the implied "correction" of Orpheus as singer, in the *Roman de la rose* in that the Orphic desire is fulfilled through recourse, not to singing, but to the creation of a concrete visual image. Although the image is once again a statue, the association of this image-making with writing is strengthened by the fact that Pynoteus is identified as a poet. As in the *Rose*, when the image speaks the artist-lover knows he has succeeded; she does not merely echo his voice, but speaks with a voice of her own.[12]

The myth of Apollo and Coronis also involves the attempted resuscitation of a beloved. Apollo fails to revive Coronis, but he does succeed in saving their child, Aesculapius, who eventually perfects the arts of medicine to the point where he actually can raise the dead. This story is analogous to that of Orpheus in interesting ways. Orpheus was unable to return Eurydice to life, so he made up a story about an artist who was able to bring a statue to life. Apollo was unable to return Coronis to life, but he brought forth a child who embodied that resuscitative power. In one case the bereaved lover-poet realizes his fantasy through narrative verse; in the other case, through procreation. The miracle of Pynoteus combines these two. His behavior recalls that of Orpheus, and insofar as he brings a statue to life, he resembles Pygmalion; but insofar as his loss of Neptisphele is glossed as the result of jealousy, he resembles Apollo, and in raising the dead he recalls Aesculapius. As the two myths are brought together, the two parts of each myth are collapsed; narrator and protagonist, father and son, are conflated. Again, the suggestion is that the lover-poet can consummate his desire only by projecting himself into a text, by becoming the protagonist of his own story. One is reminded, for example, of the *Bestiaire d'amours* and its *Response;* when both lover

12. The medieval concept of the lifelike image often centered on the appearance of speech; the miracles of Pygmalion, Pynoteus, and the hero of the *Espinette* correspond to a cultural fantasy of talking images, itself related to what I have called the performative quality of the illuminated manuscript and the tradition of oral performance. See Camille, "Seeing and Reading," especially p. 28.

and lady are textual personae, represented in image and written text, it becomes possible for her to acquire a (written) voice and reply to him.[13]

The suggestion of crossing invisible boundaries and entering the world of fiction complements the notion implied by the myths of Daphne and Leucothoë. Since the poet transforms life into art, his primary relationship is always with art rather than life. Pynoteus exemplifies this process, moving from the real Neptisphele to an artificial one. The *Prison amoureuse* forms an interesting bridge between the *Espinette*, written a few years earlier, and the *Joli Buisson de jonece*, written about a year later. In the former the poet-protagonist absents himself from his lady and then has a vision of her, generated from his own poetic creation. Once in her presence again, he is ultimately forced to ignore the empirical evidence of her disinterest in him and wilfully to project upon her the persona of his dream in order to go on believing that he even has a relationship with her. The relationship exists in the poetic dream, in the textual conjoining of complainte and confort. In the *Joli Buisson de jonece,* the narrator revives his love sentiments by returning first to the portrait and then to the dream. As implied by Philosophy's suggestion to return "Au temps passé et a tes oevres" (To the past and to your works [v. 463]), he must become once again the protagonist of his own earlier poem.

The story of Pynoteus, then, is appropriate both to the *Prison amoureuse* itself and to the codex as a whole. The poetic process is most insistently foregrounded in the *Prison amoureuse.* In a reversal of the traditional priorities of the narrative with lyric insertions, the composition of poetry becomes the frame narrative into which the love episodes are inserted; this is brought home most forcefully when the story of Rose's dream is inserted between the first three and the last nine strophes of the lay that Flos is writing. The *Prison amoureuse* shows us the love poet withdrawing from the world of lyrical encounters and performances to mediate between experience and poetry and between different sets of texts. This, the central piece of Froissart's book, represents a turning point in the poetic career there represented and prepares for the "farewell to poetry," as Michelle Freeman has termed it, that will be enunciated in the final dits.[14] Without in any way denigrating his poetic enterprise, Froissart is already affirming his identity as chronicler, one

13. The implied conflation of father and son is interesting in light of the *Bestiaire d'amours*, where, as we saw in Chapter 5, Richard states his intention to beget himself as child-lover of his lady. Froissart probably knew the *Bestiaire d'amours*, given its popularity, but it is impossible, without further evidence, to know whether he had this passage in mind in the present context. The theme of birth and lineage is extremely rich and deserves a fuller treatment than I can give it within the scope of this book.

14. Freeman, "Froissart's *Le Joli Buisson de jonece.*" See also the discussion by Dembowski, *Jean Froissart and His "Meliador,"* pp. 28–41.

whose task is to record information, to capture experience and make of it a book. The chronicler is not a Pygmalion or an Orpheus, producing purely imaginative images and hoping thereby to persuade, to rearrange, or to enlarge the shape of the world. He is, to continue the language of Froissart's mythology, an Apollo, one at whose hands the stuff of lived experience becomes a literary artifact.

The *Prison amoureuse* provides a model of literary compilation. Its various elements—prose letters, verse narratives, lyric poems—are ultimately all versions of the same underlying lyric construct of love fraught with jealousy, doubt, and separation. As a poetic construct, the compilation has a lyric coherence, consisting of a series of reformulations of the same thing. It folds in on itself in the second half, as Flos completes his lay, explains how the two intercalated stories are really versions of one another and of the letters, and compiles the book. The dit is further unified through the governing relationship of poet and patron, through whose collaborative efforts the book comes into being.[15] And it is all compiled, arranged, glossed, and in most cases written by Flos; the book is unified because it is masterminded by one person.

The *Prison amoureuse*, then, presents three sources of unity: the love story, a lyric unity; the working relationship of poet and patron; and ultimately the fact that there is a single "editor" who puts it all together. These same sources of unity operate at the level of the codex as a whole. The lyric unity derives not only from the general fact of love as the subject matter of the poems but also from the recurrence of the names "Marguerite" and "Jehan Froissart" throughout the collection. The book is framed by the opening and closing rubrics in which Froissart is named. Its first poem, the *Paradis*, closes with the ballade "Sur toutes flours j'aimme la margerite" (Above all flowers I love the daisy) and the gift of the garland of daisies; its final poem, the *Plaidoirie de la rose et de la violette*, closes with a reference to the *margherite* (daisy [vv. 333–36]). In the *Prison amoureuse*, in turn, the poet-narrator and the lady "Marguerite" are fused in the pseudonym "Flos," itself an alliterative echo of "Froissart," and his emblem, a daisy. At beginning, midpoint, and end, then, the names of the poet-lover and his lady are inscribed. The daisy is also celebrated in the "Dit de la Margherite" and in two pastourelles.[16] And the names "Jehan Froissart" and "Marguerite" are encoded in the text of the *Espinette* and the *Joli Buisson de jonece*.[17] This refrainlike recur-

---

15. Although there is no real evidence that Wenceslas participated actively in the composition of the *Prison amoureuse*—Rose's poems, for example, all appear in the lyric section of Froissart's anthologies (see n. 11)—it is generally accepted that he and Froissart actually did collaborate in the *Meliador*, into which Froissart inserted Wenceslas's lyric poetry. One might see the *Meliador* as the realization of the fantasy played out in the *Prison amoureuse*.

16. Numbers 17 and 19 in *The Lyric Poems*, ed. McGregor.

17. As Froissart himself tells us, and as Fourrier has remarked in his edition, the names

rence of the lovers' names contributes to the unification of the codex as a series of poetic formulations inspired by a single love relationship.

The relation between poet and patron, though not always explicit, also governs the collection, a series of poems written by Froissart for various noble patrons. Most important of all, the book is unified through Froissart's identity as poet, editor, and compiler. The threefold unity of the codex is formulated in the opening section of the *Joli Buisson de jonece;* here the narrator lists his poetic compositions in the order in which they appear in the manuscripts and also enumerates his various patrons before finally turning to his original love relationship for renewed inspiration. The fact of authorship within the dual context of love and patronage is stated in the frame rubrics cited in Chapter 7, where we are told that Jehan Froissart composed these poems "with the help of God and love" for the entertainment and edification of noble lords and ladies.

The foregoing discussion has served both to demonstrate the careful construction of Froissart's anthology and to clarify its poetics of lyrical writing and compilation. For Froissart's final statements, we must turn to the dits with which the book closes, the *Joli Buisson,* the *Dit dou florin,* and the *Plaidoirie de la rose et de la violette.*

## Lyricism and Escapism in *Le Joli Buisson de jonece*

In the *Joli Buisson de jonece,* Froissart reviews once more the Ovidian myths and the repertory of French courtly poetry that has informed his work. The *Joli Buisson* contains the largest assortment of Ovidian and pseudo-Ovidian material of any of Froissart's dits, as well as an impressive proliferation of lyric compositions, including not just one but two lays; it is poetic tour de force. Froissart's "farewell to poetry" in no sense entails a loss of respect for the poetic arts, nor does it imply that Froissart's own abilities are waning. It implies simply that the themes of lyricism and "courtly love" no longer serve Froissart's needs, and he turns to a different sort of literature. Indeed, as Froissart passes in review the French lyrico-narrative tradition and his own participation therein, one senses that he is not so much turning away from poetry as he is transposing poetic process into a new register.

---

"Jehan Froissart" and "Margerite" appear in the *Espinette* in vv. 3386–89: "*Je hantoie la tempre et tart, / Dont frois, dont chaus, navrés dou dart / D'Amours, et lors de flours petites, / Violettes et margerites*" (emphasis Fourrier's). The names are not explicitly pointed out in the *Joli Buisson* and are not noted by Fourrier, but they appear in the following lines: "*Je me voel retraire al ahan. / Frois a esté li ars maint an*" (vv. 930–31, emphasis mine); and "Ou nom de sainte *Margherite*" (v. 1109, emphasis mine; Fourrier does point out in his note to this line that Margherite was the name of Froissart's lady).

Froissart's last poetic dream takes place against the backdrop of Machaut's last two great dits amoureux, the *Fonteinne amoureuse* and the *Voir Dit.* As the *Joli Buisson* opens, Froissart casts himself in the role adopted by Machaut at the beginning of the *Voir Dit:* the aging poet, no longer in love, suffers from a lack of poetic material. Since Froissart was, in fact, only thirty-five when these lines were written and had composed the *Prison amoureuse* no more than a year earlier, this stance appears to be more a means of situating Froissart morally and poetically than a mark of autobiographical realism.[18] Froissart is telling us, in effect, that he has arrived at the same point that Machaut had reached when he wrote the *Voir Dit:* a learned writer and cleric, engaged in the business of producing poems and books for noble patrons, confronts the conventions of courtly lyricism and questions his own identity as lyrical writer.

The first lyric piece of the *Joli Buisson*, the virelay "Vémechi ressuscité" (Behold me here resuscitated), provides a clear point of contact with the *Voir Dit.* First of all, the protagonist composes this piece upon beholding the portrait of his lady; filled with enthusiasm, he vows to serve the portrait henceforth. Second, the opening line of the poem recalls Machaut's repeated statement in the *Voir Dit* that he has been "resuscitated" by letters from Toute Belle. Froissart, therefore, seems to begin at the same point that Machaut did in his last great love story. There is, however, an important difference between the positions of our two protagonists: Guillaume has just begun a new and initially promising love affair, whereas Froissart's persona has done nothing more than dedicate himself to the memory of a love affair that has been over for more than ten years. If Guillaume's love affair is increasingly tenuous, leading ultimately to an affirmation of textuality over experience, that of Froissart's persona is exclusively an affair of poetic imagination, right from the start. In fact, it might be more accurate to say that Froissart begins at the point where Machaut left off, or at a point even later than that. His lady does not even write letters. She is accessible only through image, memory, and dream.

In the dream, Froissart's protagonist is guided by Venus to the "bush of youth," where he finds his lady surrounded by numerous allegorical personifications. After a series of songs and games, the dreamer is so overcome with desire that he cannot refrain from pressing his suit. Waiting in the "bush of Desire," where he has hidden himself, he sends her poems declaring his love. The lady is unimpressed but allows him to rejoin her company. After a final series of poems expressing amorous wishes, which the dreamer transcribes so that they can be judged by the

---

18. Froissart dates the dream of the *Joli Buisson* November 30, 1373 (vv. 859–60). Fourrier, Dembowski, and others have assumed, there being no reason to doubt it, that the poem was composed about this time.

God of Love, he is jostled and wakes up. Realizing that such fantasies are without substance and inappropriate for one of his age, the protagonist composes a lay in honor of the Virgin.

This dream recalls both Froissart's own previous dream poetry and Machaut's *Fonteinne amoureuse*. Again, though, there is a difference. The lady with whom he interacts is hardly even the image of a real person; she is, rather, a manifestation of the portrait, for she appears in its guise, looking as she did ten years earlier. Indeed, the dreamer must consult her portrait in order to be sure that this is she; evidently his memory alone is not sufficient. And given this state of affairs, it is highly improbable that the lady herself is experiencing a similar dream of her beloved or that any sort of actual communication is taking place. This dream is a self-contained fantasy within the mind of the poet for which the primary purpose is the generation of the poetic text in which the dream is recorded.

Froissart has here taken the self-reflexivity of lyricism to its logical extreme. In the opening passage of the poem, Philosophy urges the poet to return to his craft and invokes the familiar topos that poetry is to be placed at the service of history, providing a sort of collective memory bank for human civilization. As the poem progresses, however, the priorities seem to have been reversed: experience serves poetry by providing subject matter, rather than poetry's serving experience by preserving it. If the poet can think of nothing else to write about, he can at least write about his own attempts at writing. Froissart's statement is humorous to be sure but also telling; he wishes to overcome the frivolity of lyrical poetry, its self-serving and self-contained quality.

Something of this conversion process is already mapped out within the dream itself. Initially, the dreamer is delighted to discover his lady and her entourage. Hidden in the bush of Desire, he is inflamed with amorous and poetic passion of a remarkable intensity. Whereas the narrator of the *Prison amoureuse* comments that it takes six months to compose a lay, and the dreamer of the *Paradis d'amour* resorts to a previously composed lay because it would take much too long to compose a new one, the dreamer of the *Joli Buisson* not only manages to compose a lay while hiding in the bush but dashes off a virelay as well. Yet nothing comes of all this poetic fervor. The lady remains unmoved. By the end of the poem, the dreamer has already modified his poetic function. In the final episode, he transcribes the poems composed by the other characters, without composing any of his own. This behavior, again, recalls that of the narrator of the *Fonteinne amoureuse*. Froissart has reversed the progression from the *Fonteinne* to the *Voir Dit*, acknowledging that he is finished with the fantasies of courtly love and affirming his role as writer and recorder.

Indeed, the treatment of the lyric insertions maps out a general movement from a writerly to a performance-oriented discourse in the first half of the dream, only to return to a writerly discourse in the second half. The narrator's presentation of the first virelay is an invitation not simply to listen but also to read: "Or lisiés, vous orés" (Now read, you will hear [*Joli Buisson*, v. 562]). Once inside the dream, however, he insists on the oral quality of the lyric pieces he recites for Venus and Youth and of those performed in the carol; at times he even reverts to addressing a listening audience, as for example "Or le voelliés oïr" (Now please listen to it [v. 2455]). The orality of these pieces is stressed repeatedly. For example, commenting on the beauty of a rondeau, the narrator states "car de belle bouche / En issi la vois lie et douche" (for the gay and sweet voice issued forth from a beautiful mouth [vv. 2660–61]).

Froissart here manipulates the tradition of lyric insertions, playing off his readers' expectations. The intense orality of the carol is, as we have seen, a somewhat old-fashioned trait in narratives of this sort. Froissart exploits it here in order to heighten the sense of nostalgia for a pure lyricism, an ideal associated with the past, with youth, with dream and imagination. By the time the dreamer's case is being presented to the lady, the narrator is already returning to a more writerly discourse: "Tout ensi qu'il y eut escript, / Vous en veés le contre-escript" (Just as it was written there, you see here the transcription [vv. 3994–95, introducing a ballade]). And in the final sequence of wish poems, recited by the allegorical personifications, the narrator reiterates in each case that he has transcribed the poem in its proper place. The dream thus ends with this dramatization of the passage from orality to writing.

The series of three pseudo-Ovidian myths at the beginning of the dream stresses the essentially escapist nature of the lyric idyll. The first, recounted by Venus and framed by the encoded names "Jehan Froissart" and "Margherite," may be seen as Froissart's own self-indulgent fantasy. The shepherd Telephus, who tends the flocks of Juno, is seduced and abducted by Diana, who transports him to a secret place in the forest; although Juno searches for him, his hiding place is secure. There he lives in bliss with Diana and her nymphs, and as a special gift he is granted the ability to understand the language of the birds. That Telephus is a shepherd is appropriate to Froissart's newly acquired identity as priest; that he is employed by Juno, goddess of wealth, further associates him with Froissart the writer, in the employ of the aristocracy. The fantasy that Froissart confronts, and which by the end of the poem he is ready to set aside, is the abdication of his clerical and political responsibilities. Magically freed of the demands of his profession, Froissart would retreat to a lyric paradise, where he would commune freely with that most inaccessible of ladies—one need only think of Diana's behavior toward Acteon, a story often evoked by Froissart, in order to realize just how extreme this fantasy is—and where he would be initiated into the language of purest lyricism and amorous inspiration, the songs of the birds.

The two myths recounted by Youth reiterate the deceptive powers of love and dreams: Nepti[s]phoras[19] and Ydrophus see each other as young throughout their entire lives; Architeles meets regularly with his dead love Orphane in erotic dreams, where neither of them ever ages. Both women are associated through their names with other myths that Froissart has used to exemplify the powers of poetry. Nepti[s]phoras recalls Neptisphele, the girl who was revived in the form of a statue; Orphane is identified as the sister of Daphne, symbol par excellence of the transmutation of love into poetry, and her name further recalls Orpheus. In these stories Froissart evokes the immense, virtually magical powers of the imagination to constitute a reality unto itself, one informed and maintained through desire. What is the value of this power?

The series of exempla recounted by Desire as well as the behavior of Froissart's persona upon awakening suggest that the imagination, or at least the amorous imagination, is both dangerous and seductive. The series of exempla focuses on figures who suffered pain and even death as the result of their unbridled desire. Of particular interest are the figures of Narcissus and Orpheus, both of whose stories are adapted by Froissart to the context of his own poetic corpus. Narcissus is cast in the image of the *Espinette*. Gazing into the pool, he believes that he sees the image of Echo, his dead beloved; hearing his own words of lamentation, he believes that she is addressing him. Obsessed by these delusions, Narcissus is unable to leave the poolside and so wastes away. When we recall the dream that was so central to the *Espinette*, and the resolve of the *Joli Buisson* protagonist forever to serve the image of this lady that he once beheld in a mirror, we realize that this recast tale of Narcissus constitutes a very explicit statement of Froissart's need to turn away from the poetry of courtly love. Even though Narcissus's love is honorable by courtly standards—he is not vain, he does not reject Echo or cause her death—his fixation on his own words and images has a paralyzing and ultimately fatal effect.

Orpheus, in turn, is portrayed as descending to Hell in search not of Eurydice but of Proserpine, identified as his beloved. Like Narcissus, Orpheus is redeemed of his traditional failure: it is not through his excessive desire that he loses his beloved, but through her act in eating the fruit of Hell. Again, even proper love is not enough. Orpheus's mission is doomed from the start. Like Froissart's protagonist, he has gone in search of someone who is fundamentally of another world. Since the loss of Proserpine signifies the passage from springtime to winter,

19. MS 830 has "Neptisphoras"; MS 831 has "Neptiphoras."

Orpheus's loss also resonates with the experience of the dreamer of the *Joli Buisson,* who awakens from his dream of May into the reality of November.

Yet none of these stories is simply a condemnation of lyricism or of imaginative poetry. The tales of Ydrophas and Architeles do suggest the rejuvenative powers of the imagination, the power of poetry to renew and to preserve, to keep memories alive. The story of Narcissus likewise expresses the power of words and images to preserve memories and to enable a bereaved lover to keep faith with one who has passed on. This power, although potentially dangerous, is not wholly negative. Most ambivalent of all is the treatment of Orpheus. The two stories brought together in this composite myth have very different outcomes.[20] Does Orpheus lose Proserpine forever as he did Eurydice, thereby plunging the world into an eternal winter, a cessation of all growth and certainly of all love or lyricism? Or does he gain her back for six months out of every year, as Demeter did, thereby exemplifying the power of renewal, of the periodic return of springtime, flowers, love, song? If it is poetry that retrieves Proserpine from Hell, then it is to poetry that the world owes its very life.

Clearly, this question is crucial, and I believe Froissart's point is that the real answer lies with the individual. It is the nature of the written word to be fraught with both positive and negative powers: the letter kills, but the spirit gives life. When Froissart's dreamer awakens, various options are available to him. He could follow the example of Architeles and get ready for the next dream; like Narcissus or Orpheus, he could despair. He does neither. Instead, he looks beyond the seductive surface of his dream and effects a radical transposition of its central imagery. In the *Lay de Nostre Dame,* the burning bush of sexual desire becomes the bush in the desert, burning with the presence of God, an image to be read both literally and figuratively; the Tree of Jesse, a metaphorical "bush" representing Christ's real human lineage; and ultimately the Virgin Mother of God, miraculous figure signified by the original burning bush, for those who know how to read *in spiritu.*[21] The orality of lyricism, in turn, becomes the orality of prayer: the protagonist of the *Lay de Nostre Dame* prays, "Et vous le voelliés oïr, Dame, / Car je vous offre corps et ame" (And please hear it, Lady, for I offer you body and soul [vv. 5196–97]). Through this movement from body to soul, letter to spirit, Froissart expresses his love for the Virgin, who never turns any-

---

20. Froissart does state that "Pour che demorer li couvint" (For that reason she had to stay [v. 3185]). A similar judgment, however, is passed in *Metamorphoses* 5, vv. 530–32, where Jove decrees that Proserpine may not return if she has eaten the food of Hell; the possibility remains open for this judgment to be modified.

21. Fourrier remarks on the multiple meanings attached to the image of the bush in his introduction to the *Joli Buisson,* pp. 35–36. See also Planche.

one away and through whom not just the individual but the entire human race is truly "resuscitated."

The myth of Orpheus and Proserpine can be read *in bono* or *in malo*. The Orpheus who fails through excessive desire represents the lovesick lyric poet, a figure who may enchant his audience but who ultimately cannot provide lasting fulfillment or spiritual growth. The Orpheus who succeeds is Christ; Christ's harrowing of Hell and subsequent Resurrection on Easter Sunday herald the coming of spring and so can be intimated in the myth of Proserpine. In Chapter 5 we saw that there are certain suggestive analogies between Christian imagery and that of lyricism. Froissart may be playing off these possibilities. Indeed, he would have found a model for this kind of transposition in the work of his master, Machaut, in a poem that he probably regarded with a special fondness, the *Dit de la fleur de lis et de la marguerite*.[22] In this poem, Machaut actually makes of Christ a lyric poet, author of the Song of Songs:

> Il est certein que Jhesucris,
> Si com je truis en mes escris,
> Dit dou lis en ses chansonnettes
> Paroles courtoises et nettes.

[It is certain that Jesus Christ, as I find in my writings, says courteous and clear words about the lily in his little songs.] [Vv. 43–46]

Ultimately, the corrected model for the poet (as for all humans) is Christ, lover and bridegroom of the human race, author and protagonist of historical writings and of exquisitely beautiful love poetry.

It is not, then, poetic process as such that Froissart turns from here, if we understand by the latter the generation of significant images, the construction of a mirror of memory, the ongoing linguistic renewal of the human spirit. What he turns from is the frivolous purposes to which poetry can be put, from an escapist literature that is ultimately little more than the pretext for its own creation and that centers on purely private memories. He seeks to ground literature in some larger context, some transcendent system of values. For Froissart, in practice, this meant dedicating himself to the compilation of his Chronicles.[23] Here the text once again makes contact with an external reality, which it faithfully records. Literature is no longer at the service of purely private

---

22. *Le Dit de la fleur de lis et de la marguerite*, in Fourrier's edition of *"Dits" et "Débats,"* appendix, pp. 289–301.

23. Froissart may have also included *Meliador* in this category of "serious" literature, since it addresses social issues on a large scale and portrays the values that are necessary to the working of society.

fantasies; rather, it serves the largest possible public, the collective values and experience of European civilization.

## Froissart's Epilogue

After the *Joli Buisson* Froissart no longer portrays himself in the role of lyric poet or lover but only as author. He has taken his leave of the lyrico-narrative world. He entered this world by means of a dream, and it was also a dream that spelled the end of his participation. Now he makes his farewell statement.

In the *Dit dou florin,* which follows the *Joli Buisson* in MS 830 and was probably written in 1389, Froissart portrays himself as professional poet: he writes poems and reads them aloud.[24] He is an entertainer of the nobility and he moves through society; in fact, he resembles the minstrels of nearly a century earlier. Froissart has retained the didactic first-person voice of the traditional dit, divorcing it from the lyric focus on affective experience. Significantly, the poetic work to which he refers is not one of his lyrico-narrative pieces but rather *Meliador,* a poem that operates on a vast scale comparable to that of the Chronicles, demonstrating the workings of society and the importance of collective adherence to chivalric values.

In the *Plaidoirie de la rose et de la violette,* the last piece in both manuscripts, Froissart makes his final farewell to lyricism; indeed, I believe it is possible that the poem was written as an epilogue for Froissart's book. This curious poem is not cast as a dream but as an event witnessed and recorded by the narrator. Imagination herself is personified and presides over the suit in which the rose and the violet hire attorneys to argue the question of which is the more noble flower. In the opening lines of the poem, Imagination is identified as a repository of records, before whom "on doit par droite action / Mettre memores et escrips" (one should by right action place memoirs and writings [vv. 2–3]). No longer the internalized source of poetic inspiration, Imagination is now an abstracted authority, against which diverse individual images or texts can be measured.

The rose and the violet are both lyric symbols, among the most important of the lyric repertory. The two attorneys argue their case based on the lyric associations and poetic symbolism of their respective clients. If the rose is the color of the sun and of sacramental wine, the violet is the color of the firmament. The rose is cherished by noble lords and ladies, who fashion garlands from it; the violet is equally cherished as the har-

---

24. The events described in the *Florin* indicate that it was composed in 1389: see Fourrier's comments in his introduction to the *"Dits,"* pp. 62–67.

binger of spring. Interestingly, these particular flowers can be associated with the two streams of vernacular lyrico-narrative poetry: first-person erotic dream narrative begins with the *Roman de la rose,* and the romance with lyric insertions originates with Jean Renart's *Roman de la rose* and its close imitation, the *Roman de la violette.*[25] In this sense the violet and the rose stand for the poetic tradition in which Froissart's book is inscribed, and from which he now takes his final leave. He turns from these lyrical flowers to the fleur-de-lis: a flower that can and often does have lyric connotations but evoked here for its political significance. Advising the rose and the violet to take their case to the French court, where the fleur-de-lis resides, Imagination explains that the fleur-de-lis is the "sovereign over all flowers" (vv. 293–94). As at the end of the *Joli Buisson de jonece,* Froissart has moved from one poetic register to another. In short, the movement from lyrical flowers to a heraldic flower, and from the court of Imagination to that of France, mirrors the movement from lyrical writing to chronicling.

The *Plaidoirie* is the end point of Froissart's lyrical book; in closing the poetic corpus, it carries certain reverberations with the beginning and midpoint. In the *Paradis,* there is constant reference to gathering flowers, and the dreamer's ballade opens with a list of flowers, of which rose, violet, and lily are the first three.[26] Here, they are purely lyric flowers and are subordinated to the daisy (*margerite*), preferred because of its associations with the lady. At the midpoint, the poet and his patron-protagonist are Flos and Rose, and Flos considers both Violette and Lis as possible pseudonyms before settling on the Latin generic term and the daisy emblem. In the *Espinette,* the young lover presents "Margherite" with a rose (vv. 986–1002), and later receives from her a gift of violets (vv. 3475–78). By the end of the book, then, these flowers have acquired a considerable weight of poetic associations. The revaluation of these flowers in the closing piece is an implicit retrospective on Froissart's poetic career; the reference to the daisy as a member of the fleur-de-lis's court in the last lines of the poem is a final, fleeting lyric reminiscence.[27]

25. It is hard to say whether or not Froissart would have been aware of Jean Renart's *Roman de la rose,* which does not seem to have circulated widely (it survives today in only one manuscript). The *Roman de la violette,* on the other hand, survives in several manuscripts. Although he certainly may have known Renart's poem, he may also have believed that the use of lyric insertions originated with the *Roman de la violette,* so the rose and violet, respectively, would stand for these two lyrico-narrative types.

26. This ballade opens: "Sur toutes flours tient on la rose a belle, / Et en apriés, je croi, la violette. / La flour de lis est bielle . . . " (The rose is held beautiful above all flowers, and after that, I think, the violet. The lily is beautiful . . . ). Its refrain is "Sur toutes flours j'aimme la margerite" (Above all flowers I love the daisy [Dembowski ed., vv. 1627–29, 1635]).

27. The association of the daisy with the fleur-de-lis recalls Machaut's similar pairing in the *Dit de la fleur de lis et de la marguerite.* Wimsatt argues convincingly that the latter was

In a sense, then, the book as a whole moves full circle, like a giant lyric poem. As we saw, it does have a certain lyrical unity, like the dit at its center. The self-reflexivity of lyricism becomes the self-referentiality of the written text. Again and again we read of the poet writing, making his book; again and again he addresses the reader with reference to the written page. Very often the lyric insertions are introduced as elements of the book. In the *Espinette*, we can find, among others, the following examples:

> Or lisiés, et vous verés u
> Et comment elle faite fu.

[Now read, and you will see where and how it was made.] [Vv. 925–26, introducing a ballade]

> Et droit la fis un virelay
> Tout otel que droit chi mis l'ay.

[And right there I made a virelay, just as I have placed it right here.] [Vv. 1019–20]

> Je ne sçai s'elle vous plaira,
> Mais tele est qui bien le lira.

[I don't know if it will please you, but such it is, for whoever will read it properly.] [Vv. 1467–68, introducing a ballade]

In the *Prison amoureuse*, likewise, the narrator usually addresses a reader rather than a listener, as in the following typical examples:

> Mes anchois que riens je rescripse,
> Voel qu'on voie la sienne et lise.

[But before I write anything back, I want his to be seen and read.] [Vv. 699–700, introducing Letter 1]

---

composed on the occasion of the marriage of Marguerite of Flanders and Philippe le Hardi, duke of Burgundy; see James Wimsatt, pp. 15, 54–57. Possibly it is to this latter Marguerite that Froissart refers. It is highly unlikely, however, that all of his "Marguerite" poetry is dedicated to Marguerite of Flanders, who is not even mentioned among the numerous patrons that Froissart reviews in the *Joli Buisson*. As Wimsatt notes, the name "Marguerite" was one of the most popular female names of the fourteenth century (pp. 50–51), and it is unlikely that we will ever know who Froissart's Marguerite was, if indeed there even was a single Marguerite to whom the poet dedicated his verse. It strikes me as entirely possible that the name was nothing more than an idealized feminine image, a recurring lyric motif that was part of Froissart's "signature."

> Jusques a tant que j'ai escript
> Ensi com vous ves en escript.

[Until I wrote, just as you see in writing.] [Vv. 743–44, introducing Letter 2]

> Se celles vous volés savoir,
> Le copie en poés avoir.

[If you want to know them, you can have a copy of them.] [Vv. 2034–35, introducing three ballades]

And in the *Joli Buisson,* as we have seen, Froissart manipulates the narrator's address to the reader in order to stress a movement from writing to a fantasy of pure orality, and back again to writing.

Perhaps the most curious such reference occurs in the *Plaidoirie,* where the narrator seems to be addressing us at the very moment of writing:

> . . . Vous orés comment
> Il respondi moult sagement.
> Mais ses responces faut escrire
> Avant que je les puisse dire.

[You will hear how he replied very wisely. But his replies must be written before I can say them.] [Vv. 163–66]

As was suggested by the myth of Ydoree and Papirus, the book itself is the link between the fictional world and that of the reader; the story that we read is the story of the book, and its very existence guarantees that the story is, at least at some level, true.

The lyric circularity and self-referentiality of the book is, however, tempered by the implied narrative progression from first piece to last. As the rubrics inform us, the process of poetic composition here recorded took place over a period of approximately thirty years, from 1362 to 1393 (MS 830) or 1394 (MS 831). This sense of narrative progression is heightened by references within the dits As we have seen, Froissart portrays himself growing older, modifying his poetic identity; and in the *Joli Buisson* he is explicitly identified as a seasoned poet, author of the preceding pieces. The self-contained quality of the book contrasts with the tacit acknowledgment that this record of Froissart's career is fragmentary; as the rubrics remind us, and such poems as the *Joli Buisson* and the *Dit dou florin* tell us, the man "Jehan Froissart" has done many things that are not recorded therein and will go on to do many more. We have seen that, in romances or dits with lyric insertions, the frame narrative serves to fix the lyric piece. No longer a universal statement, a timeless manifestation of song itself, the lyric poem is revealed to be a fragmentary record of experience, corresponding to a particular moment in an ongoing narrative. Similarly, the frame rubrics and references to Froissart's professional activities serve to ground the lyrical compilation in this larger context.

Froissart's anthology is even more tightly structured than those of Machaut. A devoted reader of his literary predecessors, Froissart continually refined the art of lyrical writing and compilation. He explored its power to create a reality unto itself, to mirror the dynamics of its own generation, and to record, in allegorical and mythological terms, the workings of an interior world, constituted of desire. Like Machaut and others before him, he was also aware of its limitations. Froissart's lyrico-narrative anthology is an eloquent commentary on the poetic transformation of song into book, a subtle demonstration of the enigma of lyrical writing.

# Conclusion

In the foregoing chapters I have traced a series of developments in Old French literature of the thirteenth and fourteenth centuries. The various threads of the argument have converged to demonstrate the importance of writing as the medium of vernacular poetic creation in the later Middle Ages. We have seen examples in which a narrative text is used to provide a context for lyric performance, and in which a book is arranged and decorated as if in the attempt to reproduce a performance event. This is a first step toward the establishment of a writerly poetics: songs destined for performance are written down, and books are compiled and treated as unified works of art. We have also seen examples in which a narrative records the act of written lyric composition and in which a book provides a series of interrelated texts for study or the record of a poetic career. Here, the status of song as a written text, and the identification of a vernacular corpus as a book, is more explicit. Indeed, the processes of writing and compilation, and the identification of the vernacular lyric poet as a writer, are central themes of works by Machaut and Froissart, the great poet-compilers of the fourteenth century.

This book has necessarily been somewhat narrow in scope, focusing on courtly lyric, lyrical romance, and dit. The processes that I have identified here can, however, be seen in other aspects of Old French literature as well as in the literary traditions of other linguistic areas. Chanson de geste, for example, undergoes similar transformations. The authors of late chanson de geste were conscious of their works as part of a written tradition; Adenet le Roi, as we have seen, stresses that his authority as epic poet derives from his consultation of the history books at Saint Denis. The authority of the oral tradition is challenged head on in the prologue to a French translation of the Latin pseudo-Turpin Chronicle. This latter text, purportedly an eyewitness account of the events described in the *Chanson de Roland*, was granted a high authority in the later Middle Ages partly because of its status as a written rather than an oral document. The translator reminds us that "n'est si mençonge non, ce qu'il en dient et en chantent, cil chanteor ne cil jogleor. . . . Car il n'en sievent rien for quant par oïr dire" (it is nothing but lies, what those singers and jongleurs say and sing about it. . . . For they know nothing about it except by hearsay [Bibl. Nat. fr. 124, fol. 1]). The oral tradition is subject to corruption; the written text records for all time the words of the authority.

The advent of a more writerly poetics of courtly lyric and lyrical narrative coincided with the compilation of chansonniers; similarly, the writerly approach to epic material coincided with the systematic compilation of chanson-de-geste manuscripts. As has been demonstrated in the excellent studies by Delbouille and Tyssens, thirteenth-century scribes played an important editorial role in the compilation of the great chanson-de-geste cycles.[1] Scribes frequently emended their texts for the sake of continuity and composed transitional *laisses* to explain the passage from one text to the next. At times, texts recounting simultaneous events, such as *Les Narbonnais* and *Les Enfances Guillaume,* were collated—as evidenced by erasures, the dismantling of gatherings, and the insertion of extra leaves—in order to produce a continuous narrative containing all episodes. The oral tradition of the jongleurs was reformed into a written tradition, according to principles similar to those that governed the romance anthologies analyzed in Chapter 1.

The developments traced here in Old French literature are paralleled in Italian, Provençal and German literature of the later Middle Ages. The persona of the poet is especially well defined in the Provençal chansonniers. Like trouvère manuscripts, many of them contain miniatures or historiated initials distinguishing noble, clerical, and "professional" troubadours. In addition, most contain prose vidas, or biographies, for each troubadour, and sometimes additional prose narratives, or razos, giving a narrative context for individual songs. Some chansonniers place vidas and razos all together as a special section, but most use a vida to introduce each troubadour's corpus and place the razos, if any, directly before the song that each explains.[2] While information contained in vidas varies, it usually includes at least an identification of the troubadour's birthplace and social class and often some details regarding his musical or amorous career, such as whether he was educated, whether or not he was successful in obtaining the favors of the lady for whom he sang, whether he played a musical instrument, and whether he belonged to a specific court. These troubadour anthologies therefore create a picture of the Provençal lyric tradition and its social and geographical

1. Delbouille, "Chansons de geste et le livre"; Tyssens, "Style oral."
2. See Poe, pp. 83–95.

setting. The razos in turn, by explaining the genesis of individual songs and the specific narrative events to which each refers, imply a writerly understanding of the lyric text as specifically referential. Provençal chansonniers with razos may have influenced such French works as the *Roman du castelain de Couci* or the *Dit de la panthère.* Finally, some troubadour manuscripts additionally contain treatises on Provençal grammar or on versification; those produced in Italy sometimes contain Provençal-Italian glossaries. The collections as a whole are arranged according to lyric genre, opening with the *cansos* and moving on to *sirventes, descorts,* and/or *tensos.*

Although the factual accuracy of the biographies is certainly open to question, the presence of these texts is of great importance. The Provençal chansonnier equipped with a grammatical treatise and prose commentaries could be described as a textbook for vernacular literature, a most remarkable phenomenon in the thirteenth century. A recent study, in fact, has compared the vidas to the Latin *accessus ad auctores,* which appear in schoolbooks and provide similar information regarding Latin authors.[3]

Italian lyric anthologies resemble French and Provençal collections in being arranged according to verse form (*canzoni, ballate,* sonnets), with poems of each type categorized by author. In the thirteenth-century MS Banco Rari 217 of the Biblioteca Nazionale, Florence, each canzone is provided with a historiated initial illustrating its content, and the whole is preceded by an elaborate frontispiece depicting the God of Love and his court. As a result of the illustration of the didactic or amorous content of each poem individually, author identity is subjugated to what Vincent Moleta has termed an "archaic courtly idealism."[4] In its overall effect this codex could be compared, broadly speaking, to the trouvère chansonnier *O* (see Chapter 1).

In other cases, however, Italian lyric collections manifest a far greater concern with the historical and geographical development of Italian lyric and, consequently, with the historical and regional variations of the Italian language. The late-thirteenth-century MS Vaticano 3793 of the Vatican Library presents its canzoni and sonnets in author corpora, which are in turn arranged in geographical and chronological order. The mid-fourteenth-century Vatican MS Chigiano L. VIII. 305 similarly presents each generic grouping in chronologically ordered author corpora. This treatment of the Italian lyric is similar in spirit to Dante's *De vulgari eloquentia,* which reviews the body of vernacular lyric according to the different Romance languages and dialects, giving particular attention to the regional dialects of Italian. This spirit is related, of course, to that of the Provençal chansonniers, many of which were copied in Italy. It is clear that, by the late thirteenth century, interest in the study and cod-

3. See Egan.
4. Moleta, "Illuminated 'Canzoniere.'"

ification of a vernacular lyric tradition and a generally writerly approach
to vernacular lyric poetics was a widespread phenomenon, by no means
limited to northern France.

The earliest evidence for Italian and Provençal lyric compilations
made by the authors is roughly contemporary with the Adam de la Halle
compilation in MS Bibl. Nat. fr. 25566. That certain late-thirteenth-
century troubadours may have compiled their works, or at least that
authoritative compilations existed from an early date, is suggested by the
fact that their pieces appear in the same order in otherwise unrelated
manuscripts or, in some cases, by the inclusion of dates of composition
for each song. The only explicit evidence, though, is a rubric announcing the works of Guiraut Riquier in the Provençal chansonnier Bibl. Nat.
fr. 856 (fol. 288).[5] Not only is each of his poems dated (ranging from
1254 to 1292) but also the rubric states that the pieces are copied "enaissi
adordenademens cum era adordenat en lo sieu libre, del qual libre escrig
per la sua man" (ordered just as they are ordered in his book, which he
wrote with his own hand). It is impossible to know whether the book
written in Guiraut's own hand would have been a presentation copy or
simply a notebook kept for his own use. In any case, though, it seems
that later troubadours, like their French contemporaries, were probably
influenced by the existence of chansonniers to take a more writerly
approach to their craft. And for the scribe to stress that he has preserved
the order of the autograph copy certainly implies a respect for the poet's
authority in ordering the written transcription of his works; Guiraut
Riquier is not just a singer but also the author of a book.

The earliest known Italian single-author lyric compilation is that of
Guittone d'Arezzo, preserved in the Laurentian Library MS Laurenzi-
ano-Rediano 9 (compiled about 1300). Guittone's lyric corpus falls into
two groups: his love poetry and the poetry of conversion written after
his decision, about 1265, to join the Order of the Gaudenti. This distinction is observed by the rubricator of the Laurentian manuscript, who
attributes the earlier poems to "Guittone d'Arezzo," and the later ones to
"Frate Guittone." The lyric persona as poet, lover, and religious follower
is a continuous presence in the collection, the "I" of the later poems
explicitly identifying itself with the "I" of the earlier poems in order to
contrast "before" and "after" modes of poetic composition. Although
the Laurentian manuscript includes works by other poets as well, the
careful arrangement of Guittone's poems into small-scale narrative cycles and the large-scale movement from erotic to sacred love, as well as
the self-conscious commentary on preconversion and postconversion
poetics, argues strongly for an original collection compiled by Guittone
himself.[6]

5. See Pizzoruso.
6. See Moleta, *Early Poetry of Guittone d'Arezzo*.

Petrarch, the most famous Italian lyric poet-compiler, was a contemporary of Machaut.[7] As is well known, Petrarch's *Rime sparse* manifested a very high degree of self-consciousness of the poet as writer and arranger, of the written text as the mirror of the poet's experience, and of the contrasting modes of erotic and penitential poetics. In spite of significant differences, Guittone, Petrarch, Machaut, and Froissart share certain traits in common. I have commented already on similarities between the careers of Froissart and Petrarch. Machaut likewise confronts the seductive allure of love poetry, and its quasi-idolatrous nature, in the *Voir Dit;* among his last works is the *Mass of Our Lady.* In all cases the anthology format allows later works to comment on earlier ones and, at the same time, to be informed by these. Further investigation of medieval lyric compilations could begin with a comparative study of these poets.

When we turn to the Middle High German manuscript tradition, we find again somewhat similar compilational principles. German narrative anthologies of the thirteenth, fourteenth, and fifteenth centuries resemble French codices in their frequent tendency to present independently authored texts in narrative progressions or thematically ordered groupings.[8] Anthologies of Middle High German lyric are similar to their French counterparts in their arrangement by author. Two collections, indeed, have full-page miniatures for each poet: the *Weingartner Liederhandschrift* (Stuttgart, Württembergische Landesbibliothek, Cod. HB XIII 1), compiled about 1300; and the famous *Manessische Liederhandschrift* (Heidelberg, Universitätsbibliothek, Cpg 848), compiled during the first half of the fourteenth century. Some of these miniatures illustrate an episode from one of the songs, whereas others illustrate an oral legend associated with the poet. Still others are simply amorous or courtly scenes. Noble poets are represented according to their rank and, as in French chansonniers, aristocratic poets are placed at the beginning of the collection. As in trouvère chansonniers *A, a,* and *M,* these miniatures stress the importance of the lyric poet-protagonist as well as defining the spectrum of aristocratic and "professional" members of the tradition.

The existence of somewhat similar patterns of narrative and lyric compilation in different parts of late medieval Europe does not necessarily imply identical attitudes toward vernacular poetics or toward writing. A comparative study would be necessary in order to determine the differences among the various literary traditions in question. Although such a study is clearly beyond the scope of the present work, it would be

---

7. For an exhaustive account of Petrarch's work in compiling the *Rime sparse* and the various forms that the anthology assumed, see Wilkins.

8. On anthology manuscripts of Middle High German narrative, see Becker.

useful to consider some of the directions that this study might take. One possible line of inquiry would be the study of statements regarding literary compilations. As an initial example, we can take two statements regarding lyric collections: the preface to the late thirteenth-century troubadour chansonnier *a* written by its compiler, Bernart Amoros, and a slightly later poem written by Johannes Hadlaub.

Bernart identifies himself as "clerk" and "scribe" and explains that he is a native of Auvergne, "don son estat maint bon trobador" (where many good troubadours are from). He assures us that he has "uistas et auzidas" (seen and heard) many songs, and as a result of his familiarity with oral and written productions, he has learned "tant en lart de trobar que sai cognoisser e deuezir en rimas & en uulgar & en lati per cas e per verbe lo dreig trobar d'l fals" (so much of the art of making verse that I know how to recognize and distinguish in rhymes, in both vernacular and Latin, by case and by verb, the correct verse from the false [Stengel ed., p. 6]). These credentials authorize Bernart's editorial activity in compiling and, as he tells us, frequently emending the songs; and he requests that no one attempt any further emendations unless they are well qualified for the job. He himself has refrained from emendations when the text was overly "subtle," so as not to risk damaging it through lack of understanding; this was especially important, he says, in the case of songs by the "Master" Giraut de Borneilh.

This extremely rich statement reflects the scholarly approach of the Provençal compiler; no mere copyist, he is a careful textual critic who takes pride in his work. For Bernart, vernacular and Latin poetry alike exist as a written tradition, governed by strict rules of poetic and grammatical form. His concern with textual emendations further reflects a consciousness of the poem as having a fixed form, composed by a gifted individual; the task of the copyist is to restore and preserve the work of the masters. Such an attitude can exist only within the framework of a written literary tradition; it is foreign to the semi-improvisational oral tradition.

Different priorities are expressed in Johannes Hadlaub's poem, "Wa vunde man sament so manig liet" (Where does one find gathered so many songs), written in praise of the Manesse household for the compilational activity that culminated in the production of the great *Manessische Liederhandschrift.*[9] Hadlaub does certainly conceive of German lyric as something to be found in books, commenting that nowhere else can one find "sament so manig liet / . . . als in zúrich an buochen stat (gathered together so many songs . . . as are in the books in Zurich [vv. 1, 3]). The Manesse family's compilational activity is a mark of honor (*ere*). The latter point is crucial for Hadlaub, for whom songs are important as

9. I cite from Killy ed., *Epochen der deutschen Lyrik*, vol. 1, p. 483.

reflections of social ideals. Song is "ein so gar edles gút" (a good thing, so very noble [v. 26]), which promotes noble sentiments and provides a medium for the praise of ladies. Hadlaub attributes the Manesse family's compilational activity to a desire to preserve these social ideals in the powerful form of song. In his eyes, the artistic function of the lyric anthology is more social than scholarly; rather than a learned compendium of German poetic compositions, it presents a composite picture of aristocratic ideals.

We could find analogues for either of these statements in the French texts analyzed in the foregoing chapters. Hadlaub's attitude toward lyricism might be compared, for example, with that expressed in Jean Renart's *Roman de la rose,* while Bernart's writerly preoccupations call to mind Machaut or Froissart. A more detailed study of such statements, however, might reveal distinct attitudes toward vernacular writing and lyric compilation characteristic of each literary tradition.

A second line of inquiry, equally important, is the study of authors' statements about their own poetic and compilational activity. The study of the French tradition has shown that such statements are often to be found in first-person narratives with lyric insertions. Although this literary form was particularly popular in France, the Italian and German traditions include some important examples: Dante's *Vita nuova,* written in the 1290s; Ulrich von Lichtenstein's *Frauendienst,* composed about 1250; and the anonymous *Minneburg,* composed in the mid-fourteenth century.

Narrated entirely in the first person, *Frauendienst* (Service of ladies), purportedly recounts Ulrich's amorous adventures from his earliest youth. It contains a large number of lyric poems composed by the narrator-protagonist, expressing his joy or sorrow in love. But although Ulrich may have taken pride in his ability to compose lyric and narrative verse, he was a knight and not a professional poet. Indeed, he claims to be illiterate, needing a servant to read aloud the letters he receives from his lady and to transcribe whatever he wishes to send her. Rather than serving to define a poetic career, the songs of *Frauendienst* chronicle a series of conventional roles within court society and enunciate the values of the aristocratic lover. In this respect we can say that the role of minnesinger is merely another of the various literary identities—along with those of the Green Knight, Venus, and King Arthur—donned by Ulrich's protagonist, a young man with a penchant for costumery and pageant.

Ulrich does make certain statements concerning the genesis or reception of his songs, and these tend to involve the songs as expressions of social values and their value as entertainment: they raise the spirits of the listeners and provide the ideal setting for love service. Even his discussion of the dawn song, the most extended piece of poetic commentary in *Frauendienst*, revolves around an issue of social propriety. Ulrich decides that the traditional dawn setup, in which the lovers are warned of the approaching dawn by the watchman, implies a wholly unacceptable exposure of the love life of noble ladies to members of the lower class, and he vows to compose his dawn song in different terms.

The *Vita nuova* of Dante, on the other hand, is the explicit presentation of a poetic career that evolves through distinct stylistic phases. Certainly, Dante's protagonist writes all his poetry in honor of Beatrice. But she herself is markedly different from Ulrich's capricious and at times morally wayward ladies, so the activity of serving her poetically takes on a mystical dimension wholly absent from Ulrich's account. In Dante's hands, poetic composition as love service is transposed to the new level of visionary experience, and the *Vita nuova* outlines the stages by which he develops a poetic language capable of expressing such an experience. Beyond this, the *Vita nuova* offers a kind of manifesto for vernacular poetry. Dante stresses the importance of composing in the vernacular and justifies his use of rhetorical figures on the grounds that vernacular poets are entitled to the same poetic license as Latin authors. The *Vita nuova* was surely influenced by the existence of Italian and Provençal lyric collections, and it represents a synthesis of the roles of compiler, commentator, and poet.[10] Although Dante's overall poetics differs in many ways from the French tradition, his treatment of the narrative with lyric insertions as the record of a poetic career, his writerly concept of himself as author of a book, and his vision of a continuous written tradition linking Latin and vernacular poets, are comparable to the attitudes we have seen in late thirteenth- and fourteenth-century French poets.

Several variables need to be kept in mind in the comparative study of poet-compilers. Among them the social class of the poet or compiler is crucial. Hadlaub, after all, refers to the aristocratic patron of a songbook, whereas Bernart Amoros speaks as a scribe. Similarly, Ulrich's aristocratic standing distinguishes him from Dante. In contrast to Ulrich, the anonymous author of the *Minneburg*, who does not seem to have been an aristocrat, manifests a greater interest in the poetic implications of juxtaposing different voices and different dictions. He creates an anthology of allegorical types, much of which is glossed in the course of the frame narrative by a Master of the Seven Liberal Arts whom the narrator-protagonist has summoned for that purpose. In the variety of poetic types that it presents, as well as in its alternation between narrative and nonmusical lyric discourse, the *Minneburg* could be compared to the *Dit de la panthère d'amours*.

10. For a discussion of the influence of troubadour chansonniers on the *Vita nuova*, see Moleta, "*Vita Nuova* as a Lyric Narrative."

As a lyric collection, *Frauendienst* can be compared to the other two single-author compilations of Middle High German lyric known today, those produced by Hugo von Montfort and Oswald von Wolkenstein in the early fifteenth century. All three are due to aristocratic poets and no doubt reflect motives different from those of "professional" poets. Although the protagonist of *Frauendienst* undergoes various disillusionments, culminating in the abandonment of his first lady and the selection of a second one, there is no evidence that he has changed his attitude toward the values expressed in his songs or toward his own earlier poetic or amorous exploits. Hugo's collection of songs, arranged in chronological order, is marked by a rhythm of recurring penance followed by a return to love poetry; in one song, Hugo comments that he has compiled his works into a book that reflects his changing fortunes. But this vacillation between worldly love and renunciation is not elevated to a poetic principle or used to inform an all-embracing system of metaphoric and mythological imagery, as in Petrarch's *Rime sparse;* we are given simply to understand that Hugo writes happy poems when he is happy and sad poems when he is sad. Oswald's songs, finally, are arranged in groups according to their common melodies: a purely formal ordering principle. The poems have a strong autobiographical cast, no doubt part fiction and part fact, and present a vivid impression of their author-protagonist as knight, traveler, and husband. In the Innsbruck manuscript, dated 1432, a detailed full-page portrait rounds out the picture of this poet-knight. But for all their interest as commentaries on fifteenth-century life, and their frequent playfulness and color, these poems, too, cannot be said to be informed by any systematically developed poetics of lyrical writing and compilation.

The anthologies produced by these three poets are probably analogous to the compilation assumed to have been made by Thibaut de Navarre and the later one composed by Charles d'Orléans. In each case an aristocratic poet, wealthy enough to pay the costs of making a book, decided to preserve his works. This gesture could reflect various motives. It might be the fantasy of seeing oneself as a literary hero, an exemplary lover or knight, or even a comic figure, depending on the bent of the individual author. It could be a statement of pride in poetic facility, or in the social skills of serving ladies and discoursing with eloquence and wit. It could simply be a desire to preserve a portrait of oneself for posterity. But it is unlikely that the motivations and preoccupations of the aristocratic poet are the same as those of his nonnoble counterpart, for whom the very stance of the courtly lover already represents a fiction of a very different sort and for whom the act of producing verses and books takes place in a different context.

A second variable in literary compilation is that of genre. If German lyric does not seem to offer many analogues to Old French lyrico-narrative poetics, perhaps we must look elsewhere for signs of the poet-compiler. The compilation of lyric poetry is only one part of the overall picture. Among the earliest single-author compilations in French, after all, are the collections of dits produced by such poets as Baudouin de Condé and Watriquet de Couvin. A similar phenomenon obtains in the German tradition of *Reden* or *Spruchdichtung*, which produced some of the earliest German single-author anthologies: those of Reinmar von Zweter (ca. 1240), Heinrich der Teichner (mid-fourteenth century), and his younger contemporary Peter Suchenwirt. It would be most interesting to examine the role that these anthologies played as examples of vernacular books, the extent to which the concept of poet in German-language regions was influenced by the persona of the *Reimsprecher*, and the ways in which the place of the *Reden* in the German tradition was comparable to the role of the dit in French literature. Again, the *Minneburg*, where the lyric insertions are not songs but *Minnereden* (the formal equivalent of the dit d'amour), provides an important point of comparison not only to the *Panthère* but also to the works of Machaut and Froissart.[11] Like its French counterparts, the *Minneburg* exemplifies the coming together of lyric and didactic poetics; the blend of learned and lyrical authority; the creation of an author figure who subsumes narrator, compiler, lyric poet, and protagonist.

In spite of the differences that characterize the various European literary traditions, the image of the vernacular poet as writer and compiler, and the general movement from song to book, clearly were widespread phenomena during the later Middle Ages. Naturally songs continued to be performed, but the importance of writing as the medium of vernacular poetic creation and audience consumption increased greatly, affecting vernacular poetics and book format. Can it be any accident that the century following the deaths of Machaut and Petrarch saw the invention of the printing press? A major technological innovation cannot be attributed to any one cultural trend; a complex of social, economic, and cultural factors lies behind it. Yet it cannot be mere coincidence that the printing press arrived at a moment when the literary world was so perfectly ready for it.

11. On the *Minnereden* and its manuscript tradition, see Glier.

# Appendix A

# The Rubrication of Guillaume de Lorris in MS Bibl. Nat. fr. 378

*L'aucteur*
Lors a de s'aumosniere traité (vv. 1997–99)
*Li diex d'amours*
A ceste, fest il, fermeré . . . (vv. 2000–5)
*Ci parole li amans*
Lors la me toucha au costé . . . (vv. 2006–20)
*Li diex d'amours*
Amours respont, Or ne t'esmaie . . . (vv. 2021–40)
*Li auctours*
Sire, fis je, pour dieu merci . . . (vv. 2041–48)
*Li diex d'amours*
Amours respont, Tu dis molt bien . . . (vv. 2049–54)
*Li amans*
Li diex d'amours lors m'encharja . . . (vv. 2055–74)
*Ci commencent les commandemenz / au dieu d'amours*
Vilonnie, premierement . . . (vv. 2074a–2566)

20v     *Cist parole li amans*
Quant Amours m'ot ce commandé . . . (vv. 2567–82)
*Li diex d'amours*
Biaus amis, par l'ame mon pere . . . (vv. 2583–2748)

21     *Ci se parti li diex d'amours / de l'amant qui se doulouse / tant que Bel Acueill l'apela*
Tout maintenant qu'Amours m'ot . . . (vv. 2749–80)
*Cist devise comment Bel Acueill vint / a l'amant et li fist passer la haie*
Biaus amis douz, se il vous plest . . . (vv. 2781–90)
*Ci parole li amans a Bel Acueill*
Sire, fis je a Bel Acueill . . . (vv. 2791–2878)

21v     *Bel Acueill*
Dites, fist il, vostre vouloir . . . (vv. 2879–81)
*Li amans*
Lors li ai dit, Sachiez, biaus sire . . . (vv. 2882–90)
*Ci parole li aucteurs*
Lors s'est Bel Acueill esfreez . . . (v. 2891)
*Bel Acueill*
Frere, vous beez . . . (vv. 2892–2903)
*Li amans*
A tant saut Dangiers li vilains . . . (vv. 2904–9)
*Ci parole Dangiers*
Bel Acueill, pour coi amcnez . . . (vv. 2910–26)
*Ci parole li amans*
N'osai illueques remanoir . . . (vv. 2927–81)
*Ci parole Raisons*
Biaus amis, folie et enfance . . . (vv. 2982–3056)

22     *Li amans*
Quant j'oÿ cel chastiement . . . (vv. 3057–3109)
*Amis*
Compains, or soiez . . . (vv. 3109–30)
*Li amans*

Qu'il m'a auques reconforté . . . (vv. 3131–77)
*Ci respont Dangiers*
Ta requeste point ne me grieve . . . (vv. 3178–86)
*Li amans*
Ainsi m'ostroia ma requeste . . . (vv. 3187–90)

22v  *Amis*
Or va, fist il, bien vostre afaire . . . (vv. 3191–3200)
*Li amans*
Molt me conforta doucement . . . (vv. 3201–38)
*Ci devise comment Franchise / et Pitiez vindrent a Dangier / et l'apaisierent*
La parole a premiere prise . . . (vv. 3239–68)
*Cist parole Pitiez*
Pitiez respont, C'est verité . . . (vv. 3269–3300)
*Li aucteurs*
Lors ne puet plus Dangier durer . . . (vv. 3301–2)
*Dangiers*
Dames, dist il . . . (vv. 3303–8)
*Li aucteurs*
Lors est a Bel Acueill alee . . . (vv. 3309–11)
*Franchise*
Trop vous estes de cel amant . . . (vv. 3312–22)
*Bel Acueill*
Je ferai ce que vous voudroiz . . . (vv. 3323–25)
*Li amans*
Lors le m'a Franchise envoié . . . (vv. 3326–76)

23  *Bel Acueill*
Amis, fait il, se diex m'aïst . . . (vv. 3377–90)
*Li amans*
Quant je l'oÿ ainsi respondre . . . (vv. 3391–3423)
*Ci parole Venus a Bel Acueill / pour l'amant*
Pour coi vous faites vous, biaus sire . . . (vv. 3424–54)
*Li amans*
Bel Acueill qui senti l'aier . . . (vv. 3455–3516)

23v  *Cist parole Jalousie*
Lors l'a par parole assailli . . . (vv. 3517–34)
*Li amans parole*
Bel Acueill ne sot que respondre . . . (vv. 3535–49)
*Cist parole Honte*
Pour Dieu, Dame, ne creez pas . . . (vv. 3550–82)
*Jalousie*
Honte, Honte, fait Jalousie . . . (vv. 3583–3619)
*Li aucteur*
A cest mot vint Paours tramblant . . . (vv. 3620–30)
*Ci parole Paours a Honte*
Honte, fait ele, molt me poise . . . (vv. 3631–50)
*Comment Honte et Paours vindrent / a Dangier et l'esveillierent*
A cest conseill se sont tenues . . . (vv. 3651–59)
*Cist parle Honte*

24        Comment dormez vous a ceste eure . . . (vv. 3660–93)
*Li aucteurs*
Lors aprés parle Paours. (v. 3694)
*Ci parole Paours a Dangier*
Certes, Dangier, molt me merveill . . . (vv. 3695–3712)
*Li aucteur*
Lors lieve li vilains la huce . . . (vv. 3713–17)
*Dangiers*
Bien puis or, dist il, forsener . . . (vv. 3718–36)
*Comment li amans se complaint*
Lors s'est Dangiers en piez dreciez . . . (vv. 3737–3848)

24v    *Ci devise de la tour Jalousie / ou Bel Acueill fu mis en prison*
Jalousie a garnison mise . . . (vv. 3849–4028)

25      *Ci endroit fina maistre Guillaume de Loriz cest Roumanz. Que plus n'en fist. Ou pour ce qu'il ne vost; Ou pour ce qu'il ne pot. Et pour ce que la matere enbelissoit a plusors, il plot a Maistre Jehan Chopinel de Meun a parfaire le livre. Et a ensivre la matere. Et commence en tele maniere comme vous porroiz oïr ci aprés.*
(Jean's poem follows.)

# Table of Miniatures in Selected Texts by Machaut, MSS Bibl. Nat. fr. 1584 and 1586

No comprehensive study of the illumination of Machaut manuscripts has been published. To my knowledge the only such study is the doctoral dissertation of Kumiko Maekawa, "Recherches iconographiques sur les manuscrits des poésies de Guillaume de Machaut: Les Décorations des premiers recueils personnels." A concordance of miniatures appears in Lawrence Earp's dissertation, "Scribal Practice, Manuscript Production and the Transmission of Music in Late Medieval France: The Manuscripts of Guillaume de Machaut."

## Bibl. Nat. fr. 1586

### Remede de Fortune

| Line | | Folio |
|------|---|-------|
| 1 | L'Amant, accompanied by his valet, stands to one side and watches his lady; she stands, with three attendants, in front of her castle, and points at him. The lady wears a pink hat, which she wears in every miniature except one (fol. 56v). | 23 |
| 135 | L'Amant talks to the God of Love. | 24 |
| 431 | L'Amant sits among trees, writing on a long scroll (lay). | 26 |
| 693 | L'Amant, outdoors, reads lay from a long scroll to his lady. People seated on the ground in the background. | 28v |
| 921 | *Top:* L'Amant, looking woebegone, writes musical notes on a scroll in a walled garden. | |
| | *Bottom:* Fortune and her wheel (complainte). | 30v |
| 1001 | Nebuchadnezzar asleep in bed; statue with gold head, black torso, and brown feet in background. | 31v |
| 1193 | L'Amant, seated, points accusingly at Lady Fortune. | 32v |

| 1273 | L'Amant watches his lady disappear, with attendants, into her castle. | 33v |
| 1401 | L'Amant sits on the ground, looking miserable. | 34v |
| 1481 | Hope, wearing her fluttering scarf, holds l'Amant's hand; he appears to sleep. (Hope always wears this scarf.) | 35 |
| 1671 | Hope addresses l'Amant. | 36v |
| 1821 | Hope addresses l'Amant. | 37v |
| 1881 | L'Amant and Hope sit on either side of a tree, from which hangs a blue shield, decorated with a red heart pierced by an arrow and white tear drops. | 38 |
| 1997 | Hope sings from a scroll; l'Amant sleeps (chanson royal). | 38v |
| 2039 | Hope places a ring on l'Amant's finger. | 39v |
| 2148 | Hope addresses l'Amant. | 40v |
| 2287 | L'Amant addresses Hope. | 41v |
| 2353 | L'Amant bows to Hope. | 42 |
| 2403 | Hope addresses l'Amant. | 42v |
| 2522 | L'Amant addresses Hope. | 43 |
| 2685 | Hope addresses l'Amant. | 44v |
| 2857 | Hope holds up a scroll (balladelle). | 45v |
| 2893 | L'Amant, holding scroll, watches Hope leave. | 46v |
| 3013 | L'Amant sits on the ground, writing on a scroll (ballade). | 47v |
| 3077 | Hope leads l'Amant toward the castle. | 48 |
| 3181 | With Hope in the distance, l'Amant writes on a scroll (prière). | 49 |
| 3451 | Carol (circle dance) under trees, near fountain, beside castle. L'Amant, standing next to his lady, sings; three more people watch from the side (virelay). | 51 |
| 3573 | L'Amant and his lady talk outside castle, surrounded by other couples. | 52 |
| 3729 | L'Amant and his lady talk privately, accompanied only by her attendant. | 53v |
| 3847 | L'Amant kneels before his lady while other ladies watch. | 54 |
| 3947 | Banquet scene. L'Amant, sporting a pink hat like his lady's, looks at her from across the room. | 55 |
| 4077 | As Hope watches over them, l'Amant and his lady exchange rings. | 56 |
| 4107 | At the scene of a tournament, l'Amant, scroll in hand, rides off, looking back toward the audience of ladies, None wears a pink hat (rondeau). | 56v |
| 4217 | L'Amant and his lady talk. | 58 |

*Lays*

| Lady, wearing fluttering scarf, gestures toward man, who sits on the ground and writes on a scroll ("Loyauté que point ne delay"). | 165 |
| Man stands amid flowers ("J'aim la flour"). | 168v |
| Man, seated on ground, writes on scroll ("Pour ce qu'on puist miex retraire"). | 170 |

## Bibl. Nat. fr. 1584

### Remede de Fortune

### Fonteinne amoureuse: Prologue and "Complainte a l'amant"

| 55 | Narrator (tonsured) asleep in bed. | 154 |
| 235 | Narrator writes while l'Amant speaks in a different room. | 155v |
| 539 | L'Amant sits with clasped hands, bowed head. | 157v |
| 571 | Ceyx drowned; Alcyone prays to Juno. | 157v |
| 587 | Iris hovering over Juno, who lies in bed. | 158 |
| 603 | Iris hovering over god of sleep, who sleeps in bed. | 158 |
| 619 | God of sleep, or Morpheus, sits sleepily on bed. | 158 |
| 651 | Morpheus comes to sleeping Alcyone. | 158v |
| 667 | Ceyx and Alcyone stand next to sea; two birds fly overhead. | 158v |
| 811 | L'Amant places wreath on head of god of sleep (Morpheus), who sits sleeping on the bed. | 159v |

Subsequent miniatures illustrate the meeting of the narrator and l'Amant, the fountain, the judgment of Paris, the appearance of the lady, and l'Amant's final departure by boat.

# Appendix C

# Excerpt from an Unedited Volume of *Le Roman de Perceforest*, MS Bibl. Nat. fr. 346

[The knight Lyonnel has, through the treachery of an enemy knight, lost the trophies that would have enabled him to win his beloved; he has also lost contact with the lady herself, a fairy. Riding along aimlessly in the wilderness, he engages in a lengthy lament.]

[fol. 234] ". . . Et combien que soye destourbé oultre mesure, sy feray je ung lay par quoy en aucun temps sçaront les amoureus ma mescheance." Adont se teut l'espace de .iiii. lieucs anglesches sans soy mouvoir ne mot dire. Mais aprés commença son lay en telle maniere qui s'ensuyt.

[The lay recounts Lyonnel's victories over a lion, a serpent, and a giant, his subsequent loss of the trophies of these battles, and his great sorrow. See Lods ed., *Les Pièces lyriques du roman de Perceforest.*

[fol. 235v] Quant Lyonnel eut son lay parfurny ainsi que cy dessus avez oÿ, il leva la teste et dist tout en hault, "Or vouldroie je que tous amans par amours sceussent mon lay. Sy savoient partie de mon meschief. Car il ne porroit estre qu'ilz n'eussent aucune pitié de moy; si prieroient pour moy." Tandiz qu'il disoit ces parolles, il oyt ung homme toussir par derriere luy. Lors tourna son viaire par devers luy et veyt que c'estoit ainsi comme il luy fut advis ung menestrel de la harpe. Sy luy demanda, "Sire varlet, estez vous menestrel?"—"Sire, dist il, oÿl." Adont luy demanda Lyonnel dont il venoit si prez de luy et il luy dist qu'il s'en aloit vers Bretaigne pour estre a la feste du Roy Percheforest. Mais quant il s'embaty sur luy et il le veyt ainsi embronchié, il s'aresta pour veoir a quelle fin il estoit en tel point. —"Or vous ay, sire, oÿ dire que vous avez fait ung lay que vous vouldriez que tous amans sceussent. Par ma foy se vous le me vouliez aprendre, je le joueroie encores en maint lieu."

"Varlet, dist Lyonnel, je le te diray voulentiers. Mais il n'a point de chant. Et se tu luy vouloies faire ung chant piteux selon le dit, je t'en sçaroie bon gré." —"Par ma foy, sire, [fol. 236] dist le menestrel, je le

347

feray volentiers." Adont luy dist Lyonnel le lay tant de fois qu'il le sceut par coeur. Aprés ce ala attaindre le menestrel sa harpe et ala en pou d'heure faire dessus ung chant si piteux que quant Lyonnel luy oyt harper et chanter si piteusement le coeur luy fondy, tout en larmes, et fut si destraint qu'il ne se peult soustenir. Ainçois s'embroncha sur ses mains une grant piece, de la grant douleur qu'il sentoit en son coeur. Et quant le menestrel le veyt en tel point, il en eut pitié et dist, "Ha! sire chevalier, confortez vous et ne menez tel dueil. Car il n'affiert pas a chevalier de la renommee dont vous estes selon ce que vostre lay dist. Car vous estes celluy qui a mis a mort le lyon et le serpent et le gueant aux cheveulx dorez. Mais cueilliez coeur et cerchiez tant que vous sachiez qui vous a ainsi desnué."

Quant Lyonnel entendy le menestrel, il luy dist, "Par ma foy, ainsi le feray que tu m'as conseillié." Lors monta et prist congié a luy et se mist au chemin et le menestrel demoura tout seul. Si prist sa harpe et la mist en son estuy, et puis se mist au chemin et ala tant qu'il se trouva au pilier Estonné. Lors s'assist emprés et prist sa harpe, et commença a harper le dit si hault et si bien que c'estoit une pitié a oÿr. Mais quant il eut harpé, il ne garda l'heure qu'ils s'embatirent sur luy .iii. jeunes damoiselles vestues de blanches vestures si noblement que ce sambloient deesses ou faees. Adont dist l'une des damoiselles au menestrel, "Dy moy, par amours, qui fist ce lay et qui te l'apprist?" —"Dame, dist il, il le m'aprist celluy qui le fist. Et celluy qui le fist est le chevalier a qui le fait est advenu que le lay devise." —"Par ta foy, dist la damoiselle, scez tu ou le chevalier est?" —"Par ma foy, dame, dist il, je ne sçay fors tant qu'il va querant confort de sa douleur." —"Sire menestrel, dist la damoiselle, il convient que vous venez avecques nous. Sy nous aprendrez le lay." —"Dame, [fol. 236v] dist il, je le feray voulentiers." Mais ore se taist l'ystoire a parler d'eulx.

[After an interlude focusing on other characters in the romance, the story line returns to the minstrel, whom the three maidens lead before the king.]

[fol. 242v] Quant le menestrel eut joué devant le roy, il s'en vint seoir par devers les pucelles. Car Blanche desiroit moult de sçavoir le lay de la complainte. Sy fist tant qu'elle le sceut de point en point. Cy vous dy pour certain qu'elle fut si courroucee et a tel meschief de la mesaise qu'elle sçavoit que le bon chevalier souffroit pour elle, et pour la perte qu'il avoit faicte pour le chief du gueant qu'elle ne sçavoit qu'elle peust devenir. Mais en la fin s'advisa qu'elle feroit ung lay pour resconforter le chevalier. Car autrement ne sçavoit trouver voie de luy aidier. Cy ne fina toute la nuyt de penser tant qu'elle eut finé son lay a son vouloir. Et sy tost qu'elle fut levee la matinee, elle l'aprist au menestrel et luy pria moult qu'il le jouast par tout tant que le chevalier desconforté le sceust. —"Certes, madamoiselle, dist il, je le feray. Car je ne cesseray tant que je l'auray trouvé. Mais dictes moy qui diray je qui ce lay luy envoie?" [fol.

243]—"Menestrel, dist la damoiselle, se vous trouvez le chevalier, dictes luy que la pucelle qu'il veyt baignier en l'escault l'a fait pour le resconforter. Mais hastez vous de vostre chemin, car tart m'est qu'il le sache."
—"Damoiselle, dist le menestrel, je vouldroie estre au chemin." Adont le fist la damoiselle mengier et puis le mist hors du manoir et se trouva au pilier ou les pucelles l'avoient trouvé jouant son lay. Lors se mist au chemin et erra plusieurs journees que oncques ne peult oÿr nouvelles de Lyonnel. Et sachiez que en plusieurs lieux joua le lay ou il y avoit dames et chevaliers qui le lay moult prisierent, car moult doulcement confortoit la pucelle le chevalier.

Ung jour avoit le menestrel erré en la haulte forest jusques a la nuyt, adont s'aresta au pié d'une roche et s'apensa qu'il demourroit la endroit jusques a lendemain. Quant il eut la esté assiz une grant piece, il prist sa harpe et commença a jouer plusieurs choses. Et aprés prist a jouer le lay que Blanchete avoit fait qui estoit tel.

[The lay instructs Lyonnel to seek the temple where his lost trophies are being kept for him. See Lods ed., *Pièces lyriques*.]

[fol. 244] Tandiz que le menestrel se deduisoit en chantant son lay, il y avoit assez pres de luy ung chevalier qui s'estoit tapy en [fol. 244v] une roche qui avoit oÿ chanter le lay au menestrel. Dont s'esmervelloit moult dont tel lay venoit. Lors s'apparut au menestrel dont il estoit pres et luy dist, "Sire, par amours, dictez moi qui fist ce lay que cy avez chanté si doulcement." —"Sire, dist le menestrel, je ne sçay qui vous estes, mais au dit le povez vous sçavoir puis que l'avez oÿ." —"Ha! gentil homme, dist le chevalier, je ne le demande pour nul mal, mais il semble qu'il ait esté fait aprés ung lay que je fiz n'a pas ung moys pour ung meschief qui m'estoit advenu n'a pas longtemps. Sy l'appellay le lay de la complainte."
—"Comment, sire chevalier, dist le menestrel, estes vous celluy qui feïstes le lay de la complainte?" —"Par ma foy, sire, dist il, oÿl. Ce suy je qui languiz et meurs de paour, sy que a pou ne cheÿ en desespoir de jour en jour."

"Sire, dist le menestrel, oncques ne cheÿ si bien a chevalier de lay qu'il feist comme il a fait a vous." Lors luy compta comment les .iii. pucelles l'escouterent tandiz qu'il le jouoit dessoubz le pilier Estonné, et comment elles l'emmenerent en leur manoir. Et puis luy compta comment la plus jeune des pucelles le requist qu'il luy aprist le lay. —"Et en celle nuyt mesme, la pucelle en fist ung autre et le m'aprist le lendemain et me pria que je le jouasse tant que le chevalier qui fist le lay de la complainte l'eüst oÿ pour soy resconforter. Cy m'en est bien cheü que vous m'avez trouvé le lay jouant. Et sachiez que la pucelle qui ce lay a fait est celle que vous veïstez baignier en l'escault. Et vous mande qu'elle l'a fait pour vous resconforter." —"Ha! gentil homme, dist le chevalier, je te prie que tu le vueillez jouer encore une fois tant que l'aye bien entendu." —"Sire, dist le menestrel, je le feray volentiers."

Adont commença le menestrel a jouer le lay moult piteusement. Cy devez sçavoir que tandiz qu'il le jouoit le chevalier jectoit aucunes foiz si griefs souspirs que [fol. 245] c'estoit pitié a oïr. Et sy luy filoient les larmes des yeulx aussi grosses que poix de la grant joye qu'il avoit au coeur. Mais quant le menestrel eut le lay joué le chevalier ala dire, "Certes, Sire, grandement m'avez servy a gré, et benoiste soit la pucelle qui si bien m'a resconforté par sa doulce pitié. Mais par amours me sçairiez vous mener ou elle demeure?" — "Par ma foy, sire, dist le menestrel, nennyl, car elle demeure en faerie. Mais selon le lay qu'elle a fait il fault que vous querez le temple a la franche garde. Car la recouvrerez vous vostre perte." — "Par ma foy, menestrel, dist le chevalier, vous dictes voir. Mais dictes moy, me sçairiez vous enseigner la voie?" — "Par ma foy, sire, dist il, je ne sçay."

[At this point the minstrel and the knight, finally named as Lyonnel at the end of the episode, part, and the story moves on for a time to other adventures. Eventually, Lyonnel succeeds in finding the temple described in the lay, recovers his trophies, and is reunited with Blanche.]

# BIBLIOGRAPHY OF
# WORKS CITED

## EDITIONS

Adam le Bossu. *Le Jeu de Robin et Marion suivi du Jeu du pelerin*. Ed. Ernest Langlois. Paris: Champion, 1924.

——. *The Lyric Works of Adam de la Hale*. Ed. Nigel Wilkins. Corpus Mensurabilis Musicae, 44. American Institute of Musicology, 1967.

——. *Oeuvres complètes du trouvère Adam de la Halle*. Ed. E. de Coussemaker. Paris: Durand and Pédone-Lauriel, 1872.

Adenet le Roi. *Berte aus grans piés*. Ed. Urban T. Homes, Jr. Studies in the Romance Languages and Literatures, 6. Chapel Hill: University of North Carolina, 1946.

——. *Cléomadès*. Ed. Albert Henry. 2 vols. Université Libre de Bruxelles, Travaux de la Faculté de Philosophie et Lettres, 23 and 136. Brussels: Editions de l'Université de Bruxelles, 1971.

Alard de Cambrai. *Le Livre de philosophie et de moralité*. Ed. Jean-Charles Payen. Bibliothèque Française et Romane, sér. B: Editions Critiques de Textes, 9. Paris: Klincksieck, 1970.

Alton, Johann, ed. See *Li Romans de Claris et Laris*.

Baudouin de Condé and Jean de Condé. *Dits et contes de Baudouin de Condé et de son fils Jean de Condé*. 3 vols. Ed. Auguste Scheler. Brussels: Victor Devaux, 1866–67.

Benoît de Sainte-Maure. *Le Roman de Troie*. Ed Léopold Constans. Société des Anciens Textes Français. 6 vols. Paris: Firmin Didot, 1904–12.

Bernart Amoros. *La Première Partie du chansonnier de Bernart Amoros, conservée par les MSS a, cᵃ, Fᵃ*. Ed. Edmund Stengel. Leipzig: Dieterich'sche Verlagsbuchhandlung, 1902.

Bernart de Ventadorn. *The Songs of Bernart de Ventadorn*. Ed. Stephen G. Nichols, Jr., and John A. Galm, with A. Bartlett Giametti, Roger J. Porter, Seth L. Wolitz, and Claudette M. Charbonneau. Studies in the Romance Languages and Literatures, 39. Chapel Hill: University of North Carolina Press, 1962.

*Le Bestiaire d'amour rimé.* Ed. Arvid Thordstein. Lund: Håkan Ohlssons, 1941.

*Biographies des troubadours.* Ed. Jean Boutière and A.-H. Schutz. 2d edition, revised and expanded by Jean Boutière and I.-M. Cluzel. Paris: A.-G. Nizet, 1964.

Boutière, Jean, and A.-H. Schutz, eds. See *Biographies des troubadours.*

Buchon, C., ed. *Chroniques.* See Froissart, Jean.

Châtelain de Couci. *Les Chansons attribuées au châtelain de Couci.* Ed. Alain Lerond. Paris: Presses Universitaires de France, 1964.

Chichmaref, Vladimir, ed. *Poésies lyriques.* See Machaut, Guillaume de.

Chrétien de Troyes. *Le Chevalier au lyon (Yvain).* Ed. Mario Roques. Classiques Français du Moyen Age. Paris: Champion, 1967.

——. *Le Chevalier de la charrete.* Ed. Mario Roques. Classiques Français du Moyen Age. Paris: Champion, 1971.

——. *Erec et Enide.* Ed. Mario Roques. Classiques Français du Moyen Age. Paris: Champion, 1981.

Conon de Béthune. *Chansons de Conon de Béthune.* Ed. Axel Wallensköld. Classiques Français du Moyen Age. Paris: Champion, 1921.

Constans, Léopold, ed. *Le Roman de Troie.* See Benoît de Sainte-Maure.

*Le Couronnement de Renard.* Ed. Alfred Foulet. Elliott Monographs in the Romance Languages and Literatures, 24. Princeton: Princeton University Press; Paris: Presses Universitaires de France, 1929.

Coussemaker, E. de, ed. *Oeuvres complètes du trouvère Adam de la Halle.* See Adam le Bossu.

*Le Débat sur le "Roman de la rose."* Ed. Eric Hicks. Bibliothèque du XVe Siècle, 43. Paris: Champion, 1977.

Delisle, Léopold, ed. "La Biblionomie de Richard de Fournival—Milieu du XIIIe siècle." See Richard de Fournival.

Dembowski, Peter, ed. *Le Paradis d'amour / L'Orloge amoureus.* See Froissart, Jean.

Deschamps, Eustache. *Oeuvres complètes de Eustache Deschamps.* Ed. A. Queux de Saint-Hilaire and Gaston Raynaud. 11 vols. Société des Anciens Textes Français. Paris: Firmin Didot, 1878–1903.

*Epochen der deutschen Lyrik.* Ed. Walther Killy. Vol. 1, *Von den Anfängen bis 1300.* Ed. Werner Höver and Eva Kiepe. Munich: Deutsche Taschenbuch, 1978.

Faral, Edmond, and Julia Bastin, eds. *Oeuvres complètes de Rutebeuf.* See Rutebeuf.

*Floire et Blanchefleur.* Ed. Margaret M. Pelan. Paris: Belles Lettres, 1956.

Foulet, Alfred, ed. See *Le Couronnement de Renard.*

Fourrier, Anthime, ed. *"Dits" et "débats."* See Froissart, Jean.

——. *L'Espinette amoureuse.* See Froissart, Jean.

——. *Le Joli Buisson de jonece.* See Froissart, Jean.

——. *La Prison amoureuse.* See Froissart, Jean.

Friedman, Lionel J. *Text and Iconography for Joinville's "Credo."* See Joinville, Jean de.

Froissart, Jean. *Chroniques.* Ed. C. Buchon. Vol. 3. Paris: A. Desrez, 1835.

——. *"Dits" et "débats."* Ed. Anthime Fourrier. Textes Littéraires Français. Geneva: Droz, 1979.

——. *L'Espinette amoureuse.* Ed. Anthime Fourrier. Bibliothèque Française et Romane, sér. B: Editions Critiques de Textes, 2. Paris: Klincksieck, 1972.

———. *Le Joli Buisson de jonece.* Ed. Anthime Fourrier. Textes Littéraires Français. Geneva: Droz, 1975.

———. *The Lyric Poems of Jehan Froissart: A Critical Edition.* Ed. Rob Roy McGregor, Jr. Studies in the Romance Languages and Literatures, 143. Chapel Hill: University of North Carolina, Department of Romance Languages, 1975.

———. *Le Paradis d'amour / L'Orloge amoureus.* Ed. Peter Dembowski. Textes Littéraires Français. Geneva: Droz, 1986.

———. *La Prison amoureuse.* Ed. Anthime Fourrier. Bibliothèque Française et Romane, sér. B: Editions Critiques de Textes, 13. Paris: Klincksieck, 1974.

Gautier de Coinci. *Les Miracles de Nostre Dame.* Ed. Frederic Koenig. 4 vols. Geneva: Droz; Lille: Giard, 1955–70.

Guillaume de Lorris and Jean de Meun. *Le Roman de la rose.* Ed. Félix Lecoy. Classiques Français du Moyen Age. 3 vols. Paris: Champion, 1973–75.

Guillaume le Clerc. *Le Bestiaire.* Ed. Robert Reinsch. Leipzig: Fues's Verlag (R. Reisland), 1890.

Henry, Albert, ed. *Cléomadès.* See Adenet le Roi.

Hicks, Eric, ed. See *Le Débat sur le "Roman de la rose."*

Hoepffner, Ernest, ed. *Oeuvres de Guillaume de Machaut.* See Machaut, Guillaume de.

Holden, A. J., ed. *Le Roman de Rou.* See Wace.

Holmes, Urban T., Jr., ed. *Berte aus grans piés.* See Adenet le Roi.

Jacquemart Giélée. *Renart le nouvel.* Ed. H. Roussel. Paris: Picard, 1961.

Jakemes. *Le Roman du castelain de Couci et de la dame de Fayel.* Ed. John E. Matzke and Maurice Delbouille. Paris: Société des Anciens Textes Français, 1936.

Jean de Condé. See Baudouin de Condé and Jean de Condé.

Joinville, Jean de. *Text and Iconography for Joinville's "Credo."* Ed. Lionel J. Friedman. Publications of the Mediaeval Academy of America, 68. Cambridge: Mediaeval Academy of America, 1958.

Jordan, Leo, ed. "Peros von Neele's gereimte Inhaltsangabe zu einem Sammelcodex." See Peros de Neele.

Killy, Walther, ed. See *Epochen der deutschen Lyrik.*

Koenig, Frederic, ed. *Les Miracles de Nostre Dame.* See Gautier de Coinci.

Langlois, Ernest, ed. *Le Jeu de Robin et Marion suivi du Jeu du pelerin.* See Adam le Bossu.

*Lapidaires français des XIIe, XIIIe, et XIVe siècles.* Ed. Léopold Pannier. Bibliothèque de l'Ecole des Hautes Etudes, 52. Paris: F. Vieweg, 1882.

Lecoy, Félix, ed. *Le Roman de la rose.* See Guillaume de Lorris and Jean de Meun.

———. *Le Roman de la rose ou de Guillaume de Dole.* See Renart, Jean.

Lepage, Yvan G., ed. *L'Oeuvre lyrique de Richard de Fournival.* See Richard de Fournival.

Lerond, Alain, ed. *Les Chansons attribuées au châtelain de Couci.* See Châtelain de Couci.

Lods, Jeanne, ed. *Les Pièces lyriques du "Roman de Perceforest."* Publications Romanes et Françaises, 36. Geneva: Droz, and Lille: Giard, 1953.

Ludwig, Friedrich, ed. *Musikalische Werke.* See Machaut, Guillaume de.

McGregor, Rob Roy, Jr., ed. *The Lyric Poems of Jehan Froissart: A Critical Edition.* See Froissart, Jean.

Machaut, Guillaume de. "Le Dit de la harpe." Ed. Karl Young. In *Essays in Honor of Albert Feuillerat*, 1–20. Ed. Henri M. Peyre. New Haven: Yale University Press, 1943.

——. *Le Livre du voir dit.* Ed. Paulin Paris. Paris: Société des Bibliophiles François, 1975.

——. *Musikalische Werke.* Ed. Friedrich Ludwig. Publikationen älteren Musik. 2 vols. Leipzig: Breitkopf and Härtel, 1926–29.

——. *Oeuvres de Guillaume de Machaut.* Ed. Ernest Hoepffner. 3 vols. Société des Anciens Textes Français. Paris: Firmin Didot, 1908–21.

——. *Poésies lyriques.* Ed. Vladimir Chichmaref. Paris: Champion, 1909.

Marchello-Nizia, Christiane, ed. *Le Roman de la poire.* See Tibaut.

Marie de France. *Die Fabeln.* Ed. Karl Warnke. Bibliotheca Normannica, 6. Halle: Max Niemeyer, 1898.

——. *Fables d'Ysopet.* See Marie de France. *Die Fabeln.*

——. *Les Lais de Marie de France.* Ed. Jean Rychner. Classiques Français du Moyen Age. Paris: Champion, 1973.

Nichols, Stephen G., Jr., et al., eds. *The Songs of Bernart de Ventadorn.* See Bernart de Ventadorn.

Nicole de Margival. *Le Dit de la panthère d'amours.* Ed. Henry A. Todd. Société des Anciens Textes Français. Paris: Firmin Didot, 1883.

Pannier, Léopold, ed. See *Lapidaires français des XIIe, XIIIe, et XIVe siècles.*

Paris, Paulin, ed. *Le Livre du voir dit.* See Machaut, Guillaume de.

Payen, Jean-Charles, ed. *Le Livre de philosophie et de moralité.* See Alard de Cambrai.

Pelan, Margaret M., ed. See *Floire et Blanchefleur.*

Peros de Neele. "Peros von Neele's gereimte Inhaltsangabe zu einem Sammelcodex." Ed. Leo Jordan. *Romanische Forschungen* 16 (1904): 735–55.

Reinsch, Robert, ed. *Le Bestiaire.* See Guillaume le Clerc.

Renart, Jean. *Le Roman de la rose ou de Guillaume de Dole.* Ed. Félix Lecoy. Classiques Français du Moyen Age. Paris: Champion, 1970.

René d'Anjou. *Le Livre du cuer d'amours espris.* Ed. Susan Wharton. Editions 10–18, 1385. Paris: Union Générale d'Editions, 1980.

Richard de Fournival. *Li Bestiaires d'amours di Maistre Richart de Fornival e Li Response du Bestiaire.* Ed. Cesare Segre. Milan: Riccardo Ricciardi, 1957.

——. "La Biblionomie de Richard de Fournival—Milieu du XIIIe siècle." Ed. Léopold Delisle. *Le Cabinet des Manuscrits de la Bibliothèque Nationale* 2 (1874): 518–35.

——"Li Commens d'amours de Richard de Fournival (?)." Ed. Antoinette Saly. *Travaux de Linguistique et de Littérature* 10 (1977): 21–55.

——. *L'Oeuvre lyrique de Richard de Fournival.* Ed. Yvan G. Lepage. Ottawa Mediaeval Texts and Studies, 7. Ottawa: University of Ottawa, 1981.

——. *La Poissance d'amours dello pseudo-Richard de Fournival.* Ed. Gian Battista Speroni. Pubblicazioni della Facoltà di Lettere e Filosofia dell'Università di Pavia, 21. Florence: La Nuova Italia Editrice, 1975.

*Le Roman d'Eneas.* Ed. J.-J. Salverda de Grave. Classiques Français du Moyen Age. 2 vols. Paris: Champion, 1964–68.

*Le Roman de Perceforest: Première partie.* Ed. Jane H. M. Taylor. Textes Littéraires Français. Geneva: Droz, 1979.

*Li Romans de Claris et Laris.* Ed. Johann Alton. Bibliothek des litterarischen Vereins, 169. Tübingen: Laupp, 1884.

Roques, Mario, ed. *Le Chevalier au lyon (Yvain)*. See Chrétien de Troyes.

——. *Le Chevalier de la charrete*. See Chrétien de Troyes.

——. *Erec et Enide*. See Chrétien de Troyes.

Roussel, H., ed. *Renart le nouvel*. See Jacquemart Giélée.

Rutebeuf. *Oeuvres complètes de Rutebeuf*. Ed. Edmond Faral and Julia Bastin. 2 vols. Paris: Picard, 1959.

Rychner, Jean, ed. *Les Lais de Marie de France*. See Marie de France.

Saint-Hilaire, A. Queux de, and Gaston Raynaud, eds. *Oeuvres complètes de Eustache Deschamps*. See Eustache Deschamps.

Salverda de Grave, J.-J., ed. See *Le Roman d'Eneas*.

Saly, Antoinette, ed. "Li Commens d'amours de Richard de Fournival(?)." See Richard de Fournival.

Scheler, Auguste, ed. *Dits de Watriquet de Couvin*. See Watriquet de Couvin.

——. *Dits et contes de Baudouin de Condé et de son fils Jean de Condé*. See Baudouin de Condé and Jean de Condé.

Segre, Cesare, ed. *Li Bestiaires d'amours di Maistre Richart de Fornival e Li Response du Bestiaire*. See Richard de Fournival.

Speroni, Gian Battista, ed. *La Poissance d'amours dello pseudo-Richard de Fournival*. See Richard de Fournival.

Stengel, E., ed. *La première partie du chansonnier de Bernart Amoros*. See Bernart Amoros.

Taylor, Jane H. M., ed. See *Le Roman de Perceforest: première partie*.

Thordstein, Arvid, ed. See *Le Bestiaire d'amour rimé*.

Thibaut de Champagne. *Les Chansons de Thibaut de Champagne, roi de Navarre*. Ed. Axel Wallensköld. Société des Anciens Textes Français. Paris: Champion, 1925.

Thibaut de Navarre. See Thibaut de Champagne.

Tibaut. *Le Roman de la poire*. Ed. Christiane Marchello-Nizia. Société des Anciens Textes Français. Paris: Picard, 1984.

Todd, Henry A., ed. *Le Dit de la panthère d'amours*. See Nicole de Margival.

Wace. *Le Roman de Rou*. Ed. A. J. Holden. 3 vols. Société des Anciens Textes Français. Paris: Picard, 1970–72.

Wallensköld, Axel. *Les Chansons de Conon de Béthune*. See Conon de Béthune.

——. *Les Chansons de Thibaut de Champagne, roi de Navarre*. See Thibaut de Champagne.

Warnke, Karl, ed. *Die Fabeln*. See Marie de France.

Watriquet de Couvin. *Dits de Watriquet de Couvin*. Ed. Auguste Scheler. Collection des Chroniques et Trouvères Belges. Brussels: Victor Devaux, 1868.

Wharton, Susan, ed. *Le Livre du cuer d'amours espris*. See René d'Anjou.

Wilkins, Nigel, ed. *The Lyric Works of Adam de la Hale*. See Adam le Bossu.

Young, Karl, ed. "Le Dit de la harpe." See Machaut, Guillaume de.

## FACSIMILE EDITIONS

Aubry, Pierre, and Alfred Jeanroy, eds. *Le Chansonnier de l'Arsenal: Reproduction phototypique du manuscrit 5198 de la Bibl. de l'Arsenal*. Publications de la Société Internationale de Musique. Paris: Geuther, 1909.

Beck, Jean, ed. *Les Chansonniers des troubadours et des trouvères, publiés en facsimilé et transcrits en notation moderne*. Vol. 1, *Reproduction phototypique du chansonnier*

*Cangé* (Paris, *Bibliothèque Nationale, MS français no. 846).* Corpus Cantilenarum Medii Aevi, ser. 1, no. 1. Paris: Champion, and Philadelphia: University of Pennsylvania Press, 1927.

Faral, Edmond, ed. *Le Manuscrit 19152 du Fonds français de la Bibliothèque Nationale.* Paris: Droz, 1934.

Jeanroy, Alfred, ed. *Le Chansonnier d'Arras.* Paris: Société des Anciens Textes Français, 1925.

Meyer, Paul, and Gaston Raynaud. *Le Chansonnier français de Saint-Germain-des-Près.* Société des Anciens Textes Français. Paris: Firmin Didot, 1892.

Omont, Henri, ed. *Fabliaux, dits et contes en vers français du XIIIe siècle: Facsimilé du manuscrit français 837 de la Bibl. Nat.* Paris: Ernest Leroux, 1932.


## HISTORY AND CRITICISM

Avril, François. "Un chef-d'oeuvre de l'enluminure sous le règne de Jean le Bon, la Bible moralisée, manuscrit français 167 de la Bibliothèque Nationale." In *Monuments et Mémoires de la Fondation Eugène Piot,* 95–125. Publications de l'Académie des Inscriptions et Belles-Lettres, 58. Paris: Presses Universitaires de France, 1972.

——. *Manuscript Painting at the Court of France: The Fourteenth Century (1310–1380).* New York: Braziller, 1978.

——. "Les Manuscrits enluminés de Guillaume de Machaut: Essai de chronologie." In *Guillaume de Machaut, poète et compositeur,* 117–33. Actes et Colloques, 23. Paris: Klincksieck, 1982.

Badel, Pierre-Yves. "Rhétorique et polémique dans les prologues de romans au Moyen Age." *Littérature* 20 (Dec. 1975): 81–94.

——. *Le "Roman de la Rose" au XIVe siècle: Etude de la réception de l'oeuvre.* Publications Romanes et Françaises, 153. Geneva: Droz, 1980.

Bartsch, Karl. "Zum Roman de la Poire." *Zeitschrift für Romanische Philologie* 5 (1881): 571–75.

Baum, Richard. *Recherches sur les oeuvres attribuées à Marie de France.* Annales Universitatis Saraviensis, Philosophische Fakultät, 9. Heidelberg: Carl Winter and Universitätsverlag, 1968.

Baumgartner, Emmanuèle. "Les Citations lyriques dans le *Roman de la Rose* de Jean Renart." *Romance Philology* 35 (1981–82): 260–66.

——. "Espace du texte, espace du manuscrit: Les manuscrits du *Lancelot-Graal.*" *Ecritures II,* 95–116. Paris: Sycomore, 1985.

Becker, Peter Jörg. *Handschriften und Frühdrucke mittelhochdeutscher Epen.* Wiesbaden: Ludwig Reichert, 1977.

Branner, Robert. *Manuscript Painting in Paris during the Reign of St. Louis: A Study of Styles.* Berkeley and Los Angeles: University of California Press, 1977.

Brownlee, Kevin. "Jean de Meun and the Limits of Romance: Genius as Re-Writer of Guillaume de Lorris." In *Romance: Generic Transformation from Chrétien de Troyes to Cervantes,* ed. Kevin Brownlee and Marina Scordilis Brownlee, 114–34. Hanover: University Press of New England, 1985.

——. "Orpheus's Song Re-sung: Jean de Meun's Reworking of *Metamorphoses,* X." *Romance Philology* 36 (1982): 201–9.

——. *Poetic Identity in Guillaume de Machaut*. Madison: University of Wisconsin Press, 1984.

——. "The Poetic Oeuvre of Guillaume de Machaut: The Identity of Discourse and the Discourse of Identity." In *Machaut's World: Science and Art in the Fourteenth Century*, ed. Madeleine Pelner Cosman and Bruce Chandler, 219–33. Annals of the New York Academy of Sciences, 314. New York, 1978.

——. "Transformations of the Lyric 'Je': The Example of Guillaume de Machaut." *L'Esprit Créateur* 18 (1979): 5–19.

Byrne, Donal. "A 14th-Century French Drawing in Berlin and the *Livre du voir dit* of Guillaume de Machaut." *Zeitschrift für Kunstgeschichte* 47 (1984): 70–81.

Calin, William. *A Poet at the Fountain: Essays on the Narrative Verse of Guillaume de Machaut*. Lexington: University Press of Kentucky, 1974.

——. "Poetry and Eros: Language, Communication, and Intertextuality in *Le Roman du castelain de Couci*." *French Forum* 6 (1981): 197–211.

——. "Problèmes de technique narrative au Moyen Age: Le *Roman de la rose* et Guillaume de Machaut." In *Mélanges Pierre Jonin*, 125–38. Senefiance 7. Aix-en-Provence: CUER-MA, 1979.

Camille, Michael. "The Book of Signs: Writing and Visual Difference in Gothic Manuscript Illumination." *Word and Image* 1 (1985): 133–48.

——. "Seeing and Reading: Some Visual Implications of Medieval Literacy and Illiteracy." *Art History* 8 (1985): 26–49.

Cerquiglini, Jacqueline. "Le Clerc et l'écriture: le *voir dit* de Guillaume de Machaut et la définition du dit." In *Literatur in der Gesellschaft des Spätmittelalters*, ed. Hans Ulrich Gumbrecht with Ursula Link-Heer and Peter M. Spangenberg, 151–68. Grundriss der romanischen Literatur des Mittelalters, Begleitreihe, vol. 1. Heidelberg: Carl Winter, 1980.

——. *"Un Engin si soutil": Guillaume de Machaut et l'écriture au XIVe siècle*. Bibliothèque du XVe Siècle, 47. Paris: Champion, 1985.

Chaytor, H. J. *From Script to Print: An Introduction to Medieval Literature*. Cambridge: Cambridge University Press, 1945.

Chenu, Marie-Dominique. "Auctor, actor, autor." *Bulletin du Cange—Archivium Latinitas Medii Aevi* 3 (1927): 81–86.

Clanchy, M. T. *From Memory to Written Record: England 1066–1307*. Cambridge: Harvard University Press, 1979.

Cramer-Peeters, E. *"Li Romanz de la Poire." Wetenschappelijke Tijdingen* 35 (1976): cols. 21–30.

Crosby, Ruth. "Oral Delivery in the Middle Ages." *Speculum* 11 (1936): 88–110.

Curschmann, Michael. "Hören—Lesen—Sehen: Buch und Schriftlichkeit im Selbstverständnis der volkssprachlichen literarischen Kultur Deutschlands um 1200." *Beiträge zur Geschichte der Deutschen Sprache und Literatur* 106 (1984): 218–57.

Delbouille, Maurice. "Les Chansons de geste et le livre." *La Technique littéraire des chansons de geste. Actes du Colloque internationale de Liège*. Bibliothèque de la Faculté de Philosophie et Lettres de l'Université de Liège 150 (1959): 295–407.

Delisle, Léopold. "Anciennes traductions françaises du traité de Pétrarque sur les Remèdes de l'une et l'autre fortune." In *Notices et extraits . . .* 34, pt. 1: 273–304. Paris: Imprimerie Nationale, 1891.

Dembowski, Peter F. *Jean Froissart and His "Meliador": Context, Craft, and Sense.* Edward C. Armstrong Monographs on Medieval Literature, 2. Lexington, Ky.: French Forum, 1983.

Diller, George. "Remarques sur la structure de *Guillaume de Dole.*" *Romania* 98 (1977): 390–98.

Dragonetti, Roger. *La Technique poétique des trouvères dans la chanson courtoise: Contribution à l'étude de la rhétorique médiévale.* Bruges: De Tempel, 1960.

Ducrot-Granderye, Arlette P. *Etudes sur les miracles Nostre Dame de Gautier de Coinci.* Annales Academicae Scientiarum Fennicae, B-25 (1932).

Dufournet, Jean. "La Glorification des ménestrels dans le *Guillaume de Dole* de Jean Renart." *L'Information Littéraire* 32 (1980): 6–11.

Earp, Lawrence. "Scribal Practice, Manuscript Production and the Transmission of Music in Late Medieval France: The Manuscripts of Guillaume de Machaut." Ph.D. dissertation, Princeton University, 1983.

Egan, Margarita. "Commentary, *vita poetae*, and *vida*. Latin and Old Provençal 'Lives of Poets.'" *Romance Philology* 37 (1983–84): 36–48.

Evans, Michael. "The Geometry of the Mind." *Architectural Association Quarterly* 12, no. 4 (1980): 32–55.

Fant, Carl. *L'Image du monde.* Uppsala Universitets Arsskrift. Uppsala: Edvard Berling, 1886.

Faral, Edmond. *Recherches sur les sources latines des contes et romans du moyen âge.* 1913. Reprint. Paris: Champion, 1967.

Faure, Marcel, "'Aussi com l'unicorne sui' ou le désir d'amour et le désir de mort dans une chanson de Thibaud de Champagne." *Revue des Langues Romanes* 88 (1984): 15–21.

Fleming, John. *The "Roman de la Rose": A Study in Allegory and Iconography.* Princeton: Princeton University Press, 1969.

Focillon, Henri. *Le Peintre des miracles Notre Dame.* Paris: Hartmann, 1950.

Foulet, Alfred, and Karl D. Uitti. "The Prologue to the *Lais* of Marie de France: A Reconsideration." *Romance Philology* 35 (1981): 242–49.

Foulet, Lucien. "Etude sur le vocabulaire abstrait de Froissart: *Ordonnance.*" *Romania* 67 (1942–43): 145–216.

François, Charles. "Perrot de Neele, Jehan Madot et le MS. B.N. fr. 375." *Revue Belge de Philologie et d'Histoire* 41 (1963): 761–79.

Freeman, Michelle A. "Froissart's *Le Joli Buisson de Jonece:* A Farewell to Poetry?" In *Machaut's World: Science and Art in the Fourteenth Century,* ed. Madeleine Pelner Cosman and Bruce Chandler, 235–47. Annals of the New York Academy of Sciences, 314. New York, 1978.

———. *The Poetics of "Translatio Studii" and "Conjointure": Chrétien de Troyes's "Cligés."* Lexington, Ky.: French Forum, 1979.

Glier, Ingeborg. *Artes Amandi: Untersuchungen zu Geschichte, Überlieferung, und Typologie der deutschen Minnereden.* Munich: C. H. Beck, 1971.

Grand, E.-D. "L'Image du monde: Poème didactique du XIIIe siècle: Recherches sur le classement des manuscrits de la première rédaction." *Revue des Langues Romanes* 37 (1893–94):5–58.

Günther, Ursula. "Contribution de la musicologie à la biographie et la chronologie de Guillaume de Machaut." In *Guillaume de Machaut, poète et compositeur,* 95–115. Actes et Colloques, 23. Paris: Klincksieck, 1982.

Henry, Albert. *Biographie d'Adenet / La Tradition manuscrite*. Vol. 1 of *Les Oeuvres d'Adenet le Roi*. Bruges: De Tempel, 1951.

Hillman, Larry H. "Another Look into the Mirror Perilous: The Role of the Crystals in the *Roman de la Rose*." *Romania* 101 (1980): 225–38.

Hindman, Sandra, and James D. Farquhar. *Pen to Press: Illustrated Manuscripts and Printed Books in the First Century of Printing*. College Park: Art Department, University of Maryland, 1977.

Hoepffner, Ernest. "Les Poésies lyriques du *Dit de la panthère* de Nicole de Margival." *Romania* 46 (1920): 204–30.

———. "La Tradition manuscrite des *Lais* de Marie de France." *Neophilologus* 12 (1927): 1–10, 85–96.

Hult, David F. "The Allegorical Fountain: Narcissus in the *Roman de la Rose*." *Romanic Review* 72 (1981): 125–48.

———. "Closed Quotations: The Speaking Voice in the *Roman de la Rose*." *Yale French Studies* 67 (1984): 248–69.

———. "Gui de Mori, lecteur médiéval." *Incidences*, n.s., 5 (1981): 53–70.

———. *Self-Fulfilling Prophecies: Readership and Authority in the First "Roman de la Rose"*. Cambridge: Cambridge University Press, 1986.

Huot, Sylvia. "The Book as a Literary Form: Theatricality and Textuality in *Li Romanz de la Poire*." In "The Ninth Saint Louis Conference on Manuscript Studies: Abstracts of Papers." *Manuscripta* 27 (1983): 10–11.

———. "From *Roman de la Rose* to *Roman de la Poire:* The Ovidian Tradition and the Poetics of Courtly Literature." *Medievalia et Humanistica*, n.s., 13 (1985): 95–111.

———. "The Scribe as Editor: Rubrication as Critical Apparatus in Two *Roman de la Rose* Manuscripts." *L'Esprit Créateur* 26 (1987): 67–78.

Iburg, C. "Über Metrum und Sprache der Dichtungen Nicole de Margivals." *Romanische Forschungen* 31 (1912): 395–485.

Jauss, Hans-Robert. "Littérature médiévale et théorie des genres." *Poétique* 1 (1970): 79–101.

Jeanroy, Alfred. *Bibliographie sommaire des chansonniers français du moyen age*. Classiques Français du Moyen Age. Paris: Champion, 1918.

Jung, Marc-René. "L'Empereur Conrad chanteur de poésie lyrique: Fiction et vérité dans le *Roman de la Rose* de Jean Renart." *Romania* 101 (1980): 35–50.

———. *Etudes sur le poème allégorique en France au moyen âge*. Romanica Helvetica, 82. Bern: Francke, 1971.

Karp, Theodore. "The Trouvère Manuscript Tradition." In *Twenty-Fifth Anniversary Festschrift of Queen's College, New York*, ed. Albert Mell, 25–52. New York: Queen's College Press, 1964.

Keitel, Elizabeth. "La Tradition manuscrite de Guillaume de Machaut." *Guillaume de Machaut, poète et compositeur*, 75–94. Actes et Colloques, 23. Paris: Klincksieck, 1983.

Kelly, Douglas. "'Li chastiaus . . . Qu'Amors prist puis par ses esforz': The Conclusion of Guillaume de Lorris' Rose." *A Medieval French Miscellany*, ed. Norris J. Lacy, 61–78. University of Kansas Humanistic Studies, 42. Lawrence: University of Kansas, 1972.

———. "Les Inventions ovidiennes de Froissart: Réflexions intertextuelles comme imagination." *Littérature* 41 (Feb. 1981): 82–92.

———. *Medieval Imagination: Rhetoric and the Poetry of Courtly Love*. Madison: University of Wisconsin Press, 1978.

———. *"Sens" and "Conjointure" in the "Chevalier de la Charrette."* The Hague: Mouton, 1966.

———*"Translatio Studii:* Translation, Adaptation, and Allegory in Medieval French Literature." *Philological Quarterly* 57 (1978): 287–310.

Kennedy, Elspeth. "The Scribe as Editor." In *Mélanges Jean Frappier,* 523–31. Textes Littéraires Français. Vol. 1. Geneva: Droz, 1970.

Kibler, William W. "Poet and Patron: Froissart's *Prison amoureuse.*" *Esprit Créateur* 18 (1978): 32–46.

———. "Self-Delusion in Froissart's *Espinette amoureuse.*" *Romania* 97 (1976): 77–98.

Kleinhenz, Christopher, ed. *Medieval Manuscripts and Textual Criticism.* Studies in the Romance Languages and Literatures, Symposia, 4. Chapel Hill: University of North Carolina, Department of Romance Languages, 1975.

Kuhn, Alfred. *Die Illustration des Rosenromans.* Inaugural dissertation, Universität Freiburg im Breisgau, 1911.

Lacy, Norris J. "'Amer par oïr dire': *Guillaume de Dole* and the Drama of Language." *French Review* 54 (1981): 779–87.

Långfors, Arthur. "Le *Dit des quatre rois:* Notes sur le MS. fr. 25545 de la Bibliothèque Nationale." *Romania* 44 (1915–17): 87–91.

Langlois, Charles-Victor. *La Vie en France au Moyen Age.* 3 vols. Paris: Hachette, 1927.

Langlois, Ernest. *Manuscrits du "Roman de la Rose": Description et classement.* Paris: Champion; Lille: Tallandier, 1910.

Lejeune, Rita. "A propos de la structure du *Roman de la Rose* de Guillaume de Lorris." In *Etudes Félix Lecoy,* 315–48. Paris: Champion, 1973.

Lepage, Yvan G. "La Dislocation de la vision allégorique dans la *Messe des oiseaux* de Jean de Condé." *Romanische Forschungen* 91 (1979): 43–49.

———. "Un Recueil français de la fin du XIIIe siècle (Paris, B.N. fr. 1553)." *Scriptorium* 29 (1975): 23–46.

Leroquais, Chanoine V. *Les Psautiers manuscrits latins des bibliothèques publiques de France.* Vol. 1. Macon: Protat Frères, 1940–41.

Livingston, Charles H. "Manuscrit retrouvé d'oeuvres de Watriquet de Couvin." In *Mélanges Maurice Delbouille.* Vol. 2: *Philologie Médiévale,* 439–46. Gembloux: Duculot, 1964.

Lodge, Anthony. "A New Manuscript of the *Chastelaine de Vergi.*" *Romania* 89 (1968): 544–54.

Lods, Jeanne. *Le "Roman de Perceforest": Origines, composition, caractères, valeur et influence.* Société de publications romanes et françaises, 32. Geneva: Droz; Lille: Giard, 1951.

Loomis, Roger Sherman. *Arthurian Legends in Medieval Art.* London: Oxford University Press, and New York: Modern Language Association of America, 1938.

Looze, Laurence de. "Guillaume de Machaut and the Writerly Process." *French Forum* 9 (1984): 145–61.

Maekawa, Kumiko. "Recherches iconographiques sur les manuscrits des poésies

de Guillaume de Machaut: Les Décorations des premiers recueils personnels."
Doctoral dissertation, Sorbonne, 1985.

Micha, Alexandre. *La Tradition manuscrite des romans de Chrétien de Troyes*. 2d edition. Geneva: Droz, 1966.

Minnis, Alastair. "Late Medieval Discussions of *Compilatio* and the Rôle of the *Compilator*." *Beiträge zur Geschichte der deutschen Sprache und Literatur* 101 (1979): 385–421.

Moleta, Vincent. *The Early Poetry of Guittone d'Arezzo*. London: Modern Humanities Research Association, 1976.

——. "The Illuminated 'Canzoniere' Ms. Banco Rari 217." *La Bibliofilia* 78 (1976): 1–36.

——. "The *Vita Nuova* as a Lyric Narrative." *Forum Italicum* 12 (1973): 369–90.

Nichols, Stephen G., Jr. "The Rhetoric of Sincerity in the *Roman de la Rose*." In *Romance Studies in Memory of Edward Billings Ham*, 115–29. California State College at Hayward Publications, 2. Hayward, 1967.

O'Gorman, Richard. "Un Feuillet inconnu du *Roman de la Poire*." *Romania* 103 (1982): 362–71.

Ong, Walter. *Interfaces of the Word: Studies in the Evolution of Consciousness and Culture*. Ithaca: Cornell University Press, 1977.

Paris, Paulin. "Adam ou Adenès, surnommé le Roi." In *Histoire littéraire de la France*, vol. 20, pp. 675–718.

Parker, Ian. "Notes on the *Chansonnier St-Germain-des-Près*." *Music and Letters* 60 (1979): 261–80.

Parkes, M. B. "The Influence of the Concepts of *Ordinatio* and *Compilatio* on the Development of the Book." In *Medieval Learning and Literature: Essays Presented to Richard William Hunt*, ed. J. J. G. Alexander and M. T. Gibson, 115–41. Oxford: Clarendon Press, 1976.

Payen, Jean-Charles. "Le *Dit des .vii. vertus* de Watriquet de Couvin et le *Livre de philosophie* d'Alard de Cambrai." *Romania* 86 (1965): 386–93.

——. "Le *Livre de Philosophie et de Moralité* d'Alard de Cambrai." *Romania* 87 (1966): 145–74.

Picherit, Jean-Louis. "Le Rôle des éléments mythologiques dans le *Joli Buisson de jonece* de Jean Froissart." *Neophilologus* 63 (1979): 498–508.

Pickens, Rupert T. "*Somnium* and Interpretation in Guillaume de Lorris." *Symposium* 29 (1974): 175–86.

Pinet, Max. "L'Illustration héraldique du chansonnier du Roi." In *Mélanges Jeanroy*, 521–37. Paris: Droz, 1928.

Pizzoruso, Valeria Bertolucci. "Il canzoniere di un trovatore: Il 'libro' di Guiraut Riquier." *Medioevo Romanzo* 5 (1978): 216–59.

Planche, Alice. "Du *Joli Buisson de jeunesse* au *Buisson ardent*: Le Lai de Notre-Dame dans le *Dit* de Froissart." In *La Prière au moyen-âge: Littérature et civilisation. Sénéfiance*, vol. 10, pp. 395–413. Aix-en-Provence: CUER-MA, 1981.

Poe, Elizabeth Wilson. *From Poetry to Prose in Old Provençal: The Emergence of the "Vidas," the "Razos," and the "Razos de trobar"*. Birmingham, Ala.: Summa Publications, 1984.

Poirion, Daniel. "Ecriture et ré-écriture au moyen âge." *Littérature* 41 (Feb. 1981): 109–18.

———. "Narcisse et Pygmalion dans le *Roman de la Rose.*" In *Essays in Honor of Louis Francis Solano,* ed. Raymond J. Cormier and Urban T. Holmes, 153–65. Studies in the Romance Languages and Literatures, 92. Chapel Hill: University of North Carolina Press, 1970.

———. *Le Poète et le prince: L'Evolution du lyrisme courtois de Guillaume de Machaut à Charles d'Orléans.* Paris: Presses Universitaires de France, 1965.

Räkel, Hans-Herbert. *Die musikalische Erscheinungsform der Trouvèrepoesie.* Publikationen der Schweizerischen Musikforschenden Gesellschaft, ser. 2, vol. 27. Bern: P. Haupt, 1977.

Regalado, Nancy Freeman. *Poetic Patterns in Rutebeuf: A Study in Noncourtly Poetic Modes of the Thirteenth Century.* New Haven: Yale University Press, 1970.

Ribard, Jacques. "Contribution à la connaissance de la tradition manuscrite de l'oeuvre de Jean de Condé." *Romania* 89 (1968): 125–29.

———. "Des lais au XIVe siècle? Jean de Condé." In *Mélanges Jean Frappier.* Textes Littéraires Français. Vol. 2, pp. 945–55. Geneva: Droz, 1970.

———. *Un ménestrel du XIVe siècle, Jean de Condé.* Geneva: Droz, 1969.

Robertson, D. W. *A Preface to Chaucer: Studies in Medieval Perspectives.* Princeton: Princeton University Press, 1962.

Roques, Mario. "Le Manuscrit fr. 794 de la Bibliothèque Nationale et le scribe Guyot." *Romania* 73 (1952): 177–99.

Saenger, Paul. "Silent Reading: Its Impact on Late Medieval Script and Society." *Viator* 13 (1982): 367–414.

Schapiro, Meyer. "Two Romanesque Drawings in Auxerre and Some Iconographic Problems." In *Studies in Art and Literature for Belle da Costa Greene,* ed. Dorothy Miner, 331–49. Princeton: Princeton University Press, 1954.

Schubert, Johann. *Die Hs. Paris Bibl. Nat. fr. 1591: Kritische Untersuchung der Trouvèrehandschrift R.* Frankfurt am Main, 1963.

Schutz, A.-H. "Were the Vidas and Razos Recited?" *Studies in Philology* 36 (1939): 565–70.

Schwan, Eduard. *Die altfranzösischen Liederhandschriften.* Berlin: Weidmann, 1886.

Serper, Arié. "Thèmes et allégorie dans le 'Roman de la Poire' de Thibaut." In *Acts of the Fourteenth International Congress of Romance Linguistics and Philology,* 397–402; discussion, 403. Naples: Gaetano Macchiaroli and John Benjamins B.V., 1974.

Smith, Nathaniel. "In Search of the Ideal Landscape: From 'Locus Amoenus' to 'Parc du Champ Joli' in the *Roman de la Rose.*" *Viator* 11 (1980): 238–43.

Spanke, Hans. *G. Raynauds Bibliographie des altfranzösischen Liedes, neu bearbeitet und ergänzt.* Leiden: E. J. Brill, 1955.

Stock, Brian. *The Implications of Literacy: Written Language and Models of Interpretation in the Eleventh and Twelfth Centuries.* Princeton: Princeton University Press, 1983.

Stones, M. Alison. "Secular Manuscript Illumination in France." In *Medieval Manuscripts and Textual Criticism,* ed. Christopher Kleinhenz, 83–102. Studies in the Romance Languages and Literatures, Symposia, 4. Chapel Hill: University of North Carolina, Department of Romance Languages, 1975.

Strohm, Paul. "Guillaume as Narrator and Lover in the *Roman de la Rose.*" *Romanic Review* 59 (1968): 3–9.

Thiry, Claude. "Allégorie et histoire dans la *Prison amoureuse* de Froissart." *Studi Francesi* 61–62 (1977): 15–29.

Treitler, Leo. "Oral, Written, and Literate Process in the Transmission of Medieval Music." *Speculum* 56 (1981): 471–91.

Tuve, Rosemond. *Allegorical Imagery: Some Medieval Books and Their Posterity.* Princeton: Princeton University Press, 1966.

Tyssens, Madeleine. "Le Style oral et les ateliers des copistes." In *Mélanges Maurice Delbouille,* vol. 2, pp. 659–75. Gembloux: Duculot, 1964.

Uitti, Karl D. "Foi littéraire et création poétique: Le problème des genres littéraires en ancien français." *Acts of the Fourteenth International Congress of Romance Linguistics and Philology,* 165–76. Naples: Gaetano Macchiaroli and John Benjamins B.V., 1974.

——. "From *Clerc* to *Poète:* The Relevance of the *Romance of the Rose* to Machaut's World." In *Machaut's World: Science and Art in the Fourteenth Century,* ed. Madeleine Pelner Cosman and Bruce Chandler, 209–16. Annals of the New York Academy of Sciences, 314. New York, 1978.

——. "A Note on Villon's Poetics." *Romance Philology* 30 (1976–77): 187–92.

——. *Story, Myth, and Celebration in Old French Narrative Poetry: 1050–1200.* Princeton: Princeton University Press, 1973.

Van der Werf, Hendrik. *The Chansons of the Troubadours and the Trouvères: A Study of the Melodies and Their Relation to the Poems.* Utrecht: A. Oosthoek, 1972.

——. "The Trouvère Chansons as Creations of a Notionless Musical Culture," *Current Musicology* 1 (1965): 61–68.

Verhuyck, Paul. "Guillaume de Lorris *ou* la Multiplication des cadres." *Neophilologus* 58 (1974): 283–93.

Vitz, Evelyn Birge. "The I of the *Roman de la Rose.*" *Genre* 6 (1973): 49–75.

Vitzthum von Eckstädt, Graf Georg. *Die Pariser Miniaturmalerei von der Zeit des hl. Ludwigs bis zu Philipp von Valois und ihr Verhältnis zur Malerei in Nordwesteuropa.* Leipzig: Quelle und Meyer, 1907.

Walters, Lori. "Chrétien de Troyes and the *Romance of the Rose:* Continuation and Narrative Tradition." Ph.D. dissertation, Princeton University, 1986.

——. "Le Rôle du scribe dans l'organisation des manuscrits des romans de Chrétien de Troyes." *Romania* (forthcoming).

Wilkins, Ernst Hatch. *The Making of the "Canzoniere" and Other Petrarchan Studies.* Rome: Edizioni di Storia e Letteratura, 1951.

Williams, Sarah Jane. "An Author's Role in Fourteenth-Century Book Production: Guillaume de Machaut's 'livre ou je met toutes mes choses.'" *Romania* 90 (1969): 433–54.

Wimsatt, James I. *The Marguerite Poetry of Guillaume de Machaut.* Studies in the Romance Languages and Literatures, 87. Chapel Hill: University of North Carolina Press, 1970.

Woledge, B. "Un scribe champenois devant un texte normand: Guyot copiste de Wace." *Mélanges Jean Frappier.* TLF. Vol. 2, pp. 1139–54. Geneva: Droz, 1970.

Woolf, Rosemary. *The English Mystery Plays.* Berkeley: University of California Press, 1972.

Zaganelli, Gioia. "'Amors' e 'clergie' in Adam de la Halle." *Spicilegio Moderno* 7 (1977): 22–35.

Zink, Michel. "Froissart et la nuit du chasseur." *Poétique* 41 (1980): 60–77.

——. *Roman rose et rose rouge: Le "Roman de la Rose ou de Guillaume de Dole" de Jean Renart.* Paris: Nizet, 1979.

Zumthor, Paul. "De la chanson au récit: *La Chastelaine de Vergi.*" *Vox Romanica* 27 (1968): 77–95.

——. "De la circularité du chant." *Poétique* 2 (1970): 129–40.

——. "Entre deux esthétiques: Adam de la Halle." In *Mélanges Jean Frappier.* Textes Littéraires Français. Vol. 2, pp. 1155–71. Geneva: Droz, 1970.

——. *Essai de poétique médiévale.* Paris: Seuil, 1972.

——. *La Poésie et la voix dans la civilisation médiévale.* Essais et Conférences du Collège de France. Paris: Presses Universitaires de France, 1984.

# INDEX

Modern critics are listed only when their names appear in the body of the text. Italicized page numbers refer to illustrations.

Library of Congress Cataloging-in-Publication Data

Huot, Sylvia Jean.
  From Song to book.

  Bibliography: p.
  Includes index.
  1. French poetry—To 1500—History and criticism.  2. Songs, French—History and criticism.  3. Narrative poetry, French—History and criticism.  4. French poetry—To 1500—Manuscripts.  5. Manuscripts, French—History.  6. Books—France—History—400–1400.  7. Scriptoria—France—History.  8. Poetry—Editing.  I. Title.
  PQ211.H86   1987      841'.1'09      87-47547
  ISBN 0-8014-1922-0 (alk. paper)